ILLINOIS CENTRAL COLLEGE
PN1995.9.C45G6
STACKS
The screen image
A12900 730310

W9-BQJ-230

THE SCREEN IMAGE OF YOUTH: MOVIES ABOUT CHILDREN AND ADOLESCENTS

RUTH M. GOLDSTEIN AND
EDITH ZORNOW

The Scarecrow Press, Inc.
Metuchen, N.J., & London
1980

Photo credits: Canadian Film Archive for The Effect of Gamma Rays on Man-in-the-Moon Marigolds, The Battle of the Villa Fiorita, and Bad Company; Twentieth Century-Fox for Claudine; Contemporary/McGraw Hill Films for The Game; and Zipporah Films for The Cool World.

Library of Congress Cataloging in Publication Data

Goldstein, Ruth M
The screen image of youth.

Bibliography: p.
Includes indexes.
1. Children in motion pictures. I. Zornow, Edith, joint author. II. Title.
PN1995.9.C45G6 791.43'09'09352054 80-14053
ISBN 0-8108-1316-5

Manufactured in the United States of America

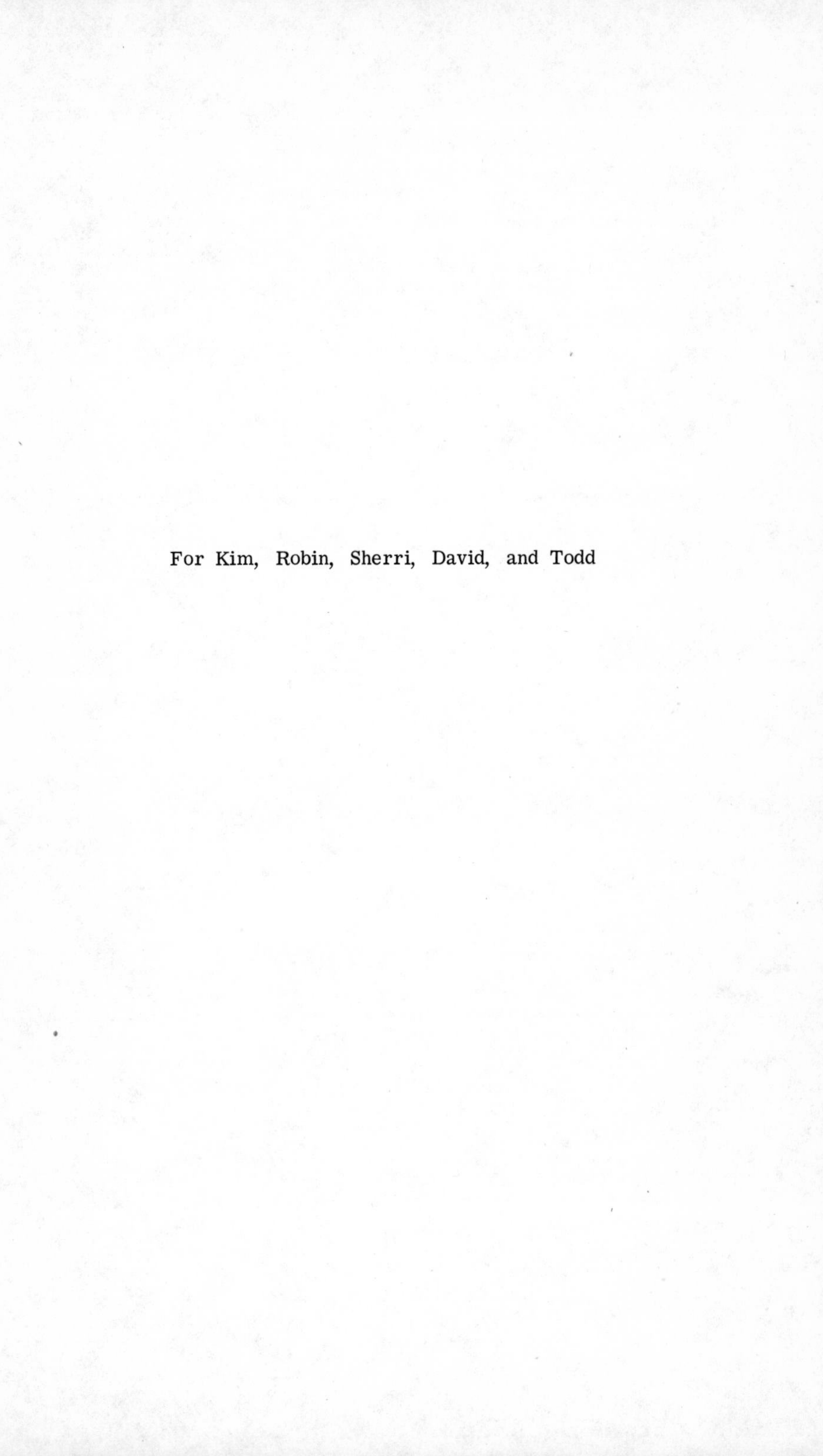

For Kim, Robin, Sherri, David, and Todd

CONTENTS

PREFACE

"Why," asked a friend who is thirteen, "are old people like you interested in movies about people like me?"

Because we've been movie watchers and child watchers for years and it's fun to combine the sports. Because children and adolescents outnumber private eyes in the population but unlike them have not yet found a place in the film-genre books. Because the image of youth on the screen has been even more tarnished than the image of women, blacks, American Indians, or Chicanos. Because we believe that "grown-up movies about children" (in Vincent Canby's phrase) have something to say to parents, grandparents, uncles and aunts; to students and teachers of psychology, education, film; to librarians, youth leaders, guidance counselors; to everyone interested in cultural mores.

As Freud pointed out, storytellers are far ahead of academicians in the search for psychological insight: they draw from sources not yet accessible to science. The living image on the screen may be a better clue to character than the textbook. *Warrendale* is worth a dozen monographs on the disturbed child. Miss Madrigal, the governess in *The Chalk Garden*, can show us better than many analysts how to reach an unhappy adolescent.

Looking at movies about children, we learn about ourselves. Do we accept Tammy or Gidget or the child in *Paper Moon* as true portraits or do we recognize them as Hollywood caricatures? Do we understand how a young girl like Anne Frank is stretching her mind and heart? In *Nobody Waved Goodbye*, do we identify with the mother unable to communicate with her son? In *The Prime of Miss Jean Brodie*, do we see ourselves as our pupils see us?

Observing children and those close to children in such films is like observing "microbehavior," the small clues to character. When Olaf in *Here's Your Life* shakes hands with the blacksmith's daughter after seducing her, we are reading a particular boy, not just a footnote to pubescent sex; when Antoine Doinel in *The 400 Blows* listens to his parents quarrel, we know from his face how completely he has retreated into independence--just as we know from his joy when they all go out to the movies how deeply he wants family closeness.

"The books we love are about growing up more than about being grown," wrote Wright Morris in *About Fiction*. So are many of the movies we love, from *Zero for Conduct* to *Small Change*.

We search them for answers to how we and the children have become what we are, how we and the children can become more than we are.

(In her introduction to the "Childhood" series on PBS-TV, Ingrid Bergman said of the films, "They remind me what it was like to be young, but perhaps they also open our eyes again to what our own children were like at all stages of their lives--one minute close to us, the next impossible to understand. And perhaps they make us think again about how we handle children--and how they handle us.")

Since the rites of passage are so familiar, some people think movies about them are outworn. Such critics remind us of the old man passing the synagogue as the bridal couple were emerging, who exclaimed, "Are they still doing that?" Initiation into love and sex and death is as trite as spring, but the poet can make spring happen again for the first time. So can the filmmaker who is an artist. He or she knows that children don't really repeat themselves; they are never exactly alike, despite their broad and deep similarities. They are people who come one by one. For each of these, out of his memory and imagination and love, the Jean Vigo or François Truffaut or Satyajit Ray or Federico Fellini makes plain what Katherine Anne Porter has called the "thumbprint" of character.

This book does not presume to be a text on child psychology. It is not a sociological study of the image of childhood in cinema. Nor is it a history of Hollywood's child stars, like the books by Marc Best, James Robert Parish, and Norman Zierold (see Selected Bibliography). Although it casts light incidentally on the way children and adolescents have been presented on the screen over a span of years, as society and acting fashions have changed, it is primarily a reference book.

We hope that we are offering a useful and even entertaining guide to movies that can be viewed and discussed profitably by anyone interested in how the young behave and how the generations may understand each other--movies that can also be seen as signposts on the cultural landscape, marking our developing attitudes toward children and adolescents.

Annotated here are more than 350 films in which a child or an adolescent is a significant character. For our purpose, "adolescent" means under twenty years of age, to exclude delayed adolescence like Dustin Hoffman's in The Graduate or Marlon Brando's and the motorcycle gang's in The Wild Ones. The list includes feature-length entertainment films, made-for-television films, and selected documentaries of a non-clinical nature.

Starting with the first important film about a child, The Kid (1921), this volume includes films about children and adolescents from that date to the present. Space and financial considerations have required us to be selective, as did the accessibility of the films for users of this reference source. We have, therefore, chosen to focus primarily on the films from the fifties to the end of 1977, with a selection of films released through May 1979. A few film classics (Road to Life), seminal films (Dead End), and films from book classics (David Copperfield) have been included from the thirties and forties; in general, we have concentrated on movies released here and abroad in the last twenty-five years. Most of the films described here are now available non-theatrically in 16mm. Some have appeared only on television and will be rerun on PBS or the commercial networks or stations.

Obviously our choices will not be everyone's. The field is vast. Our selections are very personal. From the TV dramas about adolescence, the Disneys, the formula commercial films, we have culled to our own taste. We hope we have not omitted representative films. Above all, we have been concerned not with films for children but with films that have something to tell us about children.

Some of the finest, alas, are absent because they are no longer in release: Duvivier's original 1932 Poil de Carotte; Autant-Lara's Devil in the Flesh and his The Game of Love (from Colette).

Deliberately omitted from this book are the cult films which exploit children and "religion" or occultism, Hollywood's current fixation. The most conspicuous absentee, perhaps, is The Exorcist, directed by William Friedkin from the book by William Peter Blatty, the 1973 film shocker about the demonic possession of a twelve-year-old girl. It was of little profit except to the box-office, and enough has been said of it elsewhere as a social phenomenon. As Vincent Canby wrote in The New York Times, the $10 million it cost might have been better spent subsidizing a couple of beds at the Payne Whitney Clinic. Unfortunately, its financial success spawned Exorcist II: The Heretic, with poor Linda Blair, four years later, in therapy and haunted by visions of flying. Other occult blockbusters about possessed youth that you will not find in this collection are: The Omen (1976), directed by Richard Donner, with Gregory Peck's child a real little devil, a movie utterly without class; its sequel, Damien: Omen II, released in 1978, directed by Don Taylor, and no improvement ("The first time was only a warning," the ads said); and Carrie (1976), directed by Brian De Palma, with Sissy Spacek as a repressed high school student with telekinetic powers. This last was immortalized in Sight and Sound in words that might well describe all the cult shockers: "plainly emetic ... an amalgam of old movie lore, sexual chic, and stylistic jiggery-pokery."

Arrangement

As we've indicated in the introductory chapter, "Baby, You've Come a Long Way," filmmakers have always been attracted to childhood. How film has wandered from its early visions of children and young people, and how our attitudes toward children and youth have developed through the years, can be seen when specific films are examined in detail. The main section, Features, Telefilms and Documentaries, is an extended descriptive filmography of this film genre.

The films are listed alphabetically in fifteen separate, alphabetically arranged subject categories, one comprising films taken from literature, and the others relating to some common aspects of growing up, non-clinically described. The categories overlap--for where does one draw the line, say, between Finding Oneself and Generation Conflicts?--and a single film may deal with more than one facet of childhood or adolescence. Access to film title and film category is provided with a dual system of cross references. The main entry for the film title carries the citation and the critical annotation; it is placed in the category that seemed to us most germane to the film's overall content or impact. The film title is also listed in each relevant category, with a cross reference to the page on which the main entry may be found. In addition, at the end of the annotation in the main entry there are Also references to the other categories in which the film is listed because of its relevant content. We do not claim to be definitive in identifying categories. Films, after all, can not be treated as if they were case histories. Documentaries are not treated as a separate category in the text either, but a list of the documentary films is appended for the user's convenience.

The citation for a film is given only in the main entry and includes: the title under which the film was released or is currently available in this country (with an alternate or foreign title noted in parentheses); country of origin if the film is foreign produced, or name of the film company if originally produced for first release in this country; date of first release or premiere; film length and whether color or black-and-white; major credits, such as director, author of screenplay (and name of original author and work if not originating as a screenplay), primary cast, producer, and sometimes cinematographer, art and associate directors, editor, lyricist, music composer; and a note on dubbing, subtitling, or additional scoring, if any. At the end of the citation, in parentheses, is an abbreviation for the name of the distributor(s) of the 16mm film.

For television films, films prior to the fifties, and many foreign films, the credits vary in completeness and consistency of inclusion. We have amplified data from distributors' catalogs through extensive research, but in the end we have had to sacrifice consistency and completeness for the realities of time and costs for further research. No actors' names are cited for the short (documentary) films or for some television films. For feature films, only those acting credits are included which seemed necessary for the frame of reference in The Screen Image of Youth. We have used our own discretion about mentioning minor actors in the text.

Foreign films distributed in this country are included with domestic films. Some foreign films are known only by their foreign language title; others mostly by their English title; many are known by both English and foreign language title. We follow the most widely used distributors' listings.

The distribution information in this book is based on James L. Limbacher's Feature Films on 8mm, 16mm, and Videotape, 6th edition, 1979 (R. R. Bowker Company) as well as on distributors' catalogs. An appended Directory of Film Companies and Distributors is provided as a reference aid to film users. Since distributors' rights change so often, film users should check with the catalogs of individual companies and with local library film collections.

We list in the "Selected Bibliography: Good Reading about Film" more than a hundred books which we believe will be most helpful references for further reading and critical film viewing.

We could select only a handful of the many stills we have collected from the films listed in The Screen Image of Youth. Credits for them can be found on page ii.

Acknowledgments

Among the many people to whom we owe thanks for this book, Vincent Canby, film critic of The New York Times, comes first. On July 23, 1972, we read in the Times his delightful put-on "Stop Kidding Around," in which a mythical ten-year-old boy, furious because filmmakers were lying about children, declared his intention of writing a book called The Image of the Child in Film. We decided to beat the kid to it.

We are grateful to Rohama Lee, editor of Film News, for permission to include annotations of several films which were reviewed by RMG in somewhat different form in the department "Previews and Reviews: The Feature Film in 16mm."

Our thanks to John M. Heher, who as editor of the now defunct Pflaum Publishing first believed in our book; and to Pauline A. Cianciolo, our agent, who has believed in it ever since.

Our thanks, too, to many who have been generous with time and information: Wendy Keys and Brooks Riley; Brenda Davies of the British Film Institute; Ernest Parmentier of Filmfacts; Michael Linden of the Motion Picture Association of America; Charles Silver, Supervisor of the Museum of Modern Art Film Study Center; Nadine Covert and all her staff of the Educational Film Library Association; Audrey Ryan of the Miami-Dade Public Library; Nat Chediak of the Coral Gables Cinematheque; Mrs. Kathryn Cuskley of Film & Broadcasting Review; Barbara J. Humphrys of the Motion Picture Section, Library of Congress; Robert J. Landry, Film Editor of Variety--and countless correspondents in the offices of film companies.

Jerri Seiler assisted in the preparation of the manuscript. Rose and Maxwell Nurnberg, Evelyn Gordon, and Abraham H. Lass read the Preface and "Baby, You've Come a Long Way," and offered valuable suggestions.

To Mrs. Pearl Goldsmith, RMG's sister, special thanks for the indexes and for her good counsel and constant encouragement.

New Smyrna Beach, Florida — Ruth M. Goldstein
Warren, Connecticut — Edith Zornow

May 1979

BABY, YOU'VE COME A LONG WAY -- THE SCREEN IMAGE OF YOUTH

Nobody is surprised by the first and last shots of the documentary The Invention of the Adolescent (National Film Board of Canada, 1968), in which youths are running in packs, separate from the adult herd. Today childhood and adolescence are privileged ages with special needs, language, and mores. Yet it was not always so. Century to century, the image of the child has changed with man's concept of life. Until about the twelfth century, medieval painters represented the little ones, parvuli, as dwarfed men and women with the musculature of maturity. As late as the eighteenth century, the terms "childhood" and "adolescence" were used indiscriminately in records. Not until the nineteenth century were children "in," trailing clouds of glory on every romantic page.

Our iconographc heritage is the movies. How well have they pictured the truth of childhood?

"You know," said Jean Renoir, "there is a sense in which artists have to be sorcerers twenty years ahead of their period. I don't mean that they are wiser than anyone else--only that they have more time. And, well, though it is much harder for an artist to do this in the cinema, because the cinema insists on being an industry twenty years behind the public, it can sometimes be done."

Sometimes, then, film can illuminate. Sometimes we can read on the screen the features of youth over the years.

Long before The Kid (1921), filmmakers had been attracted to the charms of infancy. In Louis Lumière's Le Dejeuner de Bébé (1898), Maman et Papa spoon-fed Bébé in a high chair and the audience ate it up. With such natural monkeys around, who needed actors? As Edmund Wilson said, Baby Peggy's public didn't want to see her act any more than they wanted to see Rin Tin Tin act.

Before the twenties, plots were straight out of nineteenth-century melodrama. In Edwin S. Porter's The Great Train Robbery (1903), a five-year-old tries to untie the unconscious railway signalman and finally brings him around by splashing water in his face. As The Moving Picture World reported, in Griffith's first one-reeler for Biograph, The Adventures of Dollie (1908), there is "the thwarting by a kind Providence of the attempt to kidnap for revenge a pretty little girl by a gypsy." Not to worry. After shooting the rapids in a water barrel, Dollie is rescued by small boys fishing near the falls. "The amazed and happy parents fold in their arms their loved one, who is not much worse off for her marvelous experience."

(The trauma-proof young adventurer is a movie tradition, all the way to True Grit, 1969. Nobody watching the Our Gang comedies thought it hurt Spanky when Baby Jane tied him to a shower curtain and put a cactus bush under his bottom. Alas, nobody thought it hurt Farina, either, when the white kids mistreated him--nobody but other black youngsters.)

Sometimes the child was dragged to the brink of death. In For Baby's Sake (1909), a child lies dying. To comfort her, a poor workingman goes out and steals a doll. When he returns, the child has expired and he is arrested. In the twenties and thirties, when Baby Leroy was one of a gaggle of gurglers that included Baby Jane, Baby Sandy, Baby Rose Marie, Baby Peggy, Baby Madge (Evans), and Baby Frances (Judy Garland), the man would be at the point of death and the baby would save him.

The omnipotent tot is part of screen mythology. In John Ford's silent Just Pals (1920), a three-year-old redeems the town bum. In C. B. DeMille's last silent, The Godless Girl (1929), a high school delinquent redeems herself. Down through the decades in Hollywood, a little child has saved them—the unhappy millionaires, the gamblers with hearts of gold, the couples drifting apart, the lonely curmudgeons--saved them by falling sick, getting hurt, running away, or just giving the grown-ups a good talking to. The archetype is Dimples (1936), in which Shirley Temple redeems her straying grandfather, Frank Morgan, while Stepin Fetchit stands by.

Before Temple, the child star with the biggest fan mail was Baby Leroy, who was hired at the age of eight months to play opposite Maurice Chevalier in A Bedtime Story (1933), and rose to become straight man for W. C. Fields. On the set, Fields reputedly spiked the infant's orange juice with gin for stealing his scenes. It's a Gift (1935) was a typical story; Fields posted a notice on a store, "Closed on Account of Molasses." After scoring nine hits, Baby Leroy retired at the age of three.

The child stars were natural candidates for sainthood in the religion of mass entertainment; the halo sat nicely on curls. But it was more than her curls that made Mary Pickford, "Little Mary of the Ringlets," America's sweetheart from 1909 until 1921 (when she was still playing child roles at the age of thirty). She charmed postwar audiences with her sweetness and pert humor as she had charmed them before the war; her miming of innocence was so good--in The New York Hat (1912), Tess of the Storm Country (1914), A Poor Little Rich Girl (1917)--that her public refused to let her grow up. After a brief flirtation with more sophisticated roles, she returned after the war to Daddy Long Legs, Pollyanna, and Little Lord Fauntleroy. In his essay on the Pickford career in Sex in the Movies: The Celluloid Sacrifice, Alexander Walker suggests that Pickford's image as "the sexual innocent" was "ambiguous": "A tough little sweetheart appeal. ... She can toss the famous curls as disdainfully as a jilted coquette stalking her next quarry."

(In 1936, Graham Greene's review of Shirley Temple's Captain January said that Shirley's popularity seemed to rest "on a coquetry quite as mature as Miss Colbert's and on an oddly precocious body as voluptuous in grey flannel trousers as Miss Dietrich's." Later, his review of her Wee Willie Winkie, which also referred to Shirley's disconcertingly sexual image, was the subject of a celebrated libel suit brought by Shirley Temple and Twentieth Century-Fox against Greene and his magazine, Night and Day. Shirley won the suit.)

Until Miss Temple became filmdom's box-office queen in 1935, the most popular child star was Jackie Coogan (see The Kid, page 89). After his appearance with Chaplin, his vehicles were not worthy of his talent.

In a class of their own were the immensely successful Our Gang comedies, a series of ninety-six two-reelers created by Hal Roach and writer-director Robert McGowan which spawned many imitations. From 1922 until the transition to sound in 1929, they exploited the "natural" antics of lively kids, unlike the earlier Fox Kiddies series, which spoofed adult plots. (Bugsy Malone in 1976 is nothing new.)

Among the best known Our Gang kids were Ernie Morrison (Sunshine Sammy) and Allen Clayton Hoskins (Farina), gifted black youngsters whose treatment by the white kids in the stories was "natural" only to the racist stereotypes of the period. Others were Mary Kornman, Mickey Daniels, Billy Thomas (Buckwheat), Carl Switzer (Alfalfa), George McFarland (Spanky), Darla Hood, Scotty Beckett, Joe Cobb (Fatty), George Wendelken (Freckles), and the young Jackie Cooper.

"The soap operas of Kiddieland," Frank Capra calls the Our Gang series in his autobiography, The Name Above the Title. During his career as a gag writer for McGowan in 1924, Capra was instructed to picture the kids as everyday small-town youngsters who "get into trouble trying to grow up." Their everyday problems? Getting their pants pulled off by Fatty's vacuum cleaner; Farina's locks being grabbed by a parrot. Only the churlish missed the charm and the mischief and the sorrows of real childhood, as gag followed gag.

And Our Gang has prospered even unto our time as television's "Little Rascals" series. It begat the Baby Burlesks (with Shirley Temple), the Mickey McGuires (with Mickey Rooney), the Kiddie Troupers (with Eddie Bracken), and the McDougall Alley Kids. For a look at the genre, see the feature-length General Spanky (1936) or the earlier shorts Mush and Milk and Shivering Shakespeare, Hal Roach comedies available from Twyman and other distributors.

Turned down by Our Gang, Shirley Temple was to hobnob with the great of the thirties. FDR thanked her for lighting the Depression with her smile; Thomas Mann and H. G. Wells visited her in her dressing room. Only a dyed-in-the-wool cynic could fail to be affected by her Little Miss Marker, said Mordaunt Hall in The New York Times.

Noncynical millions succumbed, in every sense of the words, to her Bright Eyes (1934) and Curly Top (1935) and Dimples (1936). Her collaborators included Bill "Bojangles" Robinson (The Little Colonel, 1934) and John Ford and Kipling (Wee Willie Winkie, 1937). When she gave Abraham Lincoln advice (The Littlest Rebel, 1935), few remembered that she was speaking to an actor. All over the world, mothers sighed as she danced and sang ("Baby, Take a Bow," "Animal Crackers in My Soup," "The Good Ship Lollipop"); then they went home to put little Janey's hair in curlers and sign her up for a course in tap.

Except for book movies like Heidi (1937), Shirley's "original" plots were sentimental variations on a theme: the moppet vs. the monster, or cuteness conquers all. In Baby, Take a Bow (1934), she rescued ex-convict Papa from an insurance detective; in Curly Top, she transformed a snobbish orphanage trustee by singing "When I Grow Up;" and in Little Miss Marker, she brought bookie Adolphe Menjou to his knees in prayer.

"The Sunshine Girl," they called her. "A perfect doll," she was irresistible. That she really could dance and sing and act was icing on the cookie.

With Shirley ranking among the top-ten money-making stars from 1934 to 1939, other studios got the message. From 1939 on, Jane Withers was sold as a low-budget Shirley in tearjerkers about an orphan, a vaudeville kid, a racketeers' "angel." As a counter-foil to Shirley's cherub, Virginia Weidler became MGM's and Paramount's token brat, in Mrs. Wiggs of the Cabbage Patch (1934), Freckles (1935), et al., and Ann Gillis was similarly presented in The Under-Pup (1939).

Margaret O'Brien, a child actress of great talent, won Film Daily's Critics Awards for Our Vines Have Tender Grapes (1945) and for her hair-raising Tootie in Meet Me in St. Louis (q.v.); and a Parents' Magazine juvenile acting award for her war waif in Journey for Margaret (1942).

During these years the boy stars were not neglected. MGM put three top properties--Freddie Bartholomew, Jackie Cooper, and Mickey Rooney--into The Devil is a Sissy, directed by W. S. Van Dyke. Bartholomew's David Copperfield and Little Lord Fauntleroy, and Cooper's teary The Champ, Skippy, and The Bowery, had been hits. Rooney had followed the cartoon-inspired Mickey McGuire comedies with Shakespeare (A Midsummer Night's Dream), O'Neill (Ah, Wilderness!), and Kipling (Captains Courageous), but it was

Aurania Rouverol who put him on the map. After A Family Affair, Andy Hardy was a national hero, "the epitome of all the fourteen-year-olds who hate girls until they see a pretty one in a party dress" (Frank Nugent, The New York Times). Judge Hardy's nice family in Carvel was an adman's dream. Lewis Stone in man-to-man talks with his brash but clean-cut adolescent son became the image of father-son togetherness; Mickey's teen-sized problems (Andy Hardy's Blonde Trouble, 1944) were sugarcoated digestibles for wartime audiences.

Mickey was teamed with Judy Garland in two Andy Hardys and Thoroughbreds Don't Cry before her Wizard of Oz (1939). They were the kid pros of show biz in Babes in Arms and Babes on Broadway. About the same time, apple-cheeked Deanna Durbin, a lower-key image of gifted adolescence, appeared in Carnegie Hall with Stokowski in 100 Men and a Girl (q. v.).

Andy Hardy sired Henry Aldrich (played by Jimmy Lydon), a bumbling high school editor, boy scout, and cupid. The only thing that kept changing in the Henry Aldrich movies was Jimmy's voice.

The "begats" are in the film-factory Bible. As Andy begat Henry, Gidget (1959) begat Gidget Goes to Rome and Gidget Goes Hawaiian. The teenage (or alleged teenage) beach movies begat the teenage rock movies. Penrod and Sam begat Judy and Fuffy of Sally Benson's Junior Miss, which begat Our Time (1974), in which Abby and Muffy are 1955 pre-pill junior misses talking about "doing it." Boys' Town (1938) begat Mob Town (1941) and a cycle of reformed juvenile delinquent movies with Darryl Hickman, Butch Jenkins, and Pudge Donaldson. The Courtship of Eddie's Father (1963) presented Ronny Howard as neither the first nor the last of a long, long line of prepubescent Eroses uniting their elders. Who is rash enough to trace the genealogies of other standbys like teenager hung up on an older man; teenager helping a criminal; infant adopted by unlikely bachelor men/women; children threatening adult romance?

The grandsire of them all in the "begats" is of course Dead End (1937); the descendants are listed in the annotation of the film (page 237).

Children have served time not only in formula series but in program features, as plot devices or running gags. George Winslow became known as Foghorn--he is a very small boy with a very deep voice--after being cast as Marilyn Monroe's millionaire "suitor" in Gentlemen Prefer Blondes. A poor little Greek orphan was introduced into the plot of Woman of the Year for busy Katharine Hepburn to adopt, and neglect, until she was made a true woman by Spencer Tracy; then he vanished from the story.

Youth has also been presented at the box office as "where it's at." When the social disenchantment of the young made news in the fifties, Hollywood was ready with Hot Rod Girl, Motorcycle Gang, Young and Dangerous, Eighteen and Anxious, High School

Confidential, and Juvenile Jungle. (The classic is Rebel Without a Cause, page 125.) When the "generation gap" was a cult word, we got a clinker called The Impossible Years (1968), which demonstrated how helpless a college professor could be in the toils of adolescent daughters.

Producers continue to sell us late models of the old styles--haven't the patterns been presold? After The Cowboys and Bad Company, we get Jory (1974), a pubescent Western about a boy who takes a blood bath to become a man. After the trendy characters in American Graffiti and Paper Moon, we get Rafferty and the Gold Dust Twins, about "a jaded fifteen-year-old girl going on thirty" (played by Mackenzie Phillips).

In the films that we have included in our book, there are many that tell twice-told tales about children and adolescents. They have been made to conform, in small ways or large, to the stereotypes. Their authors or directors or producers have not learned (as F. Scott Fitzgerald said in "The Rich Boy") that in life, "There are no types, no plurals."

But there are other films made not by manufacturers of products, but by artists. Over the years, some of the greatest directors and writers of cinema have given us sensitive, truthful, sometimes overwhelming pictures of childhood and adolescence.

Here in our book you will meet, each in his own right, the small brother and sister with their old, old grandmother in India (Satyajit Ray's Pather Panchali); the boy staring out at us from behind the bars of the police wagon in Paris (François Truffaut's The 400 Blows); the poor Roman billposter's son sharing his father's pain (Vittorio de Sica's The Bicycle Thief); the ambassador's child meddling in adult concerns he does not understand (Carol Reed's The Fallen Idol); the kid salvaging pop bottles on the Coney Island beach (Morris Engel's The Little Fugitive); the rancher's son crying after his departing hero (George Stevens' Shane); the boys rebelling against their masters in the French boarding school (Jean Vigo's Zero for Conduct); the children burying the dead animals in wartime (René Clement's Forbidden Games); and the adolescent planning to go with her brother and his bride on their honeymoon (Fred Zinnemann's The Member of the Wedding). You will also meet the "quiet one" in Harlem; the adolescents of "the cool world," of two worlds, of the world of ballet; the children who are emotionally disturbed, blind, mute, disoriented by war or poverty or racism; the children adrift; the children who draw; the young who are mystics, lovers, bullies, corrupters; the young who are pregnant, defenseless, vulnerable, lost, searching; and the children from the oldest books and the newest headlines.

With their parents and nannies, idols and foes, pet kestrels and tamed wild stallions, they have come a long way from Baby Burlesks and Henry Aldrich Haunts a House. Not that it's a matter of the passing of the years; Chaplin's The Kid and Truffaut's The

400 Blows could be contemporaneous. As Thornton Wilder said, every masterpiece was written this morning.

KEY TO ABBREVIATIONS

(a)	art direction
(assoc. d)	associate director
(b/w)	black and white
(c)	cast
(chor)	choreography
(col)	color
(cost)	costumes
(d)	direction
(doc)	documentary
(ed)	editing
(lyr)	lyrics
(m)	music
(ph)	photography
(prod)	producer
(sp)	screenplay
(sp. eff)	special effects

See DIRECTORY OF FILM COMPANIES AND DISTRIBUTORS, p. 333-342, for key to abbreviations of film distributors.

FEATURES, TELEFILMS, AND DOCUMENTARIES

GROWING PAINS

THE ADOLESCENTS, see p. 35

AMARCORD

Italy/France, 1973. 127 mins. col. (d) Federico Fellini (sp) Federico Fellini and Tonino Guerra (ph) Giuseppe Rotunno (m) Nino Rota (c) Magali Noel, Bruno Zanin, Pupella Maggio, Armando Brancia, Giuseppe Lanigro, Nando Orfei, Ciccio Ingrassia, Luigi Rossi, Gennaro Ombra, Josiane Tanzilli, Antonietta Beluzzi. Italian dialog with English subtitles. (FNC)

Although director Federico Fellini discourages a strict autobiographical reading of Amarcord (I Remember, in the Romagna dialect), the film's teenage protagonist Titta is in the line of his autobiographical heroes. Twenty years ago, in I Vitelloni, his somewhat older Moraldo was the sensitive observer in the town that was Fellini's Rimini, aware of the limitations of provincial life and ready to say goodbye; in La Dolce Vita, his disillusioned journalist played by Marcello Mastroianni was another Fellini figure; in 8½, Mastroianni-Fellini was the movie director at the center of things.

Amarcord, says Fellini, is "less romantic" than I Vitelloni; it is an older man's "painful goodbye.... I made Amarcord to finish with youth and tenderness."

Like all artists, Fellini is testifying about himself in Amarcord, but the memories of the world he knew at Titta's age are as much invented as recalled. This childhood is obviously close to his real childhood, in the small seacoast town at the beginning of the Fascist regime, but it is childhood recreated by a man past fifty who has always been a master of the dreamlike, the magical, the grotesque. (When Fellini was seventeen, before he left Rimini for Florence, he was a caricaturist in the cafes and on the beaches; in Rome in 1940 he was still drawing; after the war, he ran The Funny Face Shop with some friends and did caricatures of American soldiers for a few lire.)

Amarcord, his fifteenth film, caricatures teachers, students, Fascists, small town sirens, family members, priests--all larger than life, seen in the dimensions of memory. But Amarcord is a beautiful film, a picture flowing (though it is a series of vignettes) and warm (despite its director's description of it as "a painful goodbye")--a Fellini picture that is as rich in the colors of life as any other he has ever made. Somewhere between the caricatures and the fancies is truth, touched with enchantment.

Titta (Bruno Zanin), who is about thirteen in 1932, lives in a small Italian town. His mother (Pupella Maggio) is always too tired; his father (Armando Brancia), too angry. He has a little brother, full of avid curiosity, and even more interesting relatives: mad Uncle Teo (Ciccio Ingrassia), at a nearby asylum, and a fearful old grandfather (Giuseppe Lanigro), all too near at the dinner table. Such a family dinner table! Papa stamping on his hat and roaring; Mama screaming and hurling the pasta; Grandfather recalling the joys of sex, and Titta ordered to go to confession because of an especially outrageous prank. (He invents for the priest much more interesting sins than he has had the opportunity to commit.)

The story of Amarcord has two Fellini stand-ins: Titta, his adolescent self; and The Lawyer (Luigi Rossi), a commentator on the action reminiscent of the Stage Manager in Our Town, though much more pedantic in a humorous vein.

In Titta's town nothing very important happens, yet everything is important to the townspeople. Titta and his family turn out to watch the witch of winter being burned in a ritual bonfire. He delights in spring, heralded by the coming of "manine," fluff balls that float down from the sky. With the other children, Titta feels the sap in his veins and is ready for anything.

The boys at school, as Fellini remembers them forty years later, are masters of teacher-torture and scatological mischief. Did a boy really bang the teacher's desk just when the man's cigarette was making a perfect ash? Did another really give his teacher the raspberry under the pretense of pronouncing a Greek letter? Did Titta and his friends really construct paper cylinders to carry "evidence" to the front of the classroom that a boy had peed in front of the teacher? Knowing the dreams of boys, who can doubt it?

On the brink of adolescence, Titta has bawdier dreams. Sex is longing for the town's glamorous hairdresser, Gradisca (Magali Noel), and staring at her swaying hips in fascination as she makes her nightly progress to the movies (where her dreams are of Gary Cooper). Sex is also watching the beach whore, Volpina (Josiane Tanzilli); and encountering the grotesque and terrifying lady tobacconist, reminiscent of the monstrously obese La Saraghina of 8½. This mountain of a woman (Antonietta Beluzzi) makes the mouse come to her and almost swallows him whole; she insists that Titta try to carry her a few steps, then presses him to her incredible breasts until he is almost suffocated and runs in fear and humiliation from her shop.

The life of the town is Titta's life. In the ranks of the boys and girls, the pensioners, the sentimental women like Gradisca, he is on hand for the coming of a Fascist general. (Papa is a dissident; he wears a Socialist tie and is questioned by the local Fascisti, to Mama's horror.) With everyone who can take to a little boat, Titta goes out to see the fabulous trans-Atlantic liner, the Rex, passing close to their shore on her maiden voyage. When the Mille Miglia, the great race, passes through the town--tantalizingly glimpsed in the dust--Titta is uplifted almost to ecstasy: he is the champion, he is the idol of all the spectators.

Life and death, change and growth touch the boy. Gradisca settles for a policeman since Gary Cooper is unattainable, and Titta is one of the sadly resigned town swains at the wedding feast, watching her go away from them all. His mother has already left him; first there is the visit to her in the hospital with Papa, then almost without preparation there is her funeral, with Titta discovering an empty house, the real grief and the conventional grief of others, and something of himself that has just come into being.

(There have been other family surprises. His mother, who screams so at his father, is weak with the relief of love when he is freed by the Fascisti. Mad Uncle Teo, who won't come down from his perch in the tree when they go to visit him, is not really so mad as they thought.)

Nino Rota's score and Giuseppe Rotunno's cinematography make all of Amarcord sensuously lovely. But what distinguishes the film is its power to convey the sense of wonder that is part of childhood, of memory, of the poetry of life.

Some scenes are as great as any others in the best of Fellini, and are among the best of any other times-remembered scenes on the screen: the peacock coming out of the sky into the piazza where the boys and the townspeople are having a snowball fight, and spreading its magnificent tail; or the little boy going to school very early one foggy morning, his satchel on his back, and stopping suddenly because in the swirling mist he sees the marvel of a soft white buffalo. Or, to choose from among wonders more familiar: Titta realizing that one of his "inhuman" teachers is just as excited as he is by the throbbing of the motorcycle of the Mille Miglia champion.

Federico Fellini's "painful goodbye" to his adolescent self is one of the most personal films ever made about childhood.

Also: Family Relationships
Teachers and Schools

AMERICAN GRAFFITI

Universal, 1973. 109 mins. col. (d) George Lucas (sp) George Lucas, Gloria Katz, Willard Huyck (ph) Supervised by Haskell Wexler; Ron Eveslage, Jan D'Alquen (m) songs of the fifties (c) Richard

Dreyfuss, Ronny Howard, Paul Le Mat, Debbie Celiz, Charlie Martin Smith, Cindy Williams, Candy Clark, Mackenzie Phillips, Wolfman Jack. (SWA)

Four friends on a long night's journey from the way things were to the end of adolescence; from a neon-lighted, rock-loud phantasmagoria to a chilly dawn. From the fifties into the years of the Beatles, of Vietnam.

Even though it's supposed to be 1962, we know that American Graffiti is really about the last year of the fifties. The codes and rituals, the duck-tails and pleated skirts, the songs, are all of the fifties.

The small town in northern California, pieced together from Petaluma, San Rafael, and San Francisco, is director George Lucas's memory of Modesto, where he went to high school. It's the last night of summer, and the old folks are asleep in the quiet residential side streets. On the main drag, the teenagers are out cruising. From time to time they converge on Mel's Drive-In, Burger City, to sustain life with cherry Cokes, double Chubby Chucks, and Mexicali Chili Barbs brought to them by pretty carhops on skates; and to shift cars and girls for further adventures in the long electric night.

And over everything, all night long, a wolf howl shatters the sky. The legendary Wolfman Jack, disc jockey of myth and romance, hits the airwaves, blasting "Rock Around the Clock" (and forty-one other rock numbers) from the car radios: "Awwrigght, baay-haay-baay! I got a oldie for ya--gonna knock ya right on de flowa--baay-haay-hee-baay!"

Four buddies from Dewey High congregate at Mel's. Steve (Ronny Howard), last year's class president, and Curt (Richard Dreyfuss), the school intellectual, both eighteen, are slated to fly together in the morning to college in the East. Curt has some doubts about leaving his town. Steve, who has been going steady with Curt's sister, Laurie (Cindy Williams), has some trouble with her when he says he'd like to date other girls at college. The other two friends are Terry (Charlie Martin Smith), the youngest, the pimply and bespectacled Toad, and Big John (Paul Le Mat), the oldest, out of high school and the local drag-race champ with a reputation as a Lothario.

Curt, Steve, and Laurie go off to the school sock hop. Big John cruises the strip, girl hunting, and gets stuck, to his chagrin, with a sassy thirteen-year-old, Carol (Mackenzie Phillips). Trying to be sophisticated and succeeding only in being a pain, Carol goes into panic when Big John pretends he's going to make love to her. (At the end of the night, they are an oddly friendly pair, and Big John even seems aware of Carol as a kid in her own right, not a blank he drew in the sex-object sweepstakes.)

Terry, who has a Vespa scooter, is overjoyed when Steve lets him borrow his Chevy. He has a hectic time with Debbie (Candy Clark), a hot blonde who thinks she looks like Sandra Dee. He can't handle her, and he is completely agonized when the borrowed Chevy is stolen. But Debbie tells him, "You know, I had a pretty good time tonight. I mean, you picked me up and we got some hard stuff and saw a holdup, and then we went to the Canal, you got your car stolen, and then I got to watch you gettin' sick, and then you got in this really bitchin' fight ... I really had a good time."

The poetic Curt tries to find the dream woman of his life, the mysterious, beautiful blonde whom he has briefly glimpsed in a white T-Bird. Did she really mouth "I love you" to him through the closed window? Meanwhile, Curt tries to make out in the backseat with his old girlfriend Wendy (Debbie Celiz) and gets thrown out of the car. A little later, he is in the clutches of a tough local gang, the Pharaohs.

Laurie, angry with Steve, rides with an out-of-town dragster, Falfa. Falfa's car is involved in a flaming crash but Laurie ends up unhurt and in Steve's arms.

The four boys and their girls, meeting at the drive-in, the sock hop, and the drag race, are companions but are isolated in their separate dreams, searching for an elusive happiness promised in the ballads of teenage romance and the magic of Wolfman Jack.

After the long night of jockeying for position on the strip, of endless and aimless cruising, after the neon glare has faded, Curt knows he will be on the plane in the morning. He has to move on, because nothing will ever be the same where he is. Two of his dreams are shattered. The beauty in the white T-Bird is a call girl, Thirty-Dollar Sheri. The all-powerful Wolfman Jack, reputed transmitter of wild improvisations from Mexico, turns out to be a local man whose stuff is on tape. _On tape_! When Curt finds him, the real Wolfman Jack offers him a melting Popsicle and advises him to leave town.

The others will never be the same, either; never as innocent, never as believing in the songs and in their images of themselves. Terry knows that drinking bourbon is not for him and that his speed is a girl who'll be comfortable on his Vespa scooter. Steve knows that _his_ speed is Laurie; he will never leave town. And Big John knows that just before the crash in the drag race on Paradise Road, he and his '32 yellow deuce coupe were about to be nosed out by Falfa and his '55 black Chevy.

The way George Lucas directed it and Haskell Wexler supervised its dazzling kaleidoscope of neon-lighted, flashing images of cars and kids; the way the radios dinned their "Teen Angel" and "Sixteen Candles" messages into our ears -- _American Graffiti_ had to become the pacemaker in the field of movies about the high school generation of yesterday.

Enough of it is true to timeless adolescence -- the gropings of sex, and the role playing, the illusions fed by popular songs -- to make it well worth viewing. And the cinematography is a reward in itself.

Also: Love and Sex

AND NOW MIGUEL

Universal, 1966. 95 mins. col. (d) James B. Clark (sp) Ted Sherdeman and Jane Klove, from the book by Joseph Krumgold (ph) Clifford Stine (m) Philip Lambro (c) Michael Ansara, Pat Cardi, Guy Stockwell, Clu Gulanger, Joe de Santis, Pilar del Rey. (SWA, TWY, UNI)

Ten-year-old Miguel tells his older brother, Gabriel, "It's so easy to be Gabriel, but it's so hard to be Miguel."

It's hard to be treated like a child when you want to go with the men of the family into the Sangre de Cristo mountains for the summer grazing. How do you show you are ready for responsibility? By doing your everyday tasks "uncommonly well," Miguel plans.

Miguel's people, the Chavez clan, are a modern Mexican-American family in the beautiful high-plateau country in New Mexico, near Abiguin. For 400 years, since the Spaniards brought in the first flocks, sheepherding has been their way of life.

This attractive story has much insight into the generations and the impatience of a bright and lively boy to take his place with his brother, father, and uncles. It is also one of the few films which give an accurate and honest picture of the Mexican-American. The household furnishings, the statue on the village church, the importance of the terrain, Laurindo Almeida's guitar music, the authenticity of the individual characters--And Now Miguel rings true. The details of ranch life, Miguel's involvement with the shearing and branding, his rescue of the ewes from wolves, and his encounter with coyotes and rattlers, place the boy in a vivid setting.

Made from Joseph Krumgold's Newbery Medal book (later, a documentary), And Now Miguel was produced by Robert B. Radnitz, many of whose family films have won international awards.

Also: Family Relationships
From Literature

THE BACHELOR AND THE BOBBY-SOXER

RKO, 1947. 95 mins. b/w. (d) Irving Reis (sp) Sidney Sheldon (ph)

Robert De Grasse (c) Cary Grant, Myrna Loy, Shirley Temple, Rudy Vallee, Ray Collins. (FNC)

Shirley Temple was nineteen, married to John Agar, and had put on lipstick and high heels in movies three years earlier, when she played Susan, a seventeen-year-old bobby-soxer with a crush on Cary Grant, in this 1947 comedy.

And we can't buy it, as we watch it purveyed on TV these days with the other canned luncheon treats. The fault is not with Miss Temple. ("She is a sweet young girl, the audiences are enchanted with her, and that's that," said The New Republic.)

We have grown up. We've become accustomed to the face of real adolescence, in Sundays and Cybele, to mention just one. Susan is an all-too-familiar figurehead of farce. Two lines and two scenes ahead of the script, we know she will find her teenage boyfriend "so callow," that she will disguise herself in a black veil to visit Cary Grant, that she will order chocolate ice cream in the night club at the height of emotional crisis, that she will make up her quarrel with her big sister (Myrna Loy) very prettily, and that she will be over her infatuation before you can say boo to a goose. For goose she is. What actual editor of a high school paper could have been conned by a whimsical adult as she was when she interviewed Cary?

The Bachelor and the Bobby-Soxer is a wonderful reminder of how far good films have come in giving us the image of youth.

BAR MITZVAH BOY, see p. 197

BLACK PETER (a. k. a. Peter and Pavla)

Czechoslovakia, 1963. 85 mins. b/w. (d) Milos Forman (sp) Milos Forman, Ivan Passer, Jaroslav Papousek (ph) Jan Nemecek (m) Jiri Slitr (c) Ladislav Jakim, Pavla Martinovka, Vladimir Pucholt, Jan Ostroil. Czech dialog with English subtitles. (MAC)

Black Peter, Milos Forman's first feature, has the same quietly funny, engaging observations of people that characterize his later successes, Loves of a Blonde, The Fireman's Ball, and Taking Off. His genial appreciation of a fumbling seventeen-year-old in a small Czech town in the sixties is "true enough to stand for youth anywhere" (Archer Winsten, The New York Post).

Peter (Ladislav Jakim) has trouble with his parents. His father (Jan Ostroil) lectures him for being a lazy good-for-nothing without ambition, and his mother treats him like a child. His girl friend, Pavla (Pavla Martinovka), who can't communicate with her parents either, is also a problem for Peter. When they go out on a date, they keep running into a couple of other guys. It cramps Peter's style, which is not very easy at best.

And his job isn't going too well. Hired as a detective in a supermarket, Peter is supposed to keep an eye out for shoplifters. He sees one man acting suspiciously and follows him home, but he doesn't stop him (what would he say to him?). The man turns out to be the store manager's close friend.

Summertime pleasures for Peter's teenage crowd include dancing the Twist, swimming in the river or at the pool, going to a band concert or a restaurant. There are lots of songs by local talent.

Peter doesn't cope, Peter isn't really sharp--but Peter is funny, real, and easy to like. So is Forman's comedy of adolescence.

A BOY TEN FEET TALL

Paramount, 1964. 88 mins. col. (d) Alexander Mackendrick (sp) Denis Cannan (c) Fergus McClelland, Edward G. Robinson, Constance Cummings, Zia Mohyeddin, Orlando Martins. (FNC)

Made in Great Britain in 1962 by that consummate director of children, Alexander Mackendrick, Sammy Going South, as this movie was originally known, followed his Mandy (see page 257) and preceded his A High Wind in Jamaica (see page 305). An overlong, occasionally pretentious story, it often appears on TV because of Edward G. Robinson's popularity. But it is really worth a look for the sake of meeting the character Sammy, played by Fergus McClelland).

What makes ten-year-old Sammy run is the resourcefulness, often unscrupulous, of a homeless war orphan. After the death of his parents during the Suez crisis in 1956, this English boy, without a penny, sets out on a 4,500-mile trek from Port Said to Durban, South Africa, where he hopes to find his Aunt Jane.

On his journey, which is always dangerous and full of surprises, Sammy encounters four adults--a Syrian pedlar (Zia Mohyeddin); a wealthy American (Constance Cummings); a tribal chief (Orlando Martins); and an illegal diamond prospector and adventurer (Edward G. Robinson). The sly old diamond smuggler becomes his real friend; the other adults he uses more than they use him. Sammy, let it be noted, is not an endearing child hero. He is rapacious out of necessity. It's a long, hard trip.

The idyllic interlude in the diamond smuggler's hideaway, where child and man are getting along just fine, is interrupted by the police. Robinson, as the old diamond smuggler, lets the boy find his own route independently and maturely, to his reunion with security in the form of Aunt Jane in Durban.

There's a lot of Africa in the picture, a lot of insight in Robinson's grizzled nonhero father-image, and some revelation of the directness and ruthlessness of which a boy may be capable.

Also: Generation Conflicts

CAPTAINS COURAGEOUS, see p. 292

CHILDHOOD

Great Britain, Granada TV, 1974. Five 60-minute films; col. United States, PBS-TV, "Great Performances," WNET/13, New York, 1977 (PBS-TV)

The Childhood series gave us television film-making of rare quality. After viewing a variety of British productions, Cecil Smith of The Los Angeles Times wrote: "[Childhood] was the most absorbing series I saw ... each drama detailing a segment of this uneasy world as seen through the eyes of a child."

The five one-hour dramas all take place before 1935; all are set in the British Isles; all are adaptations of fiction or autobiography by well-known authors: Rudyard Kipling, H. E. Bates, George Ewart Evans, Frank O'Connor, and Barbara Waring.

"At their best," said Carol Eisen Rinzler in The New York Times, "they cut like a knife through years of adult overlay, and even at their weakest, they still rouse memories of pure emotions long since made complex, of crystalline feelings long since fragmented by intellect."

Introducing the series to American audiences when Childhood was aired by PBS in February and March, 1977, Ingrid Bergman pointed out that we adults would recognize ourselves in the situations in the dramas: situations which we often push children into, or which they often create for themselves. Even though they are seen through the filter of time and distance, these British children are familiar in every gesture--they are universal. Max Harris shouting "Punch!" triumphantly at the beginning of Baa Baa Blacksheep; Julian Wedgery, as little Herbie, tracking after the big boy and Janey in the kale field in A Great Day for Bonzo; Rosalind McCabe taking tea with her father's supposed mistress in Easter Tells Such Dreadful Lies; Paul Carey as five-year-old Michael Donovan waiting outside the pub for his father or thanking the kind nun or hating his grandmother, in An Only Child, are wonderful players. All the children in the series come straight from the classroom. The people who discovered and directed them are closer to Truffaut and De Sica than to the makers of the sit-coms and tearjerkers with child characters. It was not only the writers of Childhood who remembered what children are like in their insights and choices, and in their simplest acts, like stroking a kitten or fighting for their turn at holding a dog's leash. The magic of these films is that they seem to be happening now, everything felt or understood for the first time.

The best of the five films (separately described in the following section) are the autobiographical stories by Kipling and O'Connor, and H. E. Bates's story of three children's long summer day. Possessions is the least concerned with its child characters' attachments to an old horse and a piano, and most involved with its adults, Cassie (Mam) and Dando, the rag-and-bone man. But how beautifully it conjures up the South Wales village and its people! There is not one film in the Childhood series that does not reveal an aspect of a child's life--the fun, sadness, warmth, cruelty--through sensitive playing, and through settings photographed on location, perfectly evoking the time and place.

Also: Cultural Conflicts
Family Relationships
Generation Conflicts

Baa Baa Blacksheep

Great Britain, Granada TV, Childhood series, 1974. 60 mins. col. (d) Mike Newell (sp) Arthur Hopcraft, based on the story by Rudyard Kipling (ph) Ray Goode (c) Max Harris, Claudia Jessop, Eileen McCallum, Freddie Jones, Anthony McCaffrey. (PBS-TV)

Kipling's powerful story, written in his twenties, happened to the author himself, ninety years ago in India and Victorian England. It is full of a small boy's suffering--and endurance--in a new and shattering world.

Punch (Max Harris), the Kipling character, is six; his sister, Judy, four. Their loving parents remove them from the dangerous climate of Bombay, where they are very happy, and leave them without warning in the care of foster parents on the southern coast of England.

The boarding house of Captain and Mrs. Greenly, whom the children must call Auntie Rosa and Uncle Harry, is very different from the prospectus. Judy is made a pet, but Punch's lack of inhibition is misunderstood by Auntie Rosa (Eileen McCallum), a rigid disciplinarian obsessed by godliness. She calls his imagination "deceit" and brands him "blacksheep." Her young son, Harry (Anthony McCaffrey), bullies him cruelly. Captain Greenly understands him, but when he dies, Punch is alone. With the odds against him, he defends himself--attacking and injuring one of his tormentors at school, chasing Harry upstairs with a poker. When he weakens his eyes by insatiable reading and can barely see the blackboard, he lies to Auntie Rosa about getting good grades. But a fortuitous visit from a friend of his family with more insight than Auntie Rosa brings Punch's mother out from India to the children's rescue.

Baa Baa Blacksheep is a brilliantly played and very moving film about the vulnerability of a child to the callousness or ignorance of adults, and the ability of the child to survive on his own.

Easter Tells Such Dreadful Lies

Great Britain, Granada TV, Childhood series, 1974. 60 mins. col.

(d) June Howson (sp) Barbara Waring (ph) David Wood (c) Rosalind McCabe, Simon Griffiths, Diana Fairfax, Bernard Horsfall, Rosemary Martin. (PBS-TV)

In her pleasant, well-to-do family in Kent about 1920--with the eternal verities of the tea table and Mademoiselle and pretty Mama and her adored doctor Papa and even more adored brother Harry--Easter has all a little nine-year-old girl would want. All except romance and drama, that is. Like many other little girls, Easter imagines a wonderful story from a scrap she is told, and gets into trouble because of it.

Thirteen-year-old Harry (Simon Griffiths) comes back from his first term at school, full of his own importance, and tells Easter (Rosalind McCabe) that their father is having an affair with a patient, Nancy Thomas (Rosemary Martin). Easter sees it as a grand passion which she can help along. During Harry's absence on a camping trip, she strikes up an acquaintance with Nancy and goes often to Nancy's cottage to have tea with her and old Mrs. Thomas. In her fantasy, Easter believes that every casual word is significant, that when Papa asks her to empty the wastepaper basket, he wants her to destroy "evidence," and that Mama is the enemy. But why won't the "lovers" confide in her?

On Harry's return, Easter tells him about the developments. He has completely forgotten the idle yarn he palmed off on her. Visiting the Thomases with Easter, he cruelly tells them what she has imagined. In tears, bitterly humiliated, she runs home alone. Later she hears Harry asking her parents in the drawing room, "Why does Easter tell such dreadful lies?"

Easter is a character that tells a great deal of truth about children's romanticizing and their half-glimpses into what they imagine is the excitement of adult life.

A Great Day for Bonzo

Great Britain, Granada TV, Childhood series, 1974. 60 mins. col. (d) Michael Apted (sp) H. E. Bates, adapted by Ian Curteis (ph) Ray Goode (c) Julian Wedgery, Jennifer Cannock, Nicholas Callas, Maurice O'Connell, Barbara Hickmott. (PBS-TV)

The three children in this summer's day adventure are innocents in the remembered paradise of H. E. Bates's country childhood. "There sprung up for me out of this ordinary unprepossessing Midland earth a paradise that remains to this day utterly unblemished, a joy forever," Bates once said.

Biff (Nicholas Callas), Janey (Jennifer Cannock), and Herbert (Julian Wedgery) range from ten or eleven to about eight. Biff, who is a big boy and the leader, seems much older than Herbert, and Janey, being a woman, is far less naive. They lord it over him sometimes.

West Country children, they're playing in the hayloft of a deserted barn when they see a stranger (Maurice O'Connell) doing something mysterious with a loop of rope. To get rid of them, he gives the children his dog, Bonzo, on condition that they take him away. But Bonzo escapes into a kale field. Searching for him near the barn, Janey sees that the man is very sick and is talking of dying. Herbert is sure he will die--hasn't he drunk water from a wormy barrel?

After finding Bonzo and being refused permission by their parents to keep him, the children set off across the fields to High Farm to return him to the person named on his collar. Before the day is over, they reunite the stranger in the barn with his sweetheart (Barbara Hickmott) from High Farm, and the two go off on the train. Nobody dies and Bonzo's gone.

The children aren't sure at any given moment what it all means and they charm us in their naturalness. This is a shining little film, with every gesture right.

An Only Child

Great Britain, Granada TV, Childhood series, 1974. 60 mins. col. (d) Donald McWhinnie (sp) Frank O'Connor, adapted by Brian Wright (ph) Ray Goode (c) Joe Lynch, Kate Binchy, Paul Carey, Brian Frahill, Julie Hamilton, John Davanagh. (PBS-TV)

The most complex of the Childhood series, this is a subtle film from the book An Only Child, in which the great Irish short-story writer Frank O'Connor (whose real name was Michael Donovan) describes his unhappy boyhood. Over a span of years (from age six into the teens) we see a boy emerge from a conflict of influences with his own convictions and commitment.

In 1908, small Michael (Paul Carey) moves with his parents to Cork, near the home of his grandparents. The boy is devoted to his gentle, sensitive mother (Kate Binchy), a convent-reared orphan whose sense of responsibility and refinement (she is a valued servant in a wealthy establishment, keeping food on the table for her family) is in sharp contrast to the character of Michael's often drunken father (Joe Lynch), an ex-British Army soldier. The boy loathes the squalid home of his grandparents and is not fond of his dad, though his admiration of English virtues is inspired by the elder Donovan's tales of Queen Victoria's troops.

In 1913, adolescent Michael (Brian Frahill) has English cricket and soccer stars for his heroes, straight out of The Gem and The Magnet, the alien magazines which his playmates deride him for reading. All this changes when a new teacher arrives (John Davanagh), an Irish poet and patriot, whose influence on Michael leads to his reading Irish history and learning Gaelic. Just about this time, his father reenlists in the British Army to fight the Hun, and Michael is ostracized by his classmates as a traitor to Ireland.

When the Irish patriots who proclaimed a Provisional Government in Dublin are executed, Michael is no longer in doubt about his ideals. Out of the confusion of forces in his life, he has found his sense of personal identity. The Rebellion of 1916 has settled it for him: his heroes are Irish.

O'Connor's talent for choosing expressive details is richly evident. (The small boy who used to march behind his father's military band and imitate the British soldiers changes into the adolescent who admires his patriot Irish teacher so much that he imitates the way he limps and doffs his hat to a lady.) An Only Child is a mosaic of emotional impressions. Michael at six and even at fourteen may not be wholly clear about the meaning of events, but like most children, he is being shaped by them and coming to terms with himself, earlier than adults suspect.

Possessions

Great Britain, Granada TV, Childhood series, 1974. col. 60 mins. (d) John Irvin (sp) George Ewart Evans, adapted by Elaine Morgan (ph) Ray Goode (c) Rhoda Lewis, Anthony Hopkins, Christopher Jones, Terry Lock, David Holland. (PBS-TV)

To be a widow with three young boys in the Rhondda Valley in South Wales in the twenties depression is no joke for Cassie (Rhoda Lewis), but she is determined to hold on to as much as she can, and not to let the lightness leave her feet or those of her sons either.

The shop fittings are auctioned off to pay their father's debts; and the cherished old horse, Dick, and the piano are sold to drunken Dando (Anthony Hopkins), the rag-and-bone man, who doesn't care for them properly. The core of the film is not really in the children, but in the battle which rages between Cassie and Dando after the sale, filling the dead town with clamor. The drama fascinates Cassie's children. They don't have much of a part in it, but they are absorbing more from their Mam than the scrag-end and tripe she gives them for their dinner.

CRIA!

Spain, 1975. 115 mins. col. (d) (sp) Carlos Saura (ph) Teodoro Escamilla (c) Geraldine Chaplin, Ana Torrent, Conchita Perez, Maite Sanchez Almendros. Spanish dialog with English subtitles. Jason Allen Distribution. (WOR)

"The girl possessed a magic face," said director Carlos Saura of Ana Torrent in Victor Erice's haunting film The Spirit of the Beehive (page 275).

For this grave, lovely child with the luminous eyes, Saura wrote and directed Crfa! (Crfa Cuervos, "Raise Ravens"). It is a lyrical, perceptive evocation of a child's world, all mood and memory; a dark world in which the child is seen to move between fantasy and bizarre reality, as she tries to make order amid the half-understood disorders of adult passion and death.

The story is set in an old house in a Madrid now largely defunct, on three planes of time. Geraldine Chaplin (in a very fine performance) is the long-dead mother, narrating the past. Ana Torrent is the nine-year-old Ana, enacting it. Chaplin is also the adult Ana, about 1955.

The child is surrounded by death. Her grandmother, who has had a stroke, is speechless and paralyzed; Ana asks her whether she does not want to die. Her mother is already dead, of a painful illness. (Ana blames her father for it.) Twice Ana sees her father making love to his best friend's wife. Ana has something which she believes is poison--it was given to her by her mother with a warning, though we know it is harmless--and she administers a dose to her father. He dies, during the act of love, and Ana believes that she has caused his death. She tries to cause the death of her aunt, who is usurping her dead mother's place, with the same "poison." In fantasy, she relives the intimate relationship with her mother.

Cría! is a beautiful memory of a child's mind. Ana is wholly the child--in her moments of play as well as her moments of fantasy when she reacts in fear of the realities which surround her. There are sensitive, exact glimpses of childhood; one of the most delightful is the scene in which Ana plays, with her two sisters, who are five and eleven, "the way adults talk."

One of the subtlest recent directors of a film about childhood, Carlos Saura (winner of the Berlin Film Festival Silver Bear for _La Caza_, "The Hunt," in 1965, and again for _Peppermint Frappé_ in 1968) was awarded the 1976 Special Jury Prize at the Cannes Film Festival for _Cría!_

Also: Death

THE DIARY OF ANNE FRANK, see p. 297

DIMKA

USSR, 1963. 79 mins. b/w. (d) Ilya Frez (sp) Wolf Dolgy (ph) Mikhail Kirillov (m) Nikolai Yakevlev (c) Alyosha Zagorsky, Olga Lysenko, Vladimir Treshchalov. Russian dialog with English subtitles. (MAC)

A movie that proves some fairly incredible things: that an overlong, saccharine, and essentially implausible tale can be almost completely retrieved if the main role is played by an irresistible actor of five; and that the Gorky Studios in Moscow can defeat Hollywood triumphantly in the Infant Tearjerker Cinema Sweepstakes.

Funny thing is, Dimka (Alyosha Zagorsky), the five-year-old, leaves us quite dry-eyed. Director Frez obviously wants to make us feel deeply ("We wanted to impress upon the adult spectator that children are extremely complex, sensitive people, reacting sharply to circumstances around them and very easily hurt. And we must be extremely attentive and sensitive to them so that they are not injured through thoughtless words or actions," he has said). However, since the original premise of the movie doesn't hold water, we dismiss it almost at once. Instead of sorrowing for poor little Dimka, we focus very pleasantly on Aloysha Zagorsky--a spunky five-year-old blond boy with a masterful stride and a firm jaw, who winds the camera around his little finger. What is supposed to be a journey into the heart of a fatherless child turns into the adventure of an intriguing, tiny hero in a great city.

Dimka believes he is fatherless because his mother told him that she bought him in a store but she didn't have enough money to buy a papa, too. So Dimka takes his ice-cream money and goes shopping. He examines various male figures carefully, including the statuary on public buildings, and finally, after an unsuccessful attempt in a department store to buy a handsome window dummy, decides that the best candidate is Andrei (Vladimir Treshchalov). This friendly young man picks up the wandering child, is touched by his plight, and treats him to a meal and rides in an amusement park. When Andrei accepts Dimka's invitation to return home for tea with his mother (Olga Lysenko), the meeting is not schmaltzy at all, but understandably embarrassed. However, the possibility envisioned by the child remains; if your training in soap opera leads you to suspect that there will be future meetings, the film's denouement is just rosy enough to encourage you.

Dimka offers adults the simple pleasure of following a small boy around a big city for a day. The boy is a superb natural player, well directed, and imaginatively photographed.

Also: Family Relationships

FATHER, see p. 44

THE GO-BETWEEN

Great Britain, 1971. 116 mins. col. (d) Joseph Losey (sp) Harold Pinter, from the novel by L. P. Hartley (ph) Gerry Fisher (m) Michael Legrand (art) Carmen Dillon (c) Julie Christie, Alan Bates, Dominic Guard, Margaret Leighton, Michael Redgrave, Michael Gough, Edward Fox, Richard Gibson. (SWA)

The portrait of an adolescent boy of a bygone era, the romantic yet accurate picture of the society through which he moves, the perception of the ways in which adult ambiguity traps and scars him--these are conveyed in subtle, often beautiful cinema terms in The Go-Between.

Director Joseph Losey and playwright-scenarist Harold Pinter were interested in the screen possibilities of L. P. Hartley's novel The Go-Between as far back as 1963, when it was ten years old. Their 1971 film misses none of Hartley's insights. Unlike another period piece, The Great Gatsby, it is not only a pleasure for the eye but also a pleasure for those who treasure its source. One of the best contemporary novels about a young boy is now a very satisfying contemporary film.

Not everyone likes its style. Some have called it cold; others have been understandably confused by its device of "flash-forwards," not clear until the epilogue. The original producers, MGM, thought it wasn't good enough for the Cannes Festival. (When Columbia bought it and submitted it, it won the Grand Prix.)

The story of The Go-Between revolves around Leo Colston (Dominic Guard), who turns thirteen in the summer of 1900. Imaginative, sensitive, completely unsophisticated, Leo is the son of a bank manager who has recently died. The boy's widowed mother makes genteel sacrifices to send him to a good school, and is pleased when he receives an invitation to spend the holidays at Brandham Hall, the luxurious Norfolk estate of the family of his school friend Marcus Maudsley (Richard Gibson).

Although he is not of their class, Leo is treated kindly by the Maudsleys, and Marcus's lovely older sister, Marian (Julie Christie), makes a pet of him. Dazzled by her, and friendly with the Maudsleys' tenant farmer, Ted Burgess (Alan Bates), Leo is unwittingly enlisted as a go-between in their clandestine love affair. He carries secret letters happily between the Hall and the farm, until the day he discovers their contents by accident. He is stunned and disillusioned; how can Marian, who is engaged to Viscount Hugh Trimingham (Edward Fox), be sending passionate declarations to Ted? Since Leo is also friendly with Viscount Hugh, his loyalties are divided. In his confusion he wants only to cut short his visit and return home, but his mother will not give her permission.

During the Maudsleys' birthday party for Leo, Marian fails to appear. Mrs. Maudsley (Margaret Leighton), long suspicious, forces Leo to take her to the lovers' rendezvous. When he sees Marian and Ted making love, he has a breakdown. Afterward, someone tells him that Ted has killed himself.

We next see Leo fifty years later; he is an old man who has never married as a result of his boyhood trauma. Leo (Michael Redgrave) visits Marian, now old Lady Hugh Trimingham, and promises to carry one more message. He will tell her estranged grandson, who resembles Ted Burgess, that he should be proud to be the child of "so much beauty and happiness."

Though Leo Colston has all the naiveté of a boy of 1900 who has just turned thirteen, he is in many ways a prototype of the timeless adolescent. His dramas are the dramas of boyhood--racing up and down the double staircase of the Hall with Marcus and sharing a boy's life with him in their part of the great estate; feeling ashamed of his different clothes and manners; being jealous of Ted's adult sexuality and yet fascinated by it; demanding that Ted explain what men and women do while "spooning"; puzzling over his adored, fickle Marian; torn between triumph and regret at the cricket match because he has helped Hugh's side at the expense of Ted's; accepting the code of Viscount Hugh ("Nothing is ever a lady's fault").

In the summer of 1900, under the shimmering heat, a frost destroys a boy's innocence. Adult deceit may still mark a thirteen-year-old for life.

"The past is a foreign country.... They do things differently there." This first line of the novel is also the epigraph of the film. The story is told not from the boy's point of view but from the point of view of Leo fifty years later, revisiting Brandham Hall. That is the explanation of the "flashforwards": from the beginning of the film, the old man flashes in and out of the scene of his boyhood. This device has been called, by different critics, both convoluted and cinematically adroit.

Also: From Literature
Generation Conflicts
Love and Sex

A HERO AIN'T NOTHIN' BUT A SANDWICH, see p. 82

HOW GREEN WAS MY VALLEY, see p. 306

HUGO AND JOSEFIN

Sweden, 1968. 83 mins. col. (d) Kjell Grede (sp) Maria Gripe and Kjell Grede, based on the books by Maria Gripe (ph) Lasse Bjorne (m) Torbjorn Lundqvist (c) Fredrik Becklen, Marie Ohman, Beppe Wolgers, Inga Landgre, Helena Brodin, Bellan Roos. Swedish dialog dubbed in English. (BUD, MAC, WCF, WEL)

In the words of director Kjell Grede, Hugo and Josefin is "A summer vacation with two children and a camera.... Before it opened, I showed the film to two children. One said afterwards that it was fun because it was like a Sunday morning when one lies in bed and experiences a lot of things and one does not know whether or not one is awake or in a dream."

Grede's first feature, based on three children's books by Maria Gripe popular in Sweden, is a children's vision of their discoveries and adventures, fears and fantasies, during one summer. Marie Ohman and Fredrik Becklen, the two eight-year-olds who play

Hugo and Josefin, are appealingly innocent; it is the adult viewer (and Hugo and Josefin is a film about children more successful with adults than with children) who comprehends their experiences.

Josefin, the minister's lovely daughter, becomes fast friends with Hugo, nephew of the gardener (Beppe Wolgers) and son of a conscientious objector in prison. Hugo takes Josefin on exciting expeditions through the countryside he loves, she tries to repay him by luring him into her class at school, and they both share delightful adventures with the gardener.

The children are real and charming to watch in the beautiful Swedish countryside photographed exquisitely in color by Lasse Bjorne. They are un-self-conscious in humorous scenes like Hugo's first day in school or their farewell picnic with the gardener when they all eat hardboiled eggs whole. They are touching when they are serious as in Josefin's bewilderment about why Hugo's father is in prison, and convincing as they relish the poetry of the natural world.

From vignette to vignette, Hugo and Josefin and their friend the gardener are delicately perceived.

Also: From Literature

I WAS BORN, BUT ... see p. 86

I'M A FOOL, see p. 308

"J. T."

CBS-TV, 1969, 51 mins. col. (d) Robert M. Young (sp) Jane Wagner (m) Frank Lewin (c) Kevin Hooks, Jeanette Dubois, Theresa Merritt, Michael Gorrin. (CAR, TWY, BUD, ROA)

In this TV drama about a small black boy in Harlem, the black experience is too simply and rosily resolved. A rewarding session for any group would be a screening of "J. T." and that masterwork of realism with a similar protagonist, The Quiet One.

As the child who plays "J. T.", Kevin Hooks is often better than his formula material. We're moved when we see him alone in his dilapidated ghetto apartment while his mother is at work, loudly playing the radio he stole from a parked car under the noses of two bigger kids. (He drowns out his troubles by playing it in bed, in the bathroom, and in school.) He picks up a stray cat, starved and torn from a fight, and shelters it in an abandoned refrigerator in his hideaway, feeding it with tuna charged at the neighborhood grocery on his mother's account. The cat is killed, of course, and the radio is stolen. "J. T." is comforted in his grief when he learns that some people do care, the Jewish grocer and his family, and he may even feel less lonely soon. Anyway, that's what the ending wants us to be comforted by.

JEREMY, see p. 149

KES, see p. 280

LIES MY FATHER TOLD ME, see p. 91

THE LITTLE FUGITIVE

Burstyn, 1953. 75 mins. b/w. (d)(sp)(ph) Ray Ashley, Morris Engel, Ruth Orkin (m) Lester Troeb, Eddy Manson (c) Richie Andrusco, Rickie Brewster. (BUD, MAC, TFC)

It's slight, simple, artless. It's too long. It has no plot to speak of. Yet this shoestring production by a group of New Yorkers still has a lot. It has Richie Andrusco, a redheaded seven-year-old with an unregenerate freckled map, at large for a day and a night in Coney Island. He is as funny as only an au naturel, un-self-conscious small boy can be.

In his mother's absence, Richie runs away from home, because his brother and his brother's friends have conned him into believing he's committed a murder. After a little while on his own at Coney, he goes back and finds that all's well. That's all there is to the picture. But the show is Richie in T-shirt and dungarees, his pistol holster low-slung in dead center, knocking out the kewpie dolls; Richie devouring weenies; Richie riding herd on the merry-go-round; Richie turning a plausibly honest nickel by cornering the market in empty pop bottles.

Richie is not a child star or the 1953 model of an Our Gang kid. An uninhibited third-grader from P.S. 101 in Brooklyn, photographed doing a few of the things a seven-year-old likes to do, he's somebody for child watchers to enjoy.

LORDS OF FLATBUSH

Columbia, 1974. 86 mins. b/w. (d) Steven F. Verona and Martin Davidson (sp) Steven F. Verona, Gayle Gleckler, Martin Davidson (c) Perry King, Susie Blakely, Sylvester Stallone, Henry Winkler, Paul Mace. (SWA)

The film's weaknesses are obvious: it is another fifties nostalgia movie like American Graffiti (although it was conceived before it); it is badly lighted, grainy, and rough in texture; and it is a series of loosely constructed episodes with dialog that is not always coherent. Some of its high school seniors look more like thirty than seventeen or eighteen.

Nevertheless, Lords of Flatbush has both perception and compassion. It looks seedy, but its insight into Chico and his gang is as real as the dull and grimy Brooklyn streets that are their hangouts.

"Chico," says Stanley, "I just don't understand you."

"Stanley," Chico answers, "why can't I understand you?"

The ex-Brooklynites, Steven F. Verona and Martin Davidson, who wrote, directed, and produced Lords of Flatbush on the proverbial shoestring, understand these four young tough guys in ducktails and black leather jackets, and their bedraggled chicks in T-strap shoes and fuzzy sweaters, about as well as anyone has ever understood the late 1950s mixed-up kids. They wore their jeans low-slung and their bravado high and their hero was James Dean, the rebel without a cause.

The street gang centers around Chico (Perry King), who is crazy about a cute blonde (Susie Blakely) from a "good family" in a middle-class world he is reacting against but really is aspiring to. His not-so-bright pal, Stanley (Sylvester Stallone), is tricked into buying a $1,600 engagement ring for the strident girl he has made pregnant and is about to marry. In addition, Butchey and Wimpy stand out, as Henry Winkler and Paul Mace play them, as two guys just hanging around waiting for things to happen. They are as aimless and restless as we remember the adolescents of the period.

They all seem to be marking time until their futures as blue-collar Flatbush adults catch up with them. Meanwhile, here they are in The Lords, a social-athletic club of dingy reputation, spending more time lounging, dating, and battling other gangs than going to school. Chico will never see his blonde again; Stanley will soon be up to his neck in bills and time payments. Now, briefly, they are "doing their thing"--on a motorcycle; on the football field (brawling, mostly); in a car stolen for a pal.

The early Henry Winkler and Sylvester Stallone are players interesting to watch--and they tell us much, when we mentally subtract a few years from their age.

Also: Delinquency and Crime

MELODY, see p. 182

MY AIN FOLK

Great Britain, 1973. 55 mins. b/w. (d)(sp) Bill Douglas (ph) Gale Tattersall (c) Stephen Archibald, Hughie Restorick, Jean Taylor Smith, Bernard McKenna. (FNC)

This is the second part of the projected autobiographical trilogy produced, directed, and written by Bill Douglas, about his bleak childhood in the desperately poor mining village of Newcraighall, Scotland, in the late forties. It follows the first part, My Childhood (q. v.), and was a 1978 London Film Festival choice.

Jamie (Stephen Archibald) is an unwanted, lonely eight-year-old. His mother is in a mental hospital; the identity of his father is in doubt. With his cousin Tommy (Hughie Restorick), he is looked after by his senile maternal grandmother, until she dies. My Ain Folk carries on from her death.

The welfare people move in and take Tommy away to a home, but Jamie eludes them and takes refuge in the home of his paternal grandmother and uncle. His grandmother (Jean Taylor Smith) lets him stay but does not want him and tells him his mother had ruined her son's life. (This favorite son, the man Jamie gradually realizes is his father, is living next door with another woman, Agnes, and another son.)

Jamie is the victim of circumstances which emphasize the lack of love which brought him into the world and the hopelessness of his future. Through his child's eyes, we recognize the grimness of adult living in that sodden pit village--his pathetic grandfather's daily punishment by his wife; his uncle's affair with Agnes; his father's departure from the district with still another woman. The child is humiliated and rejected as a human being by almost everyone. In school he is broken, listless, apathetic. (Throughout the whole film, he laughs only once, when he watches Tommy pick his father's pocket and bring out a contraceptive.)

When Jamie's mother dies in hospital, his situation grows worse. His grandfather commits suicide in a fit of despair: as in My Childhood, when he lost his only friend, the German P. O. W., Jamie has been left alone again. In the end, the tenuous family relationships break up, and Jamie is sent to the welfare home. (There is a final ironic shot of the walls of that institution while a band playing "Scotland the Brave" marches past.)

This bitterly retrospective film of a childhood of rejection, isolation, and pain has terrible moments in it. One of the most chilling, perhaps, is the one in which his very drunk grandmother, for once picking Jamie up instead of the dog, croons, "Your granny loves you, your granny loves you."

The intense emotional charges in My Ain Folk come from Douglas's repeated focus on objects and gestures, like a stolen apple being replaced by a mousetrap, or a slag heap in which Jamie buries his mother's pearls, or the boy's closing his grandmother's frozen fingers around a hot, empty cup. Death, confusion, cruelty--the adult world only partially comprehended by the boy--are photographed with great clarity and imagination. (Cinematographer Gale Tattersall won the Silver Medal at the Cork Festival for his work.)

Harrowing and difficult as it is, despite gleams of humor in a few moments, My Ain Folk is not to be missed. Shown at ten festivals in 1973 and 1974, it earned critical praise for its artistic honesty. It is a stunning evocation of a remembered boyhood.

Also: Family Relationships

MY CHILDHOOD

Great Britain, 1972. 48 mins. b/w. (d)(sp) Bill Douglas (ph) Mick Campbell (c) Stephen Archibald, Hughie Restorck, Jean Taylor Smith, Karl Fieseler, Bernard McKenna, Paul Kermac, Helena Gloag. (FNC)

Like that other British film about a working-class youngster, Ken Loach's Kes (1970), with which it has some similarities, My Childhood portrays a grim childhood without sentimentality and is all the more moving for it. Precise, austere, spare of dialog--its style has been called "spartan"--it is nevertheless rich in evocative images.

Director-scenarist Bill Douglas's short feature is the first part of a projected autobiographical trilogy. (The second is My Ain Folk (q. v.), a 1973 London Film Festival choice.) It won the Best First Film award at the Venice Film Festival. Shot in less than a month, for under five thousand pounds, it is a British Film Institute production; its achievement is the triumph of imaginative simplicity over enforced economy.

My Childhood tells us about eight-year-old Jamie (Stephen Archibald), growing up in the slag heaps of the Scots mining village of Newcraighall in 1945, as the war is ending. Jamie and his twelve-year-old brother, Tommy (Hughie Restorck), are looked after, sourly, by their grandmother (Jean Taylor Smith). The exact relationship of the adults among whom Jamie finds himself is not clear to him. There are dark hints about his parentage, and he watches as the other village boys run to greet their fathers at the pit head. Is his father the man who stops him in the street and gives him sixpence? Or the man with whom he has an agonizingly short visit? His mother he knows only as the woman in the mental hospital, pulling the sheet over her head in a gesture he is to remember. His only close friend is a German prisoner of war in the village (Karl Fieseler).

Although he is bitterly poor, Jamie is not a whiner. He and Tommy have their moments, as all children do, of mystery or adventure, even of humor. They can stand on a bridge and enjoy the smoke from a passing train. Jamie has a private hideaway. He has a cat. (When it eats Tommy's canary, Tommy kills it.) He likes cheating the bus driver out of a fare, with his grandmother's help.

Mostly, though, Jamie has a hard time, in a harsh world. Bill Douglas has blocked it out for us so that the whole bleak story becomes a tribute to a child's struggle for survival. The cast, largely unprofessional, is excellent.

Also: Family Relationships

MY FRIEND FLICKA, see p. 282

MY UNCLE ANTOINE

Canada, 1971. 110 mins. col. (d) Claude Jutra (sp) Clement Perron and Claude Jutra (ph) Michel Brault (m) Jean Cousineau (c) Jacques Gagnon, Jean Duceppe, Olivette Thibault, Claude Jutra, Lyne Champagne, Lionel Villeneuve, Helene Loiselle. French dialog with English subtitles. (JAN)

My Uncle Antoine (Mon Oncle Antoine), winner of eight major film prizes in Canada, has been hailed as the coming-of-age of a major cinema talent. It is Claude Jutra's film; he is director, editor, and actor (Fernand, the clerk). But the screenplay, which he helped to adapt, is Clement Perron's own story: Perron is recalling his own coming of age, remembering himself in the character of fourteen-year-old Benoit, growing up in the poor backwoods Quebec mining town of Black Lake in the mid-1940's.

Not everyone may go along with Time's statement that My Uncle Antoine is "the best chronicle of coming of age since Truffaut's The 400 Blows." Jutra's film is sometimes off balance; it begins with a minor character and includes so many details that one can get confused. But there is no doubt of its realism, its insight into experience, and its power to move one. The boy Benoit, superbly played by Jacques Gagnon--a nonprofessional, like most of the cast, when the film was made--is a fascinating person. He stores up his observations of people as if he were a reporter from another country. His eyes are enormous, speaking with life, sly knowledge, humor. And at the climax, when he meets death and human frailty at their most shattering, he is as vulnerable as any mortal child we have ever seen.

Benoit is an orphan, raised with kindness by his aunt and uncle. The general store of Uncle Antoine (Jean Duceppe) is the world he knows, and it is a world full of human drama. Though his face remains amused, the boy is unsparing in his judgment of adults' stupidity, their boring habits. An altar boy who hungrily gobbles up the wafer and the wine, he makes the sign of the cross over the priest as the man later also takes a pull at the bottle. When he hurls snowballs at the horse of the English mine owner who is tossing Christmas gifts on the ground for children to scrabble for, Benoit is comforted by the look of approval on a woman's face. He seems to be keeping tabs on each act of hypocrisy in his environment, but he is still part child, relishing what he notes. Awakening to sex, he clumsily snatches a caress from a girl his own age, and peeps through a door at the notary's wife trying on a merry-widow corset in the store.

Christmas Eve brings his childhood to an end. Everyone in the community is enjoying the festivities when a call for help comes to Uncle Antoine. A boy has died of fever in the night in a remote farmhouse. His father is away at a logging camp and his mother is alone with the younger children. Uncle Antoine, who doubles as town undertaker, sets out with a coffin, two bottles of gin, and Benoit to assist.

The journey is the boy's passage to the deepest shocks of maturity. He helps to prepare the body of the boy--his own age--for the box, which is too small for it. Gripped by the family's grief, he is unable to eat the meal the mother has prepared; he watches Uncle Antoine gorge himself on pork and gin. On the homeward trip in a bitter snowstorm, Uncle Antoine is very drunk. The coffin slides off the sled into the snow; they cannot recover it. (One of Benoit's hands is in a cast and the drunken old man cannot help.) Railing, Uncle Antoine confesses his life's bitterness to the boy. He has always feared death and hated the task he is performing now; he is unhappy in the store and in Black Lake. When they arrive at the store, Benoit discovers his aunt and Fernand making love. He goes back to the farmhouse with Fernand to find out what has become of the body. Evidently, the father saw it from the train as he was on his way home from the logging camp. Staring through the window, Benoit sees father, mother, and children around the open coffin, transfixed in sorrow for their eldest son.

The ending, a beginning for Benoit's manhood, is one of the most powerful in contemporary films. And in every detail which has preceded it, My Uncle Antoine is alive, incisive, authentic. Much of the film is beautiful; Michel Brault's color photography of the Quebec setting makes it as much a part of Benoit as the shelves and kegs of his uncle's store.

Also: Generation Conflicts
Death

OUR HEARTS WERE YOUNG AND GAY

Paramount, 1944. 80 mins. b/w. (d) Lewis Allen (sp) Sheridan Gibney, from the books by Cornelia Otis Skinner and Emily Kimbrough (c) Gail Russell, Diana Lynn, Charlie Ruggles, Dorothy Gish, James Brown, Bill Edwards, Beulah Bondi, Alma Kruger. (UNI)

A nostalgic period piece about the zany misadventures of a pair of ingenuous teenage girls on their unchaperoned trip abroad in 1923, when "wolves were sheiks and sweater girls flappers."

It is based on the autobiographical books by Cornelia Otis Skinner and Emily Kimbrough, which were very popular for their rosy-tinted recollections of effervescent privileged youth. Though obviously out of their teens, Gail Russell, James Brown, and Bill Edwards do well enough as the older adolescents they're supposed to be. Most convincing of all is former child star Diana Lynn, who was eighteen when she played Emily Kimbrough. When she comes down with the measles you have to believe.

Though dated, coy, and farcical, the film has the virtue of reminding us of the budding flapper, who had appeared often on the screen in the forties, but never with more charm than in the characters of Cornelia and Emily.

Also: From Literature

PAPER MOON

Paramount, 1973. 102 mins. b/w. (d) Peter Bogdanovich (sp) Alvin Sargent, based on the novel Addie Pray by Joe David Brown (ph) Laszlo Kovacs (m) recordings from the thirties (c) Ryan O'Neal, Tatum O'Neal, Madeline Kahn, J. Hillerman, P. J. Johnson. (FNC)

The central relationship in Paper Moon is a movie staple, the partnership between a disreputable man and a child, in which the child learns corruption from the man and the man may learn sentiment from the child. We had Chaplin and Coogan in The Kid, Wallace Beery and Jackie Cooper in The Champ, Shirley Temple and Adolphe Menjou in Little Miss Marker.

But Tatum O'Neal, as nine-year-old Addie, is not like any of her predecessors. She is worth examining for what she tells us about today's taste in child stars. The image constructed by director Bogdanovich from Alvin Sargent's adptation of Joe David Brown's novel Addie Pray was popular with enough audiences and enough critics (though not all) to win young Tatum wide media coverage. She even got a special Academy Award.

Addie, in baggy jeans and tightly drawn knitted cap, is not winsome, charming, warm, intense, or really moving. Whether she is funny is a matter of taste, a quality which does not distinguish Paper Moon. She might pass for a boy with the light behind her. Tight-lipped and poker-faced, animated on cue, she makes one wonder what she would be in the hands of a director (and scenarist) more perceptive about real childhood and less bent on projecting a tough, trendy image. She smokes in bed, listening on her portable radio to Whiteman and Benny and "Frankie" Roosevelt (this is the 1930's). Her language suggests that she has gone to school at Polly Adler's. (She does understand floozies. To rid herself of a rival for Moses Pray's affections, the over-ripe tart Trixie (Madeline Kahn), Addie knows just what kind of sex trap to bait.) She out-cons and out-blackmails the small-time swindler, Pray (played by her real father, Ryan O'Neal), preferring to stay with him and fleece the suckers rather than let him take her to a nice, respectable aunt in St. Louis (Dullsville). Addie has a cool head for business and won't let her cigarbox of money out of her hands.

Addie is an orphan. When she meets Moze Pray at her mother's funeral, she makes up her mind (though the script never does) that he is her father. Moze palms off Bibles, "purchased by the deceased," on widows. Addie blackmails him into letting her tag along with him through Kansas and Missouri. At first she disapproves of his techniques; then she beats him at his own game. The pair are supposed to be preciously entertaining.

Paper Moon lacks conviction, Paper Moon lacks class. It isn't moving and its values are spurious, to say the least. Addie might have emerged as a real child, so lonely and yearning for tenderness that she uses her cunning to attach herself to Moze Pray, but Bogdanovich makes her a self-conscious little freak.

There's a believable adolescent in the picture--P. J. Johnson's portrait of Trixie's fifteen-year-old black maid, who helps Addie with the plot, for her own good and sufficient reasons.

Phoney as it is, Paper Moon is something to catch on television; it is the prototype road-pic-with-kid of the seventies.

Also: Family Relationships

PHOEBE: STORY OF AN ADOLESCENT PREGNANCY, see p. 154

THE RED PONY, see p. 319

THE REIVERS, see p. 320

A SEPARATE PEACE, see p. 323

SHANE

Paramount, 1953. 117 mins. col. (d) George Stevens (sp) A. B. Guthrie, from the novel by Jack Schaefer (ph) Loyal Griggs (m) Victor Young (c) Alan Ladd, Jean Arthur, Jack Palance, Van Heflin, Brandon de Wilde, Ben Johnson, Edgar Buchanan, Elisha Cook, Jr., John Dierkes, Ellen Corby. (FNC)

Into the flat valley backed by the high mountains of the Teton range in Wyoming, with a one-street town and a cemetery, the outsider descends, to the place where he will spend a brief moment before fading into the distance: this romantic legend of the ex-gunfighter, Shane, is the most lasting in the dream factory of Hollywood. But it is not we who see Shane, who is "hardly a man at all, but something like the Spirit of the West, beautiful in fringed buckskins" (Robert Warshow, The Immediate Experience). It is Joey Starrett, nine years old. When Shane comes mysteriously out of the landscape at the beginning of the film, Joey is playing at shooting deer near the cabin where he lives with his homesteader parents. Joey looks up and sees Shane. And at the end of the film, when Shane's day is over and he goes away, it is Joey he leaves behind, "the wondering little boy who might have imagined the whole thing," calling in vain for his hero to come back.

Through the eyes of a child, we have experienced the romance of the past. Brandon de Wilde, as Joey, is unforgettable in his innocence, his refusal to see things as they are or to compromise with his ideal vision of Shane. When, about the middle of the story, Shane (Alan Ladd) is talking to the leader of the cattlemen, he says to him, "Your days are over," and the cattleman replies, "Mine? What about yours, gunslinger?"

"The difference is," Shane says, "I know it."

Joey does not know it; Joey knows, as a small boy knows, that what he has dreamed is so. Shane is a beautiful film, a poetic moving study of a child's worship of a hero. It is also a realistic study of a boy's place in his family and in the adult world. Joey's parents (Van Heflin and Jean Arthur) are warm, hardworking, and brave. They understand their small son's fascination by the struggle waged so brutally between the homesteaders and the cattlemen, but they will not sanction his idealizing senseless violence. Joey, talking with his mother about Shane, is too young to understand the adult drama of husband, wife, and the stranger attractive to both as friend and potential lover. Uncomprehending, he loves all three.

George Stevens's romantic direction and Loyal Griggs's lovely color cinematography (which won him an Academy Award) make Shane the kind of movie which creates a myth for the eye to remember. At the heart of the myth is the reality of the memorably-played nine-year-old Joey.

Also: Family Relationships
From Literature

SMALL CHANGE (L'ARGENT DE POCHE)

France, 1976. 104 mins. col. (d) François Truffaut (sp) François Truffaut and Suzanne Schiffman (ph) Pierre-William Glenn (m) Maurice Jaubert; song, "Les enfants s'ennuient le dimanche," by Charles Trenet (c) Gregory Desmouceaux, Sylvie Grezel, Philippe Goldman, Pascale Bruchon, Claudio Deluca, Jean-François Stevenin, Chantal Mercier. French dialog with English subtitles by Helen G. Scott. (FNC)

We had first been enchanted by the faces--transparent, alive--on the cover of the Spring 1976 Sight and Sound. In the school playground, a boy is perched on the shoulders of a friend, his spy-glasses front center, his head slewed around to the right; a teacher is approaching, his friend's jaw drops ... When we saw Small Change, we found out whom he'd been spying on.

Truffaut never grows tired of making movies with children: "Anything a child does on the screen, it seems to be doing for the first time, and that is what gives such great value to film used to present young faces in the process of transformation."

For Small Change, Truffaut's co-scriptwriter Suzanne Schiffman tells us, he took out little pieces of paper he'd been saving for years, true stories about kids: newspaper clippings, friends' anecdotes, his own memories. They fed his curiosity, but his base is inexhaustible. "One works with what happens to one in the first twelve years of life," he said to Joseph Gelmis of Newsday. Small Change could have come only from the artist who lived and later filmed the pain of The 400 Blows, but it is far sunnier, and the artist mellower.

Not that Small Change is only funny, though it is often very, very funny. Truffaut believes that all of it--ebulliently joyous, sheer fantasy, poignant, or grim--"should animate the notion that childhood is often perilous but that it is also full of grace and that it has a thick skin. The child invents life; it runs into things, but at the same time it develops all its powers of resistance."

Small Change is a radiant mosaic of the everyday adventures in "inventing life" of about ten boys and girls, from infancy to fourteen or fifteen years, during the last month of their school year in Thiers, and in August in summer camp. Hilarious or deeply moving, the kids are spellbinding; the adults (teachers, parents, neighbors) are real people, not stereotypes. All the children are new to the screen, for Truffaut has used his Paris friends' children, his own two daughters, and two of Suzanne Schiffman's smallfry, as well as kids from Thiers and Clermont-Ferrand.

From all the faces of children in Small Change, it is hard to pick the most vivid. Here are only a few:

Sylvie, seven, is left home by mama and papa (papa is a police commissioner) because she refuses to go to a restaurant with them without a hideously dirty elephant-purse which is hers. So she opens the window, and roars through papa's bullhorn to the neighbors in the courtyard that she has been left alone starving. Food is rushed to the "victim" on a clothesline. Enjoying the chicken, she says to herself, happily, "Everybody was looking at me." Claudio, the younger of the two con-men Deluca brothers, tries to tell the other boys a dirty story, but he is half convulsed, half embarrassed, because he really doesn't understand it yet. Patrick, who is twelve-and-a-half, lives alone with his paraplegic father and is afflicted with "l'amour ardent" for the beautiful mother of a schoolmate. His first kiss, with the little girl, Martine, on the camp stairway, is not ardent but infinitely tender. Julien, who steals, and has the street wisdom of the child who must fend for himself, turns out to be the battered victim of his own drunken mother and grandmother.

And then there is Gregory, who looks about three. Gregory may be a metaphor for the whole film. All joyful experiment, he pushes a kitten out of the window, and then falls himself, down, down, down ... But he lands soft and safe. "I go boom!" he announces in delight.

There have been criticisms of the "sentimentality" of some of Small Change. But we agree with Gerald Mast of The New Republic: "The film's spiritual sunshine is as bright as its visual imagery."

It is easy to see why other commentators were taken aback by Truffaut's use of the teacher Richet (Jean-François Stevenin) as his mouthpiece. There is a schoolroom lecture in which he mades a "statement" about the fact that boys like Julien, as a compensation, may become stronger because of the abuse they've suffered; and declares, flatly, "Of all mankind's inequalities, injustice to children is the worst." While the teacher may appear didactic, he is convincing in responding with concern for his students who are frightened by their schoolmate's suffering. But Small Change is a very personal film. Truffaut is all too concerned about the Juliens, about children who suffer the four hundred blows, to be faulted for that scene. Perhaps it was an artistic error, but how much it reveals of the artist! And the teachers in this film are beautifully felt and warmly drawn: Richet, sharing with his class his excitement about the birth of his son; Mlle. Chantal, bursting into tears when she realizes she has been unjust to Julien.

We love everything about this buoyant, loving film--the slapstick, the kids' charmed lives, the innocence and absurdity of their unpredictable adventures. That may be because we share with Truffaut and Suzanne Schiffman the weakness of Victor Hugo: "Children have a way of making me go crazy. I adore them, and I am a fool."

Also: Teachers and Schools

SUMMER OF '42, see p. 156

A SUMMER TO REMEMBER, see p. 102

THE SUMMER WE MOVED TO ELM STREET

Canada, 1967. 29 mins. col. Produced by the National Film Board of Canada. (d)(w) Patricia Wilson. (CON)

In our highly mobile culture, we know how all children are emotionally dislocated when they have to leave friends and school to move out of their familiar neighborhood to a new home. How much more poignant are the needs of children like ten-year-old Doreen, who is already suffering within her unhappy family--her parents' marriage crumbling, her father an alcoholic. The Summer We Moved to Elm Street raises the question of how we can make moving easier for the Doreens and for all youngsters.

We see the tensions and bitterness in Doreen's home through her eyes, as she and her brothers witness the quarrels between husband and wife. We observe her attempts to adjust to life on Elm Street, finding a new girl friend to play with, going to lunch with her friend and her happy mother, exploring the public gardens, listening to her Sunday school teacher.

Doreen's new friendship ends in tragedy. Money is short in her home, and at the close of the film we see the van pull up at her house; the family is on the move again. In the new neighborhood to which she is going, will this lonely and sensitive child be awakened, achieve a deeper sense of life's changes and her identity, or be more alienated?

Also: Family Relationships

TO KILL A MOCKINGBIRD, see p. 326

A TREE GROWS IN BROOKLYN, see p. 103

THE WORLD OF HENRY ORIENT

United Artists, 1964. 106 mins. col. (d) George Roy Hill (sp) Nora Johnson and Nunnally Johnson, from Nora Johnson's novel (ph) Boris Kaufman and Arthur J. Ornitz (m) Elmer Bernstein (e) Peter Sellers, Paula Prentiss, Angela Lansbury, Tippy Walker, Merrie Spaeth, Tom Bosley, Phyllis Thaxter, Bibi Osterwald. (UAS)

If everyone else in the picture were as wonderful as its two fifteen-year-old characters, The World of Henry Orient would be one of the best American movies. But let us be grateful that in a glossy major production with its share of stereotypes we have two adolescents who are tart, funny, and genuine.

Tippy Walker plays Valerie Boyd, a touching screwball, wild and pathetic and hilarious. She is going through a period of adjustment with her parents; Mama Angela Lansbury is selfish and lecherous, Papa Tom Bosley, poor man, is as much in need as Valerie is. (Father and daughter will be together at the end of the film.) Valerie's best friend, Marian (Merrie Spaeth), lives with her widowed mother (Phyllis Thaxter) and wisecracking Bibi Osterwald.

Valerie and Marian, who are certain that they are madly in love with Henry Orient--a pianist from Brooklyn with a "continental" accent (Peter Sellers)--spend their days and evenings trailing him, until he is ready to collapse at the sight of them. One of his lady-loves, suburban housewife Paula Prentiss, is sure they are teenage detectives hired by her husband. When Mrs. Boyd discovers the scrapbook that the girls have been keeping during their passion for Henry, she misconstrues it and temporarily separates the pair. In the end, reunited, they are "over" Henry and ready for boys.

The teenage talk is very real and very funny, and the two girls are a delight not only on the plane of fantasy but in the very awfully-happy-in-a-sad-way moments of family emotion.

These teenagers still treat Manhattan like their own private playground. The film has a kind of Beatles grace, as the girls leap and float through the park or Washington Square or along the waterfront. The photography is often breathtaking, as it might well be; Arthur J. Ornitz was working with Boris Kaufman, who photographed *Zero for Conduct* for Jean Vigo before coming to America in 1940 and photographing such movies as *On the Waterfront* and *The Pawnbroker*.

To watch Valerie and Marian in *The World of Henry Orient* is to re-enter the world between childhood and adolescence and to fall happily under its spell. The story, incidentally, was written by Nunnally Johnson and his daughter Nora, from her novel.

Also: Family Relationships

ZOZOS, LES, see p. 166

FINDING ONESELF

A TO B

U. S., 1971. 35 mins. col. (d) Nell Cox. (TLF)

A to B is "one of the most honest, sensitive and judicious dramatic vignettes of a young girl's discovery of self." (The New York Times).

Sixteen-year-old Penny, in the last day of her junior year in high school and the first two days of her summer vacation, faces some familiar family conflicts and sexist attitudes. Dad doesn't like her to wear pants and won't let her drive him; Mom's sure Penny will never "catch a husband" if she doesn't work in the kitchen and cook. Penny hears a friend define success for his single brother: all the girls hang on him.

A documentary shot in cinéma-vérité style with nonprofessionals in Lexington, Kentucky, the filmmaker's home town--with some good bits observed in the high school and in a drive-in named the Hog Market, A to B follows Penny's encounters quietly. We do not know what her thoughts are as we watch her emerge from her home into newer relationships, but we can guess. Penny is beginning to shake off the repressions of her conditioning. The final line of the film: "To be continued."

THE ACTRESS, see p. 65

THE ADOLESCENTS (a. k. a. THAT TENDER AGE) (LA FLEUR DE L'AGE OU LES ADOLESCENTES)

Canada, France, Italy and Japan, 1964. 80 mins. b/w. (d) Michel Brault, Jean Rouch, Gian Vittorio Baldi, Hiroshi Teshigahara (sp) Alex Pelletier, Jean Rouch, Baldi, Kobo Abe (c) Genevieve Bujold, Louise Marleau, Bernard Arcand, Micaela Esdra, Esmeralda Ruspoli, Marie-France de Chabeneix, Veronique Duval, Nadine Ballot, Miki Irie. In French, Italian, Japanese, with English subtitles. (CON)

The Adolescents is a four-part film with segments by Canadian, French, Italian, and Japanese directors, about girls ranging in age from fourteen to seventeen.

Canadian Michel Brault's episode, "Genevieve," comes off best. From Alex Pelletier's slight tale, Brault (director of excellent film documentaries for the National Film Board of Canada) has created a crisp picture of a teenage charmer, pertly played by Bujold, who steals the attractive beau of her plain and vulnerable friend during a winter carnival in Montreal. This is a comedy of sex at seventeen, with good portraits.

"Fiammetta," directed by the Italian Gian Vittorio Baldi, shows the pathos of a rich girl (Micaela Esdra) isolated by her widowed mother's emotional needs in a decaying old mansion.

"Marie-France and Veronica" (by French director Jean Rouch) presents strong characterizations of young teenagers with the attitudes and behavior of adult women, one falling into easy love affairs and the other trying to find more meaningful experiences.

The Japanese "Ako," directed by Teshigahara and written by Kobo Abe, who made Woman in the Dunes together, is about a sixteen-year-old (Miki Irie) who has a monotonous job and problems with boys.

The Adolescents is fragmentary but often convincing--a show of diverse talents. Without question, Genevieve Bujold walks off with the show.

Also: Growing Pains
Love and Sex

AH, WILDERNESS, see p. 286

AL STACEY HAYES

U.S., 1970. 25 mins. b/w. (d) Joel A. Levitch. (JAS)

Al is a handsome, black sixteen-year-old of Shelby, Mississippi. He is neither radical nor militant, but is trying to formulate his own political identity. Encouraged by a recent successful boycott by blacks in Shelby, Al and other young people canvass to reelect a good black alderman. But it is difficult for Al and his friends, Elsie and Leon, to arouse the older people to develop pride in their community and to become active participants. Al says, "They just feel white people are always right and black people are always wrong."

A senior in high school, Al will soon be leaving for college. His deep concern for his people makes him say that he will return to Shelby some day, when he hopes he can "get things to move faster." Like so many intelligent youngsters trying to "change the system," he has to admit he's not going to be able to do it overnight. Meanwhile, he's going to work at it--and he is learning not only that he can't communicate with the older generation, but that these older people have fears and problems of their own. They're not ready for Al yet; meanwhile, he is growing into a deeper understanding of himself and the social climate in which he lives.

Also: Generation Conflicts

ALL FALL DOWN, see p. 67

ALL MINE TO GIVE, see p. 67

ALMOS' A MAN, see p. 289

AS WE ARE, see p. 253

BAD COMPANY, see p. 231

BALLAD OF A SOLDIER, see p. 209

BIRCH INTERVAL

Gamma III, 1976. 104 mins. col. (d) Delbert Mann (sp) Joanna Crawford, from her novel (ph) Urs B. Furrer (m) Leonard Rosenman (c) Eddie Albert, Rip Torn, Ann Wedgeworth, Susan McClung, Anne Revere, Brian Part. (SWA)

This movie has a familiar theme--a preadolescent girl involved in the complexities of adult life finds out that "Things are not what they seem." This pronouncement by the White Rabbit to Alice in Wonderland is quoted to eleven-year-old Jesse (Susan McClung) by her Uncle Tom (Rip Torn). Jesse's adventures take place in a wonderland new to the screen, which gives freshness to Birch Interval.

City-bred Jesse is sent to live with her mother's family, the Strawachers, in an Amish farming community in Pennsylvania, in 1947. Pa (Eddie Albert), Tom's wife (Ann Wedgeworth), and her young cousins, who are nine and twelve, provide an interesting summer and fall for the little New Yorker. When she arrives in the town of Birch Interval, Jesse does not encounter the stable peace she remembers. Instead she is conscious of conflict and mystery surrounding her relatives. Her loner uncle; an eccentric recluse (Anne Revere); her nine-year-old cousin Samuel who dabbles in witchcraft (Brian Part); the "crazy girl" at the window; the Amish neighhors--they take her out of her child's world and force her to look outward and to make choices. Some of her experiences are traumatic, like her grandfather's decision to send Uncle Tom to a mental institution for tests, and Tom's death from viral pneumonia, contracted when he takes refuge from his family and the community in an old mill.

Grandpa Strawacher helps Jesse to understand adult motives: "Try not to judge people so ... love them ... Try not to be seeing just good and bad in folks. Stand by them in whatever they do." She is "stretched" enough to come to terms with the questions surrounding her uncle's death.

Somewhat episodic in its vignettes of Birch Interval experience, the film offers insight into the life of the Amish--their piety and principles; a worship service sung in Pennsylvania Dutch; farming customs and dress. The beautiful photography of the late Urs B. Furrer (Part 2, Sounder and Where the Lilies Bloom) gives Jesse's story a strong sense of authenticity. Like all the other films of producer Robert B. Radnitz (Sounder), this one was shot on location. We see many landmarks of the Pennsylvania country in which the Plain People--the Amish, Mennonite, and Dunkard sects--have lived since the early 1700's. Against this pleasant background, the gradual awareness by the city youngster of different values and customs is developed clearly.

Also: Cultural Conflicts
Death
Religion

BLACK GIRL, see p. 74

BOY OF TWO WORLDS, see p. 131

THE CHALK GARDEN, see p. 116

CLAUDINE, see p. 75

CLOSELY WATCHED TRAINS (OSTRE SLEDOVANE VLAKY)

Czechoslovakia, 1966. 89 mins. b/w. (d) Jiri Menzel (sp) Bohumil Hrabel and Jiri Menzel from a story by Hrabel (ph) Jaromir Sofr (m) Jiri Sust (c) Vaclav Neckar, Jitka Bendova, Vladimir Valenta, Libuse Havelkova, Josef Somr, Jiri Menzel, Jitka Zelenohorska, Nada Urbankova. Czech dialog with English subtitles. (MAC)

"Only his mother and the audience could love the hero of Closely Watched Trains when he first comes on the screen dressed in doubts and underdrawers," said critic Joseph Morganstern, who called the movie "a gentle masterpiece."

It is during the Nazi occupation of Czechoslovakia, and a war is going on out there, but it is the daily defeats of his life--comic, and ultimately tragic--which matter for Milos (Vaclav Neckar). At seventeen, he is a shy, eager, and inexperienced trainee at a small railway station in the country near Pilston, watching with awe as his boss, the train dispatcher Hubieka (Josef Somr), seduces available females on the station-house couch. Milos is worried about his own manhood. A pretty conductress, Masa (Jitka Bendova), leans down from a train to kiss him--the locomotive yanks her away--and when Milos spends the night with her, it's a failure. He rents a room in a hotel to commit suicide by slashing his wrists, but that's a failure, too. Dr. Brabec (Jiri Menzel) prescribes an older woman--but who?

Before Milos grows from an overgrown boy in a big coat to sexual and political manhood, events catch up with him in the little station world. He is initiated into his first complete sexual experience by a woman in the resistance who has come with explosives to the station house. Early the next morning, Hubieka is prevented from blowing up a Nazi munitions train. (He has to stand trial, for using official stamps on the rear of his female telegraphist.) Milos does his job in the war as he had done it in the railway station; he takes the dynamite from under the noses of the Nazis, and from the top of the signal tower hurls the explosives onto the train. But he is killed by a Nazi soldier.

"Typical of the film's understatement is the moment of his death," wrote Stanley Kauffmann in New American Review. "... We hear the shot, then we see him sprawled on top of a freight car passing beneath the tower, being borne away. Everything gets borne away sooner or later, the film seems to say, but is that a reason not to care? By the very selection of his theme, Menzel seems to answer in the negative."

Winner of the Academy Award as Best Foreign Film in 1967, Closely Watched Trains is one of the most cherished films of the Czech New Wave. Milos is a classic portrait of a late adolescent, developed with quiet, engaging, and compassionate irony.

Also: Love and Sex
War and Its Aftermath

COOLEY HIGH

American International, 1975. 107 mins. col. (d) Michael Schultz (sp) Eric Monte (ph) Paul Vom Brack (m) Freddie Perren (c) Glynn Turman, Lawrence-Hilton Jacobs, Garrett Morris, Cynthia Davis, Corin Rogers. (SWA)

Cooley High is about growing up black in a Chicago ghetto in 1964. The movie is a funny, poignant, loving, sometimes tragic re-creation of the exuberant follies of adolescence, a particular life-style, and the moving dreams and despair of young black Americans at a point in our time.

Director Michael Schultz, himself a black, followed Cooley High with Car Wash. In both films, he literally propels his characters across the screen and into the moment.

Cooley High is about four seniors at the Edwin G. Cooley Vocational High School who are trying to achieve a sense of self. A first-rate cast brings their friendships, aspirations, and struggles close to us. These adolescents are young enough (wrote Jack Slater in The New York Times) to see themselves "without sociology's help, without clichés." Since Cooley High takes place before the activism of the late sixties, it "ignores the social and political significance of 1964 to explore instead the softer, warmer areas where young people really live."

Preacher (Glynn Turman) is a reader of poetry and history who gets terrible grades. His pal Cochise (Lawrence-Hilton Jacobs) is a basketball star. Their other friends, including Brenda (Cynthia Davis), Preacher's girl, and their families, really do live it up: cutting classes to go to the zoo, making out, drinking wine, dancing or hanging out at the local rib joint, ending a monster-movie matinee with a gang brawl, tasting the sweetness of first love, winning a scholarship, coping with brothers and sisters, even experiencing the shock of early death.

Despite such echoes of American Graffiti as the joyride in a stolen car and the epilogue showing what fate had in store for the principal characters, Cooley High is honest and important in its own right.

Also: Teachers and Schools

THE COWBOYS

Warners, 1972. 128 mins. col. (d) Mark Rydell (sp) Irving Ravetch, Harriet Frank, Jr., William Dale Jennings, from the book by William Dale Jennings (ph) Robert Surtees (m) John Williams (c) John Wayne, Roscoe Lee Browne, Colleen Dewhurst, Bruce Dern, Slim Pickens, Lonny Chapman. (GEN)

Starring John Wayne, produced by the team (Rydell, Ravetch, Frank) that did The Reivers, written by the pair (Ravetch and Frank) that authored Hud, this should have been the odds-on favorite for family entertainment in 1972, with its eleven schoolboys (aged nine to fifteen) helping Wayne get 1,200 head of cattle to market in the Old West of the 1870s.

Instead, The Cowboys caused a storm of critical controversy. "How do you feel about teenagers proving they're men by killing bad guys in an outburst of frontier vengeance?" asked William Wolf in

Cue. "It may be instructing new generations of boys in the questionable discipline of justifying unjustifiable acts," said Gary Arnold of the Washington Post.

Other critics deplored the gratuitous violence, the underlying theme (only slaughter can solve certain problems), and the suggestion that youngsters achieve maturity when they can torture and kill without flinching from their duty to the father figure (Wayne) who must be avenged.

(It is only fair to report also that hardly anyone denied the fun of the scenes of the boys learning to be cowboys or the solidity of Wayne's performance. All the furor was aroused by the film's last thirty minutes, in which the boys murder the band of cattle rustlers who had murdered Wayne.)

The story relates how rancher Wil Abderson (Wayne) has to hire and train eleven schoolboys to replace his regular cowhands who have joined the gold rush. After their grueling training session, the boys, under Wil's none-too-gentle tutelage, begin their "transformation into men." They perform hard tasks, get drunk on whiskey, encounter a band of travelling prostitutes. Long Hair (Bruce Dern), leader of the cow rustlers, shoots Wil in the back and both legs, and runs off with the cattle. With the help of the black chuckwagon cook Jebediah (Roscoe Lee Browne), the boys fulfill their commitment to the murdered Wil by ambushing the rustler and killing them off, one by one.

Rousing good fun? Simply ridiculous? A western fairy tale? Morally reprehensible? Make of it what you will. Much more to the point is the description of The Cowboys by an old Hollywood hand: "Red River with kids."

Yes, kids are "in." Of the eleven in this film, one is a Chicano, one is Jewish. Two who have no qualms about killing are still lily-pure because they are whisked away from the travelling prostitutes. One feels guilty because he's weak enough to wear glasses; another, because he stammers. (Wayne stops that by yelling at him.)

THE CULPEPPER CATTLE CO.

Twentieth Century-Fox, 1972. 92 mins. col. (d) Dick Richards (sp) Eric Bercovici, Gregory Prestiss (ph) Lawrence Edward Williams, Ralph Woolsey (m) Tom Scott, Jerry Goldsmith (c) Gary Grimes, Billy Green Bush, Raymond Guth, Anthony James. (FNC)

In a 1977 "Re-View" of under-rated films presented at London's National Film Theatre, this one by Dick Richards (Farewell My Lovely) was praised by Brian Baxter: "Of all the recent Westerns dealing with adolescents in the West, this is by far the most successful: beautifully acted and magnificently photographed...."

When Ben Mockridge, a sixteen-year-old Texan (Gary Grimes), signs on as helper to the cook (Raymond Guth) on a cattle drive to the Colorado market led by Culpepper (Billy "Green" Bush), he is full of romantic myths about what awaits him. It is just after the Civil War, and the legend of the West is a fresh dream. His experiences on the trail frighten and disillusion him. He meets the heavies (who are only sometimes funny) in a saloon shoot-out, a range war, and a sample of frontier justice for horse thieves. He has to kill a man himself. In bloody detail, the lesson is spelled out for him: "Cowboyin' is somethin' you do when you can't do nuthin' else." But when he leaves the profit-hungry Culpepper to defend a sect of religious pacifists harassed by a cruel landowner, Ben is disillusioned again when the leader of the sect, Nathaniel (Anthony James), lets him down.

At the end, riding off alone, Ben is a little older, a little wiser. At least he is following his own trail, which is neither Culpepper's nor Nathaniel's.

Gary Grimes, the Hermie of <u>Summer of '42</u>, is very believable as Ben.

DAVID: OFF AND ON

U.S., 1972. 42 mins. col. (prod)(d)(ed) Martha Coolidge. Special still photography by Haight-Ashbury Studios. (FNC)

"Martha and David Coolidge aren't fictional. She is in her mid-twenties, already rich in wisdom, and so accomplished as a filmmaker that her work becomes a prism which divides its subject, her brother David, into a hundred hues for us to look at one by one. What drives him? David is gentle, good-humored, handsome, obviously intelligent. In his first twenty-one years he has been a schoolboy, an alcoholic, a heroin addict, a convict, a mental patient, a resident of purgatory and hell. There are no fictions, no disguises, and no apologies in his sister's film biography; nothing is softened, except by love and understanding of a height which is seldom reached in film and which is rare even in life." (American Film Institute)

This prizewinning documentary traces David's problems from his childhood to the present (he is now off drugs, married, supporting a family, and planning to go to college). Interviews with him--he tells his own story--are punctuated by old family album snapshots, his own drawings, and photos of various institutions where he's been.

David appears as an infant, a child, a troubled teenager. His father died before he was born; he acquired (and resented) a stepfather when he was thirteen; he dropped out of school and "progressed" from speed to heroin. There are unsparing details of failure--of family, of institutions, of self.

"I learned from my brother," Martha Coolidge said, "that you can blame taking drugs on a lot of things, but finally you have to blame it on yourself before you can stop taking them. I then began to look for what was positive in the story and in David's personality. It was out of his search for something to live for that I had to build my film, and David had to build his life."

David emerges as charming and articulate, a sensitive artist and poet, and changed from the confused youngster of his early years. He may not know all the answers about why this particular boy, David, from an upper-middle-class family, took drugs, but he observes, "They talk about drugs as the problem, not as a symptom of everybody's problem."

David: Off and On was awarded the first John Grierson Memorial Award given to a new documentary filmmaker of outstanding talent at the American Film Festival in 1973. It is a major contribution to our understanding of young people today.

Also: Family Relationships

LE DEPART

Belgium, 1967. 92 mins. b/w. (d) Jerzy Skolimowski (sp) Jerzy Skolimowski and Andrzej Kostenko. (ph) Willy Kurant (m) K. T. Komeda (c) Jean-Pierre Léaud, Catherine Duport, Leon Dory, Paul Roland, Jacquelin Bir, John Dobrynine. French dialog with English subtitles. (CON)

Maybe Porsches aren't everything in life, after all. At the end of one of the wildest, funniest weekends in contemporary cinema, this is the truth arrived at by nineteen-year-old Marc.

Vulnerable, insecure, illogical, Marc is really a little crazy. At least he is crazy about cars. Although Marc is only a hairdresser he is frantically searching for a Porsche to race in a big motor rally. The hunt leads him through a maze of farcical adventures--half Sennett, half Godard--with a predatory older woman, with a motorcyclist, with a dog barking in a Porsche, with lovely young Michele, who gets locked with him in a car trunk.

Through all this, the boy is fascinating: endlessly in motion, and as obsessed by his hobby, as frenetic in his search for experience, as anyone else of his generation. As played by Jean-Pierre Léaud (The 400 Hundred Blows, Day for Night), he is an unforgettable young man, who is stripped down finally, when he makes love to his girl, to a realization of self.

Jerzy Skolimowski, the gifted young Polish director (Barrier, Walkover, Deep End), made this brilliant comedy in Brussels. His hero, Marc, is very French, very much of today's world, not just of sex and fast cars, but of youth's search for identity. The young

Michele who wins Marc over from his Porsches is charmingly played by Catherine Duport.

Léaud's characterization of the nineteen-year-old and Skolimowski's virtuosity add up to so much fun that one is apt to forget the truth of their modern scene. In the words of British film critic David Robinson, the movie is also about powerful cars and cool music and great blind glass buildings and Utopian advertising; the obsession with sex and the symbols of success.

Shown at the New York Film Festival, and winner of two top awards at the Berlin Festival, Le Départ proves irresistible. Under the farce, there is an authentic portrait of a young human being.

Also: Love and Sex

EAST OF EDEN, p. 77

FATHER

Hungary, 1966. 95 mins. b/w (d)(sp) Istvan Szabo (ph) Sandor Sara (m) Janos Gonda (c) Andras Balint, Miklos Gabor, Kati Solyom, Klari Tolnay, Dani Erdelyi. Hungarian dialog with English subtitles. (BUD, KAF, WRS)

In this probing drama of a boy's coming of age as he reexamines the reality and the myth of his tie to his father, director-writer Istvan Szabo may well be suggesting the maturing of his whole generation as it explored its beliefs before and after the 1956 Hungarian uprising.

In the imagination of the child Tako (Dani Erdelyi), he is the son of a hero. His father died at the end of World War II, but in his need for a glorious heritage, Tako creates the myth that he died as a brave partisan fighter during the war; and in honor of this "fact," breaks up the courtship of his mother and a suitor who would take his father's place. The legend of his father's heroism is useful to Tako as he grows up, for it makes him a leader among his friends, and later stands him in good stead with the girls.

Tako's emotional development from boy to man begins with his soul searchings when he is a university student (Andras Balint), no longer captive of his childhood dreams. Embroiled in the 1956 uprising, he acts on his own without wondering what his father would have done. While he works as an extra in a film studio, he meets Anni (Kati Solyom), and reenacts with her in the film the horrors of the persecution of the Jews--Anni's tragically real, not imagined, heritage. It moves Tako to learn the truth of his own past, and when he discovers that his father was a very ordinary doctor, decent but no hero, he is ready to respect him, but to say goodbye to the mythical image, and to live by relying maturely on his own strength as a man.

The longings of Tako as a child, his hunger for a father and a past, are shown honestly and sensitively, and sometimes with humor, first in scenes of his life as it is, then in flashbacks of his illusions about the father he makes up (Miklos Gabor).

The second feature of Istvan Szabo, the brilliant twenty-nine-year-old, who is one of the Hungarian New Wave directors, Father is almost autobiographical. It is uniformly well acted, not only in the roles of the child and the young man Tako, but in the part of the mother (Klari Tolnay) and the girl, Anni. Winner of an international festival grand prize, it offers a persuasive picture of a boy's need to reshape reality to satisfy a natural desire.

Also: Family Relationships
Growing Pains
War and Its Aftermath

FIRST LOVE, see p. 146

HAND IN HAND, see p. 198

THE HEART IS A LONELY HUNTER, see p. 303

HERE'S YOUR LIFE

Sweden, 1967. 110 mins. or 151 mins. (specify when ordering) b/w with some col. (prod)(ph)(ed) Jan Troell (sp) Jan Troell and Bengst Forslund from the novel The Story of Olof by Eyvind Johnson (m) Erik Nordgren (c) Eddie Axberg, Ulla Sjoblom, Gunnar Bjornstrand, Per Oscarsson, Ulf Palme, Ake Fridell, Allan Edvall, Holger Lowenadler, Anna Maria Blind. Swedish dialog with English subtitles. (MAC)

Olof is a working-class boy schooled by life between his fourteenth and eighteenth years, learning his lessons in work, sex, society. Like the men and women he meets, Olof is intensely alive and believable. They all move not only in the world of 1914-1918 but in the world of nature, of the harsh yet beautiful forests of northern Sweden.

Here's Your Life is the first feature of director-photographer-editor Jan Troell, whose later films, The Emigrants (nominated for an Academy Award in 1973) and The New Land, have won him an international audience. In its poetic realism, its blend of sensitivity and toughness, of humor and tragic comment, it is as fine a picture of adolescent self-realization as we have had.

Based on Eyvind Johnson's partly autobiographical novel The Story of Olof, Here's Your Life traces the development of a poor backwoods orphan through a series of difficult jobs, and personal experiences both droll and poignant, to the point of maturity where he starts off on his own.

We follow Olof, who is well played by Eddie Axberg (the brother in The New Land), from the day he leaves his foster parents' home. His first job, as a timber floater in a logging camp, is grueling, but he learns much from the older men, whether they are teasing him or sharing their lore. In a very moving dream sequence, one of the three color sequences in the black and white film, called "a tale of mist and tuberculosis," one of the loggers describes the deaths of his wife and children: "like butter you drop on the stove--a hiss and it's gone."

In winter, Olof goes to work in a brickyard-sawmill. When he protests against his boss's callousness toward an injured workman, he is fired. In his next job, candy hawker and billboard man in a village movie theater, he kisses his first girl but is disillusioned to learn he is not the only one. Promoted to assistant projectionist, he tours the summertime fairs with the chief operator, Nicke. He boasts to Nicke of imaginary sexual exploits but is too inexperienced to respond to an overture from Olivia, Nicke's mistress. After listening to them make love, Olof runs away and takes a job in a blacksmith's shop. His seduction of the blacksmith's daughter in a field ends with a handshake (the episode is as funny as it is credible) and Olof gets on a train.

After a political awakening at a rally, he develops a social conscience which costs him his job in the movie theater to which he has returned. He finds Olivia again and they set up housekeeping together. The sequence is one of the best in the film: the warm, indulgent carnival queen and her demanding adolescent lover. But Olivia's other lovers are also demanding and Olof will have none of it. He breaks off with her and gets a job on the railroad. There is an instructive, disastrous experience trying to organize support for a strike in a local trade union, and Olof decides he's learned quite a bit. "Everything is up to you--you're on your own." With his pipe stuck between his teeth, he starts walking south into a new life.

Troell's eye on the boy is unerring, whether it falls on his first kiss, his imitation of the social graces with a cigar, or just his shadow on the morning field. He neither sentimentalizes nor distorts; he cares about Olof and the people he meets. They struggle, sometimes grow, endure. We accept them as true in this climate, time, place.

In every milieu in which Olof works, there are excellent character studies by many of Sweden's best actors: Gunnar Bjornstrand's theater owner, Per Oscarsson's railroad worker, Ake Fridell's Nicke, Ulla Sjoblom's Olivia.

Originally 167 minutes, Here's Your Life was cut to 110

Eddie Axberg as Olof

for its American theatrical release in 1967, when exhibitors were more nervous about length than today. It is now available in 16mm in two versions, 110 minutes, or the clearer and more coherent 151 minutes.

Also: Love and Sex

HUD

Paramount, 1963. 112 mins. b/w. (d) Martin Ritt (sp) Irving Ravetch and Harriet Frank, Jr., from the novel *Horseman, Pass By* by Larry McMurtry (ph) James Wong Howe (m) Elmer Bernstein (c) Paul Newman, Melvyn Douglas, Patricia Neal, Brandon de Wilde. (FNC)

Continuing his series of adolescent portraits--hero worship in *Shane*, adulation that shackles him until he breaks free in *All Fall Down*--Brandon de Wilde makes a choice between two images of manhood in *Hud*.

He plays seventeen-year-old Lon Bannon, an orphan living on the West Texas ranch of his grandfather, Homer (Melvyn Douglas). He idolizes his uncle, Hud (Paul Newman), "a man without principle," as Hud's father accurately calls him. To the veteran cattleman Homer Bannon, his son is despicable: "You can talk a woman into wantin' you and a man into trustin' you," he lashes out at Hud, "but you don't give a damn ... You don't care about _people_. You live just for yourself, and that makes you not fit to live with!"

But Lon finds the irresponsible, charming Hud no worse than anyone else in town. "Everybody around here _likes_ him," he says to his grandfather.

"The country changes because of the men we admire," Homer answers. "You're just gonna have to make up your own mind one day about what's wrong."

When an epidemic of hoof-and-mouth disease strikes their cattle, Lon sees the difference between Homer and Hud. His grandfather will comply with the decision of the government vet and see his beloved longhorns destroyed; his uncle would like to sell off the herd before they're quarantined. "Try and pass bad stuff on my neighbors?" Homer asks incredulously. Hud, whose philosophy of life is dog-eat-dog and get what you can for yourself, replies cynically, "How many honest men do you know?"

After the herd are killed, Hud takes steps to have his father declared mentally incompetent so that he can gain control of the ranch. To Lon, shocked by his intentions, Hud says, "If you don't look out for yourself, the only helpin' hand you'll ever get is when they lower the box."

Lon and Hud have been sharing "manly" amusements; there is a fight in a bar and a lot of drinking one night. But when they talk about women, Hud can't get very far with Lon. "I gotta like her as a _person_," the boy insists.

One of the persons dear to Lon is Alma, the housekeeper who also lives on the ranch (Patricia Neal). A divorcee with a difficult history, Alma is warm, earthy, and devoted to the old man and the boy. Hud gets drunk and attempts to assault Alma. Lon prevents him, and the next day Alma leaves the ranch.

Homer dies of a heart attack while riding around his deserted land. After the funeral, Hud owns the ranch and offers a share of money and work to his nephew. But Lon has made his choice. He knows Hud for what he is, ruthless and sickening in his selfishness. Lon is molded closer to the image of his grandfather, perhaps a rigid man, but a man with a sense of what is right and prideful for himself and for others. The boy leaves, determined to make his own way in the world. Hud watches him go, shrugs, and opens a can of beer.

With a splendid cast of performers, striking photography by James Wong Howe, and a meaningful script that often comments provocatively on the morality of our society, Martin Ritt's _Hud_ is justly admired. One of the best things in the picture is the character of Lon, uncertain and puzzled in his adolescence, but able to grow into a man's understanding of the philosophy he wants to live by.

Also: Family Relationships

IF I HAD A GUN, see p. 214

IN THIS HOUSE OF BREDE, see p. 199

INTRUDER IN THE DUST

M-G-M, 1949. 87 mins. b/w. (d) Clarence Brown (sp) Ben Maddow, from the novel by William Faulkner (ph) Robert Surtees (c) David Brian, Claude Jarman, Jr., Juano Hernandez, Porter Hall, Elizabeth Patterson, Will Geer, Elzie Emmanuel. (FNC)

Twelve-year-old Chick Mallison is a white southern boy who rejects his traditional racial code, the code of Oxford, Mississippi, but must in the end reconcile himself to his society. Faulkner's young protagonist is well played by Claude Jarman, Jr. Faulkner (and most critics) thought that this first-class film is the best of the movies made from his novels.

The boy has been well indoctrinated in a community tradition governing race relations. Why does he go against it? He has very mixed feelings about Lucas Beauchamp--a "difficult" man, who refuses to act the way black men are expected to act in the South--but he knows he must save him from a false charge of murder and prevent his being lynched by the town mob. After Chick (with the help of old Miss Habersham and young black Aleck) clears Lucas and sees him set free, Chick still has to come to grips with the nature of the mob. He has to live among these people.

In watching Intruder in the Dust, as the distinguished black novelist Ralph Ellison has said, we have been "watching the consciousness of a young Southerner grow through the stages of a superb mystery drama.

Chick's conversations with Lucas, with his Uncle Gavin, with Miss Habersham, are very revealing. This superbly written, photographed, and directed film offers deep insight into a boy's coming to terms with social realities, and making his own moral judgment against injustice and racial bigotry.

Also: Cultural Conflicts
From Literature

I REMEMBER MAMA, see p. 308

ISLAND OF THE BLUE DOLPHINS

Universal, 1964. 101 mins. col. (d) James B. Clark (sp) Ted Sherdeman, Jane Klove, from the novel by Scott O'Dell (ph) Leo Tover (c) Celia Kaye, Carlos Romero, George Kennedy, the Manchester and Kashai Tribes of the Poma Nation, and Junior. (GEN)

How do children on their own survive, eat, and protect themselves? Scott O'Dell's Newbery Medal novel and this agreeable film version (produced by Robert B. Radnitz) tell of a young Indian girl's adventure in solitude as a modern Robinson Crusoe.

Karana is a survivor of her tribe. After many battles with sea otters, her tribe's new king decides to take his people to the mainland for help. As they get under way, Karana sees that her younger brother, only six, has been left on shore. She swims back to the island unseen by the others of her tribe. Karana and her little brother, with the dog Rontu whom they have tamed, cope very well on the remote island, which is in the beautiful Anchor Bay country of the northern California coast.

Island of the Blue Dolphins, intended as appealing and colorful entertainment for children--and Leo Tover's color camera makes a lovely thing of rocks and surf--has a glimpse for adults of the remarkable capacity of a child to make her own world when there is need.

Also: From Literature

THE LAST PICTURE SHOW

Columbia, 1971. 104 mins. b/w. (d) Peter Bogdanovich (sp) Larry McMurtry, Peter Bogdanovich, based on the novel by Larry McMurtry (ph) Robert Surtees (m) recordings from the fifties by Eddie Fisher, Phil Harris, Frankie Laine, Hank Williams, Johnnie Ray, et al. (c) Timothy Bottoms, Jeff Bridges, Cybill Shepherd, Ben Johnson, Cloris Leachman, Ellen Burstyn, Sam Bottoms, Sharon Taggart, Eileen Brennan, Clu Gulager. (PAR)

The small oil town of Anarene, Texas, is the bleakest kind of dusty flatlands town, with one main street with stores on it. In this town Sonny Crawford (Timothy Bottoms) and Duane Jackson (Jeff Bridges), high school graduates of the Class of '51, move from the late teens to the beginning of manhood.

The first shot in director Peter Bogdanovich's film is of the "picture show," Anarene's movie theater; the last shot is of the last show the house plays before closing forever. It is 1952, and Sonny goes to the movie with Duane, who is on leave before departing for Korea. The feature is Red River. Once upon a time in Anarene, as in John Wayne's big cattle drive, life had meaning and vitality. Now there is only spiritual death in the town. The adults are without hope; the young people, too, have learned "Nothin's ever the way it's supposed to be," as Lois Farrow (Ellen Burstyn) says. It is the end of a period in America, the end of the movies as the dream machine (TV has taken over), the end of a period in Sonny's and Duane's lives.

Sonny is co-captain of the worst football team in Anarene history. He and Duane and their friends hang out at the pool hall, cafe, and movie house owned by Sam the Lion (Ben Johnson), a former cowhand who is a father figure to the boys. Sonny is no longer going steady with Charlene (Sharon Taggart), who is obliging enough in the front seat of a parked car. He is having love in the afternoon with Ruth Popper (Cloris Leachman), the neglected wife of the school basketball coach. Duane is having trouble with the prettiest girl in town, Jacy Farrow (Cybill Shepherd).

The boys are not too busy to join in a typical Anarene bit of sport. With the other high school students, they force the mute Billy (Sam Bottoms) into a sexual initiation with the town whore. As punishment for the cruel joke, Sam the Lion banishes them from the pool hall, the cafe, and the picture show for a time, until he sees his waitress forgiving Sonny by serving him a hamburger.

Jacy's bored mother, Lois (Ellen Burstyn), convinces her that marriage to a poor boy like Duane is out of the question. When Jacy's rich friend, Bobby Sheen, rejects her because she's a virgin, she remedies that in a disastrous motel episode with Duane. But Bobby marries somebody else, and Jacy lets her mother's lover seduce her, then makes a play for Sonny, who deserts Ruth for her.

Returning from a spree in Mexico, Sonny and Duane learn that Sam the Lion has died suddenly. Sonny inherits the pool hall. Duane quarrels with him over Jacy and hits him with a broken bottle. During Sonny's convalescence, Duane enlists in the army. Sonny and Jacy try to elope but are intercepted by her parents and she goes away to college.

The mute boy, Billy, is run over by a truck and killed on Anarene's main street. Duane has left for Korea. Overcome with loneliness and bitterness, Sonny has nowhere to turn. He stumbles blindly back to Ruth. She is full of anger over his betrayal, but when he takes her hand she is gentle with him. Looking into her judging face, the boy feels a sense of shame for having responded so carelessly to her love.

Bogdanovich's brilliant film was hailed as a contemporary classic, a slice of authentic Americana. Photographed in Larry McMurtry's own Texas town by the first-rate cinematographer Robert Surtees, its picture of a place like Anarene in the 50's is wonderful black and white drawing.

But The Last Picture Show is one of our finest "youth movies" because McMurtry (and Bogdanovich) have observed Sonny and

Duane and Jacy with depth and insight. The young people cannot breathe in the arid air of their town; they cannot take root in its moral dust. Their alienation from reality is complete. Everything blows away--the picture show closes, their former cowhand guru Sam the Lion dies without warning. Billy is senselessly killed, Jacy is lost, Ruth Popper's husband will come home--and there is no place to go. Korea? Is that a direction?

What happens after the fifties to these young people? It is a tribute to the movie that you wonder and care.

Also: Family Relationships
Generation Conflicts
Love and Sex

THE LEARNING TREE

Warners-7 Arts, 1969. 197 mins. col. (prod)(d)(sp)(m) Gordon Parks, from his autobiographical novel (ph) Burnett Guffey (c) Kyle Johnson, Alex Clarke, Estelle Evans, Dana Elcar, Mira Waters. (GEN)

Photographer-journalist Gordon Parks, the first black director of a film financed by a major Hollywood studio, based The Learning Tree on his 1963 autobiographical novel. He not only directed it but also produced it, wrote the screenplay, and composed the score. It is "a lovely small movie about boyhood, not black boyhood or white boyhood so much as human boyhood," according to Joseph Morganstern (Newsweek). To other critics, white and black, Gordon Parks's film, in its lack of militancy, is "old-fashioned," or "sentimental," with "Garden-of-Eden pictures" in a "world of benign memory."

The Parks protagonist in The Learning Tree is called Newt Winger (Kyle Johnson). A perceptive, talented fifteen-year-old in a small rural town in Kansas in the 1920's, he is the son of a domestic who works for the local circuit judge. His father works for a kind white rancher. In a series of episodic encounters with a variety of characters--mostly played by nonprofessionals--he is initiated, like all adolescents, into sex and love and death. Because he is black he also learns about injustice. First he encounters bigoted Sheriff Kirk. Then Arcella, the pretty, new black girl in town whom he loves, is seduced and abandoned by the white judge's son and she has to move away. Finally, Newt himself is afraid to tell the truth at a black man's trial for murder because it may cause a race riot in the town.

Gordon Parks's viewpoint is that dignity and intelligence and courage all count; that one must not wallow in self-pity; that speaking the truth and acting on our best heritage from experience will make good prevail. In The Learning Tree he is on the side of morality, whether black or white. And there are ironies and ambiguities in the characters. For instance, the school principal berates a teacher for discouraging Newt's ambitions but can't (or won't) put black boys on the school teams.

The greatest moral crisis that adolescent Newt faces is at the trial. Should he tell the truth and save an innocent white man at the expense of a guilty black man? Since we've watched him grow up respecting what used to be called the eternal verities, we know what he will do.

As a movie, Mr. Parks's first effort has obvious faults--melodramatic plotting, wooden acting (except for Kyle Johnson's Newt, which is an excellent job), and frequently naive characterizations. But it is warm and moving, and the visuals, again and again, are very fine. Still-photographer Parks and his cinematographer, Burnett Guffey, have given us some lovely scenes of Kansas in the twenties.

THE LITTLE ARK

Radnitz, 1972. 101 mins. col. (d) James B. Clark (sp) Joanna Crawford, from the novel by Jan de Hartog (ph) Austin Dempster. Denys Coop (m) Fred Karlin (c) Theodore Bikel, Genevieve Ambas, Philip Frame. (GEN)

Not so well known as other productions of award-winner Robert B. Radnitz (Sounder, Birch Interval, A Dog of Flanders), this adaptation of Jan de Hartog's novel about the disastrous 1953 floods in Holland shows how two small children caught in the deluge and its aftermath are matured by the experience.

"Radnitz has learned how to make children stay believably childlike," wrote Arthur Knight in 1972, "with the result that both children and adults can identify with his characters--especially in The Little Ark, probably his best film to date."

A Dutch boy (Philip Frame) and an Indonesian girl (Genevieve Ambas) are isolated in a church steeple when the floods strike. They find a brief, idyllic refuge in an abandoned houseboat. When they are rescued by a sea captain (Theodore Bikel), they learn much from him. They take great satisfaction in helping to care for the victims of the flood. Still not quite grown up, however, they are more concerned for their pets than for people, more interested in finding their stepfather than in obtaining shelter for strangers.

The Little Ark was filmed in Holland, where ingenious use of the shallow waters of the Zuyder Zee north of Amsterdam makes the flood extremely vivid. The picture of the instinctive reactions of two youngsters to an epic experience is well done.

Also: From Literature

LOSS OF INNOCENCE, see p. 151

LOUISIANA STORY

Lopert, 1948. 77 mins. b/w. (prod)(d) Robert J. Flaherty (sp) Frances and Robert J. Flaherty (assoc. prod) Richard Leacock, Helen van Dongen (ph) Richard Leacock (ed) Helen van Dongen (m) Virgil Thomson, played by Philadelphia Symphony Orchestra members, Eugene Ormandy, conductor. (CAL, CON, KPF, PYR)

Commissioned by the Standard Oil Company of New Jersey to make a film on the romance of oil drilling, the great documentary filmmaker Robert J. Flaherty created a masterpiece, Louisiana Story. This movie, which was made from 1946 to 1948, is a photographic poem, a work of genius which rediscovers an aspect of nature at its source. Into the drama of nature comes the "monster" of the oil derrick, which in its turn is transmuted into poetry as it moves into the wilderness, probes for oil, and then moves on, leaving the land still untouched.

"We had to translate our thesis--the impact of science on a simple, rural community--into terms of people," Flaherty said. "For our hero we dreamed up a half-wild Cajun boy of the woods and bayous. To personalize the impact of industry, we developed the character of a driller who would become a friend to the boy, eventually overcoming his shyness and reticence."

Louisiana Story is Flaherty's rediscovery of the world of eleven-year-old Joseph Boudreaux of Abbeville, Louisiana, who was called, for the duration of the film, Alexander Napoleon Ulysses Latour. Strong, curious, without fear, the boy triumphs over the alligator, the beast of the bayou, and over the new machine which also invades his world. He expresses himself in primitive sounds, part French, part American, and has a natural beauty before the camera reminiscent of that other Flaherty boy, Sabu. Acting with him as the adults who take part in the events of his young life are two other nonprofessionals, Frank Hardy and Lionel Le Blanc.

There is no comment, no propaganda, and very little dialog in the film. Flaherty called Louisiana Story a fantasy, suggesting that it takes place within the consciousness of a boy who is not just a Cajun child, but almost the symbol of the childhood of the race. His enemies, the alligators and the snakes in the swamp and the werewolves and mermaids in his mind, are part of the life of primitive man.

The world of Alexander Napoleon Ulysses Latour is a world of nature--of friendly racoons, of catfish to catch and alligators to kill, of spiders' webs and cypress trees dripping with Spanish moss--but it is a world which can finally encompass the oil derrick. At first he is afraid of the drilling and of the oil men who mock his "magic" (his spit, the bag of salt inside his shirt, and his frog).

He becomes familiar with them after a while. When the blowout comes, he even tries to help the men with his magic. In the end, there is a smile on the boy's face, as he sails out to the pipe spouting oil, waves goodbye to the departing drillers, and spits into the water. His magic, not theirs, brought in the treasure! It is not the machine which is the last symbol of the film.

During the production, Helen van Dongen felt that one of the faults of the film was that the boy was always "looking"--looking at nests, looking at alligators, looking at trees, looking at birds. To most viewers, Louisiana Story is beautiful just because the camera is looking through the boy's eyes at a world he sees with ever-fresh wonder.

Also: Animals and Nature
Cultural Conflicts

ME (NAKED CHILDHOOD), see p. 119

THE MEMBER OF THE WEDDING, see p. 316

MIGUELIN

Spain, 1964. 63 mins., b/w with col. (d) Horacio Varcarcel (sp) Horacio Varcarcel, Joaquin Aguirre Bellver (ph) Francisco Fraile (c) Luis-Maria Hidalgo, Luis Dominigez Luna. Spanish dialog with English subtitles. (TWF)

"Perhaps the most delightful film about children to come out of Spain since Marcelino Pan Y Vino," said Variety about this 1965 Cannes Festival prizewinner. But Marcelino, in the 1956 film (no longer available here), gives his bread and wine to a figure of Christ that he imagines is real. Miguelin (Luis-Maria Hidalgo), who was raised not in a monastery but in the streets of a poor village, is a very different small boy. An appealing dark-eyed youngster, alive with mischief, older and more sensitive than his years, he makes a bold stab at changing the misery of the life he sees around him.

Miguelin has become an altar boy by conning the sacristan of the village cathedral into teaching him the Latin responses. Declaring a personal war against poverty, Miguelin steals the poor box from the cathedral. With his beloved burro, he tries vainly to solicit contributions from the villagers. Still in his clothes as altar boy, he even stops passing motorists on the highway. No luck. Then, in a dream (a color sequence), Miguelin is given a revelation that charity begins at home. He sells his burro and gives the money to the poor. The remorseful villagers get his burro back, though, in time for the annual blessing of the animals.

The child's discovery that there are rewards for unselfishness is well developed, and the details of daily life in the village are authentic.

THE MIRACLE WORKER, see p. 183

MY SIDE OF THE MOUNTAIN

Paramount, 1969. 100 mins. col. (d) James B. Clark (sp) Ted Sherdeman, Jane Klove, Joanna Crawford, from the novel by Jean George (ph) Denys Coop (c) Ted Eccles, Theodore Bikel, Tudi Wiggins, Frank Perry, Peggi Loder. (FNC)

Thirteen-year-old Sam Gribley of Canada, hurt when his father breaks his promise to take him on a camping trip, decides to go off by himself with his pet raccoon and live close to nature like his hero, Thoreau. He will preserve himself in the woods through the four seasons of the year.

The film is an interesting chronicle of a boy learning to be a man on his own terms. Sam (Ted Eccles) makes a home for himself in a hollow tree trunk. He conducts algae experiments and forages for food. Though he hides from passersby, he makes two adult friends, the librarian in the nearby town (Tudi Wiggins) and an itinerant folksinger (Theodore Bikel). The librarian gives him advice on how to train a falcon he has captured, and the singer adds to his knowledge of survival lore. But when the severe winter cold sets in, Sam is low in spirits. The singer shows him newspaper stories about the long search his parents have been making for their lost son, and Sam is ready to go home.

Intelligent and independent, Sam is believable. His simple, concrete comments on his experiences with nature have the ring of a real boy's memoranda on the progress of an experiment. When he is with his two adult friends, he is warm and responsive.

Beautifully photographed in the Laurentian Mountains, *My Side of the Mountain* is lovely to look at and has something to say about an adolescent enamored of Thoreau. Anyone who knows a boy who loves animals and camping would find it illuminating. Its producer, Robert B. Radnitz, has given us several good films about children, among them *And Now Miguel* and *Sounder*.

Also: Animals and Nature

PADRE PADRONE, see p. 124

THE QUIET ONE, see p. 245

THE RED BADGE OF COURAGE, see p. 221

RED SKY AT MORNING

Universal, 1971. 111 mins. col. (d) James Goldstone (sp) Marguerite Roberts, from the novel by Richard Bradford (ph) Vilmos Zsigmond (c) Richard Thomas, Catherine Burns, Desi Arnaz, Jr., Richard Crenna, Claire Bloom, John Colicos, Harry Guardino, Nehemiah Persoff, Strother Martin. (SWA, TWY, UNI)

"It comes close enough to touch us," said Charles Champlin of the _Los Angeles Times._ A strained film, handicapped by script and direction that work so hard they end by not working at all, _Red Sky at Morning_ makes some comment on a boy's growing up in the early 1940's in a town where racial and ethnic prejudices complicate his personal relationships.

Seventeen-year-old Josh Arnold (Richard Thomas, the John Boy of the Walton family on television) finds himself in the minority, as an "Anglo," in Sagrado, New Mexico, a very heterogeneous town where the largest single group is Mexican-American. Josh and his mother have been relocated in Sagrado after his father enlists in the Navy at the start of the war.

Though Josh's father (Richard Crenna) disapproves of southern racial hatreds, Josh's mother (Claire Bloom) is a bigot. In his new environment, the boy makes friends as well as enemies, and he has a first sex experience with a nonconformist classmate, Marcia (Catherine Burns). Things pile up on Josh. There are racial and ethnic conflicts at school, his mother (who has taken to the sherry bottle) alienates half the town, and he misses his father. As a substitute, he turns to a kind and eccentric artist (Harry Guardino) for advice. When he learns that his father has been killed, Josh says goodbye to Marcia, stands up to his mother for the first time, and boards a fast train out of New Mexico, on his way into the service like his father.

Red Sky at Morning is something to compare with other, better movies about growing up in the war years.

Also: Cultural Conflicts
Family Relationships
Generation Conflicts
War and Its Aftermath

THE RIVER

USA/India, 1950. 97 mins. col. (d) Jean Renoir (sp) Rumer Godden and Jean Renoir, from the novel by Rumer Godden (ph) Claude Renoir (m) M. A. Partha Sarathy (c) Patricia Walters, Radha, Adrienne Corri, Nora Swinburne, Esmond Knight, Thomas Breen, Arthur Shields, Richard Foster, Suprova Mukerjee. (MAC, PRU, SAL)

Rumer Godden's 1946 novel The River about a girl named Harriet, a "writer"-child of thirteen living with her English family in Bengal, is a work of translucent charm with deceptive simplicities and elusive lights. From this source, the great Jean Renoir made one of his most visually beautiful films, The River.

"We changed the characters," said Renoir, "and the frame--India, that is--became very important in the picture--more important than in the book."

Renoir's film is a kind of poem on India, on nature and time, but it is also a study of the subtle ways three complex and charming young girls slip into womanhood.

Flowing through the drama as a symbol of time is the Ganges. As the story is narrated by the older Harriet--looking back on her girlhood when she hid in her "Secret Hole" under the stairs--everything is bound up with the river on whose banks she lives: the shifting currents of her adolescence, her immersion in love and death and birth, her source in the deep mysteries of a very old civilization.

Harriet (played by Patricia Walters, a nonprofessional) is the awkward, gifted, vulnerable daughter of an Anglo-Indian couple (Nora Swinburne, Esmond Knight). Her Indian amah, Nan (Suprova Muskerjee), is the one, Harriet says, who "brought reality back to dream and dream back to reality."

Dream and reality coincide in the person of the American visitor, young Captain John (Thomas Breen), a maladjusted ex-Marine with a wooden leg. Harriet falls hopelessly in love with him, and so do the two other girls, older adolescents--the sensuous Valerie (Adrienne Corri), and the self-disciplined, half-Indian Melanie (Radha).

Harriet's little brother, Bogey (Richard Foster), is killed by a cobra. Harriet discovers Valerie in Captain John's arms. When Harriet tries to drown herself, Captain John fishes her out of the river and tries to console her: one of her poems might be read in 4000 A. D.

Captain John goes away, Bogey is dead, the girls will never be the same. But the eternal rhythms carry them along. Harriet's mother is awaiting the birth of another child. The festival of spring and renewal, the Kali Puja ceremony, is celebrated, ending in the Ganges.

Although The River is leisurely in pace, one sequence has dramatic tension hard to match in scenes of childhood. When Bogey becomes involved with death in the summer garden, and the play of light and shade in the fatal tree where he is wooing the cobra becomes almost unbearably accelerated, we see a great director's power to synchronize image and inner conflict. The film's final sequence is moving because it is unified; the death of Bogey is in a sense Harriet's death-as-a-child.

Perhaps the themes in The River are loosely integrated. However, Renoir's first color film (superbly photographed in West Bengal by his nephew, Claude Renoir) gives us many lovely things to look at while pondering their meaning. Not the least of these are Melanie's face as she dances to the God Krishna, Valerie's romantic vitality, and all of Harriet's search for herself within her family and within the strangeness of growing up in India.

Also: From Literature

ROOKIE OF THE YEAR

ABC/TV, 1975. 47 mins. color. (d) Lawrence B. Elikann (sp) Gloria Banta, from the book Not Bad for a Girl by Isabella Taves (ph) Richard Francis (c) Jodie Foster, Ned Wilson. (TLF)

A lively and well directed "ABC Afterschool Special" designed as entertainment for children, Rookie of the Year has value concepts for their parents and teachers, for it is a good picture of a familiar contemporary situation involving sexism and problems of adolescent identity.

Eleven-year-old Sharon Lee (Jodie Foster) plays hardball like a pro. Should she be allowed to fill in on an all-male Little League baseball team when an injured player cannot be replaced by a boy? The supportive coach (Ned Wilson) and her parents say yes. But her brother, also on the team, who cannot play as well as she does, is hostile (why can't she stick to softball like the other girls?). He is not the only one who feels threatened; irate parents pull their sons off the team when Sharon joins it, and they threaten to fire the coach. Sharon's girlfriends stop inviting her to parties (if she acts like a boy, treat her like one). When she goes up at bat, there are catcalls: "Give her a pink bat!" "Go home to Mommy, you're getting your hair dirty!"

It's no longer illegal, as it was in 1975, to recruit a girl for a contact sport; nobody can now deny a girl the right to play any sport. But the film is far from dated. Many a suburban town like Sharon's is still populated by holdouts; the old role-playing stereotypes still plague a young girl who's having more than her share of adolescent identity conflicts.

Rookie of the Year is based on an actual incident, and its portraits are recognizably true. That does not rule out plenty of dramatic invention. To protect the coach from being dismissed, Sharon pulls out of the crucial final game. But we know, when her brother admits she's great, that she will come back and wrap up the game for her team. The catcalls are still heard in the stands, but our girl steals that last base, home plate.

Sharon is home free in every sense. Withstanding the pressures and overcoming the misgivings, she's grown stronger, she understands herself better, and she's even brought some of the doubters around to accepting her as her own person.

Jodie Foster is charming as Sharon, handling her bat and her banter with spunk, and never once suggesting a Paper Moon-style brat. Consciousness-raising couldn't happen to a nicer little girl. Rookie of the Year has won an Emmy and several festival awards.

Also: Cultural Conflicts

SIXTEEN IN WEBSTER GROVES

CBS-TV, 1966. 47 mins. b/w. (p) Art Barron. Narrated by Charles Kuralt. (AIM, CAL, MMA)

WEBSTER GROVES REVISITED

CBS-TV, 1967, 53 mins. b/w. (AIM, CAL, MMA)

What are the goals of sixteen-year-olds in a wealthy American suburb? Are they in conflict with their parents' goals? According to this 1966-67 CBS television survey, there's more conformity than reform in the life-style of this stratum of youth.

Webster Groves, Missouri, a well-heeled community near St. Louis, must be more than what we see in the 1966 Sixteen in Webster Groves, but everything we see in the film is Webster Groves. A survey was taken by the National Research Center of all its sixteen-year-olds, and the statistical results, with quotations from the young people themselves, tell us that money and status are the kids' goals. They are worried about getting good grades because they can't get into college without them and they can't earn $15,000 a year without a college degree. Far from hating the Establishment, ninety percent love Webster Groves. They agree with their parents about drinking, sex, the importance of getting ahead, and having a big home and two cars. They don't worry about large issues ("I don't think any sixteen-year-old child should burden himself with the problems of the world," as one parent says); they worry about financial security. Neither rebellious nor adventurous, they want to conform to their elders, their peers, their school.

Any exceptions? One girl says that once you've had some experience, you begin to wonder if people have been honest. And a few have an inkling of what St. Louis ghetto reality is and how important learning is for its own sake.

Of course, the film was made before the thrust of the youth rebellion. Even so, it aroused such violent disagreement--in 1966 or in 1980 you can always spark a conflagration with conclusions about This Generation--that CBS conducted an experiment to allow a little talking back to the program. On the same night as the first showing of Sixteen in Webster Groves, farsighted CBS had cameras on hand to record the reactions of the young people and adults to their own images on the television screen. Webster Groves Revisited was the result--a mirror-of-a-mirror experience. One girl, watching her own interview, wept throughout.

The value of these two CBS films in encouraging study and discussion of adolescents in our culture is unquestioned, provided one remembers that they are media images of selected adolescents, as interesting as but no more conclusive than any other samples produced to bolster a generalization about a whole generation. The CBS documentary viewpoint in 1966 was clear; these sixteen-year-olds' attitudes were a sad comment not only on their own immaturity but on their country's.

Also: Cultural Conflicts
Family Relationships

SMILE, see p. 135

THE SOUND OF TRUMPETS (IL POSTO)

Italy, 1961. 90 mins. b/w. (d)(sp) Ermanno Olmi (ph) Lamberto Caimi (c) Loredano Detto, Sandro Panzeri. Italian dialog with English subtitles. (JAN)

This film could also be called Portrait of the White-Collar Worker as a Young Man. "The last sound in the film is not of trumpets; it is the slickety-whirr, slickety-whirr of the mimeograph machine," (Stanley Kauffmann) and that sound is a symbol of his defeat, his dehumanization, as the adult prison walls of his first job close in around Domenico.

A shy, sober youngster fresh from school, eighteen-year-old Domenico (Sandro Panzeri) comes up to the city to compete for a job in a huge Milan company, a job that is low paid but secure. Among the many others taking the qualifying exams is Antonietta (Loredana Detto), with whom he falls in love.

They both get jobs, but they don't see much of each other in the enormous establishment. Domenico starts humbly enough as an errand boy and assistant porter. At last a clerk dies; the young newcomer is promoted to a clerk's desk in the rear of the office, where he never sees daylight. This is his place for life; with luck, he will move up to a front desk.

Young men are not often observed in their treadmill lives with such artistry. Nothing is over stressed, nothing is false.

Writer-director Ermanno Olmi has a gentle but telling accuracy, a social realism suggestive of Vittorio De Sica's. His unprofessional actors are moving--passive in their acceptance of industrial pettiness, poignant in such moments as the boy's waiting for the girl, who never comes, at the company New Year's Eve party.

SOUNDER, see p. 100

SUMMER OF '42, see p. 156

VERONICA, see p. 137

WHERE THE LILIES BLOOM, see p. 105

THE WORLD OF APU, see p. 70

THE YEARLING

M-G-M, 1946. 135 mins. col. (d) Clarence Brown (sp) Paul Osborn, from the novel by Marjorie Kinnan Rawlings (ph) Charles Rosher, Leonard Smith (m) Herbert Stothart (a) Cedric Gibbons, Paul Groesse (c) Gregory Peck, Jane Wyman, Claude Jarman, Jr., Forest Tucker, Henry Travers, Margaret Wycherly, Chill Wills, Clem Bevans. (FNC)

Jody Baxter, like his deer, Flag, is a "yearling" who comes of age. When his father has to kill Flag, his one real companion in his lonely life on a backwoods Florida farm, it is a wrenching agony, the first real pain he has known. He cannot face it at first; he runs away into the swamp, gets lost, starves. He believes he can never again love as he has loved the dead Flag. But he knows he must go home. When he does, he shares a new understanding with his father:

"Ever' man wants life to be a fine thing, and a easy," says Penny Baxter to his son. "'Tis fine, boy, powerful fine, but 'tain't easy. Life knocks a man down and he gits up and it knocks him down again."

"I'm 'shamed I runned off," Jody answers his father. He has learned that every man is lonesome; that when he gets knocked down, he takes it for his share and goes on.

After the flight into the swamp, Jody is different not only because he has taken punishment but because he realizes, from the welcome he receives even from his stern, inarticulate Ma (Jane Wyman), that he is not alone. It was unbelievable, Jody thought. He was wanted.

There is deep tenderness in the relationship between Pa Baxter (Gregory Peck) and Jody (extremely well played by Claude Jarman, Jr., in his screen debut), and very moving insight into the friendship between two youngsters, Jody and Fodderwing, the Forresters' crippled boy.

The pioneer living of early Florida settlers, in which the youngest of the family has to accept his responsibilities, is very well filmed (the interior sets and the art direction received Academy Awards). Clarence Brown has directed Paul Osborn's script with sensitivity and power.

Altogether this is a memorable film from a famous novel about a child's maturation.

Also: Animals and Nature
Family Relationships
From Literature

FAMILY RELATIONSHIPS

THE ACTRESS

M-G-M 1953. 90 mins. b/w. (d) George Cukor (sp) Ruth Gordon, from her play Years Ago (c) Spencer Tracy, Jean Simmons, Teresa Wright, Anthony Perkins. (FNC)

As the stage-struck high school girl who overcomes her father's objection to a career in the theater, Jean Simmons is not only charming but truly and unsentimentally observed. The Actress is based on a real story, the early life of actress Ruth Gordon, who adapted the film from her stage play Years Ago.

In a Boston suburb in 1912, Ruth Gordon Jones (Jean Simmons) has felt the lure of the footlights for a long time; watching the star Hazel Dawn in the musical Beautiful Lady again and again from her perch in the gallery of a Boston theater, she has sung along with the people on the stage and felt she was one of them.

Ruth's father (Spencer Tracy), a salty, grumpy old blowhard with deeply tender understanding under the crust, is not so sure of his daughter's talent or of the wisdom of her giving up a possible career as a female instructor of physical education for the uncertainties of acting. But Ruth, with a little help from her mother (Teresa Wright), convinces her father to let her have a chance.

What makes The Actress genuinely persuasive as family drama is the fact that Clinton Jones gives in to his daughter's ambition not because a solution is needed in the last reel but because he remembers enough of his own feelings as a young man to understand exactly how Ruth feels. He, too, had felt the tug of adventure; he had gone to sea as a boy. And it is his cherished telescope, the only object of value he owns, that he sells in order to finance Ruth's trip to New York.

Ruth Gordon's script and George Cukor's direction take us inside the Jones's household. The adolescent daughter's relationship to her parents and to her raccoon-coated young beau (Anthony Perkins) are beautifully realized. Because the daughter, father, and mother in The Actress are not seen by their creators as types of family antagonists in a "You don't understand me" situation, but are clearly individuals, the film is an object lesson in how to bring people to life.

Also: Finding Oneself

ALICE DOESN'T LIVE HERE ANY MORE

Warners, 1975. 112 mins. col. (d) Martin Scorsese (sp) Robert Getchell (ph) Kent L. Wakeford (m) Richard LaSalle (c) Ellen Burstyn, Kris Kristofferson, Billy Green Bush, Diane Ladd, Lelia Goldoni, Alfred Lutter, Jodie Foster, Harvey Keitel. (SWA)

The second feature of director Martin Scorsese (Mean Streets), from an original screenplay by Robert Getchell, Alice Doesn't Live Here Any More is about a thirty-five-year-old contemporary American housewife who sets out to make some kind of new life for herself. Its protagonist, portrayed by Ellen Burstyn (who won an Oscar for the part), is a controversial figure; you can generate a lot of talk about role confusion, modern marriage, etc., by bringing up Scorsese's not-entirely-successful movie about her.

Another interesting and controversial element is the relationship between Alice and her twelve-year-old son, Tommy. You can give Tommy the award as Screen Brat of 1975 and note that Alfred Lutter is a pretty effective player himself, though there was no Oscar for him. Some people call the fast patter between Tommy and Alice a kind of act, raunchy and funny, the current version of those exchanges in the thirties comedies. However, if you accept the relationship between mother and child at face value it is recognizably true, a certain kind of abrasive but loving dialog, in which the child goes as far as he dares with his wisecracks because he is sensitive to his mother's suppressed emotions. Tommy has his problems with his father, Donald (Billy Green Bush), who bullies him, but he has enough understanding to know his mother has greater problems with Donald, and he tests the situation with open taunts.

The "road" segment of the film begins when Donald dies in an accident and Alice and Tommy, penniless, set out on a journey across the Southwest. Because she had given up her dream of a singing career to marry the male-chauvinist Donald, Alice decides to trek from their home in New Mexico to Monterey and try for a second chance.

She's not talented or attractive enough to make it. First as a saloon entertainer, then as a waitress, she has many encounters, many tests of her new independence.

Along the way, her smart-aleck son finds a companion, an even tougher youngster, Audrey (Jodie Foster). When his mother has a brief affair with the deceptively nice young Ben (Harvey Keitel), another machismo type, who is poison for his wife and for Alice, Tommy reacts with immediate antagonism to the man. He recognizes Ben is the same kind of sex salesman that Alice's late husband (and his father) was. The boy asks her point-blank whether she is sleeping with Ben. She feels she has to lie to him about that.

Providentially, a divorced rancher named David (Kris

Kristofferson) appears on the scene. It seems as if Alice has at last fallen in love with a man who can make life meaningful for her and for her son. Tommy and David work out a viable relationship. It is clear, from Scorsese's last shot, that the most important partnership in the film is not between Alice and David but between the mother and the boy; the focus is still on the pair.

Ellen Burstyn says that some of the lines in the film were lifted from exchanges she's had with her son Jefferson, who is thirteen. "Why did you marry Dad?" she says Jefferson once asked her. "Because he was a great kisser," she replied. "How great can a person kiss?" Jefferson wanted to know. "Ask me again in a few years," his mother told him.

Alfred Lutter's Tommy and Ellen Burstyn's Alice will probably strike you as authentic as any over-sharp kid and his mother around.

ALL FALL DOWN

M-G-M, 1962. 111 mins. b/w. (d) John Frankenheimer (sp) William Inge, based on the novel by James Leo Herlihy (ph) Lionel Lindon (m) Alex North (c) Eva Marie Saint, Warren Beatty, Karl Malden, Angela Lansbury, Brandon de Wilde. (FNC)

In his short career, the late Brandon de Wilde gave three memorable film performances as a boy who made a hero of a nonhero, and had to grow out of his adoration: in Shane (1953), All Fall Down (1962), and Hud (1963).

As Clint, the adolescent son of the Willart family in All Fall Down, Brandon de Wilde is playing a fifteen-year-old when he is himself twenty. He is not as much at ease as he is in Shane or in Hud, but the role is almost actor proof in its familiar psychology.

Everyone in Clint's family is lonely, unable to communicate, and some kind of emotional failure. Father (Karl Malden) is alcoholic and emasculated; mother (Angela Lansbury) is overly affectionate, overly possessive. Good-hearted as the Willart parents are, they are completely ineffectual. The older son Berry-berry (Warren Beatty) is the family problem; and it is he whom Clint idolizes.

Berry-berry's life seems all excitement to the boy. Sent to Key West with $200 on another family-rescue mission for his brother, Clint finds that he needs the money not "to go into business," as he'd wired home, but to pay a jail fine for beating up a prostitute. Exploring Berry-berry's operation for a while, in strip joints and bars, Clint finds it glamorous. When Berry-berry signs on as a gigolo "crew member" on an older woman's yacht and sends his kid brother back home, Clint loses interest in his humdrum existence and drops out of school. Everything changes when Echo (Eva Marie Saint), a charming thirty-one-year-old friend of the

Willarts, comes to visit. Clint is smitten, and believes Echo when she calls him "my guy" and suggests that he earn money so they can marry.

But Berry-berry comes home, and (after getting Clint's rueful consent) he and Echo have a love affair. Berry-berry seems to be stabilized; Clint returns to school and a part-time job.

When Berry-berry resists Echo's pressure to marry and settle down, she tells him she is pregnant but that he owes her nothing. He's ready to leave it at that. She drives away in a storm and is killed. Berry-berry's father thinks it is suicide. Clint gets a gun and seems about to murder his brother, but decides he isn't worth killing. He's already dead, only a shell of a man. ("You really do hate life, don't you, Berry-berry?" says Clint, with his new insight. "When you said it before, I went along with you because I wanted to be like you. But I love life!") Free of his illusions about Berry-berry, Clint leaves him to his loneliness.

John Frankenheimer's direction, William Inge's screenplay, and some of the original dialog of the Herlihy novel all contribute to the film's honesty. The fifteen-year-old Clint, as the outsider looking in on Berry-berry and Echo, or on his parents, and growing in understanding of the difference between his brother's real nature and his distorted idealization of him, is a portrait to place beside that of the youth in Hud.

Also: Finding Oneself

ALL MINE TO GIVE

RKO, 1956. 102 mins. col. (d) Allen Reisner (sp) Dale and Katherine Eunson, from the story "The Day They Gave Babies Away" by Dale Eunson (ph) William Skall (m) Max Steiner (c) Glynis Johns, Cameron Mitchell, Rex Thompson, Patty McCormack, Ernest Truex, Alan Hale, Hope Emerson, Royal Dano, Rita Johnson, Ellen Corby. (BUD, MAC, MOD, UNI, WCF)

On the American frontier a century ago, Scottish immigrants Robert and Mamie Eunson (Cameron Mitchell and Glynis Johns) have a pretty rough time. During their life in Eureka, Wisconsin, they have six children. After they die, their orphaned youngsters discover the tragedy of adult life.

The oldest, Robbie (Rex Thompson), is twelve when he is charged by his mother on her deathbed to take care of his five sisters and brothers. He sets out on Christmas Day to find foster homes for them, among the neighbors whose lives have touched his family's. It sometimes seems to this child that the community is as cold as the harsh Wisconsin snows; yet he succeeds in placing all the children, and leaves for the logging camp to earn his own living.

A true story, taken from Dale Eunson's family reminiscence, "The Day They Gave Babies Away," *All Mine to Give* recalls other films in which a youngster becomes the head of a family, like *Where the Lilies Bloom*. It does not suffer by comparison. Well acted, especially by Rex Thompson as Robbie and Patty McCormack as his sister Annabelle, and directed (by former television director Allen Reisner) with slow but eventually moving emotional appeal, it makes its point about necessity making a man of a boy. William Skall's photography and the characterizations of the supporting players bring the pioneer community to life.

Also: Finding Oneself

AMARCORD, see p. 3

AND NOW MIGUEL, see p. 8

THE APU TRILOGY

Pather Panchali
("Song of the Road")

India, 1954. 112 mins. b/w. (d) Satyajit Ray (sp) Satyajit Ray, based on the novel by Bibhuti Banerji (ph) Subrata Mitra (m) Ravi Shankar (c) Kanu Banerji, Karuna Banerji, Subir Banerji, Runki

Banerji, Uma Das Gupta, Chunibala Devi. Bengali dialog with English subtitles. (MAC)

Aparajito ("The Unvanquished")

India, 1957. 108 mins. b/w. (d) Satyajit Ray (sp) Satyajit Ray, based on the novel by Bibhuti Banerji (ph) Subrata Mitra (m) Ravi Shankar (c) Pinaki Sen Gupta, Karuna Banerji, Sumiron Ghosjal. Bengali dialog with English subtitles. (MAC)

The World of Apu ("Apur Sansar")

India, 1959. 103 mins. b/w. (d) Satyajit Ray (sp) Satyajit Ray, based on the novel by Bibhuti Banerji (ph) Subrata Mitra (m) Ravi Shankar (c) Sharmila Tagore, Soumitra Chatterjee, Shapan Mukherji, Alok Chakravarty. Bengali dialog with English subtitles. (MAC)

"I am always hopefully concerned to get the feeling of the movement of life itself," said Satyajit Ray to a Film Quarterly interviewer in 1958. He was coming to the end of his production of The World of Apu ("Apur Sansar"), the final film in his trilogy from the mammoth novel of Bibhuti Banerji.

What director-scenarist (and producer) Ray has achieved in the work begun in 1954 with Pather Panchali and continued in 1957 with Aparajito is a masterpiece. It is a glowing expression of Indian life; as a great naturalistic cinema poem, it also captures the movement of all life. And it is a beautiful, very leisurely, profound picture of family life. The small Apu, the adolescent Apu, and the five-year-old son of Apu, belong with screen classics of childhood.

The opening film, Pather Panchali, shows us a small brother and sister, Apu (Subir Banerji) and Durga (Uma Das Gupta), growing up in a tangled forest and small ancestral village in Bengal. Their poverty-stricken family--the dreamer-father who wants to be a writer but who works as a rent-collector; the strong and more practical mother; the ancient crone of an aunt who teaches the children to steal--struggles for existence. The children know many of the joys and sorrows of childhood. In an unforgettable moment they see their first train. They find the old aunt dead in the shade of a tree after she has been driven away by their mother. When their father returns from the city (where he has been searching for a better job), Durga is dead, a victim of the monsoon. Mother, father, and Apu set out by bullock cart for Benares.

Despite the scenes of great poverty and cruel death, Pather Panchali is not depressing. The "feeling of the movement of life"--of humor, of small daily absurdities, of tenderness within the family, of the belonging of the children to ceremony and ritual as well as to their elders--transcends the hardships.

Even with its cinematic flaws (poor sound track and subtitles),

Pather Panchali is a great human document. The music, composed and performed by Ravi Shankar, and the photography by Subatra Mitra, frame the domestic scenes in beauty.

In Aparajito ("The Unvanquished"), the sequel, the ten-year-old Apu (Pinaki Sen Gupta) is living in Benares with his mother and his father, who reads scripture on the banks of the Ganges. At his father's death, his mother goes to a village to keep house for an old uncle, a priest who begins to train Apu for the priesthood. But the adolescent son and mother, in a beautifully understated relationship, come to an understanding. She has made many sacrifices to keep him in school. When he wins a scholarship, Apu is able to go to the university in Calcutta, where he supports himself in various jobs; the mother remains behind, lonely and silent. Life in the great city has many distractions for the adolescent student Apu (Sumiron Ghosjal) that change him and estrange him from his mother and from village life. While he is studying, his mother falls ill. He comes, too late, to an empty house of death. He returns to Calcutta.

Delicate and true as is the parent-child relationship in Aparajito, there is one at the very end of The World of Apu ("Apur Sansar") which has made cinema history. Now an adult, after the end of a tragically brief marriage, a period of decline, and eventual spiritual regeneration, the new Apu (Soumitra Chatterjee) is persuaded by his friend Pulu (Shapan Mukherji) to visit the son whom he has never seen. (He had abandoned him in grief at his wife's death in childbirth.) The boy, now five, is at first hostile and distant; the man must struggle to achieve communication with him. But he succeeds. The moment when we recognize that Apu has won the boy's trust is one of the most moving father-son moments in all cinema; it is in the same class as some of the scenes in De Sica's The Bicycle Thief. Bearing his son on his shoulders, Apu is on his way back to Calcutta and to his life as a father.

The profound humanism of a great director has made The World of Apu a work of haunting and exotic beauty. Its faces are as universal as fatherhood or childhood themselves.

Also: From Literature

BAR MITZVAH BOY, see p. 197

THE BATTLE OF VILLA FIORITA, see p. 112

BAXTER

Great Britain, 1972. 105 mins. col. (d) Lionel Jeffries (sp) Reginald Rose, from the novel The Boy Who Could Make Himself Disappear by Kin Platt (ph) Geoffrey Unsworth (m) Michael J. Lewis

(c) Patricia Neal, Scott Jacoby, Jean-Pierre Cassel, Britt Ekland, Lynn Carlin, Sally Thomsett, Paul Maxwell. (SWA)

Baxter is a good job, by good people. What might have been just another film about a disturbed boy has been so well handled that Brenda Davies, in the British Film Institute Monthly Film Bulletin, found the protagonist reminiscent of Antoine Doinel in Truffaut's The 400 Blows. The director, Lionel Jeffries (The Railway Children), works sensitively with young actors; Scott Jacoby (That Certain Summer, ABC-TV) is one of the best young actors; Reginald Rose knows what to do with a script; and cinematographer Geoffrey Unsworth (Cabaret; and 2001: A Space Odyssey) uses a camera with great imagination. The result is that we have, to the life, a picture of an emotionally deprived boy of twelve whose natural spirit is blighted after his parents' divorce.

Roger Baxter (Scott Jacoby) introduces himself as Baxter because he can't pronounce his r's. His speech problem has roots in his family disorientation. He has never known a happy home; after the divorce, his bitter mother (Lynn Carlin) moves with him from Los Angeles to a luxurious, arid apartment in Mayfair in London. She sleeps all day, dabbles in art, drinks, and utterly ignores Roger except when she makes him know he is a nuisance.

In the American school in London, on his own, the boy is mocked by a sarcastic teacher because of his defect. He is sent to a speech therapist, Dr. Roberta Clemm (Patricia Neal), who is an immediate, solid comfort. He also makes friends with a pair of lovers, Chris (Britt Ekland) and Roger Tunnell (Jean-Pierre Cassel), and a girl of his own age, Nemo (Sally Thomsett), whose family life is far happier than his. Roger thaws a little and his speech improves. But he is deeply disturbed, nonetheless, for his home situation grows worse. His mother treats him with cold harshness; when he desperately telephones his father (Paul Maxwell), he gets a transatlantic brush-off. Then Nemo moves away to Bermuda. Roger withdraws almost completely from reality. At one point he says, "I thought I was going to disappear." Finally, he is hospitalized. With Dr. Clemm's help, he recovers, but on the way home, a new emotional shock--the accidental discovery of Chris's death--precipitates a withdrawal into a catatonic state. Although he seems to respond to Roger Tunnell, whose grief over Chris he shares, his recovery remains doubtful.

The film's equivocal ending, said Brenda Davies, "seems entirely right: Baxter's future is no more predictable than was that of Truffaut's Antoine Doinel."

There are memorable images in Baxter not only of the boy's alienation but of his natural zest for life: a flashback to his early childhood, listening to his parents quarrel; shots of his playing with the kooky Nemo or enjoying Roger Tunnel making lobster thermidor or romping with the lovers in the country.

Scott Jacoby's characterization is beautifully faceted--a precocious, prankish, charming youngster, torn by anguish in a loveless family.

Also: From Literature
Special Children

THE BICYCLE THIEF

Italy, 1948. 87 mins. b/w. (d) Vittorio De Sica (sp) Cesare Zavattini, from a novel by Luigi Bartolini (ph) Carlo Montuori (m) Alessandro Cicognini (c) Lamberto Maggiorani, Enzo Staiola, Lianella Carell. Italian dialog with English subtitles. (MAC)

Forget that Vittorio De Sica's The Bicycle Thief (Ladri di Biciclette) is a classic of neo-realism, that it won not only our Academy Award and the British Academy Award but also was named by the world's film critics at the 1958 Brussels Exposition one of the twelve best films of all times. After all these years, what does one remember about the little boy and his father?

Antonio Ricci (Lamberto Maggiorani) is a poor man in postwar Rome in 1946, so poor that his wife has to pawn the family sheets to buy food. When the bicycle that he needs for his new job is stolen, he spends a long, bitter Sunday trying to trace it. With him is his young son, Bruno (Enzo Staiola), as solemnly aware as Papa of the importance of the bicycle to their livelihood.

One cannot forget Bruno. Polishing a pedal of the wonderful new bike, he is unhappy when he sees it is dented and angry with his father for being unmoved. He would have complained. After it is stolen, Bruno is taut faced, staring with his chin in his hand. Chasing after Papa through the streets of Rome, he has trouble keeping up. As they take shelter from a sudden downpour, he is crushed between Papa and a cassocked monk. And when his father, unable to strike out against the indifference of the world, strikes his son, Bruno cries, runs away, returns very reluctantly: "I'm going to tell Mother."

There are two wonderful dramas of father and son. Ricci, hearing a commotion about someone's drowning, thinks it is Bruno. Overwhelmingly relieved to find that it is somebody else, he tries to help Bruno put on his jacket so he will not take cold. But Bruno, who has not forgotten the blow, insists on putting it on by himself. Later, a scene in the restaurant brings them close again. Joyously accepting Papa's offer of a fine feed, Bruno forgives all. He admires the way Papa orders two mozzarellas and wine. Under the eye of the nasty little rich girl at the next table, Bruno has a little trouble managing the long strands of cheese.

Before the film has ended, the love between the boy and the man swells almost to bursting. When Ricci, defeated and humiliated after his attempt to steal another bicycle, walks along like an automaton with his fists clenched, Bruno (almost like the father and not the child) looks up at his face from time to time, worried about him. The two sit on the curb together. Going home, the boy slips his hand into his father's.

A masterpiece, yes--of a poor man, and a poor man's son who loves him and understands his need.

Enzo Staiola, who plays Bruno, a nonprofessional like the rest of the cast, was a newsboy when he was spotted for the picture. He is one of the most expressive children ever to appear on the screen. To look at stills of him is to marvel at childhood, and at De Sica, who has never had an equal in directing children.

BLACK GIRL

Cinerama, 1972. 107 mins., col. (d) Ossie Davis (sp) J. E. Franklin, from her own play (c) Brock Peters, Leslie Uggams, Claudia McNeil, Peggy Pettitt, Louise Stubbs, Gloria Edwards, Loretta Greene, Ruby Dee, Kent Martin. (SWA)

Under Ossie Davis's direction, Black Girl has harsh, stinging reality. It is a contemporary drama of a teenaged girl trapped in her family and her society yet unwilling to give up hope.

Billie Jean (Peggy Pettitt) is the black girl, who has dropped out of school and is working as a waitress in Venice, California. She wants to move up in the world; she longs for a chance to become a go-go dancer.

Her two older half-sisters (Gloria Edwards and Loretta Greene) are jealous and resentful of the baby Billie Jean, who has a different father. They would like her to fail. If she made it, she might become Mother's favorite.

Mother (Louise Stubbs) is a bitter woman who screams at all the girls. Hardworking, deserted by her husband (Brock Peters), she has been building anger and pain over the years. She does have a favorite (Leslie Uggams), who is away at college and is not even her own daughter, but the child of a mad neighbor (Ruby Dee). Mother's other foster children have been sparked by her and have wanted to move forward; only her own children are alienated.

In this home there is really no mother but "Mu' Dear," the wise old grandmother (Claudia McNeil), who tries to fill in. The Mother's Day sequence in the movie is a passionate tearing open of all the raw wounds in the family.

Billie Jean is hard to forget. Does she have a chance?

Also: Cultural Conflicts
Finding Oneself

BORN INNOCENT, see p. 235

BOY, see p. 235

CAPTAINS COURAGEOUS, see p. 292

CHEAPER BY THE DOZEN, see p. 292

CHILDHOOD, see p. 11

CLAUDINE

Third World/Fox, 1974. 92 mins. col. (d) John Berry (sp) Tina and Lester Pine (ph) Gayne Rescher (m) Curtis Mayfield, performed by Gladys Knight and the Pips (c) Diahann Carroll, James Earl Jones, Lawrence Hinton Jacobs, Tamu, David Kruger, Yvette Curtis, Eric Jones, Socorro Stephens, Adam Wade. (FNC)

Growing up black, the Negro family, black rage, a welfare mother speaking out, an American dilemma--*Claudine* is about all these. It is a truthful and unpretentious film, full of humor--though it's no laughing matter--about a vibrant adult couple in love and six children who are very much part of the scene.

After two husbands and two almost-husbands, Claudine Price (Diahann Carroll), who is thirty-six and still lovely, is living without a man in her Harlem tenement. She is "married to the Welfare" and trying to raise her six kids against the odds. They're the most important thing in her life and she's sick of apologizing for them. The Welfare must not be told about Claudine's job as a maid in Riverdale; the caseworker asks about male visitors to her apartment and about the $2.75-worth of gifts one of them brings. If a man is suspected of being a permanent part of the household, Claudine will lose the aid she needs for the children.

Roop Marshall (James Earl Jones), the man Claudine falls in love with, is a sanitation worker. He is also over thirty-five and single. With two young boys in Ohio and a daughter in Louisville from two marriages, he's got his hands full, sending child-support payments.

To be a daddy takes a lot of money, Roop explains to one of Claudine's kids. Big, jovial, unwilling to take on any more responsibilities, Roop loves Claudine and grows closer to her all the time. But the relationship is blocked by Claudine's children, her fierce protectors. "Don't come home pregnant," says sixteen-year-old Charlene to her mother as she leaves on her first date with Roop. During the children's inquisition about that date, Patrice

comments, "It's disgusting--woman her age." Nobody will answer when Roop rings the doorbell. "We didn't hear," they tell Claudine. Charles, eighteen, refuses Roop's ice cream and warns him that every tear Claudine sheds over him will cost him a drop of blood.

When Roop begins to weigh the idea of taking over this family as his own, the kids warm to him. He gives Paul a lesson in crap shooting, talks him into staying in school, and wises him up about the realities of the life of a pimp or numbers runner. He understands why Charles needs to join the militant Kenyatta Club in his search for identity. He reaches the youngest child, Francis, who defensively used to declare that he was invisible, didn't speak, and wrote messages, but now tries to persuade Roop to remain in the family.

As far as Welfare is concerned, Roop is damned if he does and damned if he doesn't. Trouble follows trouble; Roop is accused of child neglect, though he's sent what he could to his children. On Father's Day, Roop vanishes. Francis goes back to invisibility--now nobody exists--and Charles tells his mother she should have killed her children when they were born. Charlene is discovered to be pregnant by Abdullah, a young militant. Charles moves out. When Roop meets Claudine, he tells her that he's leaving town.

In the end, the kids won't let Roop cop out, and he and Claudine do get married.

What one treasures in the movie, despite its crowding of

events and often fortuitous resolutions, are the children, and the many extremely moving moments between them and the adults. One of the best is the scene when Claudine sees that her daughter Charlene is pregnant. She beats her as if she is exorcising devils, then she weeps and cradles her in her arms, and they talk as woman to woman, lovingly, before they drop off to sleep; and the two little girls creep into bed with them. It is an infinitely tender picture of the strength and warmth of women--black women, poor women, troubled women.

"I don't know nothing; I don't have nothing; I ain't nothing," sixteen-year-old Charlene says to her mother. And Charles, hating himself and refusing to be responsible for any more like himself, undergoes a vasectomy. Francis is the child image of Ralph Ellison's Invisible Man. With Claudine and Roop to help, can the younger children grow into whole people?

Claudine's original screenplay by Tina and Lester Pine is as mordantly funny as it is pointed and frequently angry.

Also: Cultural Conflicts
Finding Oneself
Love & Sex

THE CHRISTMAS TREE, see p. 205

CORNBREAD, EARL AND ME, see p. 132

THE DARK AT THE TOP OF THE STAIRS, see p. 295

DAVID: OFF AND ON, see p. 42

DEATH BE NOT PROUD, see p. 206

THE DIARY OF ANN FRANK, see p. 297

DIMKA, see p. 16

DON'T CRY WITH YOUR MOUTH FULL, see p. 144

EAST OF EDEN

Warners, 1955. 115 mins. col. (d) Elia Kazan (sp) Paul Osborn, from the novel by John Steinbeck (ph) Ted McCord (m) Leonard

James Dean, Richard Davalos and Julie Harris

Rosenman (c) James Dean, Julie Harris, Raymond Massey, Burl Ives, Richard Davalos, Jo Van Fleet. (GEN)

This is a film, above all, of a father and son. "One hates one's father; one rebels against him; finally one cares for him, one recovers oneself, one understands him, one forgives him, and one says to oneself, yes, he is like that ... one is no longer afraid of him, one has accepted him." (Elia Kazan, in an interview in Cahiers du Cinéma)

The son in East of Eden is James Dean, best remembered as the adolescent in Rebel Without a Cause. As the younger son in East of Eden, Elia Kazan's film from the last third of Steinbeck's novel, Dean plays a rebel with a cause.

As Cal (for Caleb), the teenage son of puritanical Salinas rancher Adam Trask (Raymond Massey), and the younger brother of Aron (Richard Davalos), Dean is filled with jealousy and wrath. The world has never accepted his love or returned it. "You're the one he wants," he says to Aron, the "good" son his father has always favored. "Talk to me, please," is Cal's agonized cry, first to his father and then to the mother (Jo Van Fleet) he searched out. Lonely, sulking, violent in his sudden tantrums and laughter,

Dean is superb as the groping adolescent. His brother's fiancée, Abra (Julie Harris), whom Cal also loves, finally reaches him. We see, under the mask of Cal's rebelliousness against his father, the half-grown, sensitive boy bursting with love.

There are many memorable psychic revelations in Kazan's powerful film: the moment when the boy spies on his brother and the girl they both want, peering down from the loft between huge blocks of green ice (the symbolism throughout East of Eden is never understated); or the moment after he has fought his way down the long corridor of the brothel and for the first time confronts his mother, who is the madam. Often these moments are revelations of profound torment, like Cal's attempt to embrace his father at the end of the tragic birthday party, and Adam's rigid, embarrassed recoil.

Jo Van Fleet, who was awarded an Oscar for her portrayal of the mother embittered by her hated marriage, and Raymond Massey, the unyielding and self-righteous father unable to communicate with his younger son, are excellent. As the compassionate young girl, Julie Harris is at her best. When she brings the "bad" son together with his father at the stricken old man's bedside, she becomes an instrument of a convenient happy ending softer than the one life usually provides.

Twenty-five years afterward, James Dean's moving portrait of the confused adolescent Cal, the best role in Kazan's film, also seems, in retrospect, the best role in Dean's brief career.

Also: Finding Oneself
From Literature
Generation Conflicts

THE EFFECT OF GAMMA RAYS ON MAN-IN-THE-MOON MARIGOLDS

20th Century-Fox, 1972. 101 mins. col. (d) Paul Newman (sp) Alvin Sargent, from the play by Paul Zindel (ph) Adam Holender (m) Maurice Jarre (c) Joanne Woodward, Nell Potts, Roberta Wallach, Judith Lowry, David Spielberg, Richard Venture, Carolyn Coates. (FNC)

This is a drama of mutations. For better or worse, the two teenage daughters of Beatrice Hunsdorfer will bear all their lives the scars of Life with Mother, a "monster" of a mother who was not born, but made.

Abandoned by her husband, Beatrice Hunsdorfer (Joanne Woodward) is a sharp-tongued slattern, full of self-pity. She rents spare rooms in her rundown house on the wrong side of town to derelicts and human vegetables. The few men she encounters rebuff her overtures. Selling dance lessons over the phone,

fantasizing about getting rich in real estate and acquiring capital for her own business, she cannot accept the present or assume responsibility for her daughters. They serve as an audience for her, her only emotional outlet.

Ruth, the older girl (Roberta Wallach), to whose classmates Beatrice is the "looney," gives cabaret impersonations of her mother in school. A selfish, boy-crazy cheerleader, vulgarized by her environment, she is becoming like Beatrice. She is full of self-pity, too, and suffers from nightmares and epilepsy.

If Ruth is a carbon of her parent, a dwarf plant, the younger girl is the lovely and delicate mutant, not stunted but flourishing. Matilda (Nell Potts) is introverted, bright, and sensitive. She is deeply attached to a white rabbit given her by her science teacher (David Spielberg), in whose classes she has found inspiration.

Matilda has been studying the effect on marigold seeds of exposure to gamma rays. She is selected to be one of the five finalists in the school's science fair. Her mother, jealous of her, has been punishing Matilda for being a nuisance, for spending too much time on her homework and lab experiments, for keeping a pet that makes the house smell. Drunk, heavily made-up, and humiliated by recent experience in a bar, the mother arrives too late to see Matilda receive the prize at the science fair and creates an embarrassing scene.

The gamma rays have destroyed some of Matilda's marigolds but caused others to take on unexpected and rich new forms. The young girl is convinced that "man will one day thank God for the strange and beautiful energy of the atom."

When she returns home, Matilda finds her rabbit laid out dead at the foot of her bed. It has not come without some personal disintegration, but she is still capable of saying, at the end, "I do not hate the world." Though Joanne Woodward has emphasized the shrewishness of the mother, it seems also that her daughters do not hate her.

Nell Potts (Paul Newman and Joanne Woodward's daughter) and Roberta Wallach (Eli Wallach and Anne Jackson's daughter) are excellent, and are proof that talent can be inherited. Joanne Woodward's Mrs. Hunsdorfer is a virtuoso performance, and Paul Newman's direction is effective without strain. Most of the force of Paul Zindel's 1971 Pulitzer Prize play has been retained in Alvin Sargent's script.

The movie is an exceptionally interesting portrait of young lives developing in the shadow of a difficult parent, with subtlety between the lines and rich symbolism. The marigolds have not stopped growing in the mess of Beatrice's home.

FATHER, see p. 44

FEAR STRIKES OUT

Paramount, 1957. 100 mins. b/w. (d) Robert Mulligan (sp) Ted Berkman and Raphael Blau, from the autobiography of James A. Piersall (with Albert S. Hirshberg) (c) Anthony Perkins, Karl Malden, Adam Williams, Norma Moore. (FNC)

Most people know the drama of the adult Jimmy Piersall, big-league ball player with the Boston Red Sox, either from newspaper stories, his own book, or the television drama taken from it. Known as the club clown, Piersall insulted umpires and players and was suspended by manager Joe Cronin. After a siege of psychological and emotional problems, he was treated in a sanatorium and helped back to normalcy.

Behind Piersall's erratic behavior at Fenway Park lies the earlier story of a boy pushed to the breaking point by the impossible demands of a father's compulsion to relive his own life through the career of his son.

In the scenes of Fear Strikes Out which show the adolescent Jimmy (Anthony Perkins) and his loving but obsessed father (Karl Malden), we see a familiar relationship. The boy is not so much interested in becoming a top ball player as he is in satisying the expectations of his father, and of course he is not able to--nobody could.

In television director Robert Mulligan's hands (this was his first screen job), both the boy and the man emerge sympathetically. The picture of Jimmy is one of the few movie portraits of athletes, young or old, as people rather than symbols or heroes.

A HERO AIN'T NOTHIN' BUT A SANDWICH

Radnitz/Mattel--New World, 1977. 105 mins. col. (d) Ralph Nelson (sp) Alice Childress, from her novel (ph) Frank Stanley (m) Tom McIntosh; The Herbert Laws Group (c) Cicely Tyson, Paul Winfield, Larry B. Scott, Helen Martin, David Groh, Kevin Hooks, Kenneth "Joey" Green. (SWA)

The first two films in producer Robert B. Radnitz's "kind of trilogy, with black education, family life and restricted economic opportunity as the common denominators" Sounder and Part II, Sounder touch on the family life of black sharecroppers in the Depression. In contrast, the third film, A Hero Ain't Nothin' But a Sandwich, is about present-day urban life. It is based on Alice Childress's 1973 award-winning bestseller; its protagonist, Benjie, is a thirteen-year-old heroin addict. Originally he was from Harlem; the film sets him down in the black slum of Watts in Los Angeles.

To playwright Ed Bullins, Miss Childress's novel was an exposure of the problem of sheer survival in the black urban community. To Radnitz, Benjie's is primarily a love story, with a side story dealing with drugs: "A youngster living with a surrogate father would like to embrace him and say, 'I love you,' but like all of us he is afraid of rejection. The boy already has been rejected by his real father."

In A Hero Ain't Nothin' But a Sandwich, we see the possibility of redemption through love and forgiveness; the family is pitted against the destructive social forces of contemporary life. Benjie's anguished prayer--for a sign that somebody believes in him--is answered.

The boy (Larry B. Scott) lives with his attractive young mother Sweets (Cicely Tyson), his grandmother (Helen Martin), and his mother's lover, Butler (Paul Winfield), whom she puts off marrying because of seemingly irreconcilable tensions between the "intruder" and her adolescent son.

Benjie will not accept the reality of his real father's desertion three years earlier; nothing Butler does wins his confidence. Life in the ghetto is ugly and menacing; school is frustrating for a bright youngster with questions about attitudes and identity (when a white teacher praises his compositions by telling Benjie he could be a writer someday and become somebody, Benjie replies, "I am somebody right now"); tensions grow at home. To escape, Benjie and his friend Jimmy Lee (Kenneth "Joey" Green) get high on marijuana in their rooftop "club" and soon enough Benjie is a heroin addict. To feed his habit, he steals and runs drugs for the pusher, Tiger (Kevin Hooks).

The boy's teachers arrange for him to be put in a hospital for detoxification, and he endures agony there. He goes back on drugs, however, when he returns to the same conditions at home. Not until the end, when he and Butler bridge the gap--Benjie takes the first and most difficult step toward saving himself by reconciling himself with his family--are we reassured that the boy will transcend his problems. He and Butler, in their deep love and respect for each other, will find the strength.

The film is somewhat disunified, but it is admirable in its feel of authenticity--the dialogue; the ghetto details of the Watts scene; the playing of a fine cast and the non-professionals, the students of the George Washington Carver Junior High School and the Tarzana Psychiatric Hospital. In addition to Tyson, Winfield, and Scott, the players include Glynn Turman and David Groh, as a black and a Jewish teacher, respectively, who have a stake in the self-realization of boys like Benjie.

Revealing in its insight into a childhood in Watts, A Hero Ain't Nothin' But a Sandwich is also eloquent of child-adult relationships anywhere; the thirteen-year-old, his mother torn between two loyalties, and the surrogate father are recognizable, moving, often warm and funny, and always interesting.

Also: From Literature
Growing Pains
Teachers and Schools

FLAVIO, see p. 259

FORBIDDEN GAMES, see p. 211

THE 400 BLOWS, see p. 238

A FURTHER GLIMPSE OF JOEY, see p. 89

HENRY, BOY OF THE BARRIO, see p. 241

A HOLE IN THE HEAD

United Artists, 1959. 120 mins. col. (d) Frank Capra (sp) Arnold

Schulman, based on his television play adapted from his story "The Heart Is a Forgotten Hotel" (ph) William H. Daniels (m) Nelson Riddle, with songs by Sammy Cahn and James Van Heusen (c) Frank Sinatra, Eddie Hodges, Edward G. Robinson, Eleanor Parker, Carolyn Jones, Thelma Ritter, Keenan Wynn, Joi Lansing, George De Witt. (UAS)

"The leading man was a grandstanding, dame-chasing wastrel, rearing a ten-year-old son in an atmosphere both sinful and phony. Could I fit such a nonhero into my own style of warm human comedy?"

Frank Capra needn't have doubted himself, for he not only could, but did; A Hole in the Head works.

Who can love Tony Manetta (Frank Sinatra), the irresponsible owner of a third-class Miami Beach hotel, who has pipe dreams of breaking into the big-promoter milieu, of enjoying poolside parties and the sleekest cars? Only his kid, Ally (Eddie Hodges), who plays gin rummy with him at four in the morning and gives him unswerving devotion.

Ally belongs to that large band of children and adolescents on the screen, like the teenager in A Thousand Clowns, who are too fond of a nonconformist, highly whimsical adult (however foolish or unrealistic his life-style) to settle for ordinary family living. In the movies, they're much happier with the nonheroes.

And Ally, of course, really loves Tony. "Chiseler, cheap conniver--but that's my pop." When Ally's uncle and aunt (Edward G. Robinson and Thelma Ritter), who are respectable and sérieux, urge him to go back to New York with them and be properly cared for, you know Ally will never go, even though his father tells him he doesn't want him hanging around any more.

It doesn't hurt the nonhero's cause to be on the verge of matrimony with a most attractive widow (Eleanor Parker). She has appeal not only for father and son but for adults in the audience concerned about Ally's future; you just know that Eleanor Parker would do right by any growing boy.

"Capracorn," yes--but a believable and often colorful example. Sinatra and young Eddie Hodges make a good team. The cast is excellent, with an especially sharp portrait of a millionaire promoter contributed by Keenan Wynn. There are two hit songs by Cahn and Van Deusen: "High Hopes," which won an Academy Award, and "All Your Tomorrows."

THE HOUSE ON CHELOUCHE STREET, see p. 213

HOUSEBOAT

Paramount, 1958. 110 mins. col. (d) Melville Shavelson (sp) Jack Rose and Melville Shavelson (c) Sophia Loren, Cary Grant, Martha Hyer, Eduardo Ciannelli, Harry Guardino, Charles Herbert, Mimi Gibson, Paul Petersen. (FNC)

The Melville Shavelson-Jack Rose School of Child Psychology may be new to your local PTA, but it's a classic movie institution. Its major premise is that what every motherless kid needs is Sophia Loren, and that what Sophia needs, Sophia gets. (The theory worked so well in Houseboat that Shavelson and Rose, two years later, took it on a European seminar, for It Started in Naples. Loren is with Grant on the Potomac; later she was with Gable on the Bay.)

Cary Grant has three unmanageable kids (Charles Herbert, Mimi Gibson, Paul Petersen), who resent the fact that pop, who hasn't been around much since mom died, has taken them away from Aunt Carolyn (Martha Hyer). Lonely and unhappy, they have lots of hang-ups, like needing to play the harmonica at all times, and they tell pop off in very blunt terms. But all this is changed soon. Because of a lady-in-disguise plot device too silly to explain, Cinzia (Sophia Loren) becomes their maid on the houseboat. She smooths all the family relationships. She creates a few new problems, such as the adolescent boy's crush on her and his misery that he cannot compete with Harry Guardino or with his father for her love, but the plot takes care of them all.

Oddly, the Shavelson-Rose theory seems frequently plausible. The kids' warming up to Miss Loren's uncomplicated, direct understanding of them makes sense, as do Mr. Grant's bumbling pre-Loren efforts at parenthood. He looks just as frustrated as the fathers on "visitation days" trying to be pals with wised-up, unhappy youngsters. Oh, for a Sophia Loren in every broken home!

HOW GREEN WAS MY VALLEY, see p. 306

HUD, see p. 47

THE HUMAN COMEDY, see p. 307

I REMEMBER MAMA, see p. 308

I WAS BORN, BUT . . .

Japan, 1932. 89 mins. b/w. (d) Yasujiro Ozu (sp) Yasujiro Ozu, with Akira Fushimi and James Maki (ph) Hideo Shigehara (c) Hideo Sugawara, Tokkan-Kozo, Tatsuo Saito. Silent with English subtitles. (MAC)

"I started to make a film about children and ended with a film about grown-ups," said Ozu of this silent comedy, which is so full of rich detail. Though his film is bright, funny, and charming, it is basically serious. Once the two little boys recognize the hypocrisies of their father's world, a world with problems for which they are not quite ready, they will never be the same again. "One is born, then the trouble begins."

Ryoichi, ten (Hideo Sugawara), and his brother, Keiji, eight (Tokkan-Kozo), are the children of a white-collar worker, Yoshi (Tatsu Saito), who moves the family to a Tokyo suburb close to the home of his boss. Ryoichi and Keiji are picked on by the boss's son, Taro, and snubbed by the other kids in the new neighborhood. School isn't much better, until their classmates accept them as leaders because a friend of theirs overpowers a bully.

What hurts the most is the revelation that papa is not a great man; papa is a clown who grovels to his boss. The fact is clear as the kids watch a home movie at the boss's house, in which papa is trying to be amusing. They are full of shame. Why can't _he_ be the boss? There's a big family showdown. The brothers go on _a_ hunger strike. Mama-san tempts them with rice balls and the strike ends--but papa makes the point that his pleasing the boss is what fills their bellies.

Well, maybe when they grow up, they will also have to toady to the boss. But meanwhile, the brothers can take small-boys' revenge on Taro, the boss's son. They make him lie down in the dust. Some day they may have to work for him to earn _their_ children's rice balls--but right now, Ryoichi is stronger _than_ he is and smarter in school.

As the small brothers, Hideo Sugawara and Tokkan-Kozo are as delightful as miniature Keatons, as real as if caught unaware by the camera.

Of Ozu's fifty-three films, _I Was Born, But . . ._ seems to many people his definitive study of children, their innocence, and their compromise by social forms. In 1959, he reworked the theme in _Good Morning_ (Ohayo), in which the emphasis shifted from the boys to society in general, and the boys are too easily won over to acceptance of the way things are when their parents buy them a TV set.

Called "the most Japanese of directors," the late Yasujiro Ozu was a film artist whose treasures are accessible to us all. _I Was Born, But. . ._ is universal. Very accurate and very funny are such things as low-angle shots from the boys' eye-level, intercut with higher shots from their father's, as he lectures them, while he is undressing, about getting high marks.

Also: Growing Pains

THE ISLAND (HADAKA NO SHIMA)

Japan, 1961. 96 mins. b/w. (d)(sp) Kaneto Shindo (ph) Kiyoshi Kuroda (m) Hikaru Hayashi (c) Nobuko Otowa, Taiji Tonoyama, Shinji Tanaka, Masanori Horimoto. No dialog; music and sound effects only. (MAC)

Kaneto Shindo watched his own mother toiling in the rice fields. His film about a poor family is a lyric to their endurance. It has no dialog, only natural sound and music. Every shot is beautiful in its simplicity.

Two small boys, Taro and Jiro, live with their parents, who are farmers, on an island in western Japan--a tiny steep hill without water. In summer, every day they all go to the mainland to collect water, carrying it up the hillside and carefully ladling it around the roots of their crops. Even when the mother takes Taro to school, she must bring back water. When she spills some, Taro's father strikes her. The older boy contracts a fever and dies. (The doctor comes too late.) After the funeral, his brother and their parents resume their watering. Suddenly the mother hurls down her bucket, tears up the plants, and falls to the ground. After a while, she stops sobbing, rises, and they go on with their work together.

Together. "It is impossible to imagine these children growing up lost and bewildered," said Stanley Kauffmann (A World on Film). We remember the day Taro and Jiro catch a fish: the family sells it on the mainland and enjoys a meal in a restaurant. Self-sufficient, equally needed and important in the small world they share, children and parents are very close. There is no generation gap here.

ISLANDS IN THE STREAM

Paramount, 1977. 110 mins. col. (d) Franklin J. Schaffner (sp) Denne Bart Petitclerc (c) George C. Scott, David Hemmings, Gilbert Roland, Claire Bloom, Hart Bochner, Michael-James Wixted, Brad Savage. (FNC)

"About the only normal--or normally neurotic--children to be seen in a recent American film," commented Vincent Canby in the Times on May 29, 1977, "are the three boys in ... Islands in the Stream, and the film isn't really about the boys. It's about their Hemingway-like dad and what he feels about them."

In an otherwise undistinguished movie, there is insight into the relationship between children and divorced parents. From Hemingway's autobiographical novel, published posthumously in 1970, Islands in the Stream presents "Thomas Hudson" (George C. Scott) as a twice-divorced artist, self-exiled in the Bahamas after a successful career in Paris. His guilt and regrets over past mistakes surface when his three attractive teen-age sons, whom he hasn't seen in four years, spend a summer with him. Two adore him; Davy, the middle boy (Michael-James Wixted), resents him for mistreating his mother. Realizing that he cannot live apart from them, Hudson decides to return to the mainland and be a better father. However, he is accidentally sidetracked: he has to "attend a war," as Hemingway once wrote of himself.

The adolescent macho profanity of the youngsters trying out their wings is believable. But whether you swallow the marlin episode depends on your own Papa quotient. Davy emerges a MAN from the struggle with the giant fish. It is the Hemingway code: he has hunted and killed and "loved" his prey--and in his newly-won maturity, no longer resents his father.

Well, what one comes away with is a reminder that sons are often ambivalent in their love and need for the divorced parent.

Also: From Literature

JOEY

Canada, 1965. 28 mins. b/w. (d) Graham Parker (ph) Paul Leach (c) Miles McNamara, Irene Mayeska. (IFB)

A FURTHER GLIMPSE OF JOEY

Canada, 1966. 27 mins., b/w. (IFB)

These two documentaries by the National Film Board of Canada, made with the cooperation of the Children's Aid Society, dramatize through one boy, Joey, the experience that a seven-year-old has with adoption.

Placement is easy for infants. For the older child, there are problems on both sides. A likeable youngster, Joey has already had several traumatic episodes in his short life; after being abandoned by his parents, he was first placed in a foster home. He is full of fears and scars. But we are glad to see that now he is with new parents, and they are learning to accept each other.

In the second film, A Further Glimpse of Joey, we see him a little later in his new home, getting used to family routines, with adjustments being made on both sides.

THE KID

First National, 1921. 60 mins. b/w. (d)(sp)(m) Charles Chaplin (assoc d) Chuck Riesner (ph) Rollie Totheroh (c) Charlie Chaplin, Jackie Coogan, Edna Purviance, Carl Miller, Tom Wilson, Chuck Riesner, Albert Austin, Nellie Bly Baker, Henry Bergman, Lita Grey. Silent. Score added by Chaplin in 1971. (PAR)

"His eyes speak," wrote Francis Hackett about Jackie Coogan in 1921. "No child that I have ever seen on the stage created so full a part before. Most of the children one sees are limited to one or two postures. They appear but do not represent. This 'Kid' represents, and with a lovely mobile countenance, a countenance that is at once quite childlike and deep as an Italian masterpiece."

Now almost sixty years later, after Baby This and Baby That and curls and cuteness and child stars and even a few real child actors, the five-year-old gamin in *The Kid* is still unique. The boy with a natural gift was tutored by a genius; between them they made a great motion picture. It is wonderfully funny, of course, but it is also wonderfully moving--the love between the kid and the tramp who is both foster father and foster mother to him holds all the gags firmly in place.

In his autobiography, Chaplin tells how he went to the Orpheum in Los Angeles and saw a four-year-old brought on at the finish of his father's act to take a bow with him. The boy broke into a few amusing steps, looked knowingly at the audience, waved and ran off. Brought on again when the crowd went into an uproar, he did a different dance. Chaplin notes that it would have been obnoxious in another child but Jackie Coogan was charming. When he later asked the elder Coogan to let him have the boy for one picture, Jackie's father said, "Why, of course you can have the little punk."

Begun in 1919 and completed in 1920, *The Kid* grew without a script. Chaplin built a story which was almost a chapter out of his own boyhood in the London slums; even the garret room was said to be a copy of the one in which he had lived with his mother.

Gouverneur Morris, one of Chaplin's literary friends and a seasoned script writer, warned Chaplin that the form *The Kid* was taking, keying slapstick with sentiment, would never work. But Chaplin knew it would work if the artist believed in it. Raw slapstick and sentiment, the premise of *The Kid*, was something of an innovation; but the artist who wrote, directed, and acted in *The Kid*--then cut it in a hotel bedroom to foil lawsuits and sold it to skeptical First National smart-money men--was right. Chaplin's first production of a feature-length film not only pleased critics and audiences all over the world but made a fortune and launched Jackie Coogan on a career as the most popular child star before Shirley Temple.

Jackie's talent was genuine. He demonstrated it in *Peck's Bad Boy* (1921); *Oliver Twist*, *Trouble*, and *My Boy* (all in 1922); *Circus Days*, *Daddy*, *Long Live the King* (all in 1923); and *A Boy of Flanders* (1924). He was honored on Jackie Coogan's Day in Brooklyn in 1924, and did yeoman service in the Children's Crusade, selling Mercy Bonds for Near East Relief. There were ovations all over Europe on his tours. And there were the legendary lawsuits, when his mother and her husband displayed a rapacity shocking even in Hollywood, and Jackie's great wealth went down the drain; and the decline of his popularity, when such pictures as *Old Clothes* (1925) and Buttons (1927), revealed an awkward teenager without the early appeal.

In The Kid, Jackie seemed to match Charlie in emotional intensity, in light-hearted zest. He was not "cute" but genuine. "A picture with a smile--perhaps a tear" was the First National come-on, and for once the promise was richly fulfilled.

The story? The Tramp, debonair as ever, is on promenade, swinging his cane, carefully selecting a butt from his sardine-can cigarette case. He is stuck with a bundle--the baby of an unmarried mother (Edna Purviance). He contrives to care for it in his wretched garret. Five years pass. The Kid and the Tramp are in business together: the Kid throws stones at a window and runs; the Tramp "happens by" and is hired to repair the damage. There is some trouble with a suspicious cop (Tom Wilson) but they soon shake him. Meanwhile, the mother has become a rich and famous opera star. She accidentally finds the Kid. There are complications; the authorities try to take the child away from the man, but Charlie and he run away. A flophouse owner (Henry Bergman) steals the Kid for the reward. Charlie is awakened from a fantastic dream of "Fairyland" (Heaven) where the slum inhabitants sprout wings, and the policeman takes him to the Kid and his mother for a warm reunion.

Some of the most famous sight gags from this film include: the baby in the garret, swinging in a homemade hammock with a nursing bottle made from a coffeepot suspended on a string; Charlie patting the hammock bottom and wiping his hands, then carving a hole in the seat of a chair, putting the chair under the hammock and a spittoon under the chair; Jackie making pancakes; Charlie sticking his head through a hole in a dirty blanket and turning it into a dressing gown, then giving Jackie a lesson in good manners; Charlie examining Jackie's hands and ears before setting out to break windows; Charlie shaking Jackie off like a puppy to outwit the suspicious cop; Jackie sitting on the curb manicuring his nails with all of Charlie's aplomb.

They are a pair--man and boy, "father" and "son", tutor and pupil--both exquisite and coarse, natural and fantastic. Always loving, always close, they lift up the spirit forever.

To see the gamin miming the manners of the tramp he adores is to see every small boy walking like his father. And, incredibly, to see the Tramp care for the baby in the garret is to see every mother who ever tended an infant. The difference, of course, is comic genius.

THE LAST PICTURE SHOW, see p. 50

LIES MY FATHER TOLD ME

Columbia, 1975. 102 mins. col. (d) Jan Kadar (sp) Ted Allan (ph)

Paul van der Linden (m) Sol Kaplan (c) Yossi Yadin, Len Birman, Marilyn Lightstone, Jeffrey Lynas, Ted Allan, Barbara Chilcott, Carole Lazare, Cleo Paskal. (SWA)

This picture is writer Ted Allan's Roots--his memories of his childhood in a Russian-Jewish immigrant family in the Jewish quarter of Montreal in the 1920's.

Bursting with emotion, amusing and touching, the film succeeds in the broadest human terms. Made in Canada by Czech director Jan Kadar, under a grant from the Canadian Film Development Corporation, Lies My Father Told Me reminds us that he is one of the so-called "Czech film renaissance" directors who produced such films as Closely Watched Trains (q. v.). Some of its best scenes have the texture of The Shop on Main Street, for which Kadar won an Academy Award.

The keystone of the story is the relationship between David (Jeffrey Lynas), who is seven, and his wise old grandfather (Yossi Yadin), a junk man. It is joy for the boy to ride with his Zaida and to shout, "Rags! Clothes! Bottles!" as ancient Ferdelah draws the creaking wagon through the back alleys, or (on Sundays) through the countryside. Zaida has so many wonderful things to give him--explanations of the rituals, the traditions and the faith; Biblical parables; tall tales; quotations from the Talmud (really quotations from Zaida). And David's father has only "lies" to give him--the "practicality" of money-making schemes that fail, as luckless Harry Herman (Len Birman) struggles to invent creaseless trousers and scrounges loans from the old man. Ingenuous and adoring, David looks to his Zaida for the truth, for dreams and imagination and the answers to many of the things that puzzle him.

His neighborhood provides a great deal of drama: the local scold (Barbara Chilcott) incensed by stable matters; the gentle Marxist (Ted Allan); the prostitute (Carole Lazare) and the little girl (Cleo Paskal) who are both his friends. Everything and everyone touching him helps him to grow.

But it is grandfather who is closest. One day, David spies on a buxom lady nuzzling a lusty gentleman to her naked breast. Then he sees his mother (Marilyn Lightstone) nursing her newborn baby, of whom David is intensely jealous. Pointing to her breast, David insists, "I want that." When she turns him down, grandfather tries to explain matters.

Finally, the boy must face the terrible reality of his Zaida's death. There is a very moving scene when Zaida dies and David chases after him in fantasy, seeing him in the distance, always losing him at the spot where he thought he saw him last.

Israeli actor Yossi Yadin is a strong, tender Zaida; Jeffrey Lynas is genuinely convincing as David; and the Canadian actors play people as real as the settings in which Kadar has placed them.

Also: Death
Generation Conflicts
Growing Pains

THE LITTLE KIDNAPPERS

Great Britain, 1953. 95 mins. b/w. (d) Philip Leacock (sp) Neil Paterson, from his own story (ph) Eric Cross (m) Bruce Montgomery, played by the Royal Philharmonic Orchestra (c) Duncan Macrae, Adrienne Corri, Vincent Winter, Jon Whiteley, Jean Anderson, Theodore Bikel, Francis de Woolf. (JAN)

"Vincent Winter, with all the innocence of a five-year-old, has momentarily obliterated the happy memories I used to harbor of Jackie Coogan in The Kid, Jackie Cooper in The Champ ... Enzo Staiola in Bicycle Thief, Christian Fourcade in Little Boy Lost and Brandon de Wilde in Shane," said Paul Dehn, British film critic.

Vincent's innocent charm is one of many fresh and appealing things in director Philip Leacock's film of an interesting Nova Scotia family in the 1900's. With his big brother, Harry (Jon Whiteley), who is eight, five-year-old Davy goes to live with his dour Scottish grandfather MacKenzie (Duncan Macrae), his grandmother (Jean Anderson), and beautiful Kirsty MacKenzie (Adrienne Corri) in the Nova Scotia countryside.

The small orphaned boys, whose grim grandfather has turned down their request for a dog, find a lost baby in the woods. Overjoyed, they make it their pet, hiding it and feeding it. Young Harry is charged with kidnapping, but is acquitted. The baby's father, Boer farmer Jan Hooft, has spoken on his behalf, and grandfather MacKenzie not only sees the light about his Boer neighbors (his son had been killed in the Boer War) but about his little grandsons' need for love. He sells his best pair of boots to get them a dog.

Very well acted, written and photographed (in Scotland), The Little Kidnappers has lasting quality. Neil Paterson's dialog is real, not coy, so much so that we sometimes have a little trouble understanding the genuine Scottish accents of the children as we eavesdrop on their privacy. Even the drama of the adults of the family, usually intrusive in films about children, is well handled. Daughter Kirsty's romance with the local Boer doctor, Willem Bloem (Theodore Bikel), is brought to a dramatic, plausible climax. The rigid Calvinist household of the MacKenzies, with its gentle mother and repressed daughter dominated by the stern yet not unkind old man, is vividly drawn.

The Little Kidnappers is a delightful picture of the natural instincts of small children breaking out of the vise of adult convention. Director Philip Leacock went on to make other films about children and adolescents (The Rabbit Trap, Hand In Hand, Take A Giant Step, Reach for Glory), none as fine as the first, but all marked by the naturalness of the performances he obtained from his young actors.

LITTLE WOMEN, see p. 312

LOVERS AND LOLLIPOPS

Trans-Lux, 1956. 83 mins. b/w. (d)(sp)(ph) Morris Engel and Ruth Orkin (c) Cathy Dunn, Lori March, Gerald O'Laughlin. (MAC)

Having demonstrated in Little Fugitive that nothing is so hilarious as a child who takes the immediate goal seriously, Morris Engel and Ruth Orkin did it again in Lovers and Lollipops.

Seven-year-old Peggy (Cathy Dunn) is the daughter of a young war widow (Lori March) who is thinking of getting married again to a young man named Larry (Gerald O'Laughlin). The child resents the intrusion of a suitor for her mother, and does everything to complicate the courtship before she is won over by the young man.

Though the theme is unremarkable, the Engel-Orkin treatment hasn't a single false note. Its adult lovers are awkward, natural, and full of tenderness as well as exasperation during the child's ploys. The little girl is perfectly delightful. Whether she is getting lost in a parking lot, or causing havoc in Macy's toy department or in the garden of the Museum of Modern Art, or delaying bedtime in her mother's Upper West Side apartment, or trying to consume an entire package of lollipops which she has stuck in the sand at the beach in Rye, she is a person to reckon with, not just to laugh at.

MEET ME IN ST. LOUIS, see p. 315

MURMUR OF THE HEART (LE SOUFFLE AU COEUR)

France, Italy, West Germany, 1971. 118 mins. col. (d/sp) Louis Malle (ph) Ricardo Aronovich (m) Charlie Parker, Sidney Bechet, Gaston Freche, Henri Renaud (c) Lea Massari, Daniel Gélin, Benoit Ferreux. French dialog with English subtitles. (BUD, IMA, WRS, WHO, KPF)

This collective autobiography (his friends' and his own) of adolescence by director Louis Malle (The Lovers, Zazie in the Metro) has a climactic episode of mother-son incest. The mother and the son are miserable one Bastille Day. In an inebriated glow, they make love almost by accident. Afterward she tells him gently that the experience will not be referred to again.

This is not one of the standard crises of puberty, admittedly. The French authorities condemned the original screenplay; the Cannes jury ignored the film; the French public flocked to the theater. Here and abroad, many have found Malle to be concerned not with incest but with the often funny, often painful relationships between an adolescent and his bourgeois, provincial family in the mid-fifties. They have called the scene of incest discreet and inoffensive. Wrote Pauline Kael about Malle, "He looks at this bourgeois bestiary and sees it as funny and appalling and also--surprisingly--hardy and happy." But others have found the director's intention offensive: "The whole sunny _ménage_ is poisonous," said critic Robert Hatch. "What [Malle] appears to be saying is that life is a great joke because nobody gets hurt. That point of view is bad enough in Tom and Jerry cartoons; when applied to alleged human beings it becomes moronic."

The sexual education of Laurent (Benoit Ferreux), who is fifteen, takes place in Dijon, in 1954, where he lives with his gynecologist father, his demonstrative Italian mother (Lea Massari), and his two elder brothers. Laurent's priest is a pederast; his mother is having an affair; his brothers take him to a brothel for initiation and humiliate him brutally at the crucial moment. When an attack of scarlet fever leaves Laurent with a heart murmur, his mother takes him to a mountain spa. She flirts with another young patient, until her lover arrives and there is a quarrel. Laurent sizes up a couple of girls, Daphne and Helene. After mother and son make love on Bastille Day, Laurent leaps from his mother's bed and makes for Helene's room; on being repulsed, he moves down the hall to find Daphne more willing. In the morning, back in his own room, very pleased with himself, Laurent finds the family reunited--his father and brothers have arrived during the night--and everyone greets him with good-natured teasing, sharing the joke.

Whether or not one is inclined to enjoy Malle's style, or Laurent's situation, there is something interesting in the boy's feeling about his shameless, free, and sensual young mother. He loves her for what she is, careless of all the bourgeois forms. Laurent is a spoiled brat, and his mother, Clara, says she grew up like a savage; the tie between them is knotted very fast.

Also: Love and Sex

MY AIN FOLK, see p. 22

MY CHILDHOOD, see p. 24

THE NANNY, see p. 121

NAVAJO GIRL

Bobwin Associates, 1973. 21 mins. col. (XER)

In this documentary, a point made in many films about happy children, that family love, not wealth, sustains them, is made effectively about a little Indian girl whose family barely subsists on an Arizona reservation, where their survival depends solely on sheep and goats.

Kathrine Begay, ten, has a close-knit, warm, and loving home. This is the way of life of a Navajo child more fortunate than many children in less primitive situations.

Beautifully photographed and told without sentimentality, Navajo Girl was an American Film Festival Blue Ribbon winner.

NOBODY WAVED GOODBYE, see p. 122

OUR VINES HAVE TENDER GRAPES

M-G-M, 1945. 106 mins. b/w. (d) Roy Rowland (sp) Dalton Trumbo, from the novel For Our Vines Have Tender Grapes by George Victor Martin (c) Margaret O'Brien, Jackie "Butch" Jenkins, Edward G. Robinson, Agnes Moorehead, Morris Carnovsky, Sara Haden, James Craig. (FNC)

Hardly a classic, but a very pleasant M-G-M production of vignettes of family and community life in a Norwegian farming settlement in Wisconsin, this is one of the most fondly remembered films featuring children.

Margaret O'Brien is glowing as seven-year-old Selma, and Jackie "Butch" Jenkins is her freckled, towheaded little brother Arnold. They do such things as explore the spring-thaw flooded farm in a tub that is swept into the river, and spend loving times with their grandfather, Martinius Jacobson (Edward G. Robinson). When he asks Selma to pray for a new barn as good as neighbor Bjornson's, she exclaims, "Gosh! What's one more barn to God?"

Though it sometimes smells of the studio klieg lights, Our Vines Have Tender Grapes has its heart in the right place, and the family is tenderly handled. James Agee, an old admirer of Margaret O'Brien, liked the movie. "Several scenes and many details," he wrote, "are as gracious and touching as the intention of the whole film."

Also: From Literature

PAPER MOON, see p. 27

THE PARENT TRAP

Disney, 1961. 124 mins. col. (d)(sp) David Swift (ph) Lucien Ballard (m) Paul J. Smith (sp. eff) Ub Iwerks (c) Hayley Mills, Maureen

O'Hara, Brian Keith, Charlie Ruggles, Una Merkel, Leo G. Carroll, Cathleen Nesbitt. Title song sung by Tommy Sands and Annette Funicello. (CWF, EPC, MAC, TWY)

The Parent Trap gives us a double helping of Hayley Mills. She plays thirteen-year-old identical twins who meet for the first time at summer camp. (They have grown up on separate coasts with their respective parents, who are separated from each other. Got it? It takes the girls some time to sort it out.)

This vehicle is the American model of Das Doppelte Lottchen (Lisa and Lottie), by Erich Kastner, tooled here by David Swift, who had directed Hayley in Pollyanna. Since Kastner is the author of Emil and the Detectives, a much better story, it is possible that The Parent Trap has lost something in translation. The American version is broad and predictable and occasionally tiresome as it follows the little girls in their efforts to reunite their parents (Maureen O'Hara and Brian Keith).

Little girls they are, however, and some people will thank heaven for their lively, winning, and often recognizable adolescence. In double-exposure and split-screen scenes, Hayley differentiates the personalities of Sharon and Susan. The New York Times thought the film should be appealing to parents.

PART 2, SOUNDER, see p. 185

POPI

United Artists, 1969. 113 mins. col. (d) Arthur Hiller (sp) Tina and Lester Pine (ph) Andy Laszlo (m) Dominic Frontiere (c) Alan Arkin, Rita Moreno, Miguel Alejandro, Ruben Figueroa. (UAS)

How many films do you know that recognize the wealth of material to be found in El Barrio, New York's Spanish Harlem, or that have Puerto Rican children as protagonists?

Popi is really Alan Arkin's picture. He is superb as the young widower, Abraham (Popi) Rodriguez--handyman, attendant in a hospital morgue, plumber, waiter--trying to raise two very lively cubs in the ghetto jungle. But the kids themselves have a way of taking over. Miguel Alejandro and Ruben Figueroa, as Junior and Luis Rodriguez, do not seem to be aware of the fact that they are disadvantaged members of a neglected minority group living in squalor. They attack abandoned cars and other slum litter with zestful recognition of their possibilities for play, roll with the punches sometimes administered by their weary father, and are prepared to wait outside when he wants to make love to his girl (Rita Moreno). They are very happy.

But their father is not happy at all. He schemes crazily, hilariously, to get them out of El Barrio and into a better life. We will not spoil the tale by giving it away.

If you do not analyze it sociologically, Popi has a family portrait that you will remember: a nutty, ever-loving, harried father, and two small Puerto Rican boys, wonderfully themselves.

THE QUIET ONE, see p. 245

THE RAILWAY CHILDREN, see p. 318

REBEL WITHOUT A CAUSE, see p. 125

RED SKY AT MORNING, see p. 57

THE RUSSIANS ARE COMING, THE RUSSIANS ARE COMING

United Artists, 1966. 126 mins. col. (d) Norman Jewison (sp) William Rose, from Nathaniel Benchley's novel The Off-Islanders (m) Johnny Mandel (c) Alan Arkin, Carl Reiner, Eva Marie Saint, Brian Keith, Jonathan Winters, Theodore Bikel, Paul Ford, Ben Blue, Tessie O'Shea, Andrea Dromm, John Phillip Law. (UAS)

One of the funniest comedies of recent years, about how some of us got overheated in the Cold War, this has a glimpse of a father-son relationship that is not only funny (since Carl Reiner plays the father) but a good reminder of how children are brainwashed in ways that are surprising to their parents.

A pigheaded commander of a Russian submarine grounded on a sandbar off a New England island has trouble getting away, because the islanders include would-be Paul Reveres, vigilantes, and just plain flappable citizens who think the crew are desperate invaders instead of the ludicrous (and embarrassed) blunderers they really are. One of the chief incendiaries, in his small way, is the lively young son of Walt Whittaker, a vacationer on the island. The boy has been so conditioned by newspapers, spy stories, and the Cold War atmosphere, that he cannot understand why his father does not immediately blow all the Russians' heads off. And his father--nervous, but cooler--simply cannot understand where his boy has picked up his bloodthirsty ideas.

Later on, when Whittaker shows real courage in defending his family, in a true rather than an imaginary crisis, the boy is proud of him. This incident gives us a small insight, perhaps, in the larger context of the movie. But you'll be feeling no pain if you catch The Russians Are Coming, The Russians Are Coming, next time around on TV, because it is full of delightful performances by Reiner, Alan Arkin, Theodore Bikel, Ben Blue, and Tessie O'Shea.

SATURDAY MORNING

U. S., 1971. 90 mins. col. (d) Kent Mackenzie. (CHA)

Saturday Morning is the diary of an encounter session involving a group of twenty California adolescents from every background, inner-city to suburbia, and from every kind of home.

For six days, under the guidance of their role-play leader--Michael Solomon, Director of Training, California Institute of Psychodrama--they reveal their emotional problems. From different social milieus, these young people have the same concerns: their relationships with their parents, their relationships with the opposite sex, their sense of identity, their sense of alienation. They act out the roles of their parents, express their anxieties about sex, and try to break down one another's defenses.

On Saturday morning (the sixth day), most of the defenses are down. Two weeping girls admit they are bewildered about their identity. A boy, describing his relationship with his parents, admits he is unable to love. A defiant black girl tells of her father's rejection of her effort to reach him, and her decision afterward; she turns away from the encounter group, still not "open."

Occasionally funny, more often poignant, and always honest, this documentary can be helpful to adults in their exploration of the emotional world of the younger generation. The role-play format has been interestingly employed by director Kent Mackenzie.

Also: Generation Conflicts

SHANE, see p. 28

SIXTEEN IN WEBSTER GROVES, see p. 60

THE SOUND OF MUSIC

Twentieth Century-Fox, 1965. 174 mins. col. (d) Robert Wise (sp) Ernest Lehman, from the musical play by Howard Lindsay and Russel Crouse (ph) Ted McCord (m) Richard Rodgers (lyr) Oscar Hammerstein II (c) Julie Andrews, Christopher Plummer, Eleanor Parker, Richard Haydn, Peggy Wood, Charmian Carr, the Bill Baird Marionettes. (FNC)

There is no point in being snide about the winner of five Academy Awards, including Best Picture of 1965, which is also the third highest grossing entertainment in Hollywood annals, after Gone with the Wind and The Godfather. As Richard F. Zanuck said, "It has everything: children, religion, high society, royalty, Nazi Germany, and Julie Andrews as the fairy on top of the Christmas tree." Not to speak of songs by Rodgers and Hammerstein ("My Favorite Things," "Sixteen Going on Seventeen," "Climb Every Mountain," "Do-Re-Mi").

Set "in Salzburg, toward the end of the Golden Thirties," with color by De Luxe, The Sound of Music is based on the true story of the Von Trapp Family Singers, modified for musical comedy. There are seven children in the story, all belonging to the widowed Baron Von Trapp. Soon they are won over by Maria (Julie Andrews), a singing postulant nun whom the Mother Abbess sends to be their governess.

The question is whether there is insight to be gained from observing the seven young Von Trapps. We say they're moppets--sugar-candy "Kiddies," these Baby Trapps--and W. C. Fields would know just what to do with them: spike their edelweiss with gin, 'e would.

SOUNDER

Twentieth Century-Fox, 1972. 106 mins. col. (d) Martin Ritt (sp) Lonnie Elder, III, from the novel by William H. Armstrong (ph) John Alonzo (m) Taj Mahal (c) Cicely Tyson, Paul Winfield, Kevin Hooks, Carmen Mathews, Taj Mahal, James Best, Janet MacLachlan. (FNC)

In rural Louisiana during the depression of the '30s, a black sharecropper, Nathan Lee Morgan (Paul Winfield), is struggling to provide for his family by working the land and hunting for game with the hound, Sounder. His wife, Rebecca (Cicely Tyson), takes in laundry; the children, David, the eldest (Kevin Hooks), and little Earl (Eric Hooks) and Josie Mae (Yvonne Jarrell) help out. David walks every morning to a white school because Nathan Lee and Rebecca are determined that their son should "beat the life they got laid out for you" by getting an education.

Nathan Lee steals some meat from a white man's smokehouse to keep his family going and is sentenced to a year on the chain gang. Rebecca and the children, to meet their landlord's produce quota and still have something left for themselves, plant and harvest the crop together. David, with the help of Mrs. Boatwright (Carmen Mathews), the white lady who has loaned him The Three Musketeers, learns the location of his father's work camp, and when the planting is finished sets out to visit him. He gets lost and is sheltered by a young black teacher, Miss Johnson (Janet MacLachlan). She gives him a notion of his own culture, instilling in him a sense of pride and an even stronger desire for education.

David returns home and one day (with his mother and the other children) has the joy of seeing his father return, wounded but smiling. The family takes up life--until the moment when David has to decide whether he will remain with his beloved father as a help and support to everyone, or accept Miss Johnson's invitation to study at her school far away.

This is the outline of a beautiful movie that belongs with warm family stories like The Sundowners and The Yearling and To Kill a Mockingbird, where the love between the older and younger members of the family is what keeps body and soul alive in a hard time. In Sounder, the wife and husband love each other with deep tenderness. The moment when she runs to meet him, after a year's separation, explodes on the screen (thanks to Cicely Tyson's magnificent performance); and the moment, the morning after their reunion, when the children show their delight in their parents' exuberant physical embrace is an added comment. The father and son love each other with growing understanding. In one of the most moving father-son scenes in movies, Nathan Lee explains to David that he will be cherished by his family wherever he is, so he must go to Miss Johnson's school to better himself.

The black child growing to manhood in his father's absence, and the magnificent black mother with bedrock pride and courage make Sounder an experience familiar to anyone who has known a loving, strong family. Director Martin Ritt thought that Nathan Lee's and Rebecca's determination to give David an education was like that of his own immigrant parents. But Sounder also manages, as no other film has done in quite the same way, to make clear the special experience of a black family, its trials and its stamina.

Cicely Tyson's portrayal of the mother (for which the National Society of Film Critics named her Best Actress of 1972) is a total revelation of the nobility of a woman. Paul Winfield and Kevin Hooks are admirable as the father and son. In the sensitive screenplay made by dramatist Lonnie Elder, III ("Ceremonies in Dark Old Men") from William Armstrong's 1970 Newbery Medal novella, there aren't many words, for these are simple, illiterate people. But Sounder is full of meaning, through the artistry of director and cast.

As Pauline Kael wrote of it, "One could do an iconography of smiles from this movie; often it is a smile that ends a scene, and it always seems a perfect end, just what was needed--an emblem of the spirit of a people, proof that they have not been destroyed."

Produced by Robert Radnitz (And Now Miguel, My Side of the Mountain), the film was photographed by John Alonzo in the East Feliciana and St. Helena parishes of Louisiana, where the look and accents of the people (and Taj Mahal's playing of his own songs) ring true.

Also: Finding Oneself
From Literature

SOUNDER, PART 2, see PART 2, SOUNDER, p. 185

THE SPANISH GARDENER

Great Britain, 1957. 97 mins. col. (d) Philip Leacock (sp) Lesley Storm and John Bryan, based on the novel by A. J. Cronin (ph) Christopher Challis (c) Dirk Bogarde, Jon Whiteley, Michael Hordern, Cyril Cusack. (ICA)

A strained relationship between a lonely child and his overpossessive father which leads to the child's rebellion is the crux of The Spanish Gardener, directed by Philip Leacock (The Little Kidnappers, Hand in Hand, Reach for Glory).

Towheaded Jon Whiteley, who was the eight-year-old in The Little Kidnappers, is twelve here, the son of a minor counsular official (Michael Hordern) stationed in a small town on Spain's Costa Brava. The father is a soured man; he is separated from his wife, and he has been passed over for promotion because he can't get along with people. He needs to monopolize little Nicholas' affection, and so he forbids him to make friends with other children, and refuses to give him a formal schooling. Inevitably, Nicholas finds a friend for himself: José, the warm and sympathetic young peasant gardener (Dirk Bogarde), who understands the boy's needs for robust fun and companionship. Their friendship arouses his father's jealousy, and matters come to a melodramatic climax.

As the boy torn between his love for his father and his admiration for another adult with more perception, Jon Whiteley is very appealing. The Spanish Gardener is a quiet film, but its British understatement is not without compassion for the characters. There are colorful shots of the Costa Brava mountains and beaches, and the villagers put on a rousing game of jai alai on Sundays.

Also: Generation Conflicts

THE SPIRIT OF THE BEEHIVE, see p. 275

SPLENDOR IN THE GRASS, see p. 155

A SUMMER TO REMEMBER

USSR, 1960. 80 mins. b/w. (d) Georgy Daniela, Igor Talankin (sp) Vera Panova, Georgy Daniela, Igor Talankin, from Vera Panova's novel Seryozha (ph) Leonid Kosmatov, Anatoly Nitochkin (m) Boris Chaikovsky (c) Borya Barkhatov, Sergei Bondarchuk, Irina Skobtseva. Russian dialog with English subtitles. (MAC)

Not since Vincent Winter, the Davy of The Little Kidnappers, has there been a five-year-old as winning as Borya Barkhatov, the Seryozha in A Summer to Remember. With great naturalness, he conveys the true feeling of a child whose world has been overturned by the arrival of a stepfather and a new baby.

Seryozha lives with his widowed young mother (Irina Skobtseva) on a collective farm in the Soviet Union. When she remarries, Seryozha resents the stranger who has pushed him out of her life. But the stranger, the farm director Korostelyov (Sergei Bondarchuk), meets every test of a new father. When he gives Seryozha a bicycle, and Seryozha and a friend demolish it by running it into a goat, he understands. And he does not punish Seryozha even when he calls a foolish uncle a fool. Just as Seryozha is settling down to adore this newcomer, another turns up to shatter his peace--an infant! His parents have to leave the farm, in winter, to move to a new post, and plan to deposit him with an aunt until the summer, because he has been ill. Seryozha is brokenhearted. They have rejected him. But Korostelyov realizes what is happening and decides to take his son along.

The relationship of a stepfather to a child and the problems of sibling rivalry have never been screened with more light and less artificiality than in this charming picture. And there is humor, too. When Seryozha's sea-captain uncle arrives covered with tattoos and the farm children play with the dangerous possibility of getting tattooed themselves, we have a richly funny Tom Sawyer-on-a-collective episode.

Also: Growing Pains

THE SUMMER WE MOVED TO ELM STREET, see p. 31

A THOUSAND CLOWNS, see p. 265

TO KILL A MOCKINGBIRD, see p. 326

A TREE GROWS IN BROOKLYN

Twentieth Century-Fox, 1945. 128 mins. b/w. (d) Elia Kazan (sp) Tess Slesigner and Frank Davis from the novel by Betty Smith (ph) Leon Shamroy (m) Alfred Newman (art) Lyle Wheeler (c) Dorothy McGuire, James Dunn, Peggy Ann Garner, Joan Blondell, Lloyd Nolan, James Gleason, Ted Donaldson. (GEN)

In his first film, director Elia Kazan (East of Eden, On the Waterfront) realizes powerfully not only the atmosphere of the tenements and slum streets of Brooklyn's Williamsburg sixty years ago, but the family relationships that are the heart of Betty Smith's best-selling autobiographical novel. Life in the big cities has changed and contemporary films are more realistic, but the father-daughter, mother-daughter, sibling relationships in this picture are as moving as ever.

The tree across the tenement courtyard that twelve-year-old Francis Nolan (Peggy Ann Garner) can see from her window is a symbol of herself, rooted in dust and poverty, growing strong in the struggle toward light.

Francie adores her feckless father, Johnny Nolan (James Dunn), full of drink and poetry, who delegates the harsh facts of existence to his indomitable wife, Katie (Dorothy McGuire). Little Neeley Nolan (Ted "Pudge"Donaldson) is his mother's boy, Francie thinks, as she is her father's. There are alliances and differences within the family. Francie leans on her father, but he is unable to give her real support, though he invents a ruse, deceiving her mother, that enables her to get into the school she longs to attend.

When her father dies, Francie at first cannot bear the truth: "Maybe it was a dream. But no, no dream lasted that long. It was real. Papa was gone forever."

Francie sobs, alone in the world. "Mama doesn't love me the way she loves Neeley ... I can't make her love me the way papa loved me."

But Francie loves mama. She begins to realize how good mama is, how hard she works, how brave she is despite her grief. What would Neeley and she do without mama?

Daughter and mother draw closer. "I can't tell you how much I'm counting on you," says the pregnant young widow. "I can't count on Neeley--a boy's no use at a time like this."

And Francie grows up a little: "Maybe she doesn't love me as much as she loves Neeley. But she needs me more than she needs him and I guess being needed is almost as good as being loved. Maybe better."

Peggy Ann Garner is quite wonderful as the plain, intense, creative adolescent so sensitive to every experience. She and James Dunn won Academy Awards for their performances, but everyone in the cast from Dorothy McGuire and Joan Blondell (as problem Aunt Sissy) down to Ted Donaldson is excellent.

The film (like the novel) is a penetrating glimpse of family life, and an affecting study of an adolescent on the verge of maturity.

<u>Also</u>: From Literature
Growing Pains

TWO WOMEN, see p. 225

LES VIOLONS DU BAL, see p. 226

WHERE THE LILIES BLOOM

United Artists, 1974. 97 mins. col. (d) William Graham (sp) Earl Hamner, Jr., from the novel by Vera and Bill Cleaver (ph) Urs Furrer (m) Earl Scruggs (c) Julie Gholson, Harry Dean Stanton, Sudie Bond, Tom Spratley, Alice Beardsley, Jan Smithers, Matthew Burrill, Helen Harmon. (UAS)

The mixture as before, for admirers of writer Earl Hamner, Jr. ("The Waltons") and producer Robert Radnitz (Sounder, My Side of the Mountain, And Now Miguel). Adapted by Hamner from the 1969 Newbery Award novel by Vera and Bill Cleaver, Where the Lilies Bloom tells us again about a loving family whose poverty is not poverty of spirit, and about an adolescent growing in strength.

Mary Call Luther (Julie Gholson) is fourteen. She doesn't have time to write in her diary and longs for the day when she can be "all the things inside me no one else can see." She loves her shiftless father despite his weakness, as Francie loves hers in A Tree Grows in Brooklyn. When he dies, she promises him that she will keep neighbor Kiser Pease (Harry Dean Stanton), whom he hates, away from her sister, Devola (Jan Smithers), and that she will keep the family together without taking charity or losing pride.

Although she's not the oldest of the Luther children, Mary Call is the sturdiest, and she copes. It isn't easy, on their 200-year-old sharecropper's farm in the Appalachians (Boone, North Carolina). They just about manage, keeping up the sharecropping and existing on a little fatback and potherbs. To avoid being sent to the orphanage, they must keep their father's death secret. Storekeeper Connell (Tom Spratley) helps out by giving them a chance to earn money by wildcrafting--collecting and preparing roots and plants used in folk medicine.

Mary Call, the other children think, is a little hard on them. But it's a big assignment for a fourteen-year-old, being father and mother to a brood. And things get involved; Kiser Pease is hospitalized after an accident and when his sister, Goldie (Alice Beardsley), comes out from the city, she orders the Luthers off the land.

Not to worry: this is the land of Hamner and Radnitz. Goldie isn't really any meaner than Liv Walton's neighbors. Storekeeper Connell (blood brother to Ike Gadsey in "The Waltons") will dance to a Watauga County fiddler's tune at the wedding of Kiser Pease and Devola. And Mary Call, who wants to be a writer (like John-Boy), will be freed from her adult burden so that she can start to fulfill the promise that her teacher (Sudie Bond) has glimpsed.

The Luthers' cabin is papered with newspapers, their diet is peppered with a kind of spinach called "lamb's quarters," and their talk about God's sense of humor is authentic Appalachian, but their characters sometimes seem less mountain-grown than media-sprung. In the never-never haze, one character is made real by Julie Gholson, playing her first role at thirteen. We've seen that toughness before in a little girl who has to keep a family going. We can follow her growth from blind loyalty to the dead father to her own knowledge that living people need compassion and that Kiser Pease isn't such a bad egg after all.

Also: Finding Oneself
From Literature

THE WILD DUCK. see p. 332

THE WORLD OF HENRY ORIENT, see p. 32

THE YEARLING, see p. 62

THE YOUNG STRANGER, see p. 128

YOURS, MINE AND OURS

United Artists, 1968. 111 mins. col. (d) Melville Shavelson (sp) Melville Shavelson and Mort Lachman, from a story by Madelyn Davis and Bob Carroll, Jr. (ph) Charles Wheeler (m) Fred Karlin (c) Henry Fonda, Lucille Ball, Van Johnson, Tom Bosley. (UAS)

There were only a dozen children in Cheaper by the Dozen, and they all had the same father and mother. Here, a widow (Lucille Ball) with eight young children marries a widower (Henry Fonda) with ten--and they have another one together, making nineteen.

The logistics of raising all these youngsters in a modern San Francisco middle-class home can be milked for comedy, and Melville Shavelson (director and co-scripter) is not a man to refuse to look a gag in the face, particularly with Lucille Ball on hand. Some of this movie is very, very funny. But underlying Yours, Mine and Ours is the true story of the California Beardsley family, and many of the children emerge as very real people, not just cardboard pop entertainers.

There's the little boy who shakes his sibling's pet ant farm and yells, "I HATE ANTS!" There are the kids who doctor the lady visitor's drinks when Lucille Ball comes calling (how dare she think of replacing their lost mother!). There is the rice-throwing fight right after the wedding. Particularly touching is the final realization of all the children that they are one family named Beardsley.

Though the film has a problem hardly universal, the hostility of children to the remarriage of their parents is not rare. The

Norths and the Beardsleys give one insight into the changes in attitude that can take place, given a lot of love and rolling with the punches.

GENERATION CONFLICTS

ABIDE WITH ME

BBC/TV, 1976. 60 mins. col. (d) Moira Armstrong (sp) Julian Mitchell, based on Winifred Foley's A Child in the Forest (c) Cathleen Nesbitt, Anne Francis, Iris Allen, Phyllida Law, John Nettleton, Geoffrey Bayldon, Denis Carey, Denise Hoskins. (TLF)

This beautifully played and directed film, presented in the "Great Performances: Childhood" series by the Public Broadcasting Service, shines with truth. Cathleen Nesbitt, as a lonely dowager of 90, and Anne Francis, as a remarkable girl of 14, throw light on a complex relationship between two strong women of disparate generations and backgrounds who begin in conflict and end in closeness.

Based on Winifred Foley's autobiographical A Child in the Forest, the action of the film takes place in 1928 in a small village in the lovely Cotswold Hills of Gloucestershire (where it was filmed). Living alone in her great house filled with treasures and memories, Mrs. Hollins (Cathleen Nesbitt) can afford few luxuries in her impoverished gentility. She engages Winnie Mason (Anne Francis), a miner's daughter, to serve for six months as maid, cook, and housekeeper.

It's not only the work that keeps Winnie on her toes. She must remember to say "ma'am," must eat with the old lady, and even sleep in her bed so she will be near at hand when Mrs. Hollins cries out in fear in the night. She must go to church in her place when she is ill (though the gentry frown when she sits in her mistress's pew), and repeat the vicar's sermon verbatim when she returns.

At the end of six months, Winnie has grown completely loyal and protective. Mrs. Hollins is no longer terrifying, but a frail woman waiting for death who leans on her young companion. Winnie frustrates the attempts of the gardener and the village shopkeeper to steal from Mrs. Hollins, and rejects the offers of the vicar and Mrs. Hollins's relatives--whose hypocrisy is transparent to her--for better positions. In turn, Mrs. Hollins has become wholly attached to her.

The old woman has no intention of letting the homesick girl leave her. When Winnie's older sister answers her plea for help in getting home, and the moment of desertion comes, Winnie is reluctant. She writes a note, and steals away through a window.

Abide with Me has superlative performances and sensitive writing. What is most memorable is the portrait of Winnie--wise in the ways of people, her father's staunch daughter, full of humor and independence, and a match for anyone. Her loving comprehension of Mrs. Hollins is a beautiful thing to see.

Also: From Literature

AL STACEY HAYES, see p. 36

ALICE IN THE CITIES (ALICE IN DEN STATDEN)

West Germany, 1974. 110 mins., b/w. (d) Wim Wenders (sp) Wim Wenders, Veith von Furstenberg (ph) Robby Muller, Martin Scafer (c) Rudiger Vogeler, Yella Rottlander, Elisabeth Kreuzer. German dialog with English subtitles. (BAU)

Philip (Rudiger Vogeler) is a thirty-one-year-old German journalist on assignment in America. He is emotionally and creatively burned out, alienated by what he sees. On his way home, at the airport in New York, a nine-year-old girl, Alice (Yella Rottlander), is abandoned to his care. They embark on a complex odyssey together; to his dismay, he must go on a long journey to find her grandmother, whose name and home are a mystery.

Before Philip meets Alice, he is at a dead end. Travelling with her, he is often irritated with her, and she finds him wanting, too. But it is largely through the child that the man regains his bearings. Alice serves as a medium between Philip and the world he lives in. Their understated relationship gives both of them greater strength than they had separately.

Wim Wenders's film inevitably invites comparison with Bogdanovich's Paper Moon (q.v.). But this fourth feature by the subtle director of The Goalkeeper's Fear of the Penalty (also about alienation) is immeasurably superior. The Bogdanovich film is a put-on, in which the adult's first distaste for the child is predictably followed by his ultimate affection, as the boy-meets-girl formula movies always went from first tiff to final kiss. Alice in the Cities is without sentimentality. Its hero is more of a person, and so is its nine-year-old. One believes that the man who is suffering from what Wenders calls "everyday schizophrenia" is slowly able to give more of himself to the little girl he's saddled with--cheerful, bright, snobbish, charming Alice.

The film's success, as Nigel Andrews (Financial Times, London) wrote, "is in turning a potentially 'cute' and whimsical little tale into an absorbing, complexly funny parable of the problems of communication."

Wenders makes his points in beautifully controlled images. When Alice escapes from the police station, she climbs into Philip's car, announcing "Now I know where Grandma lives," though she has no better directions than before. Philip laughs in sudden delight and drives off with her without another word. They are treating each other as they did from the beginning, but he has found himself in the process of their journey. Difficulties do not seem so arid and desperate.

Alice in the Cities was selected for the Edinburgh, Melbourne, London, and New York film festivals, where critics and audiences welcomed the stylistic assurance of Wenders, and the sensitivity and naturalness of his people. Yella Rottlander's Alice is no quirky nine-year-old like Tatum O'Neal. At the end of the Wenders film, the man and child resume lost identities. We believe that Philip will write again and that Alice will have a reunion with both her mother and grandmother. At the end of *Paper Moon*, all we were sure of was that Tatum was a hot property who would be exploited in another quirky movie soon. See *The Bad News Bears*.

BAA BAA BLACK SHEEP, see p. 12

THE BAD NEWS BEARS

Paramount, 1976. 102 mins. col. (d) Michael Ritchie (sp) Bill Lancaster (ph) John A. Alonzo (m) Jerry Fielding; themes from Biset's *Carmen* (c) Walter Matthau, Tatum O'Neal, Vic Morrow, Joyce Van Patten, Ben Piazza, Jackie Earle Haley, Alfred W. Lutter. (FNC)

If it hadn't been directed by Michael Ritchie (*Smile*, *The Candidate*, *Downhill Racer*), this would have been a standard exploitation film. The trendy things are here--an odd couple made up of Oscar-winner Tatum O'Neal (*Paper Moon*) and ever-reliable Walter Matthau; Little League games driving kids into stress traumas; teams discriminating against girls; foul mouthed small fry batting out one-line gags. That's Entertainment.

But *The Bad News Bears* has pleasant surprises, thanks to Ritchie and scriptwriter Bill Lancaster (Burt's son). It is often a very funny film about children, and it makes its point about what adults do to them to fulfil their own drives and aspirations.

"Everybody assumes we're doing some kind of scathing indictment of the Little League, but we're not interested in that," said Ritchie during production. "It's not a Disney movie, yet it's the kind of movie I hope will make the audience feel good at the end."

The Bad News Bears, despite its director's declaration that baseball is simply "a metaphor for these scruffy kids coming to terms with life," zeroes in on its satirical target clearly enough.

This is the vanity of adults in a championship Little League game, as rival coaches suddenly see that their pressures to make all-American winners out of the kids have led them to the brink of destroying them, psychologically and even physically. But the ending, unlike that of Smile, does make the audience feel good, to the extent that it shows how even the worst baseball weakling can make the grade.

Matthau, once a baseball pro, and now a beer-swilling swimming-pool cleaner, is hired to coach a misfit Little League team of boys. He's willing to take the money and slide, until the Bears are massacred and he becomes emotionally involved. He helps the team climb steadily up the League by acquiring two whiz kids, pitcher Tatum O'Neal and Jackie Earle Haley. At season's end, the Bears are slated to play the top-dog team for the championship. Tensions have risen, however, and when Matthau realizes what's been done to the kids by pressuring them to win The Big Game, he withdraws his stars and substitutes his worst players. The Bears lose, but amaze themselves by putting on a good show and by looking forward to next season.

Ritchie handles the kids extremely well. Despite the gags and the comic set-pieces, such as Tatum's Friday night date and ride on a motor scooter, or her conning the tourists, they emerge as really funny (if somewhat repellent) kids, caught without condescension. Alfred W. Lutter (Alice Doesn't Live Here Any More) and Jackie Earle Haley (the dreadful infant prodigy of Day of the Locust) have some sharp moments. Most humorous of all are the baseball scenes themselves--for The Bears drop, miss or fumble every ball that comes along.

Whether you respond to the film's satirical intent, to show how competitive adults can push children beyond sane limits, or watch the Bears as if they were a team of grisly Buster Keatons, it is entertaining. Not without manipulation, not without vulgarity, but entertaining.

BAR MITZVAH BOY, see p. 197

THE BATTLE OF THE VILLA FIORITA

Great Britain, 1965. 111 mins. col. (d)(sp) Delmer Daves, from the novel by Rumer Godden (ph) Oswald Morris (m) N. Spoliansky (art) Carmen Dillon (c) Maureen O'Hara, Rossano Brazzi, Richard Todd, Phyllis Calvert, Olivia Hussey, Elizabeth Dear, Martin Stephens, Ursula Jeans, Finlay Currie, Ettore Manni. (ARG, CCC, TMC, WCF, WEL)

Have you ever thought that little Seryozha, Anna Karenina's son by her husband, could have broken up the affair between mama and Count Vronsky, if he had put his mind to it? No follower of movies about children would doubt it.

The battle in The Battle of the Villa Fiorita is between three kids and some adulterous goings-on in the Via Fiorita between mama and papa, who are not married to each other. Guess who wins.

Moira (Maureen O'Hara) feels neglected by husband Darrell (Richard Todd) in the home near London which they share with fifteen-year-old son Michael (Martin Stephens) and eleven-year-old daughter Debby (Elizabeth Dear). During one of Darrell's frequent absences, she falls in love at an arts festival with Lorenzo, a widowed Italian composer (Rossano Brazzi). Before divorce proceedings, Moira runs away with Lorenzo and lives with him in a luxurious villa near Lake Garda. Darrell gives the children an edited version of their mother's departure.

But these precocious and self-reliant youngsters are hard to fool. They sell Michael's prized coin collection and Debby's beloved pony and set out for Italy to bring mama home from her infatuation. When they arrive, dusty and half-starved, from their journey through Dover, Calais, Paris, and over the Alps, they find an ally at the Villa, Lorenzo's thirteen-year-old daughter, Donna (Olivia Hussey), who doesn't like the liaison any more than they do.

After some guerrilla warfare, including the children's hunger strike, the adults are weakening; but the coup de guerre is an unplanned accident on the lake in a storm, when two of the children are almost drowned. Moira and Lorenzo realize that their real responsibility is to their offspring and that their affair must end. Lorenzo promises to be a better father to his motherless daughter; Moira returns to England with her brood.

Directed and adapted by Delmer Daves from the much less soapy novel by Rumer Godden, with outstanding photography by Oswald Morris, The Battle of the Villa Fiorita is not one of the best of recorded skirmishes in the war between the generations. It is too full of Hollywood dialog and motivation. But the three adolescent actors are all good, with the prize going to Olivia Hussey as Donna. Three years later, she was playing Juliet in Franco Zeffirelli's film about two more famous lovers (q. v.).

Also: From Literature
Family Relationships

BLESS THE BEASTS AND CHILDREN

Columbia, 1971. 106 mins. col. (d) Stanley Kramer (sp) Mac Benoff, from the novel by Glendon Swarthout (ph) Michel Hugo (m) Barry de Vorzon and Perry Botkin, Jr., with title song by the Carpenters (c) Bill Mumy, Barry Robins. Miles Chapin, Darel Glaser, Ken Swofford, Bob Kramer, Marc Vahanian. (GEN)

First, the children. At their camp in Arizona, they're nicknamed "The Bedwetters" and ostracized because they're "dings"--they don't fit in, they're no good at sports. They share a bunkhouse under the supervision of Wheaties (Ken Swofford), the kind of brutal counselor that kids write home about.

But these six teenagers have home problems, too. The group's resourceful leader, Teft (Bill Mumy), is neglected by his rich father. His response up to now has been to steal cars. Cotton (Barry Robins), who'd like to be like Teft, is the son of a mother who's a tramp and a father who's a martinet in the Marines; he acts as much like his father as he can. Schecker (Miles Chapin), who's overweight, tries to be as funny as his father, a popular TV entertainer, but he always lays an egg. The timid baby of the six, Goodenow (Darel Glaser), is mama's and papa's boy. Lally 1 (Bob Kramer) is resentful of his brother, Lally 2 (Marc Vahanian), because Lally 2 is mama's boy.

Now, the beasts. As a treat, Wheaties takes his bunkload of misfits to a government preserve to watch the thinning out of the herd of buffalo--the weaklings herded into a pen and killed by hunters who pay for the sport. Wheaties, taking part in the shoot-out, tells the boys the bison are "dings" just like themselves, and have no right to live.

The six children vow to free the beasts before the carnage begins the next day. They steal a pickup truck and release the

buffalo. But when Cotton tries to stir the animals, he causes a stampede. Wheaties and the hunters, enraged, try to halt the stampede by firing at the truck. A bullet pierces the windshield and kills Cotton. The hunters and the boys are stunned; the buffalo thunder away to freedom.

What to make of all this? With very few exceptions, critics found Bless the Beasts and Children heavy-handed, with the medium failing to deliver the message. The message, according to Charles Champlin of the Los Angeles Times, is not only that hunts requiring no skills turn into slaughters; it is also that "children have a way of surviving no matter how hard we adults try to louse them up."

The six teenage boys, unfortunately, do not survive the treatment they've been given in the movie. Each one is drawn with a spray gun--a grotesque caricature of a disturbed child. Their parents, seen in flashback, are equally overstated and underperceived. Our sympathy for the youngsters' cruel humiliations in the Box Canyon Boys Camp ("Send us a boy, we'll send you a cowboy") would be keener if Mr. Kramer hadn't nudged us so hard every minute of the way. They're very unappealing, these six young "dings." Couldn't somebody have made them human in their mixed-up way, not just like the weaklings in the herd?

Also: Animals and Nature

BLUE DENIM

Twentieth Century-Fox, 1959. 89 mins. b/w. (d) Philip Dunne (sp) Edith Sommer and Philip Dunne, from the play by James Leo Herlihy and William Noble (ph) Leo Tover (c) Carol Lynley, Brandon de Wilde, Macdonald Carey, Marsha Hunt. (FNC)

In the play from which Blue Denim is taken, fifteen-year-old Janet, pregnant by sixteen-year-old Artie, has an abortion, shocking their parents into the knowledge that they've failed to reach their children. In the film, the parents prevent the abortion just in time, send Janet out of town to have the baby, and help Artie join her for the wedding.

Accused of taking on a Hollywood ending, producer Charles Brackett denied it was a happy one; he said it was the saddest of any picture he'd ever made, because the teenagers were forced into the roles of marriage and parenthood long before they were ready. So much in Blue Denim is contrived and slipshod that one may be forgiven for doubting Mr. Brackett; the ending is convenient, to say the least.

Blue Denim contributes little today to the question of teenage love and sex. However, it is still interesting for two reasons. One is its picture of the way Artie (Brandon de Wilde) and his pals play at what they think is manhood, drinking, playing poker, talking big and bad. Another is its still-valid insight into the gap between the youngsters and their parents. The kids wouldn't dream of confiding their dilemma to their parents; the adults have no real idea what their kids are like. And when Artie's father (Macdonald Carey) asks, in the final scene, "Their childhood, their innocence--all those straight A's gone right up the flue. Why did it happen, Mother?" and she answers, "I don't know," they don't sound so dated after all. The terrible isolation of the generations from each other is well illustrated by daughter Carol Lynley and mother Marsha Hunt.

Also: Love and Sex

A BOY TEN FEET TALL, see p. 10

THE CHALK GARDEN

Great Britain, 1964. 106 mins. col. (d) Ronald Neame (sp) John Michael Hayes, from the play by Enid Bagnold (ph) Arthur Ibbetson (m) Malcolm Arnold (art) Carmen Dillon (c) Deborah Kerr, Hayley Mills, John Mills, Edith Evans, Felix Aylmer, Elizabeth Sellars. (UNI)

In the role of adolescent Laurel, who grows out of hysteria and fantasy into a small figure in need of love, Hayley Mills has an opportunity to display her talents.

Laurel, at sixteen, is an extremely difficult child, living with her grandmother, Mrs. St. Maugham (Edith Evans), in a luxurious country house in Sussex. Mrs. St. Maugham has trouble raising anything in her chalk garden because the earth is sour. Laurel is like a human garden choked with weeds: she hates her mother (Elizabeth Sellars), who she believes abandoned her when she divorced and remarried; she defies adult authority, behaves eccentrically, and lives in a semireal world of her own vivid creation. She is understood by the new governess, Madrigal (Deborah Kerr), whom Mrs. St. Maugham has hired without references because she knows something about gardening. It is Madrigal, who has a conviction for murder and a prison sentence in her hidden past, who recognizes Laurel as the young girl she once was herself--and it is Madrigal who is able to weed out the fears that are souring Laurel. By a combination of honesty and unflappable directness, the difficult woman reaches the difficult child, and Laurel realizes that she has never been rejected and is ready and willing to go with her mother when she comes to take her home.

The relationship between the possessive, domineering grandmother and Laurel, so similar to that of Mrs. St. Maugham and Laurel's mother, is well established. But the cruel, touching, even funny relationship between the young girl and her governess is the heart of Ronald Neame's film. Laurel, a precocious adolescent who lies pathologically but who recognizes reality, learns the "accidents of truth" from a teacher who has bitter knowledge of them.

Adapted from Enid Bagnold's stage play, The Chalk Garden lacks the macabre brilliance of the original--Laurel is less sadistic and more malleable than the girl Miss Bagnold drew--but it still offers us some glimpses of adult and adolescent time bombs going off in some exceptionally lovely scenery. Arthur Ibbetson's color photography of the manor house and the nearby cliffs is so beautiful that we know the ending will be happy; of course Madrigal will make this garden bloom.

Also: Finding Oneself
From Literature
Teachers and Students

CHILDHOOD, see p. 11

A CLOCKWORK ORANGE, see p. 271

THE DIARY OF ANNE FRANK, see p. 297

EAST OF EDEN, see p. 77

THE FORGOTTEN VILLAGE

Mexico, 1941. 60 mins. b/w. (d) Herbert Kline and Alexander Hackenschmied (Hammid) (ph) Alexander Hammid (sp) John Steinbeck (m) Hanns Eisler. Narration in English by Burgess Meredith. (MAC)

In this classic story documentary the conflict of young people with their elders is dramatized in the course of a larger conflict, that between science and superstition.

In the primitive Mexican mountain village of Santiago, the new clashes with the old. When the little brother of Juan Diego--and all the other village children--become ill, the local Wise Woman (the curandera) Trini blames "the bitter airs" and prescribes chants and lotions. Trini turns the villagers against the village teacher, who speaks of typhoid from polluted well water. When Juan's brother Paco dies and his mother suffers from a premature birth brought on by anxiety, adolescent Juan takes matters into his own hands. Courageously he bypasses the Wise Woman and seeks out the government doctors of the Servicio Medical Rural. Though the villagers resist modern medicine, gradually the ideas of youth--of Juan as well as his teacher--prevail over the superstitions as old as their Aztec ancestors.

Acted by nonprofessionals of Santiago, with Juan and the younger children drafted from the local government school, The Forgotten

Village is a beautifully photographed, powerful documentary that shows how the ancient life that has persisted for a thousand years finally changes because the young inevitably take issue with their elders.

Also: Cultural Conflicts

THE 400 BLOWS, see p. 238

GO ASK ALICE, see p. 240

THE GO-BETWEEN, see p. 17

HIGH SCHOOL, see p. 178

IF ..., see p. 180

IN THIS HOUSE OF BREDE, see p. 199

THE LAST PICTURE SHOW, see p. 50

LIES MY FATHER TOLD ME, see p. 91

THE LONELINESS OF THE LONG DISTANCE RUNNER, see p. 243

ME (L'ENFANCE NUE) ("NAKED CHILDREN")

France, 1968. 83 mins. col. (d) (sp) Maurice Pialat (ph) Claude Beausoleil (c) Michel Terrazon, René and Marie Louise Thierry, Marie Marc, Henri Puff, Linda Gutemberg, Raoul Billery, Pierrette Deplanque. French dialog with English subtitles. (MAC)

Maurice Pialat's first film was sponsored by a number of important French directors; François Truffaut and Claude Berri head the list of the producers. ME, originally called L'Enfance nue (Naked Childhood), resembles Truffaut's The Four Hundred Blows in that it is a semiautobiographical story of a boy's encounters with the older generation. It is also like Berri's The Two of Us, in that it gives us a picture of a tender understanding between a child and someone who might have been his grandparent. Pialat's style is his own, however. In his quiet, probing study we come to know as much about François as about any other ten-year-old in cinema.

François (Michel Terrazon), father unknown, has been unwanted as long as he can remember. Though his mother will not give him up for adoption, she has placed him under state care. Known as File 7693 in the records, François has had a problem history in two foster homes when we meet him. Now he is under the temporary care of his third foster parents, a miner (Raoul Billery) and his wife, Simone (Linda Gutemberg). They have a child of their own, Josette (Pierrette Deplanque).

From the beginning, François feels that he will never be accepted as one of the Joignys. Their pampered little Josette has a lovely new bedroom; he has a cubbyhole on a landing. It has always been like this for him, François thinks, rejection, loneliness. Under the pretence of indifference, he rages. When he turns to such destruction as flushing a stolen watch down the drain and hurling a cat downstairs, the Joignys send him away. The director of the state agency, deciding to give François one more chance though he is "unmanageable," discovers, on the train to the next foster home, that the boy is as responsive as any other boy of his age when he is with someone he feels he can trust.

In the home of the Minguets (René and Marie Louise Thierry), an elderly couple who are professional foster parents, François takes an instant dislike to the fifteen-year-old Raoul, another state charge (Henri Puff), a placid student type. But he appreciates the affection of the Minguets, and he at last has a room of his own.

The most interesting relationship of the film is between the very old Minguet grandmother (Marie Marc) and François. An invalid, with a delightful repertoire of songs and stories which she uses to break down the boy's guard, she warms him tenderly into a kind of peace he has not known before. However, to win the friendship of a gang at his school, François steals a box of chocolates from a movie usher and is beaten up by some of his schoolmates.

The grandmother dies; François is violently jealous when the Minguets consider taking in a little girl; he turns to destructiveness again and with two older boys causes a serious auto crash. Finally, he is placed in an institution. But he has realized that the Minguets have meant something very important to him. He sends them a letter: "Dear Parents: I am writing to you from my room. I am well. I often think of you. I have made a friend."

Unsentimental, often objective, Me has a great deal of truth about childhood, about old age, about loneliness. It won the Prix Vigo, a French award for films of social value.

Also: Delinquency and Crime
Finding Oneself

MILES TO GO BEFORE I SLEEP

Tomorrow Entertainment (CBS-TV), 1975. 78 mins. col. (d) Fielder Cook (sp) Judith Parker, Bill Svanoe (ph) Terry K. Meade (c) Martin Balsam, Mackenzie Phillips, Pamelyn Ferdin. (LCA)

"I've got to tell you--I don't like old people," says Robin (fourteen). "That's okay, I don't like teenagers," says Ben (one of the old people).

Robin (Mackenzie Phillips), a car thief, is in a home for delinquent girls. Ben (Martin Balsam), a widower with grown children, roams the streets aimlessly, looking at "the old store" and "the old car." They are brought together by the Foster Grandparents Program in the home. Despite initial distrust, their relationship develops slowly. Robin is planning to steal a car and run away with her pal (Pamelyn Ferdin), who's mixed up in drugs and prostitution. But she realizes she needs help and accepts it from Ben, whom she has learned to trust more than her young friend. There seems to be a future for Robin and Ben; they are best friends now.

The playing by Mackenzie Phillips (American Graffiti; TV's "One Day at a Time") and Martin Balsam (A Thousand Clowns) is better than the pat story. As they relax their defenses and find each other, they are a believable pair.

Also: Delinquency and Crime

MY UNCLE ANTOINE, see p. 25

THE NANNY

20th Century-Fox, 1965. 93 mins. b/w. (d) Seth Holt (sp) Jimmy Sangster, from the novel by Evelyn Piper (c) Bette Davis, William Dix, Pamela Franklin, Wendy Craig, James Villiers, Jill Bennett, Jack Watling, Alfred Burke, Maurice Denham. (FNC)

What adult will take a child's word against that of another adult? It is always difficult for a child to get through to Them. In The Nanny, a brilliant young actor (William Dix) dramatizes this common predicament, raised to the nth-degree in a melodrama. Master Joey, an exceptionally clever and resourceful ten-year-old, almost doesn't break through the communication gap between himself and his parents in time to save them all from a woman's madness by making plain his own innocence and an adult's guilt.

In one of her best-modulated roles, Bette Davis is the devoted, middle-aged nanny, a model of correctness. Master Joey is rude, arrogant, disobedient, and emotionally disturbed. He is returning home from a custodial institution after the mysterious death of his little sister had triggered erratic behavior. Nanny says the drowning was Joey's fault; Joey still says that it was Nanny's, and that she's out to get him, too. Father, a stern Queen's Messenger (James Villiers), and mother (Wendy Craig), a neurotic still coddled by Nanny as if she were a child, are dismayed that Joey is incorrigible. His hatred and distrust of Nanny are implacable. He will not let her feed him (poison!) or enter his room (which he keeps barricaded). Until the conclusion, the odds are in Nanny's favor in the battle of wits between her and the child.

As the strongly defined and credible Joey, William Dix is a fascinating boy: shrewdly protecting himself against an enemy shielded by his parents' blindness; striking out against the parents he says he hates but actually needs. His only confidante, a teenage neighbor, Bobbie (Pamela Franklin), alternately ridicules and believes his story. They taunt each other, like every other ten-year-old boy and fifteen-year-old girl, but they are allies against adult obtuseness.

The Nanny recalls The Window (RKO, 1949; 73 mins., b/w, FNC), from a novel by Cornell Woolrich, in which Bobby Driscoll vainly tries to convince adults that he is not being fanciful again and that a murder really has been committed. The Window has more suspense; The Nanny has better characterization. Its director, Seth Holt, used to be a producer for the Ealing Studios, where excellent child actors appeared in films like The Magnet (no longer available here). In William Dix's Master Joey, The Nanny presents one of the most truthfully drawn boys in screen fiction.

Also: Family Relationships

NOBODY WAVED GOODBYE

Canada, 1964. 80 mins. b/w. (prod) Don Owen and Roman Kroitor for the National Film Board of Canada (d) (sp) Don Owen (ph) John Spotton (m) Eldon Rathburn (c) Peter Kastner, Julie Biggs, Claude Rae, Charmion King. (AIM, CHA, MAC)

This National Film Board of Canada cinéma-vérité feature directed and written by Don Owen has sparked controversy from the beginning. When it won the 1965 Robert Flaherty Award, many film lovers saw its special virtues (improvised dialog and near-impromptu performances, natural sound, the nuances of real speech patterns--all making for a sense of honest immediacy). Many other film lovers saw its flaws (dialog occasionally dull, content and characters often clichéd, theme superficially explored, camera undistinguished--all making for something less than art).

None of the early difference of opinion has prevented Nobody Waved Goodbye from establishing itself as a classic social-problem film. It turns all youngsters and most adults on, sparking heated and sometimes enlightening discussion of the relationship between teenagers and their parents.

"Don't you ever get the feeling that your parents are sort of working on the opposite team?" asks Peter of Julie--and away go the questions. What causes suspicion and hostility between the generations? How does one achieve understanding, communication, even agreement?

"I don't know where I want to go and what I want to do, but I can tell you what I don't want to do," says Peter another time. Whose fault is it?

"It's your decision," Julie tells Peter. When he steals, and will not accept responsibility for Julie's pregnancy--is society to blame? His parents?

"You can get kicks out of other things," is something else that Julie tells Peter. She finally says no to him; could she have said it earlier?

There is a lot to argue about in Nobody Waved Goodbye.

The main character is Peter (Peter Kastner), eighteen, a high school senior in a prosperous Toronto suburb, completely at odds with the moral and material values of his parents (Claude Rae, Charmion King). Without defining his own values, he rebels against theirs--cutting school, staying out till dawn, getting jailed overnight for driving his father's car all over town like a maniac. His girl friend, Julie (Julie Biggs), though sympathetic, is a little more realistic and mature.

After the night in jail, Peter quarrels bitterly with his parents. He moves out to a rented room, takes a job in a parking lot, and is soon supplementing his salary by shortchanging the customers. His parents offer private tutoring (he has failed three high school exams) but Peter doesn't like the conditions--no more Julie, and law school--and refuses to go home. He decides to go away with Julie. When his father refuses him a loan, Peter steals a car and some cash from the parking lot. Julie insists that he return both. She tells him also that she is pregnant but that she won't marry him for that reason. She begs him to face up to their problems. When he refuses to be persuaded, Julie gets out of the car and Peter drives off alone.

Boyish rebel and angry and bewildered parents are familiar subjects. They are not explored in depth by Don Owen. The best things in the movie are the quasi-documentary, small reminders of teenage behavior: Peter and Julie groping for closeness, making love on a summer's day (in discreet 1964 style); Peter unable to listen for the space of a meal to his mother, who cannot listen to him; teenagers strumming folk songs on a deserted subway platform late at night.

Nobody Waved Goodbye has provoked especially interesting discussion from mixed audiences--the older and younger generations--

who have viewed it together. Are Peter's difficulties due to his parents' warped values? Are the pressures on this family the fault of society? How "free" is Peter?

The film ventilates a serious, recognizable situation in many middle-class homes and should have a stimulating effect on most groups.

Also: Delinquency and Crime
Family Relationships
Love and Sex

PADRE PADRONE (MY FATHER, MY MASTER)

Italy, 1977. 111 mins. col. (d) (sp) Paolo and Vittorio Taviani, based on the book by Gavino Ledda (ph) Mario Masini (m) Egisto Macchi (c) Saverio Marconi, Omero Antonutti, Marcella Michelangeli, Fabrizio Forte, Marino Cenna, Stanko Molnar, Nanni Moretti. Italian dialogue with English subtitles. (CIV)

The first film to win both the Grand Prize and the Critics Prize at the Cannes Film Festival, Padre Padrone is a work of great power and beauty--the true story of a son imprisoned in his father's pattern of ignorance and isolation until he breaks the pattern through education, learning words to think and to break both silence and isolation.

Padre Padrone is emotionally gripping from the key opening scene (which is repeated toward the end). Gavino's father, a brutal Sardinian peasant (Omero Antonutti), comes to take his six-year-old son out of school. Gavino is heartbroken; in his fear and agony, he wets on the floor. As the other students begin to laugh at his plight, Gavino's father shouts, "Today it is Gavino's turn; tomorrow it will be yours." We are then given a series of close-ups of the faces of the children and hear their inner voices; they know it is true. They too will be the victims of poverty and ignorance. They must follow the pattern, first obey and then command their own children.

The boy Gavino (Fabrizio Forte) is sent off to a desolate, ruggedly magnificent mountainside, to tend, in solitude, the flock of sheep that are the family's living. Though the father has a few moments of softness when he shares perceptions of nature with Gambino or realizes he has tortured or beaten the boy beyond endurance, he is in the main a man so harsh that poverty is no rational excuse; the child's helplessness against the man's cruelty is every child's passivity against adult machismo.

The child Gavino would live in one's mind as a symbol of the tragic human condition, except that he is a symbol of triumph; his story sings. The child becomes a man. In late adolescence, he chafes against his father's tyranny and seeks an escape. At twenty he becomes a soldier, then a scholar. The illiterate Sardinian peasant boy is now Professor of Linguistics Gavino Ledda, whose autobiography is the source of the film.

The Taviani brothers' direction is both tough and innocent (like the shepherds on the mountainside), juxtaposing incidents crude and poetic. They have reminded viewers of Rossellini and De Sica and the Fellini of Amarcord; of Boccaccio and Chagall. Goats talk, peasants burst into song, statues come to life (the heavy Christ figure carried by Gavino in the procession turns into his father). The combination of the coarse and the lyrical seems to work; the effect is lucid, stirring, inspirational.

And nowhere in film, outside of De Sica and Fellini, perhaps, are there children like those in Gavino's classroom, or like Gavino, alone on the mountainside.

Also: Finding Oneself

ONE SUMMER OF HAPPINESS, see p. 153

AN ONLY CHILD, see p. 14

REBEL WITHOUT A CAUSE

Warners, 1955. 111 mins. col. (d) Nicholas Ray (sp) Stewart Stern, from a story by Nicholas Ray adapted by Irving Schulman (ph) Ernest Haller (m) Leonard Rosenman (c) James Dean, Natalie Wood, Sal Mineo, Jim Backus, Ann Doran, Corey Allen, William Hopper, Rochelle Hudson, Nick Adams. (GEN)

A month before the release of Rebel Without A Cause, James Dean was killed, at the age of twenty four, in his speeding Porsche. Already a teenage idol because of the image he projected in East of Eden and in his private life, after his death he was a cult figure for many years. To adolescents, he was the symbol of their rebellion against their elders.

Nicholas Ray's film, anticipating the youth cycle by ten years, is a director's triumph. With a far from subtle script, Ray created some still-memorable scenes--the "chicken run" when three boys test their manhood by driving as near as possible to the edge of a cliff, and the scene in the deserted house when Jim and Judy, with Plato, try to find solace by acting out a family closeness. Ray undoubtedly shaped its youth prototypes.

Jim (James Dean) is a middle-class problem boy in his teens. Whenever he gets into fresh trouble, his weak father (Jim Backus) and domineering mother (Ann Doran), who drive him up the wall, move on to a new town. In jail on a drunk-and-disorderly charge, Jim meets two other troubled adolescents with whom he has an immediate rapport: Plato (Sal Mineo), the child of divorced parents who is ripe for hero-worship of Jim; and Judy (Natalie Wood), whose father has withdrawn his affection from her. Jim would like to get off to a good start in his new high school, but he becomes involved in violence when Judy's tough boy friend, Buzz (Corey Allen), and his gang slash his tires. There is a fight and then the famous "chicken run" with stolen cars. Buzz is killed and his gang beats up Plato in an empty swimming pool. Later, running in panic from the police and his parents, Plato is killed by a cop's bullet. Afterward, Jim's and Judy's parents achieve some understanding of their children's problems.

Neither Jim, whose father is henpecked, nor Plato, whose father has all but abandoned him, nor Judy, whose father has rejected her, has a male figure to look up to. Jim's mother is an unlovely person, Plato's leaves him to be raised by a maid. So much for the script's explanation of underlying causes. What a whole generation saw in the James Dean character--the sullenness, inarticulateness, alienation--they recognized as belonging to themselves, violence's own excuse for being. Analogies have been drawn between the self-destructiveness, the death wish, of Dean's character on and off the screen, and the parallel direction of many young people who worshipped him.

Whatever you make of the James Dean-Sal Mineo-Natalie Wood syndrome as Nicholas Ray records its fitful fevers, it represents a facet of youth in the fifties and sixties. The acts of anger, madness, and death in Rebel Without A Cause were to be repeated in dozens of films that came later and in untold numbers of young lives.

Also: Delinquency and Crime
Family Relationships

RED SKY AT MORNING, see p. 57

SATURDAY MORNING, see p. 99

SMILE, see p. 135

TAKING OFF

Universal, 1971. 92 mins. col. (d) Milos Forman (sp) Milos Forman, John Guare, Jean-Claude Carriere, John Klein (ph) Miroslav Ondricek (m) Songs by Mike Heron, Robert Wright and George Forrest, Ike Turner, Nina Hart, Mike Leander, Bobo Bates, Carly Simon and Tim Saunders, Tom Eyen and Peter Cornell, Catherine Heriza, Shellen Lubin (c) Lynn Carlin, Buck Henry, Linnea Heacock, Georgia Engel, Tony Harvey. (SWA, TWY, UNI)

In the credits of Taking Off, one name makes the difference: Milos Forman. His first American film, about the total inability of young people and their parents to enter one another's worlds, it might have been--well, listen to the plot-germ and you'll be able to imagine what it might have been: A sixteen-year-old girl leaves her comfortable home, and her suburbanite father and mother to embark on a search which ends in the hippy East Village. Can't you just see the patronizing of either or both generations, the stereotypes, the implicit denunciations, of the other youth-exploitation movies?

But director Milos Forman (Loves of A Blonde, The Fireman's Ball) has his own style, an affectionate, sympathetic irony. He doesn't take sides; old and young are equally ridiculous; better to laugh than to scold. The result is one of the best satires of the generation gap one could wish for. The comedy is the classic kind: admit that human beings are funny and observe them in character. Some people found Taking Off pessimistic because nobody wins in this war of the generations. Perhaps it is pessimistic in the sense of Mark Twain's many dismissals of the entire human race; he too thought that we are all laughable.

There is so much in this film that one does not wish to spoil the surprises. But here are some of the things Forman sees on the parent scene: the Tynes numbing themselves with liquor but attacking their young for seeking out drugs; a fictitious Society for Parents of Fugitive Children whose members, experimenting with grass, play strip poker; parents as lost in their marriage as their children are lost in their adolescence, groping for renewal of values; and more, much more.

On the youth scene? An audition for rock singers, with exploiters of the young, and the exploitees; many, many faces of the runaway and lost street girls (nonprofessionals and actors); and lovely, introverted, sad Linnea Heacock (one of the nonprofessionals) as the runaway sixteen-year-old Jeannie Tyne.

The photography of Miroslav Ondricek captures wonderful minutiae of both scenes. If what you are looking for is insight into the younger generation, you will find it, tangentially, in this satire of their parents.

A TASTE OF HONEY, see p. 158

TO DIE OF LOVE, see p. 164

TORMENT, see p. 165

VISIT TO A CHIEF'S SON, see p. 138

WILD IN THE STREETS, see p. 277

THE YOUNG RUNAWAYS

M-G-M, 1968. 91 mins. col. (d) Arthur Dreifuss (sp) Orville H. Hampton (ph) John F. Warren (m) Fred Karger (c) Brooke Bundy, Kevin Coughlin, Lloyd Bochner, Patty McCormack, Lynn Bari, Norman Fell. (FNC)

The Young Runaways is a sample youth-exploitation product of Hollywood in the sixties, in the large economy size (dramas of three teenagers and their families), packaged with the commercial expertise of director Arthur Dreifuss (The Love-Ins, For Singles Only), and with the predictable proportion of artificial additives.

A great deal happens to three adolescents when they leave their parents, for different reasons, to live in Chicago's hippy district. Shelly (Brooke Bundy), who splits from her success-driven adman father (Lloyd Bochner), is kidnapped and beaten when she poses a threat (innocently, of course) to a call-girl operation. She is then offered a haven by a second runaway, Dewey (Kevin Coughlin). Dewey has left his rigid Nebraska father back on the farm and is already disenchanted with hippy life because of his friendship with Terry (Richard Dreyfuss), a draft-dodging slum kid who believes in the rip-off as a way of survival. Deanie (Patty McCormack), the last of the trio of runaways, who left her parents because she thought they repressed her socially and sexually, embarks on a couple of affairs, simultaneously, with a jealous musician and his roommate, and ends up being identified in the morgue by her parents. (Somewhere in the plot, the draft-dodging Terry steals a car and expires in one of those crashes the movies save for Flaming Youth.)

In the end, Dewey concedes that his father is capable of understanding him, and Shelly can think of a number of reasons for going home. They are both reunited with their parents.

Although the three young players are engaging enough, the mishmash of stereotypes and contrived melodrama in the script defeats one's effort to believe that these are true runaways and true families. The one glimpse of reality in this "youth scene" is the Chicago hippy district itself. Shot on location, The Three Runaways is a record of a place and a life-style as truly of the sixties as Haight-Ashbury, the Sunset Strip, or the West Village in New York. A rock group called The Gordian Knot sings "Ophelia's Dream" and "Couldn't We," by James Weatherly.

Also: Delinquency and Crime

THE YOUNG STRANGER

RKO, 1957. 84 mins. b/w. (d) John Frankenheimer (sp) Robert

Dozier (c) James Daly, Kim Hunter, James MacArthur, James Gregory, Jeff Silver. (MAC, UNF, WCF)

In 1957, when movies and other media were exploiting sensational stories of juvenile delinquency, a refreshing exception was The Young Stranger, a quiet little picture which still holds up. Its creators were able to take a story of a sixteen-year-old's minor brush with the law and, by not breathing too heavily, turn it into a revealing picture of his relationship with his father. It's not the best written story in the world, but you may still like it as well as bigger and more complicated but not necessarily more sensitive explorations of generation misunderstanding.

Hal Ditmar (James MacArthur), the bored and restless son of a Hollywood producer (James Daly), gets into a scrap with the manager of a movie theater one night, and his father refuses to believe he was acting in self-defense. The boy's tensions grow because of his inability to reach his father or his mother. Finally, a detective reads his father a lecture, and things clear up a little in this actually very nice home.

Director John Frankenheimer and scriptwriter Robert Dozier were in their mid-twenties when they brought this agreeable and convincing film out of the studio mill. James MacArthur was nineteen, but he looks and sounds a most convincing sixteen-year-old; Jeff Silver is good as his pal, Jerry. But what Frankenheimer carries off best are those family scenes in a home we recognize, where youth and the no-longer-youthful talk across a chasm.

Also: Delinquency and Crime
Family Relationships

CULTURAL CONFLICTS

BIRCH INTERVAL, see p. 37

BLACK GIRL, see p. 74

BOY OF TWO WORLDS (a. k. a. PAW)

Denmark, 1960. 88 mins. col. (d) Astrid Henning-Jensen (sp) Astrid and Bjarne Henning-Jensen (ph) Henning Bendtsen (m) Herman D. Koppel and the Danish State Symphony Orchestra (c) Jimmy Sterman, Edvin Adolphson. Danish dialog with English subtitles. (BUD, IVY, MOD, WCF, WEL)

"He is different, so he needs a good whacking," wrote Hans Christian Andersen. A century afterward, we have this story of little Paw (Jimmy Sterman), whose color is like his West Indian mother's, not his white sea-captain father's, and who knows more about animals and the jungle than about the manners of blonde and blue-eyed classmates. He has a funny name, he was born in a funny place, he looks funny--and so Paw gets his whacking when he comes to live in a Danish town.

At first he makes his home with his father's sister. After her death, he becomes a ward of the town. The mockery of other children and the coldness of adults drive him into the forest. For a short, happy time, he finds refuge with another outcast, a poacher (Edvin Adolphson). When Paw is caught and sent to a reform school, he escapes again, and lives like Robinson Crusoe on an island, with a fox cub for companion. Not until the townspeople finally come to their senses does the boy agree to give human beings another try and to return to the community.

A film of sensitivity and cinematic loveliness, *Boy of Two Worlds* (originally known as *Paw*) has been widely honored: Grand Prix for Cinema Technique (Cannes); International Catholic Prix; Academy Award nominee (1960); and the Gold Medal, Strasbourg, for its contribution to better understanding between people of different races. It was made by the distinguished Danish filmmakers Astrid and Bjarne Henning-Jensen, whose earlier collaborations (*Ditte, Child of Man*; *Palle Alone in the World*; *Where Mountains Float*; *Ballet Girl*) also centered on the problems of young people. "It's with the children everything begins," says Mrs. Henning-Jensen.

The little boy Paw is always alive, learning, and growing. We remember Jimmy Sterman's face, peering out of the friendly woods alongside his friend the poacher (Edvin Adolphson is a veteran Swedish player attracted to this Danish film by its theme), or nestled close to the baby fox draped around his neck. A nonprofessional, Jimmy is half Dutch and half West Indian.

This movie is recommended for its insight into conflicts of race and culture on the level of a small boy's experience.

Also: Finding Oneself

CHILDHOOD, see p. 11

CLAUDINE, see p. 75

CORNBREAD, EARL AND ME

American International, 1975. 95 mins. col. (d) Joe Manduke (sp) Leonard Lamensdorf (ph) Jules Brenner (c) Moses Gunn, Rosalind Cash, Madge Sinclair, Keith Wilkes, Tierre Turner, Larry Fishburne, Bernie Casey, Vincent Martorano. (SWA)

When eleven-year-old Wilford, the "Me" of the title, sees his idol die in a senseless street killing by the police, he faces a moral dilemma which epitomizes the social problems of his black family and neighbors.

Wilford's hero is everyone's hero in the black community: Cornbread (Keith Wilkes), the star of high school basketball, winner of an athletics scholarship to college, untainted by dope or gangs or the numbers. As often as they can, Wilford (Larry Fishburne) and his buddy Earl (Tierre Turner) spend time with Cornbread, being coached or just rapping.

One dark, rainy night, the boys are with him in a store when a gunman shoots a woman nearby. Running home, Cornbread is mistaken for the gunman by two cops, one black and one white, and is killed by them as his friends look on.

Everyone is enraged. Cornbread's parents' lawyer (Moses Gunn) knows how many witnesses there are to Cornbread's innocence. But there is a political cover-up to protect the police, and witnesses are intimidated.

Wilford's mother (Rosalind Cash) refuses to be intimidated. Living on welfare because of illness, afraid to lose the payments by marrying her lover, she has tried to instill values in her son. Because of her, he tells the truth on the stand and Cornbread's name is cleared. In the movie's last frame, Wilford is passing on to

Earl what he has learned from Cornbread, not only about basketball but about the way to live even in the ghetto.

Cornbread, Earl and Me is frequently contrived, but well acted, and provocative for discussion.

Also: Family Relationships

THE FORGOTTEN VILLAGE, see p. 118

THE GAME

U. S., 1966. 17 mins. b/w. (d) Roberta Hodes (sp) Roberta Hodes from a play by George Houston Bass. Produced in cooperation with Mobilization for Youth. (GRO)

Amateurs of acting--black and Puerto Rican youngsters on the Lower East Side of New York--give us a close, real, terrifying glimpse of their own society. Restless and bored, they are playing near their ghetto homes, in demolition sites and school yards that look like prisons.

As they relive their own lives in their games, a stranger appears. First they taunt the newcomer cruelly, rejecting him from their circle: they trap him, crying, "You can't get out, you can't get out." Later, he displaces their leader and takes over.

Like a poem of violence, The Game tells us a great deal through its symbolism about the emotions seething within. This is the way these adolescents feel about being cut off from the American life beyond the ghetto. This powerful film statement about the dislocation of youth was produced by Roberta Hodes in cooperation with Mobilization for Youth and won the silver plaque of the Lion of St. Mark at the Venice Documentary and Short Film Festival in 1967.

GERONIMO JONES

U. S., 1970. 21 mins. col. (d) Bert Salzman. (LCA)

Made by Bert Salzman on the Papago reservation in Arizona, Geronimo Jones introduces us to a reservation child caught between the values of his Apache heritage, taught him by his grandfather (an actual descendant of the Geronimo), and the possibilities for the future in the world of his cousin, an astronomer in a nearby observatory.

The boy is exploited when he steps off the reservation. The town storekeeper tricks him into trading a treasured Apache amulet given to him by his grandfather for a secondhand television set "to please the old man." But the old man and the boy feel only grief and pain when they turn on the set and see, in Stagecoach, the "bad guys," the Indians, being wiped out by the "good guys," the U. S. Cavalry.

Winner of several American awards, Geronimo Jones has beautiful color photography of the Papago location and is long on good will even if it is short on subtlety. The complexities of the reservation child's situation are glossed over, but the simple outlines of injustice and stereotyping, of inner conflicts, are there.

HALLS OF ANGER, see p. 177

HENRY, BOY OF THE BARRIO, see p. 241

INTRUDER IN THE DUST, see p. 49

IT STARTED IN NAPLES

Paramount, 1960. 100 mins. col. (d) Melville Shavelson (sp) Melville Shavelson, Jack Rose, Suso Cecchi d'Amico, from a story by Michael Pertwee and Jack Davies (m) Alessandro Cicognini, and Carlo Savino (ph) Robert L. Surtees (c) Clark Gable, Sophia Loren, Vittorio De Sica, Marietto. (FNC)

It Started in Naples is a large piece of pizza washed down with Coca Cola. Filmed at the Cinecitta Studios in Rome and on other Italian locations, it has Italian seasoning (Sophia Loren and Vittorio De Sica, music by Alessandro Cicognini, and dialog by Suso Cecchi d'Amico) and the Hollywood mixture as before (Melville Shavelson and Jack Rose directing and writing; Clark Gable; and Robert Surtees photographing the Bay and the Grotto). The unexpected tidbit in this pasta is the small boy Nando, played by somebody called, simply, Marietto.

A tough Philadelphia lawyer (Gable), in the usual American rush, is on a quick visit to Naples to look up his late brother's belongings. They seem to include a son, Nando, who has been raised by his Aunt Lucia (Loren) in her own way, which is very Neapolitan, highly unconventional, and deeply loving. Aunt and nephew strike the American as scandalous, but he cannot deny that they are getting a lot more fun out of life than he is. At any rate, he wants to bring up the boy properly, according to his own standards, and he sets siege to the lady to obtain guardianship. If you can't guess how it ends, you haven't seen Sophia Loren in Technicolor.

Nando is quite a street urchin. He has been embroidered a little by the scriptwriters, but Marietto breaks through. Outrageous, as many ten-year-olds are, Nando-Marietto is a special, memorable

Neapolitan model, a poor postwar orphan reared by a Neapolitan night club dancer. He smokes, drinks wine, curses fluently, scorns school (who can get up that early, after selling Aunt Lucia's pictures to the customers half the night?), cons the tourists, and is fiercely, passionately attached to his aunt. When Mike (Gable) gets off that train to rejoin his new family of Lucia and Nando and to live happily forever after in Naples, we know it's a Paramount fable, but we have had a glimpse--just a glimpse--of something real, the difference between Nando and what Mike was certain a ten-year-old boy should be.

Next time the film is on television, you will enjoy taking a look at the encounter between the starchy lawyer from the States and the precocious kid of the Naples streets.

LOUISIANA STORY, see p. 54

AN ONLY CHILD, see p. 14

RED SKY AT MORNING, see p. 57

SIXTEEN IN WEBSTER GROVES, see p. 60

SMILE

United Artists, 1974. 113 mins. col. (d) Michael Ritchie (sp) Jerry Belson (ph) Conrad Hall (m) Daniel Orsborn, Michael Ritchie, Will Schaefer (c) Bruce Dern, Barbara Feldon, Michael Kidd, Geoffrey Lewis, Denise Nickerson, Jean Prather, Nicholas Pryor. (UAS)

Director Michael Ritchie (Downhill Racer, Prime Cut, The Candidate, The Bad News Bears) uses the phenomenon of a teenage beauty contest as a metaphor for the attitudes of small-town America. As in Milos Forman's Taking Off (q. v.), we follow the vicissitudes of adolescents to gain insight into the foibles and hypocrisies of adults.

Smile covers the three days and two nights building up to the annual "Young American Miss" Beauty Pageant in Santa Rosa, California, in which thirty-three high school girls are competing. The proceedings are pointless, grotesque, trashy; by the time the pageant is staged (in the actual Veterans' Memorial Auditorium of Santa Rosa, with Santa Rosans as audience), the contest has brought out the worst and the best in everyone.

The Great American Dream has turned slightly sour for the young girls, rehearsing their individual and collective performances and being interviewed by a panel of judges. At one point, Miss Antelope Valley (Jean Prather) suggests to her roommate and competitor that perhaps beauty pageants are demeaning. Miss San Diego (Denise Nickerson) replies, "Boys get money for making touchdowns, why shouldn't girls get money for being cute?" Then a light dawns slowly: "Yeah, but maybe boys shouldn't get money for playing football!"

Around the edges of the pageant, the adults are going crazy. The man who makes the trophies (Nicholas Pryor) is becoming the town drunk; his wife, a former pageant winner who is now the queen bee of the contest (Barbara Feldon), is frigid and monstrously lacking in sensitivity. There is more than sexual conflict tormenting the husband; he is revolted by the Exhausted Rooster Ceremony for local men like himself who have just turned thirty-five. In flight from the ceremony, he finally takes a pot shot at his wife. The codirector and head judge of the pageant is car dealer "Big Bob" Freelander (Bruce Dern), a right-thinking Babbitt whose idealism about the pageant is shaken when his youngster, "Little Bob," is caught with his polaroid while the girls are undressing. (He's entrepreneur for the school kids; the price of a nude snapshot is high.) The boy is taken to a psychiatrist by his father. Professional choreographer Tommy French (Michael Kidd) arrives to train the girls in dance routines. When one of the contestants falls off the stage during rehearsals because a ramp has been removed, French forfeits $500 of his $2000 fee to compel the businessmen sponsors to put the ramp back.

The last shot in the picture--after the winners have been declared, the publicity photographs taken--is of the nude snapshot taken by "Little Bob": it's clipped to the sun visor in a police car.

Ritchie's throwaway style, his scatter-shots at many targets, won both praise and adverse criticism. What one carries away from <u>Smile</u> is his complex response to a particular attitude toward life and to the people who hold it. John Russell Taylor wrote in <u>Sight and Sound</u>: "The teenage beauty contest in Santa Rosa which forms the central matter of <u>Smile</u> is and remains throughout the film absurd and grotesque. But the people who believe in it are not dismissed because of that; Ritchie even seems to see something touching in their dedication."

Examples of this are found in the adult and the adolescent characters. "Big Bob" remembers the rules by which the Young American Miss has to be charming, talented, concerned with others--and he asks, <u>aren't</u> they good, desirable qualities? And despite the ludicrousness of the events in the contest, our laughter is not directed against the hapless young girls wandering briefly in and out of them--the girl with the butter churn; the girl whose one talent is packing suitcases; the girl who doesn't know there's a difference between singing a Rodgers and Hart song with live musicians and with tape; the girl who is asked by the sugary judge, "Why do you like to play the flute, dear, in your own words?"

As in American Graffiti, popular songs set the tone as well as the time, for their sentiments are the real basis for the "ideals" of contestants and judges alike. Among them are Nat King Cole's "Smile," Ringo Starr's "You're Sixteen," The Beach Boys' "California Girls," and Nacio Herb Brown's "You Were Meant for Me."

Smile is an excellent film, in which the young and the mature together show us how much dedication is wasted on some of the sillier values in American life. Not the least of Ritchie's achievements is our recognition that these muddled, sometimes awful Young American Misses are quite nice youngsters putting their hearts into it. After all, "It" was not their invention, but the dream of the Chamber of Commerce, the Rotary, and the PR men.

Also: Finding Oneself
Generation Conflicts

TWO LOVES, see p. 330

THE TWO OF US, see p. 224

VERONICA

U.S., 1969. 27 mins. b/w. (d) Pat Powell. (JAS)

One of her best friends says of Veronica, "The blacks are pulling at her and the whites are pulling at her."

This bright and pretty seventeen-year-old has many problems, trying to be the person she wants to be. A black girl in a chiefly white high school (New Haven, Connecticut), president of the student congress, Queen of the school parade, she'd rather get involved with individuals than with groups. Talking with a white friend ("with a different background but the same kinds of problems"), she feels a kinship, and concludes that skin color makes little difference; everyone has problems with people, and we all need to free ourselves from suspicion and distrust. In her African literature class, her uncertainties are intensified: forces seem to be shaping her identity solely as a black.

As the hand-held camera draws its portrait of Veronica, she emerges as a sensitive high school senior who will probably be able to resist the pressures of stereotypes and conformism to be her own woman.

Also: Finding Oneself
Teachers and Schools

VISIT TO A CHIEF'S SON

United Artists, 1974. 92 mins. col. (d) Lamont Johnson (sp) Albert Ruben (ph) Ernest Day, James Wells (m) Francis Lai (c) Richard Mulligan, Johnny Sekka, John Phillip Hodgdon, Jesse Kinaru, Chief Lomoiro, members of the Masai tribe in Kenya. (UAS)

This story of what an African safari did for an American scientist and his self-absorbed young son began as a photomontage by _Life_ photographer Robert Halmi which described, in pictures rather than words, the developing friendship of his own stepson and the son of a Masai chieftain in Kenya. For the film, Halmi and director Lamont Johnson returned to the bush, using only two professional actors for the drama of a culture crossing which hastened a boy's maturation.

The father, Robert (Richard Mulligan), remains in Kenya--according to Albert Ruben's script--after covering the 1973 solar eclipse, in order to have more time with his adolescent son, Kevin (John Phillip Hodgdon), who's having growing pains, and to study and photograph Masai folkways.

Robert fails to get off to a good start; Chief Lomoiro forbids him to film secret rites, and Kevin becomes increasingly estranged. But the American boy finds a close companion in the Chief's son, Kodonyo (Jesse Kinaru), with whom he watches the ceremony of initiation into manhood. They go off to Lake Nakuru, where their mutual education continues, and where they perform the Masai test of courage (plucking a flamingo feather). Eventually, father and son grow to understand each other better, reaching an accord with their Masai counterparts.

Quietly entertaining, with lovely color shots of the African bush, _Visit to a Chief's Son_ owes its insights not to its dialog or story, but to its two young actors, John Phillip Hodgdon and Jesse Kinaru, whose adventures, both tribal and personal, have a natural grace.

Also: Generation Conflicts

WALKABOUT

Australia, 1971. 96 mins. col. (d) (ph) Nicolas Roeg (sp) Edward Bond, from the novel by James Vance Marshall (m) John Barry (c) Jenny Agutter, Lucien John, John Meillon, David Gumpilil. (FNC)

"I've got a lot of children," said director Nicolas Roeg to an interviewer, "and I've been tremendously conscious each time of this question of identity and destiny ... Here [in _Walkabout_] were two people who by this curious moment of fate were at a point where they could have been in love with each other. They had everything to offer each other, but they couldn't communicate and went zooming to their own separate destinies, through the odd placement of identity, the identity that other people had put on them. The girl came nearly to the point where she could have changed, but then in one moment when they see the road she slipped all the way back, tumbled into this mould. So nearly ... and there was still doubt in her right at the end of the film."

The title Walkabout refers to a tribal initiation into manhood in which the adolescent aborigine in Australia must survive alone in the desert for six months. In Roeg's film, the aborigine (David Gumpilil), who is about fourteen, is joined by two middle-class European children, a girl of his own age (Jenny Agutter), and her six-year-old brother (Lucien John). They have been abandoned in the outback when their father commits suicide.

Lost, hungry, and frightened, the children are protected by the young aborigine hunter, who guards them at night, hunts for their food, and starts back to civilization with them. Meanwhile, in their primitive and beautiful surroundings, they all swim and play together, in harmony with nature and with one another. But after the aborigine has seen the girl naked, he covers his body with leaves and feathers and begins a frenzied dance of courtship. She pretends not to understand and ignores him. The next morning, she and her brother find his body in the cleft of a tree, laid out in the manner of the aborigine death ritual. Years later, when she is a grown woman married to an ambitious businessman in the city, the girl remembers the interlude in a primitive paradise when three children were free and joyous.

Critics have praised Roeg's striking photography and faulted Walkabout for its straining for symbols. (Much is made of the contrasts between the noble savage and the corrupt city dweller.) Though it often lacks directness and simplicity, it is illuminating about the things shared and unshared by the adolescents of different cultures. When the girl is upset because her little brother tears his blazer in the middle of the desert ("We don't want people thinking we're a couple of tramps"), we know she will reject and wound the young aborigine.

The acting by the three children is excellent, though Jenny Agutter seems mature for fourteen. Playwright Edward Bond, who wrote the script, has given the small boy some lyrical yet very childlike dialog. ("There's the sea. It's the sea. It is the sea, isn't it?")

WEST SIDE STORY

Mirisch/Seven Arts, 1961. 155 mins. col. (d) Robert Wise and Jerome Robbins (sp) Ernest Lehman from the Broadway musical by Arthur Laurents (ph) Daniel L. Fapp (m) Leonard Bernstein (lyr) Stephen Sondheim (chor) Jerome Robbins (c) Natalie Wood, Richard Beymer, Russ Tamblyn, Rita Moreno, George Chakiris, Marni Nixon (voice), Jimmy Bryant (voice). (UAS)

Though often compared with Romeo and Juliet, this magnificent musical--which got nine Academy Awards and still sets the standard for dance and music on the screen--is not a revelation of youthful innocence stained by society. These teenage hoods and their rumbles are not romantic. The film's intention, moreover, is not to give us a serious study of such contemporary problems as slum violence and juvenile delinquency, problems not best illuminated in ballet or musical comedy. What West Side Story is, and promises to be for years, is a superb utilization of all cinematic means, with the Jerome Robbins dance numbers playing to the camera with excitement still unmatched and the pictorial quality as thrilling as the score by Leonard Bernstein.

Yet the animal energy of the Jets and the Sharks is the energy --restless, embittered--of the teenage members of rival gangs in the slums of Manhattan's upper West Side, where racial tensions erupt into violence and crime.

A new arrival in this atmosphere is the young Maria (Natalie Wood), whose brother, Bernardo (George Chakiris), is the leader of a Puerto Rican street gang, the Sharks. Maria falls in love with Tony (Richard Beymer), a young Polish boy who belongs to the enemy gang, the Jets. Their love affair fans the feud between the gangs and leads to a rumble in which the Jet leader, Riff (Russ Tamblyn), is stabbed to death by Bernardo. Tony fatally wounds Bernardo in a fit of passionate revenge and is in turn killed by one of the Sharks. As Maria sobs over her dead lover, the incredible waste of three young lives affects both gangs, and they join in carrying the dead Tony from the playground.

The teenagers lounging against a mesh fence of a city playground; their "muscle" (in both senses) and insolent grace; their alienation from their elders (like the candy-store owner who yells, "You kids make this world lousy! When will you stop?"); their mockery of the Establishment (in "Gee, Officer Krupke")--these are all memorable, valid glimpses of adolescence.

Just don't buy the suggestion in West Side Story that these teenage hoods are ultimately innocent, that society is entirely guilty. The film transcends its sociological limitations by the terrific theatrical intensity of its images and rhythms, and intensity as hot-blooded as youth.

Also: Delinquency and Crime

WILD BOYS OF THE ROAD, see p. 248

LOVE AND SEX

ADIEU PHILIPPINE

France, Italy, 1960-1962. 111 mins. b/w. (d) Jacques Rozier (sp) Michèle O'Glor and Jacques Rozier (ph) René Mathelin (m) Jacques Denjean, Maxime Saury, Paul Mattei (c) Jean-Claude Aimini, Yveline Céry, Stefania Sabatini, Vittorio Caprioli. French dialog with English subtitles. (NYF)

Michel is nineteen, Juliette and Liliane, eighteen. Their whimsical pursuit of romance is completely immature; yet we watch this attractive trio of Parisian teenagers with indulgence. We know their light-hearted adventures must end when Michel is called up for military service, probably in Algeria. As the two girls wave good-bye to his boat from the dock, they are all bidding farewell to adolescence.

The title refers to a wishing game that French children play; _philippine_ means "sweetheart." In this story he is Michel Lambert (Jean-Claude Aimini), an assistant of doubtful value on a television camera crew. One day, Michel picks up two very pretty girls who are inseparable, Juliette (Stefania Sabatini) and Liliane (Yveline Céry), and since he can't decide which he likes better, he romances them both. They spend time together in Paris, and then after he loses his job and decides to take a holiday before his call-up, in the Club Mediterranée in Corsica. There is a subplot involving a crooked film producer, Pachala (Vittorio Caprioli), whom they chase to recover the money he owes them, but most of the Corsica stay shows Michel growing more involved with the girls. He makes love first with Juliette and then with Liliane, so that they become jealous and angry at each other. They would like Michel to make a choice between them, but when he is informed he must report for service, he leaves without making a decision.

Wholly fresh and spontaneous, the girls flaunt their budding sexuality in some charming scenes. Since _Adieu Philippine_ has very little plot, these joyous moments are the film's excuse for being. Drying each other's hair, plotting to tease Michel, dancing on the sands of Corsica, Juliette and Liliane are delightfully genuine--and so is Michel, driving with his pals in their jointly owned car and looking for pickups, or eating at home and ignoring his folks' and the neighbors' boring conversation.

Long regarded as one of the most enjoyable of the New Wave films, _Adieu Philippine_ relies on improvisation by its nonprofessional actors. The music that director Jacques Rozier used to underline each sequence is infectious, his invention (more in the Paris television studio scenes than in Corsica) often highly entertaining. In one of the best scenes, Juliette and Liliane frisk along the Paris streets, and the spectators relish the sight, all to the beat of a tango on the sound track.

Throughout the film, we feel the beat of youth.

THE ADOLESCENTS, see p. 35

AH, WILDERNESS!, see p. 286

AMERICAN GRAFFITI, see p. 5

BADLANDS, see p. 233

BALLAD OF A SOLDIER, see p. 209

BLUE DENIM, see p. 116

BUSTER AND BILLIE

Columbia, 1973. 99 mins. col. (d) Daniel Petrie (sp) Ron Turbeville and Ron Barton from a story by Ron Turbeville (ph) Mario Tosi (m) Al De Lory (c) Jan-Michael Vincent, Joan Goodfellow, Pamela Sue Martin, Clifton James, Robert Englund, Jessie Lee Fulton. (SWA)

Writer Ron Turbeville has said that he was returning to the scene of his own high school memories in the story of Buster and Billie. However, since the movie takes place in "Georgia, 1948" (which was the first title of the movie), and Mr. Turbeville was twenty-seven when he wrote the script, he was two years old when these particular adolescents were drinking Orange Crush and reading Captain Marvel. Maybe what he was really returning to was the well-plowed land of high school nostalgia movies.

There's a little bit of everything in Buster and Billie. In Greenwood High School, class leader and big man on campus is farm boy Buster Lane (Jan-Michael Vincent). Buster is as nice a senior as ever had a school loner like the albino Whitey (Robert Englund) for his friend, or the prettiest girl in school, Margie (Pamela Sue Martin), for his fiancée. Margie is certainly a nice girl; she lets Buster go only so far in their nightly tryst in the front seat of his pickup truck.

While Margie is preserving her maidenhood, a bovine, dull, homely blonde named Billie Joe (Joan Goodfellow) is putting out for all the boys in school. The only attention the retarded Billie ever gets is when Buster's pals force her to have sexual relations with them.

One day Buster also turns to Billie, furtively. Later a real affection springs up between them, and he dates her openly. He sees her as a person, and she has changed, but neither Buster's friends nor the townspeople have changed. Tongues wag when the two turn up at Sunday service. Buster's parents struggle to understand why their son has broken his engagement to Margie. Buster's friends ostracize him at the poolroom. Then there is violence--Billie is set upon in the woods by Buster's friends, gang raped, and dies. Discovering her body, Buster returns to the poolroom and kills two of the boys with a pool stick. He is jailed, but manages to drive out to the local cemetery to deck Billie's grave.

Is this the way things were in Stateboro, Georgia, in 1948? Are Buster and Billie and their schoolmates to be believed?

Oddly enough, Billie is--thanks to the playing of Joan Goodfellow. The silent, passive town tramp is capable of a moving relationship with another teenager, a boy who senses her loneliness.

It is a pity the rest of Buster and Billie borrows from so many nostalgia-with-violence cycle pictures. Only fleetingly do we recognize true rituals of youth: posing for the senior class picture, driving fast on dusty country roads, swimming naked as jaybirds.

CLAUDINE, see p. 75

CLOSELY WATCHED TRAINS, see p. 38

DEEP END

Paramount, 1971. 87 mins. col. (d) Jerzy Skolimowski (sp) Jerzy Skolimowski, J. Gruza, B. Sulik (ph) Charly Steinberger (m) Cat Stevens (c) Jane Asher, John Moulder-Brown, Diana Dors, Karl-Michael Vogler, Christopher Sandford. (FNC)

As in his Le Départ (q. v.), Polish director Jerzy Skolimowski is focusing on youth in a contemporary urban mileu. Made in London, Deep End turns its eccentric but perceptive eye on a run-down public bath and swimming pool in a seedy quarter, where an adolescent boy is introduced to some of the facts of life by a slightly older female attendant. Not a new theme, of course, but in this film, the corruption of innocence seemed to the critics remarkably well presented --mischievous, funny, revealing, and with recollections of Truffaut, Godard, and Polanski.

Mike (John Moulder-Brown), fifteen, takes his first job out of school as an attendant at the baths. He promptly falls in love with another attendant, Susan (Jane Asher), twenty. Lovely, cynical, perverse, she leads him on and refuses him by turns. He is undeterred by her acid tongue, her fiancé (Christopher Sandford), or her lover (Karl-Michael Vogler). He pursues her everywhere.

The baths are filled with sexual fantasists, and the leading one is Mike, eager to play out his dreams. There are some very weird situations, some very funny ones (like the one with soccer-fan Diana Dors), and an ironic climax. Somehow, Mike treads water in the depths represented by the baths.

Jane Asher and John Moulder-Brown are nothing less than superb in their roles. Skolimowski's personal vision makes Deep End an exceptionally observant film about youth and its encounters. "Terrifyingly observant," wrote Penelope Gilliatt in The New Yorker, "about discomfiture; comic and melodramatic; flagrantly inconsequential but furtively in praise of the indestructible."

LE DEPART, see p. 43

DITTE, CHILD OF MAN, see p. 298

DON'T CRY WITH YOUR MOUTH FULL (PLEURE PAS LA BOUCHE PLEINE)

France, 1974. 116 mins. col. (d) Pascal Thomas (sp) Pascal Thomas, Roland Duval, Suzanne Schiffman (ph) Christian Bachmann (m) Vladimir Cosma (c) Annie Colé, Bernard Menez, Frédéric Duru Friquette, Alain Perceau, Jean Carmet, Christiane Chamaret, Hélène Dieudonné, Daniel Ceccaldi, Isabelle Ganz. French dialog with English subtitles. (NYF)

Country matters, around Thouars, south of the Loire. A comedy of fifteen-year-old Annie's summer deflowering, Don't Cry with Your Mouth Full reminded Stanley Kauffmann, who liked it nevertheless, of an Andy Hardy story, and kept Archer Winsten "happily suspended somewhere between Andy Hardy and Deep Throat."

Annie, who is played by Annie Colé, a nonprofessional from the French provinces, is buxom and sweet. Spring into Summer was the title for the film's British release; Annie ripens in the sun as carelessly as the flowers in the garden of her carpenter-farmer Papa (Jean Carmet).

Her family is direct and earthy. Good-tempered Maman (Christiane Chamaret) enjoys love in the afternoon with Papa. Annie's uncle, who is also her godfather (Daniel Ceccaldi), unsuccessfully tries to make her during a visit. Nature takes its frank and open course; Annie's little sister Friquette begins to menstruate; her father has to double as an undertaker when her aunt dies; Grand-mère, a wise old party, finds the obituaries dull reading. None of the physical functions are unmentionable (or omitted from the sound track).

There are two young men in Annie's life. Two days before Frédéric (Frédéric Duru) is drafted, he declines to sleep with her; it will interfere with a bike race the next day. While Frédéric is gone, Annie decides she has been virginal long enough. The lucky swain is Alexandre (Bernard Menez), a rich, nervous young man without the aplomb that the town's reputed Lothario should have.

The film ends on a note which suggests the simple acceptance of the natural: Annie tells Maman about her giving in to Alexandre; Friquette joins them in the field. Freeze frame on the three women in the sunshine.

The tone of Don't Cry with Your Mouth Full is light and its insight unstressed. "We're happy, aren't we?" Annie asks her mother. "Enjoy it," her mother responds.

Annie Colé's puppyish, often overgrown adolescent is not hard to take. More diverting is the portrait of a young country rake by Bernard Menez, who was the prop boy in Truffaut's Day for Night.

This second feature of young director Pascal Thomas (Les Zozos), suffers by comparison with Renoir, Pagnol, and Truffaut--whose names were mentioned with Thomas's in French publicity--but it has some pleasant interest as a portrait of a bucolic fifteen-year-old bursting into bloom one summer.

END OF INNOCENCE (a. k. a. THE HOUSE OF THE ANGEL) (LA CASA DEL ANGEL)

Argentina, 1957. 76 mins. b/w. (d) Leopoldo Torre Nilsson (sp) Beatriz Guido and Torre Nilsson, from Beatriz Guido's novel (ph) Anibal Gonzales Paz (m) Juan Carlos Paz (c) Elsa Daniel, Lautaro Murua, Guillermo Battaglia. Spanish dialog with English subtitles. (MAC)

The film with which Argentinian director Leopoldo Torre Nilsson won international recognition, End of Innocence was the first of many script collaborations with his wife, novelist Beatriz Guido. Their work usually centers on sexually repressed women who live shut away from reality, in a milieu of bourgeois suffocation in which the air is stirred by intrigue, passion, and remorse.

The woman here is only sixteen, the daughter of a rich and influential Argentinian family in Buenos Aires in the early 1920s. Denied normal emotional development by a fiercely puritanical mother, the girl is bewildered by the awakening of passion when a handsome colleague of her father, involved with him in a political plot, spends the night in the family mansion. (There is to be a duel in the morning.) Afraid the young man will die, she goes to his room and allows him to seduce her. Guilt and shame possess her, condemning her to spinsterhood.

Script, direction, and Elsa Daniel's exquisite performance as the adolescent girl (which won a Cannes Best Actress award) distinguish the film. It is an elegant, intelligent portrait of youth in a social and psychological trap, youth dislocated and doomed.

FIRST LOVE

Germany, 1970. 90 mins. col. (d) Maximilian Schell (sp) Maximilian Schell and John Gould, based on the novella by Ivan Turgenev (ph) Sven Nykvist (m) Mark London (c) John Moulder Brown, Dominique Sanda, Maximilian Schell, Valentina Cortese, Marius Goring, Dandy Nichols, Richard Warwick, Keith Bell, Johannes Schaaf, John Osborne. English dubbed sound track. (BUD, MAC)

Through artistry, the story of a youth's first brush with desire and his disillusionment seems as fresh as if it had never been told before. Sixteen-year-old Alexander (John Moulder Brown) is a character out of a Russian novel in every sense. Originally, of course, he was the creation of Ivan Turgenev, from whose novella the film has been loosely adapted. But we know this moody, shy, ardent boy. His infatuation is classically doomed.

The scenes of director Maximilian Schell, whose first film this is, and the beautiful pictures of photographer Sven Nykvist, Ingmar Bergman's cinematographer, ensure that not a scintilla of romantic nostalgia has been lost in the process of transforming the pages of Turgenev into a film. A few things have been added, perhaps. Schell has developed the heartless Sinaida's social background, so her flirting takes place on the thin ice of a society destined for dissolution. And in casting the sexually provocative Dominique Sanda, whose intriguing face we have met in the films of Bresson, Bertolucci, and De Sica, Schell has made the boy's passion a little more sensuous, a little more painful, than in the 1860 original. Score one for the suggestive power of contemporary cinema in the hands of fine craftsmen. Though First Love does not take advantage of our sexual permissiveness to exploit sensuality, it is all there, romantic and vital but delicate.

Alexander is in love, against all hope, with the impoverished, wild young Princess Sinaida, who is a little older than himself. She is toying with him. She becomes the mistress of his father (Maximilian Schell), and she is surrounded by older suitors (played by the German director Johannes Schaaf and the British playwright John Osborne as well as actor Marius Goring). It is a desperate love, but it is beautiful, and it is the making of his manhood.

The cast, which is internationally polyglot (dubbed in English), is superb. In addition to John Moulder Brown's fine portrait of the boy, one remembers two good ones of mothers: Valentina Cortese's as Alexander's and Dandy Nichols's as Sinaida's.

Also: Finding Oneself
From Literature

FRIENDS

Paramount, 1971. 102 mins. col. (d) Lewis Gilbert (sp) Jack Russell and Vernon Harris, from a story by Lewis Gilbert (ph) Andreas Winding (m) Elton John (c) Sean Bury, Anicee Alvina, Pascale Roberts, Sady Rebbot, Ronald Lewis. (FNC)

Despite beautiful photography of La Camargue, charming young performers (Sean Bury and Anicee Alvina) in the main roles, and the efforts of director Lewis Gilbert (whose film Loss of Innocence in 1961 was a delicately handled adaptation of Rumer Godden's novel The Greengage Summer) Friends is a very poor movie which represents the lowest point in the cycle of teenage-love idylls.

With incredible sentimentality, incredible dialog, and incredible plotting, Friends tells us about fifteen-year-old Paul and fourteen-year-old Michelle. Both feel unwanted by their families. Meeting at the Paris zoo, they run away to a cottage in La Camargue. Paul works in the local vineyard, Michelle becomes pregnant. Rather than risk discovery, they deliver their baby themselves, with the help of a medical manual. But two detectives have tracked down Paul and are waiting for him. . . .

Slow motion shots, lovers leaping hand in hand, a first kiss in a field of corn, bathing scenes where they scrub each other, archness about sex--need one go on? Friends is one of the best examples on the screen of the manipulation of youth for cloying effect. If Lewis Gilbert is not being commercial, he is astonishingly lacking in a sense of the absurd.

The story is told to the accompaniment of songs by Elton John.

THE GAME

Canada, 1966. 27 mins. b/w. (d) (sp) George Kaczender (ph) Paul Leach (m) Don Douglas (c) Mira Pauluk, Robert Fairley. (CON, MMM)

The Game is about sexual activity among high school students, from the point of view of Peter, a cocky teenager in the eleventh grade who takes a dare from his peer group to "get" Nicky, one of the school's most attractive girls.

Peter's male ego challenges him to pursue Nicky from the first dates to an all-night beach party to a ride in his father's car along a secluded beach. What used to be called "the inevitable" takes place on the front seat.

Afterward, Peter is troubled; he has seduced a virgin who (he realizes) is a sensitive, trusting human being. He does not confide in his gang, and he lies around his lonely room, thinking. The film ends with a phone call to Nicky and the suggestion that Peter may be ready for a relationship that is not a game.

The Game is a documentary interesting for its focus on the factors in an adolescent boy's sexist conditioning. Peter's subsequent internal struggle is worth discussing: what enables him to overcome his male chauvinism?

THE GO-BETWEEN, see p. 17

HERE'S YOUR LIFE, see p. 45

THE HOUSE ON CHELOUCHE STREET, see p. 213

JEREMY

United Artists, 1973. 90 mins. col. (d) (sp) Arthur Barron (ph) Paul Goldsmith (m) Lee Holdridge (c) Robby Benson, Glynnis O'Connor, Len Bari, Leonardo Cimino. (UAS)

Arthur Barron, professor of film at Columbia University and Brooklyn College, got mixed grades for his first feature, _Jeremy._ It won Best First Film Award at Cannes, was chosen for the Edinburgh Festival, and impressed Rosalyn Drexler (_The New York Times_) as "a BIG 'little' movie." To some, it is a sensitive idyll of the awakening of adolescent love. To others, in the words of _Film & Broadcasting Review_, it is an "extraordinary pretentious latter-day _Love Story_ which, apart from the winsome faces of its two unknown principals ... is fantasy of the sort that projects adult wish fulfillment upon the minds and sensitivities of the young. _Jeremy_ is so phony in its contrivances that it should make any self-respecting teenager retch."

Jeremy (Robby Benson), a nice sophomore at the High School of Music and Art in New York, is warned by his teacher (Leonardo Cimino) that he will never make it as a virtuoso cellist unless he swears off basketball and the _Racing Form._ At sixteen, Jeremy is so shy that he has to enlist his pal Ralph (Len Bari) to introduce him to Susan (Glynnis O'Connor), a ballet student. After she is warmed up by Jeremy's performance at the school concert, Susan responds to his advances. They drop the cello and the dance, eat pizza, walk dogs, go to the track, share confidences about their alienation from their stupid parents, and make love. (The cut comes before he removes her bra.) But Susan must return to Detroit with her father. The lovers part at the airport.

What we wanted to ask Robby and Glynnis was, "What's a bright pair of students from Music and Art doing in a plot like this?"

Also: Growing Pains

THE LAST PICTURE SHOW, see p. 50

LAST SUMMER

Allied Artists, 1969. 97 mins. col. (d) Frank Perry (sp) Eleanor Perry, from the novel by Evan Hunter (c) Barbara Hershey, Richard Thomas, Bruce Davison, Cathy Burns, Ernest Gonzalez, Peter Turgeon. (CIN)

It begins as a Fire Island sailing-and-swimming idyl of three apparently innocent teenagers; it becomes a horror story, in which their attack on a fourth teenager marks the last summer of innocence.

"The best thing about the movie," said Vincent Canby of The New York Times, who thought it as flawed as other films by the Perrys, but equally hard to dismiss, "are the performances that Perry has gotten from his new players. They manage to seem variously awkward and strident, dense and dumb, and sometimes very innocent, without ever being self-conscious about it."

The adolescent trio who make a kind of closed community are Peter (Richard Thomas), basically the nicest; Dan (Bruce Davison); and their neurotic girl friend, Sandy (Barbara Hershey). When they corrupt Rhoda (Cathy Burns), a fifteen-year-old who has fallen into their hands, the film raises questions it never answers. How did Peter and Sandy and Dan get that way?

Like Evan Hunter's novel, the screenplay by Mrs. Perry does not tell us. The focus is on the adolescents, isolated on Fire Island for their "last summer." Parents, teachers, everyone outside the circle of their friendship (and their conspiracy) are only noises offstage.

Also: From Literature

THE LEATHER BOYS

Great Britain, 1963. 103 mins. b/w. (d) Sidney J. Furie (sp) Gillian Freeman, from the novel by Eliot George (ph) Gerald Gibbs (c) Rita Tushingham, Colin Campbell, Dudley Sutton, Gladys Henson, Avice Landon, Betty Marsden. (MAC)

Some of the things in this movie may seem removed from our scene: the "leather boys"--a respectable cockney cycling club--and their cross-country race to Edinburgh; the working-class London parents; and Dot's peroxided beehive hairdo. But the teenage marriage of Dot and her mechanic boy friend, Reggie, is wholly accurate, alive and moving, the best in contemporary movies.

Dot (wonderfully played by Rita Tushingham) is sixteen, a little slut, tart and yet vulnerable. She pops out of school and into wedlock mostly to get away from her Mum. She hasn't a thing on her mind but pleasure. Even on the honeymoon, at a holiday camp, Dot and Reggie (Colin Campbell) have different ideas about good times. After-marriage sex begins to pall (though there is one joyous scene in a bed filled with crackers and chocolates) when Reggie comes home to a messy flat and baked beans for supper, with Dot out or reading True Romance. There are rows and brief reconciliations, but the marriage breaks up when Reggie shares a room at his grandmother's with Pete (Dudley Sutton), another one of the leather boys, with whom he has some companionship. Dot has another man in her bed when Reggie drops by at the flat one day.

Hostile to Pete, Dot says scathingly to Reggie, "You're like a couple of bloody queers!" Reggie and Pete plan to sail to New York, but there is a development which surprises nobody except innocent Reggie: Pete has a homosexual past. Reggie leaves him in revulsion. At the end, all three of the young people are alone.

Dot is a superb adolescent portrait. Directed by Sidney J. Furie with authority and feeling, The Leather Boys tells us much about its young people, cut off in their blindness to one another's needs.

LOLITA see p. 313

LOSS OF INNOCENCE

Great Britain, 1961. 99 mins. col. (d) Lewis Gilbert (sp) Howard Koch, from the novel The Greengage Summer by Rumer Godden (ph) Frederick A. Young (m) Richard Addinsell (c) Kenneth More, Susannah York, Danielle Darrieux, Claude Nollier, David Saire. (MAC)

"Little Joss," says the man to the sixteen-year-old girl, "in this summer you grew up. You've become a woman."

Like the title, the words suggest soap opera. But nothing else in this film does. From Rumer Godden's novel The Greengage Summer, it has taste and delicacy, and it offers us insight into the elusive psychology of feminine adolescence. Director Lewis Gilbert is not Jean Renoir, but Loss of Innocence sometimes recalls The River (q. v.) the film from an earlier Rumer Godden novel about adolescent womanhood in its first, uncertain experience of love.

When their mother is hospitalized, four children are stranded in an old chateau hotel on the Marne, in the champagne and greengage valley of France. The eldest, Joss (Susannah York), takes charge. Their summer is filled with sightseeing and other pleasures, in the company of another boarder, a mysterious Englishman, Eliot (Kenneth More). Eliot begins to take more than a casual interest in the maturing Joss, and Zizi (Danielle Darrieux), his lover and one of the hotel proprietors, creates a scene. Joss is jealous of Zizi, too. In an adolescent reaction, she gets drunk with the scullery boy, Paul (David Saire), and later correctly reports Eliot to the police as a wanted jewel thief. Paul attempts to rape Joss and is prevented by Eliot, who not only escapes from the chateau ahead of the police but sends an SOS to the children's uncle to come get them.

Despite the melodramatic tinge, the proceedings are not lurid. There is a soft bloom on the whole picture--on the color photography (by Frederick A. Young) of the serene Marne Valley in summer, on Richard Addinsell's romantic music, and on the excellent acting of the French and British players.

Loss of Innocence is understated and has a good portrait of the urgencies of a young girl. The three other children are engaging British youngsters; red-haired Jane Asher is a little girl of special charm.

Also: Finding Oneself
From Literature

MÄDCHEN IN UNIFORM

Germany, 1931. 89 mins. b/w. (d) Leontine Sagan (sp) F. O. Andam and Christa Winsloe, based on Christa Winsloe's play Gestern und Heute (ph) Reimar Kuntze, Fritz Weihmayr (m) Hanson Milde-Meissner (c) Dorothea Wieck, Ellen Schwannecke, Emilie Lunda, Herta Thiele. German dialog with English subtitles. (CON, JAN)

Although it was remade in 1958 in West Germany (in color, by director Geza von Radvanyi, starring Lilli Palmer and Romy Schneider) Mädchen in Uniform in its original 1931 version is the one that matters. This is the classic study of an adolescent girl's sexual fixation on a woman teacher, beautifully directed by Leontine Sagan and acted by Herta Thiele and Dorothea Wieck.

Manuela (Herta Thiele), a boyish, intense, rather charming adolescent, has just lost her mother. She feels emotionally imprisoned in her boarding school. For the daughters of poor army officers, this Potsdam school in the Imperial era is dedicated to training the future mothers of soldiers for the Vaterland. Frau Principal (Ellen Scwannecke) keeps rigid discipline. The schoolgirls in their striped uniforms are overheated by their urgent need to rebel against repression, as well as by their natural sexual needs.

In this atmosphere, Manuela secretly nurses her passion for beautiful Fraulein Professor von Bernburg (Dorothea Wieck), who does not discourage it (perhaps because of a leaning of her own). Chastely but violently, Manuela lives with her obsession, until a little too much wine after her success (in a boy's role) in a school play loosens her tongue. Her confession of love is an open scandal in the school, which Frau Principal deals with summarily. The result is a near tragedy, for in her grief Manuela attempts suicide and is saved by her classmates in the nick of time.

Some scenes remain in memory: the struggle on the issues between the young Fraulein Professor and the old Prussian Frau Principal, and the moment when Manuela looks down into the abyss of the great stairwell into which she longs to throw herself.

The title of Christa Winsloe's play from which the film is taken is Gestern und Heute ("Yesterday and Today"), which suggests that even in the years before the Nazi regime Winsloe was worried about the German fondness for military repression. Mädchen in Uniform is a splendid picture of a certain kind of school, as well as a certain kind of young love.

Also: Teachers and Schools

LA MATERNELLE

France, 1932. 86 mins. b/w. (d) Jean Benoit-Levy and Marie Epstein (ph) G. Asselin (m) Edouard Flament (c) Madeleine Renaud, Mady Berry, Pauline Elambert. French dialog with English subtitles. (MMA)

The passion of a child for a mother, the passion of a woman for a child--yes, La Maternelle is about love. It is one of the most delicately tender stories in the treasury of film classics.

The child (Pauline Elambert) is neglected by her own mother, a prostitute, who abandoned her. Placed in a day school for children from poor homes, the little girl, desperate in her need for a mother's love, becomes attached to Rose (Madeleine Renaud), a qualified teacher who prefers to work as a maid, and who is also hungry for love after being jilted by her fiancé.

The child's adoration for Rose is so deep that she cannot bear to see her accept a proposal of marriage from the director of the school board. She tries to drown herself, but is brought back to life and to new trust in her foster mother, Rose.

Directors Jean Benoit-Levy and Marie Epstein made La Maternelle with humor and profoundly touching detail. What might have been only an earnest essay in documentation--for this is a real school, these are the real children who attend the school, and the directors are truly concerned with educational goals--is a glowing drama of the human spirit. Not only are the child and the maid beautifully drawn; every youngster (and how many different little ones there are!) stands out as himself, from the one who doesn't smile to the one who swallows the coin and must be made to pass it. This film is a rare experience for all who love children.

Also: Teachers and Schools

MURMUR OF THE HEART, see p. 94

NOBODY WAVED GOODBYE, see p. 122

ONE SUMMER OF HAPPINESS

Sweden, 1951. 92 mins. b/w. (d) Arne Mattson (sp) Wolodja Semitjov, from the novel by Per Olof Ekstrom (ph) Goran Strindberg (m) Sven Skold (c) Folke Sundquist, Ulla Jacobsson, Edvin Adolphson, John Elfstrom, Irma Christenson, Gosta Gustavsson, Berta Hall. Swedish dialog with English subtitles. (MAC)

Viewed today, it is hard to believe that the single modest and lyrical scene in which the naked young lovers make love in a field could have made an international sensation of Arne Mattson's Swedish film. However, it was released in 1951.

One Summer of Happiness ("Hon dansade en sommar") is interesting now not as an archive curiosity but as a still-vital drama of the passion of adolescence in a bigoted community. The tragedy of a love affair between a seventeen-year-old farm girl and a college student from the city, with the sense of guilt which hangs over both of them because of the social standards of the girl's family, still has its parallels in small towns. A contemporary director would screen it with fewer inhibitions, especially in Sweden, but he would be lucky to find a better actress than the young Ulla Jacobsson to play the adolescent Kerstin.

Goran (Folke Sundquist) comes to his uncle Anders' farm for a rest one summer. Anders (Edvin Adolphson) is a tolerant man in an intolerant, staid village, where most of the young people are at odds with the clergyman (John Elfstrom) and their rigidly conventional parents. Anders allows Goran and a neighbor's daughter, Kerstin, to meet in his barn. There is a complex, melodramatic plot--Anders is hurt in an accident, Kerstin and Goran are discovered, she is sent away, there is a motorcycle crash and Kerstin is killed, Goran is blamed by the vicar at the funeral--but the core of the story is the sweet torment of the young lovers, unable to consummate their desires without fear.

Rediscovering One Summer of Happiness in the eighties, one is reminded that sexual relationships have never been simple when one of the lovers is seventeen and the other lover threatens the social and moral conventions of her people.

Adding to our pleasure in the film are Ulla Jacobsson's portrayal of the lovely and impulsive seventeen-year-old and the rich sense of the country scene achieved by Goran Strindberg's photography.

Also: Generation Conflicts

PHOEBE: STORY OF A PREMARITAL PREGNANCY

Canada, 1964. 28 mins. b/w. (d) (sp) George Kaczender. (CON, MMM)

This excellent National Film Board of Canada documentary about an unwed teenager's pregnancy, written and directed by George Kaczender (The Game), vividly communicates to us a sixteen-year-old's feelings in the course of one day.

Unfortunately, Phoebe cannot communicate her problem to her boyfriend, Paul, to her mother, or to her school counselor. In a stream of consciousness, shifting back and forth in time, she projects in her mind the way it might be if she tried to tell them, but she cannot bring herself to do it. Paul cannot sense her feelings and acts like a kid, not an adult. Is he any readier to assume responsibility, to face the reality of a new life, than she is? And her mother--does she really listen to her daughter?

The moment in Phoebe that is most provocative occurs when, frightened and at sea, she suddenly phones Paul, blurts out the fact that she is pregnant, and hangs up at once.

An excellent source of discussion about the central dilemma, which is not premarital pregnancy but a failure of communication, and about an adolescent's unpreparedness for mature experience.

Also: Growing Pains

ROMEO AND JULIET, see p. 322

SPLENDOR IN THE GRASS

Warners, 1961. 124 mins. col. (d) Elia Kazan (sp) William Inge (ph) Boris Kaufman (m) David Amram (c) Natalie Wood, Warren Beatty, Pat Hingle, Barbara Loden, Audrey Christie, Zohra Lampert, Sandy Dennis, Phyllis Diller, Fred Stewart, Gary Lockwood, Joanna Roos, Charlie Robinson. (GEN)

"The torment of two late-adolescents, yearning yet not daring to love, is played against the harsh backdrop of cheapness, obtuseness, and hypocrisy in a socially isolated Kansas town of the 1920's." This is Bosley Crowther's description of a film which, he believed, "makes the eyes pop and the modest cheek burn." That was in 1961. Today, Splendor in the Grass makes the eyes pop, all right, but if the modest cheek burns, it is with embarrassment for William Inge's script and Elia Kazan's direction. Though Inge won an Oscar for it and said the story was based on an incident from his youth, the plot of this movie is True Confessions with sitcom trimmings, and Kazan's handling of it can only be called frenetic.

The high school students, Wilma Dean Loomis (Natalie Wood) and Bud Stamper (Warren Beatty), are crazy about each other. They pet like wrestlers (that's what bothered Mr. Crowther), but they are frightened to go "all the way." Wilma's mama (Audrey Christie) hates men and teaches her daughter that no nice girl ever feels "that way." Bud's father (Pat Hingle) advises his son to take up with the "other kind" of girl until he finishes Yale and is ready for marriage. If you think all this is stereotyped Inge and stereotyped Kazan put-down of small-town thinking, you're right. None of the people in Splendor in the Grass persuade you that they're real. Undoubtedly the attitudes toward sex, given the time and place, are real enough; it is the thundering sententiousness of the film's style that deafens you to its truth.

But on with the story. At the prom, when Wilma is unable to endure the advances of another date, she finally pleads with Bud to make love to her. He balks and she is shattered by her guilt; she feels soiled by her own desires. She tries to drown herself and is rescued by the police. She has a breakdown. (Madness overwhelms her in her bath.) She is sent away to a mental institution in Wichita.

Meanwhile, Bud gets pneumonia, takes up with the town tramp, flunks out of Yale, and marries a lovely Italian girl (Zohra Lampert). He has been released from his father's domination; pop killed himself during the 1929 crash, soon after the death in an auto accident of Bud's sister Ginny, who always went all the way. Out of the sanitarium--cured by the Freudian doctor and her fellow patient Johnny (Charlie Masterson), who proposes--Wilma has a last meeting with Bud, now a farmer. They discover they are strangers.

Oh, what a tangled web we weave, when once we practice nickel psychiatry in the movies!

The themes of Puritan repression, parental inhibition, and sexual guilt in adolescence are all so valid that _Splendor in the Grass_ can hardly fail to be interesting for effort if not for achievement. Under the bathos, the emotional _sturm und drang_, are some fine moments of insight in Natalie Wood's playing of the girl who is aghast at the devil in the flesh.

Also: Family Relationships

SUMMER OF '42

Warners, 1971. 102 mins. col. (d) Robert Mulligan (sp) Herman Raucher (ph) Robert Surtees (m) Michel Legrand (c) Jennifer O'Neill, Gary Grimes, Jerry Houser, Oliver Conant, Katherine Allentuck, Christopher Norris, Lou Frizzell, voice of Maureen Stapleton. (SWA)

Summer of '42 is a matter of taste. Now that it's on TV, you can decide whether it is a contrived exercise in nostalgia, with lush music and sentimental photography, that reaches for easy laughs and is essentially unconvincing (as most of the critics thought); or a warm and moving recreation of the "first time" of sex and death of three recognizable adolescents (as most of the audiences thought).

Herman Raucher wrote the autobiographical screenplay in ten days and then (like Erich Segal with _Love Story_) turned it into a novel. Both movie and book were best-sellers.

The film opens with a narrator (the voice is director Robert Mulligan's), a middle-aged man, reminiscing about a small island off the New England coast and the summer he spent there in 1942, when he was fifteen and everybody called him Hermie.

Hermie (Gary Grimes), his friend Oscy (Jerry Houser), and the bespectacled kid Benjie (Oliver Conant) raided the Coast Guard station four times, saw five movies (among them Now, Voyager with Bette Davis), and had nine days of rain. "Benjie broke his watch, Oscy gave up the harmonica, and, in a very special way, I lost Hermie forever."

So much for what the narrator tells us. We get to see Hermie and Oscy at Now, Voyager with their teenage dates, Aggie (Katherine Allentuck) and Miriam (Christopher Norris). Mostly, we share the boys' fumblings with the life force. With the help of an illustrated sex manual that Benjie has filched from his parents, Oscy is making a list of the steps in how to do it. Hermie, more sensitive, is emotionally involved with a very lovely twenty-year-old soldier's wife (Jennifer O'Neill) who lives on the island. Though she gives him coffee and sympathy and small, friendly assignments like putting big boxes in the attic, Dorothy, Hermie thinks, might as well be on Mars. His romantic adoration is an obsession--but it doesn't prevent him from seizing reality. At the movies, he clocks what he thinks is a record fondling of Aggie's breast (it turns out it was her arm) and with Oscy he prepares for a double date on the beach by going to the drugstore for contraceptives.

Hermie never gets to use them. (He and Aggie are not ready for what they glimpse behind a sandbar, where the more adventurous Oscy and Miriam are making out.) The next evening, visiting Dorothy, he finds in the empty living room the crumpled telegram announcing her husband's death. The shattered girl clings to Hermie, dances with him, and then leads him to the bedroom. His initiation into sex is half-shown. The following morning he finds a note from Dorothy tacked to the door of the deserted house; she hopes that some day he will find the proper way to remember their relationship. Silent, changed, Hermie scarcely listens as Oscy tells him how Miriam's appendicitis has put an end to *his* summer dreams.

Scenarist Raucher and director Mulligan have made Summer of '42 with a minimum of subtlety. There is an elbow in your ribs (get this--teenagers buying rubbers and talking about foreplay); there is heavy, gagged-up underlining of scenes like Hermie's attempt to buy contraceptives. What appears to be restraint--the coupling of Oscy and Miriam behind the sandbar is not shown, except in Hermie and Aggie's flight from the sight; Dorothy's seduction of Hermie is not spelled out by the discreet camera--may be a hazing over the truth of experience.

But, you may object, this is only boyhood experience recalled to life over many years.

Yet, other films of reminiscence are keenly perceived such as Truffaut's short, Les Mistons and Losey and Pinter's The Go-Between. Where Raucher and Mulligan fail is in the concept of the boys' characters. There is a smell of situation comedy about Summer of '42, a reminder of too many stereotypes. (Joseph

Gelmis, in Newsday, said the picture might be called Andy Hardy Meets Tea and Sympathy.) It's a pity, for the young actors have been perfectly cast and often rise above their material; their appearance and their mannerisms, at the beginning of the film especially, promise more than we get.

If it is a romanticized version of boyhood's encounter with sex and sorrow, Summer of '42 sometimes evokes a sense of recognition. Now and then--Oscy telling Hermie about Miriam's ill-timed appendicitis, for instance--it reminds us of the pangs of distant summers.

Also: Finding Oneself
Growing Pains

SUNDAYS AND CYBELE (LES DIMANCHES DE VILLE D'AVRAY)

France, 1962. 110 mins. b/w. (d) Serge Bourguignon (sp) Serge Bourguignon, Antoine Tudal, based on Bernard Eschasseriaux's novel Les Dimanches de Ville D'Avray (ph) Henri Decae (m) Maurice Jarre (c) Hardy Kruger, Patricia Gozzi, Nicole Courcel, Daniel Ivernel, Michel de Ré, André Oumansky. French dialog with English subtitles. (SWA)

This picture is an idyll of intense and innocent love between a lonely twelve-year-old girl who is almost a woman and a lonely, amnesiac man who is in some ways a child. It sustains them both until it is misunderstood and interrupted by outsiders in a small town, and it ends in tragedy.

Françoise (Patricia Gozzi), the twelve-year-old, has been placed by her father in the convent school in Ville d'Avray. Wandering around the same town is Pierre (Hardy Kruger), a former pilot in the French-Indonesian War who became a victim of amnesia as a result of his fear that he had killed a young girl on a bombing mission. Pierre has moved in with his mistress Madeleine (Nicole Courcel), and is living an aimless and friendless life in Ville d'Avray. He and Françoise--who tells him that her name is Cybèle which means "earth goddess"--develop a warm attachment. They walk every Sunday near the lake; they share a loving, nonphysical closeness in this "home" and speak of symbolic objects like the weathercock, bird of Apollo, god of light. (At the end of their idyll, an evergreen, tree of Dionysus, god of darkness, is above Pierre's dead body.) Strength seems to flow into Pierre from the child's warmth. For the child, Pierre is part father figure, part imagined lover; the first stirrings of womanhood in this child-earth goddess prompt her to be flirtatious with Pierre and to be jealous of Madeleine.

To others in Ville d'Avray--a friend of Madeleine's in particular--the relationship between the psychotic man and the child-woman is not only ambiguous but potentially dangerous to the girl. Afraid that Pierre is about to assault her during their Christmas celebration at the lake, the police kill him. After his death, when they ask the child what her name is, she says, "I no longer have a name."

Winner of the 1962 Academy Award for Best Foreign Film, it was overpraised on its importation from France. However, it was extremely popular for its qualities of delicate half-sexual tenderness. Sundays and Cybèle does not stand up on re-viewing. Much of it now looks artificial, for writer-director Serge Bourguignon was straining for effect. The story is cluttered with symbolism, the camera is busy and self-conscious.

What remains--and it is well worth looking at--is an unmatched performance by Patricia Gozzi as the child-woman. She has an overpowering effect; the role has subtlety and range and gives us a screen adolescent to remember. At thirteen, this Cybèle may not be the earth goddess of legend that Bourguignon insists on, but she is a fascinating revelation of nascent sexuality--no Lolita, but a girl more recognizable to those who know how sensitive and intensely vulnerable a twelve-year-old girl can be.

A TASTE OF HONEY

Great Britain, 1961. 100 mins. b/w. (d) Tony Richardson (sp) Shelagh Delaney and Tony Richardson, from the play by Shelagh Delaney (ph) Walter Lassally (m) John Addison (c) Dora Bryan, Rita Tushingham, Robert Stephens, Murray Melvin, Paul Danquah, David Boliver. (BUD, IMA, KPF, ROA, TWY, WHO, WRS)

Shelagh Delaney was a Lancashire working-class girl of nineteen when she wrote the play from which her script of A Taste of Honey is taken. Her protagonist, Jo, whom Time called "Oliver Twist in a maternity dress," is a girl of seventeen, just out of school, who lives in the grimy canal town of Salford in the industrial north of England.

The "more" that this Oliver Twist hungers for is love. Jo (Rita Tushingham) is left out of the existence of her mother, Helen (Dora Bryan), who moves from man to man and one dingy furnished room to another. Now Helen is thinking of marrying Peter (Robert Stephens) and leaving Jo entirely to her own devices.

Moody, lonely, unlovely in every conventional sense, but thoroughly appealing in her honesty, Jo has untapped stores of warm feeling and a kind of wild inner freedom. On the Salford docks, after her mother's departure, she makes friends with a black sailor, Jimmy (Paul Danquah), and sleeps with him. After his ship has sailed, Jo takes a job in a shoe store and lives alone in a big, bare room until she meets Geoffrey (Murray Melvin), who is homeless, and invites him to move in with her. Geoff, too, is lonely and a misfit. He is a homosexual and like Jo is sad, shy, and childlike in his whims.

Jo is going to have the sailor's baby. Geoff is like a mother hen in her pregnancy, taking care of her and the "house." He even offers to marry Jo, with whom his relationship has never been sexual, but she does not wish it. The two odd friends share their taste of companionship--which is both poignant and funny--until Helen returns. Abandoned by Peter, she moves in with Jo. She is shocked by the news of the black baby on the way. Domineering as ever, she overrides Jo's protests that she needs Geoff and throws him out of the home he has made.

Marvelous to watch, Jo is unique among film seventeen-year-olds. Rita Tushingham is perfect as the gawky Lancashire girl trying to find loveliness in an unlovely world. The private retreat from adults she builds with Geoff has the poetry of a child's fantasy; they are playing house. The sound track echoes the theme with its children's songs, and it is underlined by Geoff's last scene, in which he is fascinated by the children playing in the street and then moves off alone again.

A Taste of Honey won most of the '61 British Academy Awards, and Rita Tushingham and Murray Melvin were awarded Cannes prizes as best players of the year. A first-rate version of the play, Tony Richardson's film has much to offer in emotion and meaning. It has many stock contemporary problems--teenage pregnancy, generation conflict, adolescent isolation, interracial sex, slum child's deprivation, homosexuality--but there is nothing stock about the way the problems have been transmuted into art.

Also: From Literature
Generation Conflicts

TEA AND SYMPATHY, see p. 325

TERM OF TRIAL

Great Britain, 1962. 113 mins. b/w. (d) (sp) Peter Glenville, from the novel by James Barlow (ph) Oswald Morris (m) Jean-Michel Demase (c) Laurence Olivier, Simone Signoret, Sarah Miles, Hugh Griffith, Terence Stamp. (SWA)

Term of Trial is worth seeing because of three extraordinarily perceptive characterizations: Laurence Olivier, as a teacher; Simone Signoret, as his wife; young Sarah Miles, as a sixteen-year-old pupil who falsely accuses him of rape. Though it won an award at the Venice Festival, the film is otherwise undistinguished, for Peter Glenville's direction and screenplay are often contrived.

As Olivier plays him, Graham Weir is a somber man, compassionate and high principled, too weak to control his unruly north-of-England slum students (especially the bully, Terence Stamp) or to cope with his sluttish French wife, Signoret. When she taunts him with his spinelessness, he takes to drink. Into this household comes a precocious adolescent, Shirley, who wants private tutoring from Weir. It is patently a ruse, as the wife sees; Shirley is infatuated with Weir. During a school trip to Paris, she goes to his room and asks him to sleep with her. When she is rejected--he is gentle--she is humiliated and enraged and eggs on her mother to bring Weir to trial on the rape charge. He is convicted. In the end, the girl admits to her lie, but Weir's contemptuous wife mocks him for not having seduced Shirley and to save their marriage he tells her the girl's accusation is true.

Before this sleazy resolution, Olivier and Signoret, in minutely observed characterizations, are very absorbing in their private drama of adult sexuality. Sarah Miles holds her own in this company surprisingly well for so untried a player. The adolescent who has fallen in love with an older man is a well realized portrait. She is recognizable in all her moods, with her schoolmates as well as with the teacher and his wife.

Oswald Morris, who photographed the film, is the excellent British cinematographer responsible for such interesting camera jobs as The Entertainer and The Pumpkin Eater, among many others.

Also: Teachers and Schools

THIEVES LIKE US

United Artists, 1974. 121 mins. col. (d) Robert Altman (sp) Robert Altman, with Calder Willingham and Joan Tewkesbury, based on the novel of the same name by Edward Anderson (ph) Jean Boffety (m) songs and radio programs of the thirties (c) Keith Carradine, Shelley Duvall, John Schuck, Bert Remsen, Louise Fletcher, Ann Latham, Tom Skerritt. (UAS)

We have seen this mixture before: a highly regarded director, Robert Altman (M*A*S*H, McCabe and Mrs. Miller), goes back to the thirties for a story of star-crossed lovers who are bank robbers and killers. Unlike Bonnie and Clyde, with its Freudian and sociological underlining, and Badlands, with its alienation motif, Thieves Like Us presents its young pair outside a frame of reference. Of course, they make love while "Romeo and Juliet" is playing on the radio, and they are very much in the mode of the thirties.

The 1937 novel by Edward Anderson from which the title and the characters are derived tells the story of three life-term convicts, seasoned but not very competent bank robbers: T. W. Masefield (T-Dub), Elmo Mobley (Chicamaw), and young Bowie Bowers (Bowie). Their adventures predictably end in capture and violent death. At the core of the book is the love affair of Bowie and a poor Southern country girl, Keechie.

In 1949, Nicholas Ray based his first feature, They Live by

Night, on Anderson's novel, with Farley Granger and Cathy O'Donnell as Bowie and Keechie. Altman reputedly had not seen Ray's film before making his own. He most certainly had seen Penn's Bonnie and Clyde.

For Altman, as for the novelist, the phrase "thieves like us" refers to the bank robbers' conviction that they are doing nothing more heinous than what socially acceptable Americans with a sharp business sense do every day. There is no comment about the multiple killings committed in the course of "business."

The convicted "kid murderer," Bowie (Keith Carradine), is the youngest of the three escaped men and is paradoxically the one with most scruples about killing. Chicamaw (John Schuck) and T-Dub (Bert Remsen) are unstable and rather nasty characters. Chicamaw is captured and T-Dub is killed some time before Bowie is trapped by the police inside his cabin and is blasted apart while Keechie watches in horror.

(Déjà vu? The film has other reminders of Bonnie and Clyde: folksy, deep South relatives and friends; the fugitives' car racing across a beautifully photographed landscape; the radio blaring the songs of the thirties.)

Shelley Duvall, as a younger and plainer Keechie than Cathy O'Donnell was in Ray's film, is an immensely appealing, natural, homely waif. Her love story is not a short-lived and superficial Teen Romance game playing like that of the adolescent Holly in Malick's Badlands; it is a real love story. The relationship between Keechie and her gangly Bowie is equated three times by Altman with the "Romeo and Juliet" music coming over the radio as they lie in bed; you may take it as sentimental or as cynical, but we think the nonprofessional Shelley Duvall makes it credible.

Thieves Like Us is an interesting glimpse of strays who cling to each other. Bowie, who would rather be like the innocent Keechie than what he is, asks a dog on the road, "Do you belong to someone or are you a thief like me?" Bowie and Keechie belong to each other. This is so clear and moving that even though Thieves Like Us is in a too-familiar genre, their love story is worth looking at. The acting of the rest of the cast, Altman's direction, and Jean Boffety's camera work make it easy enough.

Also: Delinquency and Crime
From Literature

THIS SPECIAL FRIENDSHIP

France, 1965. 115 mins. b/w. (d) Jean Delannoy (sp) Jean Aurenche and Pierre Bost, from the novel Les Amitiés particulières by Roger Peyrefitte (ph) Christian Matras (m) Jean Podromides (c) Francis Lacombrade, Didier Haudepin, Lucien Nat, Louis Seigner, Michel Bouquet, François Leccia. French dialog with English subtitles. (CON)

Roger Peyrefitte's novel Les Amitiés particulières scandalized France in 1945 with its story of the homosexual love affair between two boys in a Roman Catholic boarding school in 1930. In Jean Delannoy's gentle and sensitive film, Georges and Alexandre never get further than holding hands, although the homoerotic overtones in their special friendship are strong.

A good deal of the quality of this unsensational film is owing to the screenplay by Jean Aurenche and Pierre Bost, for whom the subject of adolescent love is not new. They wrote two of the best postwar French films: Devil in the Flesh (Le Diable au corps, 1947), about a schoolboy's passion for a young married woman, and The Game of Love, also known as Ripening Seed (Le Blé en herbe, 1954), Colette's story about a preadolescent boy and girl in their first sexual experience. (Unfortunately, neither of these films is now available in 16mm in this country.)

Georges (Francis Lacombrade), who is sixteen, and Alexandre (Didier Haudepin), a much younger boy, are drawn together in the chilling atmosphere of a harshly regimented authoritarian academy. They nurture as much warmth as they can in private meeting places. When Alexandre's confessor, Father Lauzon (Louis Seigner), catches them smoking and playing together in a shed, he threatens to expel them unless they break off their intimacy. Georges agrees, but Alexandre, crushed by his friend's desertion, commits suicide by jumping off the train that is carrying him home. The tragedy turns Georges away from Father Lauzon's moral precepts and convinces him of the goodness of his love for Alexandre.

The boys are sympathetically presented. Francis Lacombrade, as the older boy, is full of radiance, and Didier Haudepin, as the younger, has a great deal of charm. But the ending is melodramatic, for Alexandre is not convincing as a candidate for suicide.

Director Jean Delannoy, so powerful in his early films L'Eternel retour (1943) and La Symphonie pastoral (1946), is not successful in making This Special Friendship especially noteworthy. If you see it, you will respond to the vulnerability of the young boys and to the fact (understated) that their relationship is taken for granted by everyone at the school except the fathers.

Also: Teachers and Schools

TIGER BAY

Great Britain, 1958. 105 mins., b/w. (d) J. Lee Thompson (sp) John Hawkesworth and Shelley Smith, from the novel Rodolphe et le revolver by Noel Calef (c) Hayley Mills, John Mills, Horst Buchholz, Yvonne Mitchell. (BUD, LCA, MAC, TWY)

The girl is ten, the man is an escaping killer--but Tiger Bay *is* a love story, and a very affecting one, about the love between a lonely child and a lonely man.

Gillie (Hayley Mills) is a tomboy in the Tiger Bay slum of Cardiff. If she had a gun, it would impress the other kids when they played cowboys and Indians. And so when Gillie, peering through a mail slot, sees a young Polish sailor (Horst Buchholz) shoot his fickle sweetheart (Yvonne Mitchell) in a jealous rage, Gillie manages to steal the murder weapon, and she lies to the police superintendent (John Mills) about what she has witnessed. Buchholz pursues her. Trapping her in a church attic, he threatens to kill her unless she gives him the gun. But, oddly, a strong attachment develops between the two. Gillie offers to help him. They hide out in the hills; she sees him aboard a freighter bound for South America. Before their story is over, she has refused to identify him to the police, and he throws aside his chance for freedom by saving her life. (It's a thriller with its own tensions.)

For her superb performance as Gillie, Hayley Mills won a special award at the Berlin Festival and a prophetic accolade from Variety: "This disarming, snub-nosed youngster ... appears to have a great career ahead of her."

Without mannerisms, Hayley is wholly convincing as the pre-adolescent girl, hungry for affection, who responds to an unhappy, desperate man and is fiercely loyal to him. She was never better, in all her child roles, than she was in her first part in Tiger Bay.

TO DIE OF LOVE (MOURIR D'AIMER)

France, 1970. 108 mins., col. (d) André Cayatte (sp) André Cayatte, Albert Laud (ph) Maurice Fellous (m) Louiguy (c) Annie Girardot, Bruno Pradal, François Simon, Nathalie Nell. French dialog with English subtitles; English dubbed. (FNC)

André Cayatte (Justice Is Done, We Are All Murderers), the lawyer-turned-director, relates as a complete flashback the tragic story of the thirty-two-year-old teacher (Annie Girardot) who has a love affair with her seventeen-year-old pupil (Bruno Pradal). Browbeaten by his parents' opposition, legal harassment, and the destruction of her career, she commits suicide.

To Die of Love is based on the actual cause célèbre in 1969 involving Gabrielle Russier, a Marseilles teacher, and her pupil, Christian Rossi. If one reads The Affair of Gabrielle Russier (New York, Knopf, 1971), it becomes clear that Cayatte made several changes in the politics, profession, and motives of the Rossi parents, in order to bolster the case he makes in his film against bourgeois narrow-mindedness.

The most popular film in Europe in 1971, To Die of Love reminds some of Claude Autant-Lara's Devil in the Flesh (Le Diable au Corps, 1947), a story about an adolescent's passion for a young married woman whose husband is at war, based on Raymond Radiguet's autobiographical novel. However, Bruno Pradal is no Gérard

Philipe, though he is tall, bearded, and handsome. His parents charge the teacher with seducing him, but it is not difficult to believe--as the boy escapes from all manner of restraints to rush to her arms--that this adolescent has been seduced by love itself. His character is interesting enough, a reminder that a minor may suffer from a major passion. We are moved; we accept the situation. The artistry of Annie Girardot's strong and tender portrait of the teacher is compelling.

Also: Generation Conflicts

TORMENT (HETS)

Sweden, 1944. 90 mins., b/w. (d) Alf Sjoberg (sp) Ingmar Bergman (ph) Martin Bodin (m) Hilding Rosenberg (art) Arne Akermark (c) Alf Kjellin, Mai Zetterling, Stig Jarrel. Swedish dialog with English subtitles. (JAN)

Ingmar Bergman's first screenplay, Torment (sometimes also known as Frenzy), introduces some of his favorite themes: the conflict of the young generation with the old, the need for the young to rebel against their surroundings, the torments of love. One of the great Swedish films, it gives us a classic portrait of an adolescent schoolboy's first, tragic passion.

Jan-Erik (Alf Kjellin) is a student in the Latin class of a sadistic teacher, Caligula, who has made him his butt. When Jan-Erik falls in love with a shop girl of easy virtue, Bertha (Mai Zetterling), he does not know that the older lover whom she fears is Caligula (Stig Jarrel), but Caligula knows the boy is his rival and intensifies his persecution. Jan-Erik, deeply involved with Bertha, neglects his work. One day, he finds Bertha dead in her room and Caligula hiding in her hallway. He accuses him of being responsible for her death and calls for the police. An autopsy gives heart failure as the cause of death and Caligula is released. After Jan-Erik strikes Caligula in the presence of the school principal, the Latin teacher prevents Jan-Erik from sitting for his matriculation exams. The boy goes to live by himself in Bertha's apartment. Caligula comes to him, seeking some kind of forgiveness, appealing to him, in his now-broken state, for companionship. But--in the kind of revenge that is an adolescent's dream of wish fulfillment--Jan-Erik refuses him and symbolically goes out into the new day.

Under Alf Sjoberg's direction, the three protagonists give superb characterizations. Mai Zetterling's performance as the young woman only a little older than her adolescent lover led to her international career. As Caligula, Stig Jarrel (made up to resemble Himmler, then head of the Gestapo) suggests the brutality of the totalitarian personality, whether in a school room or a state. Jan-Erik, as the boy whose first experience of passion is tragically ended by an adult's cruelty, is not Romeo any more than poor little Bertha is Juliet, but he belongs with all the star-crossed young lovers destroyed by an older generation.

Almost all the scenes between Jan-Erik and his parents--poor, well-meaning people who have struggled to provide him with his education and who are helpless to understand him in his torment--or between Jan-Erik and Bertha or the other students ring true. After almost forty years, the grim story still has impact.

Also: Generation Conflicts
Teachers and Schools

TWO WOMEN, see p. 225

VALERIE AND HER WEEK OF WONDERS, see p. 276

LES ZOZOS

France, 1972. 105 mins. col. (d) Pascal Thomas (sp) Pascal Thomas, Roland Duval (ph) Colin Mounier (m) Vladimir Cosma (c) Fréderic Duru, Edmond Raillard, Jean-Marc Cholet, Annie Cole, Virginie Thevenet, Daniel Ceccaldi. French dialog with English subtitles. (BAU)

Les Zozos ("The Rascals") are not delinquents, you understand, only Fréderic and François doing what comes naturally to seventeen-year-olds in a French provincial boys' school in about 1960. They are not planning how to settle the Algerian question but they *are* planning how to cajole girls into bed. And then they do not know *just* what to do with them. Plaguing their teachers and the smaller boys they are, like poor "Venus," also being plagued themselves by the unaccountable ways of adults.

Fréderic (Fréderic Duru), tall and handsome, is not much of a scholar, but he is a well-meaning boy. His friend François (Edmond Raillard), at the top of his class, is a schemer. They're not doing very well on the home front. After eight months of dating François, lovely Martine (Virginie Thevenet) is still holding out. Blonde Elisabeth (Annie Cole) just tags along. The boys do not have enough sense yet to see what a little beauty she is.

Fréderic and François have a master plan. There is a girl in Sweden who has been writing to François. *Eh bien*--they will go to Sweden for their Easter holiday and lose their virginity.

It doesn't quite work out that way. The Swedish pen pal has a formidable boy friend. The weather is freezing, the food strange. Stomach distress interrupts *l'amour*.

Home again, broke and sick, the long trip a bust, the boys are still crowing in the lycée lavatory sessions. What lies they tell! Oh, that blonde of thirty who gave them a lift in her car!

(Next year, they promise each other, they will try Spain.)

Les Zozos is the first feature of director Pascal Thomas, released after the success of his Don't Cry with Your Mouth Full (q. v.). It has the same provincial inspiration and some of the same nonprofessional actors, including the charming Annie Cole. Many of the actors are friends of the director, who was twenty-seven the summer of '72; perhaps that's why Les Zozos is both spontaneous and familiar. We immediately recognize the truth of the episode of the boys' stay with "that blonde of thirty who gave them a lift"--all adolescents are bewildered by what adults expect of them--but we are wholly delighted by the surprise of the boys' individual behavior. The scene is lovingly hilarious.

Roger Greenspun of The New York Times, like everyone else who enjoyed Les Zozos in the New Directors/New Films series at the Museum of Modern Art, found the tone of the film refreshing: "Nothing like the soft-focus, soft-headed nostalgia recently so popular ... It is lucid, ironic, unillusioned...."

The first in a trilogy on youth planned by Thomas, Les Zozos is a delicious apéritif.

Also: Growing Pains

TEACHERS AND SCHOOLS

ADOLESCENCE, see p. 253

AMARCORD, see p. 3

AS WE ARE, see p. 253

BALLET GIRL, see p. 254

THE BELLES OF ST. TRINIAN'S

Great Britain, 1955. 80 mins. b/w. (d) Frank Launder (sp) Frank Launder, Sidney Gilliat, Val Valentine, based on the Punch cartoons of Ronald Searle (c) Alastair Sim, Joyce Grenfell, Hermione Baddeley, George Cole. (CTH)

The little female horrors who go to school at St. Trinian's, originally conceived for Punch by cartoonist Ronald Searle, have appeared in four Launder and Gilliat films, but none is as gruesomely satisfying as this first one.

The St. Trinian's girls are exceptional. You'll never find them smoking in secret. Whether they are stealing a racehorse for their dormitory or a silver challenge cup to pawn, they are unswervingly loyal to the school motto, In flagrante delicto. They bring the classics to mind, particularly Edgar's immortal lines in King Lear: "My face I'll grime with filth; / Blanket my loins; elf all my hair in knots."

The school administration is special, too. When a prospective pupil, about to be rejected as overage, points out that a girl in the school is older and is married, besides, headmistress Millicent Fritton (Alastair Sim) corrects her: "Not officially, dear!"

The faculty includes a mistress of scripture and needlework (a stunning Charles Addams type) who's filling in before serving a prison term; a chemistry mistress whose class is making gin; and a French mistress who's living in the gardener's cottage with a former inspector from the Ministry of Education. Nothing escapes the eye of P.W. Sgt. Joyce Grenfell, who's making an interesting report on the white squares of the linoleum in the fourth form lavatory.

In a wonderful British cast, Alastair Sim has the dual role of the headmistress and her gambler brother, Clarence.

Is this to be regarded as "Regressive Education in Britain" (Time)? We think it is a fierce, funny, macabre romp.

THE BLACKBOARD JUNGLE

M-G-M, 1955. 101 mins. b/w. (d) (sp) Richard Brooks, from the novel by Evan Hunter (ph) Russell Harlan (m) Charles Wolcott; Bill Haley and the Comets ("Rock Around the Clock") (c) Glenn Ford, Anne Francis, Sidney Poitier, Margaret Hayes, Louis Calhern, John Hoyt, Vic Morrow, Rafael Campos, Dan Terranova, Danny Dennis. (FNC)

Acts of terrorism by young hoods in the schools have been headlined frequently in the years since The Blackboard Jungle appeared (1955); its revelation is not the scandal it was when Evan Hunter's best-seller and Richard Brooks's movie were as new as "Rock Around the Clock." Encouraged by the success of The Blackboard Jungle, producers have been turning out school-horror films ever since. As the prototype, The Blackboard Jungle deserves a sober look.

The original novel, by Evan Hunter, was autobiographical, about a young man who had taught in a big city vocational school for half a year and had quit in anger and frustration. Understandably, his account was full of exaggeration, telescoping, self-justification, and the modish mixture of sex and mayhem. Less understandably, the protagonist was moved by very little love or compassion for those who teach and those who are taught--or who perhaps could be taught. The Blackboard Jungle was a hot best-seller; but it did not strike a blow in the long fight against the hundreds of social evils which produce juvenile delinquency.

Nor does the movie. Rick Dadier, the teacher (Glenn Ford), lacks not only love, compassion, and experience, but perception of the real goals and the real problems. To him, his students are The Enemy or The Enigma. His colleagues, without exception, strike him as dupes, cynics, boors, or fools. Parents, employers, school and community leaders, police, and school boards simply do not exist in his students' world. When Rick breaks through to his class one day, is it because he is reaching out to his students' real problems and concerns? Well, believe it or not, he gets to senior students with a Disney short about Jack and the Bean Stalk. If you can accept that, you can also believe that his students know the correct choice in the sentence, "If I were (he, him), I wouldn't say that."

Some of the gnats we found especially irritating in this jungle include; the scene in which Rick overcomes the dope addict in his classroom, knocks his head savagely against the blackboard, and then wins over to the side of law and order the erstwhile pals of the beaten student; and the Good School shown briefly in contrast to North Manual Trades High. The Good School students are white and upper middle-class, and the school has palms waving around it: the whole thing suggests that the kind of kid and the kind of horror we've seen belongs solely to those foreigners in New York.

The students in The Blackboard Jungle, played by some unprofessionals, fit right into the dirt-encrusted corridors; their tough young faces are as insistently real as "The Jazz Me Blues" and "Jungle-E-Bop" under the scenes. Vic Morrow, as a younger Brando, and Sidney Poitier, as a natural leader who'd like to be the teacher's ally, are fine.

As for the rape attempt on the teacher, the knife attack on a man in his classroom, the complete anarchy of the school--they have been a model for every movie melodrama set in a school since 1955.

Also: Delinquency and Crime
From Literature

BOYS IN CONFLICT, see p. 255

THE BROWNING VERSION

Great Britain, 1951. 90 mins. b/w. (d) Anthony Asquith (sp) Terence Rattigan, from his own play (ph) Desmond Dickinson (art) Carmen Dillon (c) Michael Redgrave, Jean Kent, Wilfrid Hyde-White, Brian Smith, Nigel Patrick. (JAN)

There are so few good movies about teachers and students that we cannot afford to pass up one with as much insight as The Browning Version, though it is a thirty-year-old story of a classics teacher in a snobbish British school--a teacher named Andrew Crocker-Harris, for heaven's sake--and dated in many ways. Despite its typical assumptions of class differences, it remains rich in sympathy and brilliant in characterization. The school world of young Taplow and the Crock is not the school world of today. (The boy's parting gift to his teacher of Greek is Robert Browning's version of the Agamemnon of Aeschylus.) But some portraits are timeless: a teacher whose coldness is armor against defeat and a student who is sensitive enough to see deeply into an adult's pain and to respect a man his classmates deride.

Crocker-Harris (Michael Redgrave) is a deeply unhappy man who has retreated into an unattractive shell. He should have led the sheltered life of the scholar; instead, he teaches for his livelihood. We have all met someone like him, the teacher whose bitter marriage and private wounds follow him into the schoolroom. Dubbed The Crock and Himmler of the Fourth Form, he is incompetent and unloved. Under his dreadful academic sarcasm, children wither.

Yet one boy intuitively understands him and breaks down his defenses, so that in the end the Crock is able to confess to the whole school, "I have failed."

Behind the teacher's locked-in nature is a history of personal and professional defeat. His wife, Millie (Jean Kent), despises him and spits the venom of her lovelessness at him as she rages across the school grounds in a picture hat. She is having an affair with one of his colleagues, the science master (Nigel Patrick). His headmaster, Frobisher (Wilfrid Hyde-White), refuses him a pension and points out that he can live on his wife's money after he retires.

When his student Taplow (Brian Smith) gives the Crock the gift of a special book, Millie is sure the boy wants to butter up his master for a passing grade. Her contempt for her husband is not shared either by the boy or by her lover. They genuinely understand and like him for himself. The boy's belief, especially, restores the Crock to self-awareness.

In the end, the Crock frees himself from Millie, defies Frobisher, and is moved to explain to all the students what a teacher should be and how he has not measured up. It is not only Taplow who accepts the apology and cheers him for it. In an unsentimental and restrained scene, all the boys respond with youthful fairness to the man's sincerity.

Winner of Cannes Festival awards for best actor (Redgrave) and best screenplay (Terence Rattigan, from his own play), The Browning Version was directed by Anthony Asquith in his admirably polished, unobtrusive style. It is a film which says a great deal about two human beings, a teacher and a student whom we can recognize. The Crock might still be on your local high school faculty, unlike Mr. Chips, that nice old stereotype who was wired for sound and accompanied by the orchestra even when he was calling the roll.

Also: From Literature

THE CHALK GARDEN, see p. 116

CHILDREN WHO DRAW

Japan, 1956. 44 mins. b/w and col. (d) Susumu Hani (sp) Shizuo Komura (m) Norihiko Wada. English narration. (MAC)

Early in his career, the noted Japanese director Susumu Hani (She and He, Bad Boys), whose mother and grandmother were teachers, won the Robert J. Flaherty Award for this loving documentary about the art activities of some Tokyo first graders during one school year.

Under the guidance of their teacher, a young man of great sympathy, the children express themselves individually and in groups through the media of oils, crayons, paint, and clay. We see them at home as well as in school and come to understand how their family experiences influence what and how each child draws and how self-expression affects character.

Children Who Draw is illuminating about how a child sees and expresses his world. Since the youngsters are Japanese, the film has the added charm of introducing us to many cross-cultural similarities and a few differences. The children were unaware of being photographed; the use of the telephoto lens for intimate close-ups of their lives is most effective.

CHILDREN WITHOUT

U.S., 1964. 30 mins. b/w. (d) Charles Guggenheim. (NEA)

The children in this documentary are without food, without clothing, without love, without stimuli for learning, without many of the things they need. How do public schools in the slums help such children and their parents? How do they give them both a second home and an antidote against the poverty of their after-school home?

The National Education Association focuses attention on a little girl who has to play mother to two younger children while going to school herself. In her home, she is not only without a mother but is almost without a father, for hers is an alcoholic.

The beauty and effectiveness of Children Without are rooted in the director's loving handling of all the children in it. They are children without basic human necessities but not without eloquence or worth, and part of the film's achievement is to educate teachers to that fact. Children Without was nominated for an Academy Award in 1965.

CHILD'S PLAY

Paramount, 1972. 100 mins. col. (d) Sidney Lumet (sp) Leon Prochnik, from the play by Robert Marasco (ph) Gerald Hirschfeld (m) Michael Small (c) James Mason, Robert Preston, Beau Bridges, Ronald Weyand, Charles White, David Rounds, Kate Harrington. (FNC)

"He's a devil," kids say about a teacher they loathe. "They're possessed," teachers say about students inexplicably out of hand. In Child's Play, a gothic melodrama, director Sidney Lumet leads us down the garden path wondering who is the devil and who are the possessed.

At St. Charles, a Catholic boarding school for boys, strange forces have been causing a reign of terror. There have been six unexplained student accidents in the winter term. Obscene notes are written and an obscene phone call made to a master's dying mother. In the gym, one boy allows his eye to be gouged out. Another boy is beaten and hung on the cross in chapel. Teachers are warned not to leave their classes unattended; the headmaster is thinking of closing the school.

Three of the lay teachers are part of the malevolent scene. Old Lash (James Mason), rigid disciplinarian of his Latin students, and hated by the boys, accuses his rival, a very popular English teacher (Robert Preston), who is genial and easygoing, of causing all the trouble. Mr. Malley and Mr. Dobbs hate each other bitterly, as only James Mason and Robert Preston can hate, when the first is clearly paranoid and the second (despite his red shirts and grin) is clearly no good for his students, since he exacts blind obedience from them.

The young teacher Reis (Beau Bridges), observing the hatred between Malley and Dobbs, understands the focus of infection in the school: it is not Malley's madness but Dobbs' evil. The corruption of the innocents is not the work of Old Lash but of the popular master who manipulates his boys.

That's what the film seems to be saying. It's not all that easy to tell since we have been manipulated, too. Lumet's tricks of style suggest until the end that some psychic mystery is responsible for the students' possession. The final explanation, as one critic put it, is part Biblical, part Freud.

No critic was very happy about what Lumet and the scriptwriter, Leon Prochnik, and possibly the producer, David Merrick, had done with the Broadway play of Robert Marasco on which _Child's Play_ is based. Apparently, a literate chiller had been souped up, with loss of subtlety in characterization and meaning.

James Mason's portrait of the Latin teacher, however, cannot be faulted; it is as complex as it is intense. The pupils, some unprofessional and some stage children, are not bad. The setting of the action is perfect, for the movie was made on location at Marymount, the magnificently Victorian girls' school at Tarrytown-on-the-Hudson.

Some Catholic reviewers have objected to the lack of truth in portraying the Catholic teachers in the film, who fail to see into the hearts of their lay colleagues and do a great deal of infighting in the chapel.

Violence, madness, suicide, and evil dwell in _Child's Play_. Enter these halls of poison ivy at your own risk.

Also: From Literature

CONRACK

Twentieth Century-Fox, 1974. 106 mins. col. (d) Martin Ritt (sp) Irving Ravetch and Harriet Frank, Jr., based on the novel by Pat Conroy, The Water Is Wide (ph) John Alonzo (m) John Williams (c) Jon Voight, Paul Winfield, Hume Cronyn, Madge Sinclair, Tina Andrews, Antonio Fargas. (FNC)

Seven of his twenty-one pupils don't know the alphabet; three can't spell their own names; two don't know how old they are; five don't know their birthdays; four can't count to ten; twenty-one think the earth is flat, have never heard of Asia, and have yet to see a movie or ride on a city bus.

The black principal tells the new white teacher that colored children are slow and need the whip. "Treat your babies stern ... Step on 'em everyday when they get out of line. I know colored people better 'n you do. That's because I'm one myself."

(Later, she attempts to justify her philosophy: "They're going out into a world where they gotta please the man and see him smile ... When I was a Negro, I knew I was colored. Now that I'm black, I know which color it is ... I just try to please the man--and then everything rolls along just fine.")

The "man" the principal has to please, the white superintendent of schools, considers that everything which is not customary educational procedure is both radical and dangerous. Since he is a redneck, he states his philosophy in barnyard terms.

But, as Carl Sandburg said, "The young men keep coming on." And the young white teacher, Pat Conroy (Jon Voight), comes on, all right. It is his first job, and the sad darkness of ignorance and apathy that he finds on first meeting his fifth to eighth graders in the dilapidated two-room school on Yamacraw Island off the coast of South Carolina shocks him into a crusader's passion. He will move these kids across the water, metaphorically, and into the world.

(Conrack is an adaptation of Conroy's autobiographical novel, The Water Is Wide, about his own experience in 1969.)

Conroy is a convert, with a convert's special zeal. He explains himself to Mad Billy (Paul Winfield), whom he is teaching to read in exchange for moonshine whiskey: "I used to wear Brylcream in my hair and chuck watermelons at black kids and call 'em niggerheads. Then I did a 360 degree turn--and if a black man handed me a bucket of (deleted) and told me to drink it to rid my soul of the stench of racism, I'd only have asked him for a straw ... Now I'm just teaching school."

Conrack, as the children call him, is related to the teacher in the classic French film Passion for Life; he breaks the furniture of the conventional curriculum and opens the windows to life. He blows a horn to get attention, sits on the bough of an oak tree and drops an apple on a kid's head to illustrate Newton's law, tramps the class through the woods for wild flowers, uses a tape recorder for their poetry and music making, shows them Bogart movies, and introduces them to Willie Mays, football, and Beethoven's Fifth. He sticks a feather in his hair and whoops a war dance around the room. He comes to school barefoot. Do his children respond? Well, what do *you* think?

To the old superintendent, this is no idealist adored and trusted by awakened children; this is a menace. He warns him not to take the kids to Beaufort on the mainland to celebrate Halloween. Of course Conroy takes them--the kids have the time of their lives--and Conroy is fired.

Not everyone has warmed to *Conrack*. Some people have wondered whether the liberal white teacher bringing the light to the poor deprived blacks might not have given the youngsters a sense of pride in their own identity and heritage, instead of Bogart movies. Others have found the Yamacraw community half-drawn, not seen fully in relation to social and political reality.

Most viewers, however, enjoy *Conrack*, and think that Jon Voight and the children (locals from the Georgia island where the film was made), are wonderful. Voight makes such an exuberant teacher--cocky, free wheeling, more than a little nutty, inspired by love--that one can believe the children are so good not because Martin Ritt directed them but because Voight really turned them on. It's great to see them in Beaufort on their excursion, on a bus, in the library and a department store, trick-or-treating down the stately southern avenues.

Conrack may not have the special quality of director Martin Ritt's *Sounder*, but it has unpretentiousness, vitality, and warmth. It is the fifth collaboration between Ritt and the screenwriters Ravetch and Frank (*Hud*, *Hombre*, *The Sound and the Fury*, *The Long Hot Summer*). John Alonzo, the cinematographer for *Sounder*, has photographed *Conrack* beautifully; the cast includes not only those remarkable youngsters and Voight, but Madge Sinclair as the embittered principal, and Hume Cronyn doing what he can with the role of the superintendent of schools.

Visually, *Conrack* is a pleasure, not only because it has so many lovely long shots of water and land, but because it has so many loving shots of children--and of at least one adult--who light up the screen.

COOLEY HIGH, see p. 39

CRASH OF SILENCE (MANDY), see p. 257

HALLS OF ANGER

United Artists, 1969. 98 mins. col. (d) Paul Bogart (sp) John Shaner, Al Ramrus (ph) Burnett Guffey (c) Calvin Lockhart, Janet MacLachlan, Jeff Bridges, Rob Reiner, James A. Watson, Jr., Dewayne Jesse. (UAS)

Like so many other movies about schools, Halls of Anger is full of oversimplification and inaccuracy. In this ghetto high school, supposedly "the way it is" (in '69), there are no drug problems; the reading problems disappear as soon as the hero-teacher introduces a sexy paperback; none of the other teachers know why they're there; and the curriculum and tests, without exception, denigrate blacks. When were scriptwriters Shaner and Ramrus last in an inner-city school? Have they learned anything about the things that good people, not necessarily heroic, have been trying to do in integrated schools in the last decade?

What makes Halls of Anger interesting is its cast of black adolescents, many recruited from Watts and other Los Angeles neighborhoods. Their problems, unlike the movie's solutions, are not dated; they give humorous, involved, and forceful performances.

In the story, sixty whites are involuntarily transferred into an all black school and the racial scales are reversed, with the blacks giving the whites a hard time until the situation erupts into a strike. The film calls for racial understanding. If the adult characters were as real as the students, the message might be effective. But Calvin Lockhart, as the ex-basketball champ who is the only one who cares, and Janet MacLachlan, as the pretty teacher who cares for him, are cardboard people; it doesn't help to color them black.

Not cardboard at all are James A. Watson, Jr., and Dewayne Jesse, as bright problem students. They know their roles only too well, and they play them down to the wire.

Also: Cultural Conflicts

THE HAPPIEST DAYS OF YOUR LIFE

Great Britain, 1950. 81 mins. b/w. (d) Frank Launder (sp) Frank Launder and John Dighton, from a play by John Dighton (c) Alastair Sim, Margaret Rutherford, Joyce Grenfell. (MAC)

If the pupils of Nutbourne and St. Swithin's resemble anyone--outside the nightmares of school boards, teachers, and parents--they bring to mind the scholars of St. Trinian's, that hall of horrors which producer Sidney Gilliat and director-scenarist Frank Launder created five years after the success of The Happiest Days of Your Life. (Ronald Searle, who provided the drawings for the titles of this first film, was the cartoonist whose Punch caricatures inspired the four St. Trinian's films.)

The trouble at Nutbourne and St. Swithin's begins, where so much school trouble begins, at headquarters. Through a bureaucratic error during World War II the Ministry of Education assigns a select girls' school, St. Swithin's (headmistress Margaret Rutherford), to be billeted at a select boys' school, Nutbourne (headmaster Alastair Sim). Since coeducation is a scandal in this period in Britain, the situation must be concealed when both sets of parents and a trustees' investigatory committee descend on Nutbourne at the same time.

The two student bodies prepare for the joyous fray with exuberance, and brouhaha is triumphant. Even mistress Joyce Grenfell, clutching her New Statesman like a talisman, is swept up by the wild rotation of classes and games schedules.

It is all very British, very broad, very inventive, and very funny. The adolescents in The Happiest Days of Your Life will never sit for yearbook pictures in any schools we know, but we recognize them, just the same. We have seen that boy's locker pinups before, and we have tasted that little girl's cementlike muffins, which one of the boys has sent to a laboratory for analysis. The Grecian dances are not familiar, but we have been in that spectacular dormitory pillow fight.

A HERO AIN'T NOTHIN' BUT A SANDWICH, see p. 82

HIGH SCHOOL

U. S., 1968. 75 mins. b/w. (prod)(ed) Frederick Wiseman (ph) Richard Leiterman (m) song, "The Dangling Conversation" by Paul Simon, performed by Simon and Garfunkle. (ZPH)

The documentaries of Frederick Wiseman (Juvenile Court, Hospital, Basic Training, Law and Order, Essene, The Cool World, Primate) seem most effective as the voyages of discovery that he intends, when there is the least staginess of scenes. Juvenile Court, for example, gets very close to the judge; he is understandable in his various roles as arbitrator of cases, adviser to the young, consultant with specialists, etc. But High School, at least to those whose professional lives have been spent in American high schools, good and bad, is a voyage of controversy rather than discovery. To many it seems rigged from the first shot--a close-up of a teacher's mouth lecturing the kids: Authority vs. Captive Audience.

However, High School is all things to all people. You can choose your weapons. The highly favorable professional reviews are echoes, interestingly enough, of the following comment by Monte R. C. Freeman, a sixteen-year-old high school junior from Washington, D. C., who reviewed it for Engage, the United Methodist Church magazine: "An unveiling of what most high school students already know: that our high schools are bustling graveyards." Richard

Schickel in Life called the documentary "wicked, brilliant," and Joseph Morganstern in Newsweek said it was a "terrifying, inestimably important" film. In Great Britain, on the other hand, Caroline Lewis, in the British Film Institute Monthly Film Bulletin, echoed other English critics of Wiseman's film: "As in deficient sports reporting where the camera only follows the ball, much of the game which impinges on the rules is obscured." And the principal of the school Wiseman "discovered" called the film "slanted, cruelly middle-class debunking."

When High School was shown by its producer to an audience of parents and students in a Boston suburb, some of the youngsters denounced their own school, because, they said, it was just as coercive, boring, and lacking in relevance as the school in the film. But then their parents said, "What are you talking about? It's a good school--it teaches respect for hard work and for authority, and has a realistic attitude toward college!"

High School is intended as a study of middle-class values. The school administrators' values are surrogates for the parents' values: pound the kids into shape. Wiseman spent two months in Philadelphia's Northeast High, which is a largely white and middle-class institution.

And "institution" is the mot juste. None of the kids smile. Nobody seems to be enjoying his education. What education? An English teacher murders "Casey at the Bat," a jock sex counselor offers crude machismo jokes to an all-boys class, history is spoon-fed into empty heads and blank notebooks. Supervisors equate wearing the "wrong dress" at the senior prom with "an insult to the entire school." Moronic teachers handling petty infractions of discipline make federal cases of them. In scene after scene, the cumulative effect is one of supreme futility, of utter lack of communication between so-called educators and their bored, suffering charges. At several points, the school's failure to relate to life (the Vietnam war, for example) is underlined. The very few instances of good teaching and sensitive counseling are quickly forgotten in the collage of mediocre-to-worse. The students come off as more intelligent and more human than the faculty.

Critics of Wiseman's bias suggest that he has stacked all the cards against the school. Where, they ask, is evidence of what an objective visitor finds in almost any high school: the kids' inquisitive questioning in some classes and their teachers' encouragement of active response in others; the kids' eagerness to take part (with cooperation from the faculty) in extracurricular activities; the administration's introduction of aids and resources (film, for one) to keep pupils interested; the offering of electives, optional courses, etc., etc.

No, say many who know our high schools, High School isn't a picture of a normal school, but of a really horrifying school, if one thinks only of the vast gap between the young and their elders. See it for yourself, and use it for a measuring rod for your own children's schools.

"It's a good sign," Pauline Kael said of High School, "when a movie sends us out wanting to know more and feeling that there is more to know." Amen.

Also: Generation Conflicts

IF....

Great Britain, 1968. 111 mins. b/w and col. (d) Lindsay Anderson (sp) David Sherwin, based on the original script "The Crusaders" by David Sherwin and John Howlett (ph) Miroslav Ondricek (m) Marc Wilkinson (c) Malcolm McDowell, David Wood, Richard Warwick, Christine Noonan, Robert Swann, Mona Washbourne. (FNC)

A Cannes prizewinner, If.... was the youth-rebellion art film of the late sixties; it had radical chic. How dated it seems now! It recalls activist Jerry Rubin's dictum, "Until you're prepared to kill your parents, you're not really prepared to change the country, because our parents are our first oppressors." (That was 1970; in 1974, Jerry Rubin said, "You have to rebel against your parents to discover your identity, and then you have to love yourself, because you are your parents.")

The enemy in If.... is not the parents, but a posh British boarding school with traditions 500 years old. Lindsay Anderson pictures it as utterly dead. What life do the student guerrillas envision? The leader, Mick, declares, "Violence and revolution are the only pure acts." The adolescent terrorists in the film are undoubtedly acting out many other fantasies of power common to student revolutionaries in the high schools and colleges of the sixties. Pauline Kael has commented, most acutely, that the rebels in If.... (whose motto seems to be, no quarter to anyone) are less like principled insurrectionists than like the University of Texas boy who climbed up a tower and exploded his rage by shooting at everyone in sight below.

In 1969, If.... reminded people of Jean Vigo's Zero for Conduct. Both films romanticize a student uprising against a hated school, both are surrealistic. But Zero for Conduct does not date; it is a lyrical masterpiece, all of a piece, a beautiful evocation of boyhood's rebellion against authority. If.... is the work of an interesting director who is not a master; Lindsay Anderson fragments his theme. The shifts from realism to fantasy, from black and white to color, from one attitude toward the young protagonists to another--these defeat the most earnest viewer.

One strains to follow If.... What does the title mean? There is the obvious reference to Kipling's poem, of course. Why not go further? If the realities of the school situation were stretched a little, *if* the students were to react thus and so--then we'd have the grotesqueries of the plot?

Cinema buffs never fail to enjoy talking about *If. . . .* because Lindsay Anderson, critic as well as director, has made bows in the direction not only of Vigo's classic, but Godard's *La Chinoise*, and Brecht's technique of epic theater, which aims at keeping the viewer at an objective distance.

Youth buffs have enough to interest them in the atmosphere of this British school. It is a hotbed of sadism, masochism, homosexuality, snobbism, hypocrisy, militarism. The Whips (the upper-form prefects) tyrannize over the Scum (the new boys, known sometimes as fags) in the name of discipline and are protected by the administration in the name of tradition.

The Hero, Mick (Malcolm McDowell), and his two roommates, Johnny (David Wood) and Wallace (Richard Warwick), are seniors, nonconformists who despise the Whips as cold-blooded hypocrites and brutes. The three boys steal a motorcycle and sneak off to town to cavort with a barmaid (Christine Noonan).

The "realism" gives way to surrealism just about here. After the boys are humiliatingly punished by a flogging in the gym administered by the Whips, they decide on open rebellion and commit (or fantasize?) an act of murder against the Chaplain during a field exercise. (The headmaster, in the course of an interview when he rebukes the boys, takes the chaplain's body out of a desk drawer.)

Now the boys find a store of arms and ammunition under the stage of College Hall and bide their time. On Speech Day, when General Denson (a parent as well as a pillar of the establishment) is pontificating to the massed students, faculty, and guests, Mick and his allies (including the barmaid from town) start a fire under the floorboards, and take to the roofs, gunning down the audience as it pours into the Quad. "Trust me!" shouts the headmaster. He is greeted by a barrage from our boy heroes. General Denson mounts a counterattack. Undaunted, their backs to the wall, Mick and his friends continue the war.

Whatever you make of *If. . . .*, you will be interested in such things as the hazings; the sight of a youngster falling in love with an upper-form hero whom he worships; the seniors in their rooms, playing very successfully the games of power; the suppressed eroticism of the faculty; and the decadence that passes for loyalty and tradition.

Most of all, you will gain a chilling insight into some types of boyhood: the bullies, the hypocrites, the nihilists, the cowards, and the rebels.

Also: Generation Conflicts

THE LONELINESS OF THE LONG-DISTANCE RUNNER, see p. 243

MÄDCHEN IN UNIFORM, see p. 152

LA MATERNELLE, see p. 153

MELODY

Great Britain, 1971. 107 mins. col. (d) Waris Hussein (sp) Alan Parker (ph) Peter Suschitzky (m) The Bee Gees and Richard Hewson (c) Jack Wild, Mark Lester, Tracy Hyde, Sheila Steafel, Kate Williams, Roy Kinnear, James Cossins. (FNC)

Reuniting Jack Wild and Mark Lester (_Oliver!_) in a charming comedy with music about rebellious preteens in a London grade school, _Melody_ pleased most critics. Its wild and hilarious student revolution is hardly on a par with those in _Zéro de Conduite_ and _If...._, but the director, Waris Hussein, has handled his eleven-year-olds with tenderness and humor.

Two lonely youngsters in a South London elementary school strike up a close friendship--Daniel Latimer (Mark Lester), a well-bred introvert neglected by his middle-class parents, and Ornshaw (Jack Wild), an aggressive young cynic who lives with his impoverished grandfather. Their companionship is affected when Daniel falls in love with eleven-year-old Melody Perkins (Tracy Hyde) while she is doing exercises in ballet class. There is a fight; when Daniel wins, the friends come to a new understanding.

The decision of Daniel and Melody to get married--greeted by parents and headmaster with incredulous ridicule--is interpreted by the other students as a rebellion against the establishment. They decide to help them. At a makeshift chapel by the railroad tracks, Ornshaw "marries" Melody and Daniel just as carloads of adults arrive to prevent the ceremony. In retaliation, the children attack teachers and parents with homemade bombs and even blow up Daniel's mother's car. During the melee, the "newlyweds" escape in a hand car. We are left to wonder: do they live happily ever after?

Is this a preteen _The Graduate_? Fluff and nonsense? Or a refreshing look at eleven-year-olds at a recognizable school? See it and decide. The songs, performed by The Bee Gees, include "Teach Your Children," "In the Morning of My Life," and "Give Your Best to Your First of May."

Also: Growing Pains

THE MIRACLE WORKER

United Artists, 1962. 107 mins. b/w. (d) Arthur Penn (sp) William Gibson, from his play, based on Helen Keller's The Story of My Life (ph) Ernest Caparros (m) Laurence Rosenthal (c) Anne Bancroft, Patty Duke, Victor Jory, Inga Swenson, Andrew Prine. (UAS)

"The real subject of The Miracle Worker is not deafness nor blindness or even, centrally, teaching or communication, but the life principle itself." (Robin Wood, Arthur Penn)

In Anne Sullivan, the teacher of Helen Keller, life was so passionately strong that she never gave up--not even in her own blind childhood, prisoned in an orphanage with her crippled brother, Jimmy. In seven-year-old Helen Keller, blind and deaf, the will to possess her own life raged so savagely that it almost tore her apart. Unable to escape from her inner darkness, she clawed and gasped like an animal.

When Miss Annie met her first pupil, in the unhappy Keller home in the South in 1887, two extraordinary human beings literally came to grips with each other. "To disinter the soul" was Miss Annie's fierce, profoundly believing goal for Helen. That is what she did, in a battle royal. The iron will of the spoiled child, the overprotective love of her parents, and the inexperience of Miss Annie herself made it a superhuman task.

As we all know, the teacher was successful. The moment when Helen realized the connection between the finger-spelt word "water" and the reality it indicated--the moment when she grasped the key to learning about the world--is one of the great moments in the history of children who are "impaired," in Mrs. Keller's phrase. Miss Annie knew that there was no impairment of Helen's mind, no absence of the needs and hungers shared by all children.

Anne Sullivan, who became Mrs. Macy years after, and Helen Keller, who became one of the world's wonders, were matched in a profound understanding of what they wanted. The miracle celebrated in their story is the miracle of the meeting of two minds of equal temper. The triumph, despite the implied disclaimer in Robin Wood's statement, was a triumph of teaching, of a teacher's finding, through unswerving faith in the child's right to her highest fulfillment, the breakthrough to a seeking mind and its plea for life.

Arthur Penn's superb film has all the values right. The emphasis is on the emotional power of the struggle between these two exceptional people. In Anne Bancroft's performance as Miss Annie--proud, yet often lacking in self-confidence; full of humor as well as the scars of her own childhood; unrelenting in her expectations for her pupil--there is true greatness of spirit. In Patty Duke's performance (which won an Oscar) as the stumbling, battling youngster, there is a miracle of perception; she is the epitome of all handicapped children aching for self-expression.

The Miracle Worker is the achievement not only of director Penn and two magnificent actresses. The excellent screenplay by William Gibson is the ultimate form of several earlier efforts. From Helen Keller's The Story of My Life, first came the ballet (unproduced) in 1953; then the Playhouse 90 production in 1957; finally, the Broadway play in 1959. From the last, producer Fred Coe took Anne Bancroft and Patty Duke to recreate their roles in Arthur Penn's film.

As the bewildered parents and half-brother of the child Helen, Victor Jory, Inga Swenson, and Andrew Prine give sensitive performances.

Also: Finding Oneself
Special Children

MORE THAN A SCHOOL

U. S. 1974. 55 mins. col. (d) (ed) Martha Coolidge (ph) Peter Aaron. Narrated by Jack Robertson. (FNC)

Martha Coolidge won the first John Grierson Award in 1973 for best young documentary-film director for her David: Off and On. In More Than a School, she has produced a superb documentary on a free community school which is "an experiment in life styles."

Ms. Coolidge felt that what was happening in Herricks Senior High's Community School ("C. S.") was very special: "The lack of peer pressure ... and the honesty of the students and the teachers with each other and with me. It is this honesty which is the key to the film."

A pioneer effort in 1972-1973, when the documentary was made, this suburban Long Island school illustrates the influence on student-family-community relations of C. S., in contrast with past educational institutions which alienated young people. Students plan the curriculum, teach some of the courses, work in the community, and attempt to solve their own school problems. In unrehearsed interviews, the young people themselves tell us how keenly they are motivated, how intensely they understand their responsibilities as learners and teachers.

More Than a School is extremely interesting for the spark it gives to discussion of the need to reassess our curricula to awaken the creativity of students, parents, and teachers. Martha Coolidge herself became involved as a community resource person for C. S. and joined its women's consciousness-raising group.

NO REASON TO STAY

Canada, 1965. 28 mins. b/w. (d) Mort Ransen (sp) Christopher

Nutter and Mort Ransen (ph) Mike Lente (c) Raymond Wray, Cathy Wiele. (CON, FNC)

Written by a high school dropout, Christopher Nutter, this National Film Board of Canada production presents the reasons Christopher Wood (Raymond Wray) decides that his school has nothing to offer him except a job-training card (the diploma) and forced feeding of conformist attitudes.

"Education is to encourage; you discourage. Education is to interest; you bore," is Christopher's reaction to his teachers. A very bright boy, he resents being told to stop reading Dylan Thomas while the class is plowing through "The Highwayman." He daydreams; he finds his history teacher authoritarian, the school counselor unhelpful, and the urging of his girl friend, Joan (Cathy Wiele), to remain in school unconvincing.

Strongly slanted, both cinematically and thematically, to prove that Christopher's needs are never met by the adults in charge of the learning factory so unappetizingly drawn, No Reason to Stay dramatizes the repulsion toward their educators that drives many boys and girls like Chris to leave school. It is especially effective in pointing up such major obstacles to sensitive education as the profit motive base of educational philosophy, teachers' lack of imagination and reliance on lockstep methodology, and the neglect of individual differences among young people. Though No Reason to Stay is one-sided, it is good provocation for lively discussion of what the quality of school life should be if it is to make Chris and his like find a reason to stay.

PART 2, SOUNDER

Gamma III, 1976. 90 mins. col. (d) William Graham (sp) Lonne Elder III, based on the Newbery Award novel by William H. Armstrong (ph) Urs B. Furrer (m) Taj Mahal (c) Harold Sylvester, Ebony Wright, Taj Mahal, Annazette Chase, Darryl Young, Erica Young, Ronald Bolden, Barbara Chaney. (MOD, SWA, WHO)

The beautiful Sounder is a hard act to follow. Like most sequels, Part 2, Sounder is disappointing in some ways. But despite its talkiness and lack of dramatic tension, it is an honest and often moving story of a strong father's unshakable vision of a better future for his little son who has found joy in learning. This man and boy are black; their dream could be anyone's. Producer Robert B. Radnitz doesn't really know how to make a bad movie, and Part 2, Sounder, like all the other Radnitz movies, is close to the heart of the matter.

Nathan Lee Morgan (Harold Sylvester), a 1933 sharecropper, lives in the Louisiana bayou country with his wife, Rebecca (Ebony Wright), their oldest boy, David Lee (Darryl Young), and a younger boy and girl. A loving family, they support one another in back-breaking toil in the cane fields. Their poverty has not crushed them.

In Sounder, we saw David Lee discovering the excitement of study through Miss Camille, a fine teacher in a neighboring parish. But now her school is closed and Miss Camille (Annazette Chase) is thinking of going north to teach in Cleveland.

Nathan Lee and his friend Ike (Taj Mahal) and other neighbors want to keep Miss Camille in their own town. They will make a school. Since the white owner of their church won't let them use his building, they will build another, supply books, and pay her salary--all in four weeks, before she must give an answer to those people in Cleveland.

But they can't do it. They have to work their own farms before they work on the school building, they can't meet the lumber yard's demands for cash, a storm destroys their crops, and Rebecca and Nathan Lee have a quarrel when he wants to use their savings for the school instead of food.

Just before Miss Camille is due to leave, Nathan Lee drives her to the crude structure they've started, its walls and roof unfinished, its floor bare. Is she going to run away? If she can't win her fight to educate the children right here, where the need is desperate, will she win it anywhere?

Of course she stays. The day she was supposed to leave for Cleveland, school opens for David Lee and the other children of the community.

David Lee's father, an impoverished black man despised or ignored by local and state officials, tells his son, "That school is a chance to find your way out of here. If there's anyone who can tell you what it's like not to have a chance, it's me and your mama. It's like being in a jailhouse all your life."

The boy understands very well what his father and mother have done, and what Miss Camille is doing to get him out of that jail.

Part 2, Sounder, like the first film, was shot on location in the East Feliciana and St. Helena parishes of Louisiana. Delving more deeply into the role of the father and the teacher, it offers a natural, memorable picture of the young boy as well--the boy whose escape in the depth of the depression from Louisiana black poverty is the dream of his elders.

Also: Family Relationships

PASSION FOR LIFE

France, 1948. 85 mins. 1948. (d) Jean-Paul Le Chanois (c) Bernard Blier, Juliette Faber, Dany Caron, Delmont, twenty-five children of

Salezes, Provence. French dialog with English subtitles. (MAC)

Almost forty years after it was produced--in cooperation with the French Ministry of Education and under the sponsorship outside of France of the Film Board of the United Nations--this classic about a compassionate and courageous teacher and his village children still throws a warm light on the subject of education.

Perhaps the reason lies in the truth with which the twenty-five youngsters of the village of Salezes, Provence, were introduced to us. No faded daguerreotypes, but still recognizable, are Firmin, who used to do nothing but daydream and is now setting up type for a class book; Jacquot, that former authority on the number of flies on the ceiling, who is now reading up on crayfish; and Michel, who never used to draw anything but caricatures of teacher, who is now at work on the cover of the class publication. They can be found in any good school where a loving teacher has enjoyed bringing excitement and a passion for life to pupils formerly embalmed in chalk dust.

The story (based on a real story in Provence after World War I) begins with the arrival of the new schoolmaster, Monsieur Pascal (Bernard Blier), who is rather fat and isn't wearing good clothes. Eh bien, he is a war hero. Climbing up the hill from the railway station, he can hear the shouts of children in the brook below. He smiles at the antics of his new pupils and walks down to the edge of the stream. Albert--an unreconstructed young savage--sees M. Pascal first. The town Huck Finn, whose sister has an unsavory reputation, Albert is an orphan accustomed to fear and hostility, certain that life holds special injuries for him. (Once, when all the children were photographed, only Albert's picture came out dark.) Now, a fish wriggling in his grasp, Albert is defiant. Although M. Pascal has not said a word, Albert bursts out rudely that he hasn't done anything wrong. The teacher smiles again, admires the fish, tells Albert his name, and holds out his hand.

M. Pascal knows how to reach Albert and the others. His method is compounded of assurance and maturity. He prizes the emotions of his pupils rather than the leaves of their copybooks. He listens, talks, reads to them; before anyone quite knows what is happening, they are taking walks here and there and everywhere. L'école buissonière, "the hooky-playing school," is investigating its world. The parents, at first bewildered, are soon contributing to the children's experiences.

In the end, Albert, who does not remember the date of Agincourt, learns how to build a power plant, knows what the people of Marseilles do for a living, and is passed by the examiners.

It was in 1920, and M. Pascal's miracles may seem impossible today to the harried teacher in an inner-city school, or in any other school where life and education seem very far apart to the pupils. But the film is still basic. All children challenge this teacher, who says: "Behind each face ... what are his thoughts? what will interest him? Gaston, with his mother threatening the dark closet; and Jeannot, timid and submissive. And the little ones, with their mouths open .... And over there, Albert, almost a man ... How should I reach him?"

When M. Pascal comes into his classroom for the first time, he objects to its antiquity and its smell. He tears up the platform in order to put wood in the stove. Conrack, today, would understand him.

The naturalness of the children in Passion for Life is one of the film's lasting delights; so are the French actors (Blier as the teacher is supported by a number of character players as the villagers: Maupi, Aquistapace, Arius, Ardisson). Pierre Coste is excellent as the adolescent Albert. In his direction, Jean-Paul Le Chanois displays the humor and the humanism characteristic of the French cinema in its golden age.

THE PRIME OF MISS JEAN BRODIE

Great Britain, 1969. 116 mins. col. (d) Ronald Neame (sp) Jay Presson Allen, based on her play from the novel by Muriel Spark (ph) Ted Moore (m) Rod McKuen (c) Maggie Smith, Robert Stephens, Pamela Franklin, Gordon Jackson, Celia Johnson, Jane Carr, Diane Grayson, Shirley Steedman, Rona Anderson. (FNC)

The fascinating, the monstrous Miss Jean Brodie in her prime--and the charming Brodie set of schoolgirls--are the creation of Muriel Spark. Those who know her witty 1961 novel prefer it to the stage and screen adaptations by Jay Presson Allen. But if the movie is not pure gold to all appraisers, it is studded with gems. Maggie Smith's portrait of Miss Brodie, which won an Oscar, is brilliant. Celia Johnson's Miss MacKay, the headmistress, is a subtle triumph. And Pamela Franklin's Sandy is a pupil who makes you believe that only she could have put a stop to Miss Brodie.

The setting is Edinburgh in the thirties. The conservative Marcia Blaine School for Girls is a private day school where the well-bred pupils do not remove their panamas near the gates because hatlessness is an offence and where a poster of Stanley Baldwin captioned "Safety First" adorns one wall.

"Safety does not come first," Miss Brodie tells her girls in the Junior school, who are not yet twelve. "Goodness, Truth, and Beauty come first. Follow me."

And follow her they do. Under the influence of her intensely personal and more than slightly mad ideas of goodness, truth, and beauty, they are more Miss Brodie's than Marcia Blaine's. By the time they are old enough for the Senior school, one adolescent has had an affair with a painter and another is killed in Spain.

"Give me a girl at an impressionable age," is Miss Brodie's dictum, "and she is mine for life.... I am putting old heads on your young shoulders, and all my pupils are the crème de la crème."

Utterly dedicated to her girls, Miss Brodie lectures them on subjects not in the curriculum: her European travels, her preferences in art and food, her philosophy of sex, her heroes Mussolini and Franco, her lovers past and present. Her account (imaginary?) of the death of her first sweetheart brings them to tears; when a surprise visit from the headmistress threatens to compromise their teacher, Miss Brodie's girls say they are weeping over her account of the Battle of Flodden. The little clique whom she treats to theater and gallery excursions, and to the most intimate confessions of her life--Jenny, the prettiest girl; Monica, the most histrionic; Mary McGregor, the most malleable; Sandy, not after all the most dependable--enjoy being the crème de la crème. It does not prevent them, however, from making fun of Miss Brodie's mannerisms and obiter dicta. When they are past sixteen and in the Senior school, they see through the dazzling exterior of this exciting personality to the neurotic fantasist that Miss Brodie is.

Growing up with their own curiosity about sex, Miss Brodie's girls learn that her romantic passion is for the art instructor, Teddy Lloyd (Robert Stephens), though she keeps a crèpe de chine nightdress under the pillow in the bed of the music instructor, Gordon Lowther (Gordon Jackson). Sandy and Jenny divulge this fact, and give vent to their soaring imaginations in the fictitious love letter from Miss Brodie to Mr. Lowther that they compose, and the headmistress finds it and presses for Miss Brodie's resignation. That formidable lady, however, cows her by threatening to take the case to court.

Miss Brodie's very odd attempt to substitute Jenny for herself in Teddy Lloyd's bed is foiled; he takes Sandy instead. But she succeeds in inflaming the impressionable Mary McGregor with her own passion for Franco. When the girl runs away to Spain and is killed, the whole house of cards falls, for Sandy tells the headmistress all about the lectures on fascism, and the Board of Governors dismisses Miss Brodie. (Mr. Lowther, timing it badly, announces his engagement to the science mistress, Miss Lockhart.) In the final scene of the film, Sandy confronts Miss Brodie, and tells her it is she who is the informer. Miss Brodie screams, "Assassin! Assassin!"

Literate and superbly cast, The Prime of Miss Jean Brodie is a memorable drama of a teacher-as-self-appointed-goddess and a shrewd young pupil capable of seeing through her. The headmistress, who seems to come off so badly in the beginning when she is compared with the colorful Miss Brodie, comes off best in the end: she understands so much better than Miss Brodie what is sane and honorable in dealing with children.

The "Brodie set" are not only attractive girls, they are extremely funny in such moments as dancing together and speculating about sexual intercourse (if it's a matter of uncontrollable impulse, isn't it dampened by the pause when one takes off one's clothes?) and extremely perceptive in their final estimate of Miss Brodie.

Warmly recommended for its picture of a highly individualistic teacher and some pupils who really are the crème de la crème.

Also: From Literature

THE QUIET ONE, see p. 245

THE ROAD TO LIFE (PUTYOVKA Y ZHIZN)

USSR, 1931. 100 mins. b/w. (d) (sp) Nikolai Ekk (ph) Vasili Pronin (m) Y. Stolyar (c) Nikolai Batalov, Mikhail Zarov, Tzyvan Kryla. Re-released 1957, re-edited by Ekk with a new sound track, 98 mins. Russian dialog with English subtitles. (MAC)

The classic Russian film about the rehabilitation of the bezprizorni (neglected) or "wild boys of the road" is admired not only as the first Soviet sound film but as a still-effective dramatic exposition of social casework. "The simple humanist position of the film has kept it valid far beyond the immediacy of its problem," wrote Jay Leyda in Kino, pointing out how Ekk had avoided oversimplification. The band of boys is a tangle of good and evil. On one side, they are influenced by a hardened criminal; on the other, by a teacher who encourages every good instinct.

In 1923, the Children's Commission (VGIK) rounds up a group of bezprizorni, homeless children abandoned or orphaned during the Revolution and Civil War, who have been roaming in packs, stealing, begging, and resisting capture. One band is led by Mustafa (Tzyvan Kryla), a Mongolian.

Under the leadership of a genial and sympathetic teacher, a VGIK inspector named Sergeyev (Nikolai Batalov), the children go to the country to establish their own cooperative school. They learn trades, and Sergeyev puts them to work building a railroad to connect their school with the outside world. (The kids don't turn into angels: when the school is cut off by floods, they stage a riot.) The underworld tries to lure the boys back; Zhigan (Mikhail Zarov) tries to regain his influence by forming his own gang and kills Mustafa. But the boys come through. The railroad is triumphantly completed. Mustafa's body is carried back to camp on the front of the locomotive.

The Road to Life is full of memorable images like this one, or like the figure of the teacher walking alone and unguarded among the wild boys. Ekk's use of sound in 1931 was minimal; there is little dialogue.

The character of Sergeyev was based on that of the Soviet teacher Anton Makarenko. In 1955, Makarenko's book, Pedagogicheskaya Poema, was the basis of a remake of The Road to Life which was called Pedagogical Poem. It's talky and ineffective compared to the Ekk original.

Though the bezprizorni in the opening sequence of The Road to Life seem like players in an ancient history, the child victims of war, revolution, and famine are still in the world, and Sergeyevs are still needed.

Also: Delinquency and Crime
War and Its Aftermath

SARAH, see p. 264

A SEPARATE PEACE, see p. 323

SMALL CHANGE, see p. 29

TERM OF TRIAL, see p. 160

THIS SPECIAL FRIENDSHIP, see p. 162

TO SIR, WITH LOVE

Great Britain, 1967. 105 mins. col. (d) (sp) James Clavell, from the novel by E. R. Braithwaite (ph) Paul Beeson (c) Sidney Poitier, Judy Geeson, Christian Roberts, Lulu (Marie Lawrie), Suzy Kendall. (GEN)

Can the adolescent louts in this London slum school, who have defied discipline, baited authority, behaved outrageously during lessons, turn so soon into attractive, well-mannered young people ready to take their place in the world outside?

Well, their teacher is Sidney Poitier, and if anyone could bring about instant education, he could. Sir has class. Dignified, firm, restrained, he is warmly responsive to youth. He doesn't believe these boys are near hoods or these girls are sluts; he thinks they're playing East End roles and can be taught different roles, if they are appealed to as young adults. And so he gives them a model of decency and discusses with them the subjects they are most concerned with.

The movie is based on the real experience of E. R. Braithwaite, a qualified engineer who could not get a post when he came to London, because he was black, and took an interim job in a tough school. (Mr. Braithwaite later became the delegate of his country, Guyana, to the United Nations.) Like Mr. Braithwaite, the Mr. Thackeray of the film that Poitier plays so well has a background which qualifies him to respect his students' problems.

Among the young Londoners who act in the film are some fine examples of teenage psychology. There is Pamela (Judy Geeson), who gets a crush on Sir that he handles with delicacy; Denham (Christian Roberts), who has to be out-boxed in the gym before he can respect the teacher enough to give up his role as class ringleader; and all the members of the class who defy East End racial codes by attending the funeral of the mother of a Negro classmate. An actress named Lulu (as Barbara, who presents Sir with the students' endterm-party gift) is not only a good singer but a reminder of many other eighteen-year-old girls about to burst out of school and into a world they already know very well.

The happy ending, when Mr. Thackeray tears up the offer of an engineering job to remain in the school, and the many too-simple, too-sweet resolutions which precede it have not prevented the film from becoming an extraordinary box-office success. Perhaps, as Time said, a valid point has been made: "the world can use more Sirs."

TORMENT, see p. 165

TWO LOVES, see p. 330

UNMAN, WITTERING AND ZIGO

Great Britain, 1971. 100 mins. col. (d) John Mackenzie (sp) Simon Raven, from the radio and television play by Giles Cooper (ph) Geoffrey Unsworth (m) Michael J. Lewis (c) David Hemmings, Douglas Wilmer, Cary Farthingale, Carolyn Seymour, Michael Howe, Colin Barrie. (FNC)

Zigo is permanently absent. Unman and Wittering are two students in Lower Five B, as sinister a group of adolescents--if you believe them--as the screen has seen.

John Ebony (David Hemmings), in his first teaching post at a secluded English boarding school near the sea, is stunned when his sixteen pupils threaten to murder him as they murdered his predecessor. (Their previous master fell to his death over a nearby cliff.) They promise him safety if he will accede to their demands: little work, passing grades, his help in placing their bets at the track. Incredulous, John faces the truth when the boys produce the dead teacher's bloodstained wallet and shoe. But when he is told he is not to be rehired, he loses interest in the job and refuses to comply with the boys' conditions. He reads a newspaper in class while they beat up Wittering, the school scapegoat.

To reassert their domination, the boys attempt a mass rape of Ebony's wife, Sylvia (Carolyn Seymour), choosing Wittering to begin. When he proves incapable, she escapes. The next morning, Wittering is missing and the boys fear he has gone to the authorities. Despite Sylvia's protest, the teacher leads the search for Wittering. His dead body is found at the bottom of the cliffs. A suicide note reveals that Lower Five B did murder their former teacher; it was Wittering's plan, a futile, desperate move to end his classmates' bullying.

If you can swallow the original premise of the film and the melodrama you can decide how you feel about these students. To Judith Crist, they are "vulnerable children buried within sinister adolescents." To Andrew Sarris, the attempt of the film to indict a vague Establishment as the creator of these boys is trumped up. To Gary Arnold, the whole situation is "faintly ludicrous--sort of St. Trinian's without laughs."

Easily recognizable, however, is the inexperienced teacher vainly struggling with a rough gang of delinquents; many of the classroom encounters are frighteningly real.

Excellent British cinematographer Geoffrey Unsworth (2001: A Space Odyssey) brings to life the physical atmosphere of the school, a real establishment near Llandudno.

Also: Delinquency and Crime

UP THE DOWN STAIRCASE

Warners-7 Arts, 1967. 123 mins. color. (d) Robert Mulligan (sp) Tad Mosel, from the book by Bel Kaufman (ph) Joseph Coffey (m) Fred Karlin (c) Sandy Dennis, Patrick Bedford, Eileen Heckart, Ruth White, Jean Stapleton, Sorrell Booke, Roy Poole, Jeff Howard, Ellen O'Mara, José Rodriguez, John Fantauzzi, Elena Karam, Florence Stanley. (GEN)

"From a Teacher's Wastebasket" was the title of the Saturday Review article by Bel Kaufman which grew into her best-selling book, on which this film is faithfully based. The horrors of that basket--memorabilia of the bureaucratic paperwork and authoritarian idiocy of an overcrowded and out-of-date urban high school--are on the screen, unleavened by Miss Kaufman's earlier humor. More importantly, the central drama of neophyte Sylvia Barrett's struggle to reach her pupils remains undiluted. Scriptwriter Tad Mosel lets it all hang out in the school itself (an actual New York City run-down building) and doesn't digress to give us a love story or unrelated violence.

There is enough love in this young woman's desire to "gladly teche" the youngsters who come out of the ghetto into her classroom, some to learn, most to mark time. And there is enough violence in the confrontations between her college idealism and the brutal realities of the system.

Calvin Coolidge High School seems familiar to anyone who has ever done time in a real city school: the administrator bent on law and order (Roy Poole), the harassed principal (Sorrell Booke), the deafening noise, the challenge of resuscitating A Tale of Two Cities for young people who couldn't care less. The teaching staff, as seems inevitable in movies about schools, is a collection of over-familiar types: the emotional woman (Eileen Heckart), the hopeless ignoramus (Elena Karam), the cynical poseur (Patrick Bedford), the pompous theoretician (Florence Stanley). The students, on the other hand, are wonderful: problem boy Joe Ferone (Jeff Howard), who misunderstands Miss Barrett's interest and almost attacks her; embittered Ed Williams (John Fantauzzi), sure that no black can ever get a break; shy José Rodriguez (José himself), flowering into self-confidence, albeit implausibly, in time to convince Miss Barrett that she has reached at least one of her pupils.

The best thing in Up the Down Staircase, worth all the effort, is the picture of Alice Blake (superbly played by Ellen O'Mara, beautifully directed by Robert Mulligan). Alice is the poignant incarnation of every unattractive adolescent schoolgirl who ever had a crush on her English teacher and was rebuffed by him in a particularly crass and teacherish way. Alice's attempt to kill herself after Mr. Barringer corrects the grammar of her love letter to him is not very realistic. But the moment at the school dance when she looks adoringly at the man who dances with her as an act of pity, and the moment the next day when the same man cuts her to ribbons in the composition lesson--we see her hand clutching the sleeve of her coat in agony--are delicate, true moments of insight.

Though she won a Best Actress award at the Moscow Film Festival, Sandy Dennis is not our idea of a teacher; she is mannered, lacking in presence, often silly. But the Pakula-Mulligan team of producer and director (which also gave us To Kill a Mockingbird), with assistance from Tad Mosel's screenplay and a cast of naturals taken from the streets of New York City, has achieved a creditable picture of a large problem-area school. Up the Down Staircase does not go into any of the reasons mass education is so hopeless, or how it might be improved, but its "teacher's wastebasket" is absorbing, and a few of its students' faces are unforgettable.

Also: From Literature

VERONICA, see p. 137

THE WILD CHILD, see p. 269

ZERO FOR CONDUCT

France, 1933. 44 mins. b/w. (d) (sp) Jean Vigo (asst. d) Henri Storck, Albert Riera, Pierre Merle (ph) Boris Kaufman (m) Maurice Jaubert (c) Jean Dasté, Robert Le Flon, Du Veron, Delphin, Mme. Emile, Larive, Louis Lefebre, Gilbert Pruchon, Coco Goldstein, Gerard de Bedarieux. French dialog with English subtitles. (MAC)

How can you find out what goes on in a schoolboy's head? For a brief spell, Zero for Conduct invites you to explore the reality of fetish, dream, metaphor, and myth. There is nothing out-of-Freud-by-René Clair that is quite like this school satire; and despite the passage of time and the later imitations (like If. . . .) there is nothing which surpasses it.

"Under pretext of civilization and progress," said André Breton in the first Surrealist manifesto from the Café Cyrano in 1924, "we have come to banish from our mind anything that, rightly or wrongly, might be considered superstitious or chimeric, and to proscribe any search for a truth that does not conform to convention. I believe in the future resolution of two states (in appearance so contradictory) --dream and reality--into a sort of absolute reality: 'Surréalite'."

Zero for Conduct has the profound reality of the two states. Everything is photographed in two ways; as the boys see it, and then as it would appear normally. When Caussat goes to spend a long Sunday away from school with his harsh guardian, he is shown blindfolded in an uncomfortable chair, tortured by the little girls allowed to move about freely at the piano. In the beginning of the film, when the boys are in the train on their way to school, they are photographed as if their third-class compartment were cut off from the outside world. (Like all children, they are in their special compartment of experience, protected by their own magic.) Symbolic toy balloons soar out of their pockets, cigar smoke wreathes them in clouds, quills decorate them. A grown-up who has been asleep topples over in his seat. "He is dead!" the boys shout.

The logic of the film concerns a rebellion in a French boarding school. The teachers are tyrants, monsters. Do you doubt it? Look at the gargoyles kids draw in their notebooks. The exception is Huguet, the young master, pictured by the boys as an acrobat imitating Chaplin. The headmaster is seen as a black-bearded dwarf in a bowler hat, his assistant as a menacing Groucho Marx type.

A brave boy organizes the conspiracy. Why? Because the school cook, who happens to be his mother, cooks beans every day. His friend rebels too; his mother dresses him shamefully. A third boy joins up because he has no mother, a fourth because he is in school. Who can endure the rules?

The students plan to take over the school when the governors convene for Speech Day. The night before the great event, there is a pillow fight in the boys' dormitory. The triumphant climax comes when in a snowstorm of feathers, a teacher in bonds is carried through the sea of white. Photographed in slow motion, it is a lyric of revolution, of freedom from oppression.

The boys of Zero for Conduct will not come to terms with the tyranny of things-as-they-are. Down with the reality of school! Fight it with pillows, hide your marbles from it, hurl rubbish at its ceremonies, hold a procession, raise a flag over its downfall. Above all, trust none of them.

Considering these schoolboy acts of defiance an open invitation to anarchy, the authorities banned the film in France for twelve years, until 1945. Mark Twain would have understood the rationale; his Tom Sawyer so offended the ladies of Brooklyn that they banished him from the public library. Huck Finn was also condemned as subversive of the morals of youth.

An unmatched tour de force acclaimed for its brilliant insight into child psychology, Zero for Conduct, as James Agee pointed out, is "one of the most visually eloquent and adventurous" achievements of pure motion picture style. It goes more deeply into the nature of the schoolboys--their quasi-criminal guile, their gaiety, their need for liberty--than any film we have, and it achieves its effects with the originality of a surrealist poem.

Zero for Conduct was the first full-length film of Jean Vigo, whose early death in 1934 was a great loss to world cinema. The extraordinary photography by Boris Kaufman and the music of Maurice Jaubert contributed to Vigo's art.

Also: Fantasy

LES ZOZOS, see p. 166

RELIGION

ALL THE WAY HOME, see p. 203

BAR MITZVAH BOY

Great Britain, BBC-TV, 1976. 75 mins. col. (d) Michael Tuchner (sp) Jack Rosenthal (ph) Elmer Cossey (c) Jeremy Steyn, Adrienne Posta, Maria Charles, Bernard Spear, Jonathan Lynn, Cyril Shaps, Jack Lynn. (TIM)

At thirteen, about to be initiated into manhood in his Bar Mitzvah ceremony, Eliot Green (Jeremy Steyn) is a bright lad. He wise-cracks in French and Latin and is a quick study. What he studies with disenchantment is his middle-class London Jewish family.

The night before the Bar Mitzvah it is not at its best. Mother (Maria Charles), a tangle of nerves over the catered affair, nags to deaf ears at dinner. Father (Bernard Spear), a taxi driver, not much help at the best of times, barks, "In the morning he gets Bar Mitzvahed, in the evening we have the dinner dance, then on Sunday it's all over, thank God." Grandpa (Cyril Shaps) is his usual doting, silly self. Eliot's sister, Leslie (Adrienne Posta), nervy too, snaps at Eliot to go right out and get a haircut and brushes off her milk-sop fiancé, Harold (Jonathan Lynn), without a kiss ("My hair...."). Does anyone in this family know how to communicate love?

Nobody reads the danger signals Eliot is flashing. He mimics Grandpa and Harold behind their backs. He does not go out for a haircut. And he objects to riding to the synagogue on the Sabbath. "Everyone does it," says his father. "I'm not thinking of everybody," says Eliot.

All the conflicts erupt during the ceremony; he walks out. A family crisis is precipitated. "What usually happens in cases like this?" Leslie asks. "There are <u>no</u> cases like this," the rabbi replies.

After Eliot runs away, he buys a mask, gets the haircut, has a soda with a girl. Leslie finally reaches him in a playground and listens to him. "I don't think I want enough to be Bar Mitzvah," he says. "I haven't the qualifications." The men he knows are not men. "They're babies ... If that's being a man--I don't want to do it." To prove he could have done it, he stands on his head and recites the Hebrew fluently.

"Do you think I'm a man already?" he asks her. "You're well on your way, " answers Leslie. He agrees to go home; to save face for the family, she'll tell the lies. ("I've had the practice; I've been grown-up for years. ") Rabbi Sherman (Jack Lynn) finds a Bible text to prove that Eliot has already satisfied the Bar Mitzvah requirements for God. That night, 117 relatives and friends hear the Bar Mitzvah boy deliver the conventional speech of thanks to his parents.

The best things in the film are the playground scene with brother and sister, and such accurate observations as the boy's taking out of the wastepaper basket the plane models he'd discarded when he thought he was too old for toys.

If you accept the major premise, Bar Mitzvah Boy offers a glimpse of adult obtuseness to a boy's soul searching not limited to the London-Jewish scene.

Also: Generation Conflicts
Growing Pains
Family Relationships

BIRCH INTERVAL, see p. 37

FORBIDDEN GAMES, see p. 211

HAND IN HAND

Great Britain, 1959. 75 mins. b/w. (d) Philip Leacock (sp) Diana Morgan, from an adaptation by Leonard Atlas of a story by Sidney Harmon (ph) Frederick A. Young (m) Stanley Black (c) Loretta Parry, Philip Needs, John Gregson, Derek Sydney, Sybil Thorndike, Finlay Currie. (GEN)

Is this a fragile and saccharine fairy tale or a fresh and delicate observation of youthful innocence?

One of the few pictures dealing with children's attitudes toward religion, Hand in Hand has always divided critics and audiences. Winner of an Edinburgh Festival Award, a Parents' Magazine Medal, and several interfaith amity awards, it has nevertheless been called contrived and pretty-pretty by other less-impressed viewers, including Bosley Crowther of The New York Times.

It makes for good discussion, especially in connection with other films on the subject, such as Whistle Down the Wind or the episode of the crosses in Forbidden Games.

A bond springs up between two eight-year-olds, a Roman Catholic boy (Philip Needs) and a Jewish girl (Loretta Parry), who are close companions until older children point out their religious differences. With trepidation they make the experiment of attending each other's places of worship and find only cause for greater understanding. Later, a boating accident makes the boy afraid of the Lord's vengeance, but he is reassured by a priest (John Gregson) and a rabbi (Derek Sydney), who are friends, like Rachel and himself. Although some adults have pointed up the religious differences between the children, both sets of parents are free from bias.

Director Philip Leacock, responsible for The Little Kidnappers, Reach for Glory, and other good films about children and adolescents, has handled his two attractive child players with skill. We see the world through their eyes. The awe in their faces when they visit the synagogue and the church is good camera language, more persuasive than the often stilted, didactic screenplay.

A veteran British cast, which includes Dame Sybil Thorndike and Finlay Currie, does its best to support the children.

Also: Finding Oneself

IN THIS HOUSE OF BREDE

Tomorrow Entertainment (CBS-TV), 1975. 105 mins. col. (d) George Schaefer (sp) James Costigan, based on the novel by Rumer Godden (c) Diana Rigg, Judi Bowker, Gwen Watford, Pamela Brown. (LCA)

Inside the cloistered walls of Brede Abbey, the dedicated Benedictine sisters move in the discipline of their order. When a new postulant of sixteen (Judi Bowker) turns to a much older nun (Diana Rigg) as a substitute for the mother she felt did not love her, she is rejected. The only special friend of a nun is God, and all the nuns must care for one another equally. Young Joanna questions her vocation, until Dame Philippa helps her find strength and understanding.

Dame Philippa has renounced her London life as a sophisticated widow with a successful career and bitter secret memories. On her way to Brede, she sees the girl Joanna in the street. A few years later, Joanna is a novice in the Abbey, eager to form a bond between herself and Philippa. At first Philippa resists, but gradually they grow close, until the Mother Abbess, Dame Catherine (Gwen Watford), cautions Philippa against showing favoritism. Philippa's reaction is to sever her relationship with Joanna completely. When she avoids all personal contact with her, Joanna is profoundly hurt and troubled and doubts her ability to measure up to the Benedictine vows. Philippa decides to tell her about her past and why she has said, "Don't love me. I can't cope with it." Philippa's one child, a daughter also named Joanna, had been killed in an accident, and this shattered Philippa's marriage and her life. Brede had become a place of refuge until Joanna came and reminded Philippa so much of her own daughter. The older and the younger woman come to grips with the depth of their mutual need and their religious duty--to care less for each other and more for all the rest. In time, they both succeed.

Readers of the novel by Rumer Godden from which the film is derived will not recognize the character of the young novice Joanna; she is not in the book. And Philippa never had a daughter; it was her small son, Keith, who was killed.

What makes the screen version moving in its own right is the caliber of the production. Diana Rigg is excellent as the austere woman warmed and deepened by her claustral experience. Director George Schaefer and scriptwriter James Costigan have presented Miss Godden's world of nuns with taste and perception. Filmed on location in England and Ireland, the Abbey scenes are lovely settings for this story of women who find faith and renewal in their Order.

Also: Finding Oneself
From Literature
Generation Conflicts

AN ONLY CHILD, see p. 14

LES VIOLONS DU BAL, see p. 226

WHISTLE DOWN THE WIND

Great Britain, 1960. 98 mins. b/w. (d) Bryan Forbes (sp) Keith Waterhouse, Willis Hall, from the novel by Mary Hayley Bell (ph) Arthur Ibbetson (m) Malcolm Arnold (c) Hayley Mills, Alan Bates, Bernard Lee, Alan Barnes. (JAN)

Mary Hayley Bell may not have had her daughter Hayley Mills in mind when she created the character of Kathy in her novel Whistle Down the Wind, but it is one of her best screen roles. As the thirteen-year-old on a North of England farm who believes that the vagrant in her father's barn is Christ returned to earth, she is tender and eloquent.

Kathy is the eldest of three motherless youngsters. They are hiding some kittens in the barn when they discover the man (Alan Bates). His face is covered with a dark beard, and when he is asked who he is, he mutters a startled "Jesus Christ!" before he faints. That is enough for Kathy. " 'E has cum back," she tells her younger sister and brother. With the "disciples," the other children of the countryside, Kathy reverently takes bread and wine to the visitor, keeping the wonderful secret of his presence from the adults. Kathy's six-year-old brother, Charlie (Alan Barnes), is the one skeptic, and when the man lets his sick kitten die, Charlie knows he cannot be the Saviour and betrays him.

The difference between the children's and the grown-ups' attitudes, the beauty of Kathy's innocence ("You missed him this time, but he'll come again"). and the accuracy of little Charlie's reactions make this a sensitive and genuine picture of childhood faith. Director Bryan Forbes has quietly drawn extraordinary performances from the large cast of children.

DEATH

ALL THE WAY HOME

Paramount, 1963. 103 mins. b/w. (d) Alex Segal (ph) Boris Kaufman (sp) Philip Reisman, Jr., based on the novel A Death in the Family by James Agee and the play All the Way Home by Tad Mosel (m) Alec Wilder (c) Jean Simmons, Robert Preston, Pat Hingle, Aline MacMahon, Thomas Chalmers, John Cullum, Michael Kearney, Lylah Tiffany, Georgia Simmons, Edwin Wolfe. (FNC)

In Knoxville, Tennessee, in 1915, a seven-year-old named Rufus shares a special world of delight with his father, a world of Charlie Chaplin movies and "their place," a vacant lot where they watch the trains go by. When his father is killed in an automobile accident, Rufus's world falls apart.

After her husband's death, Rufus's mother, who is pregnant, is hysterical with despair and self-pity. Rufus is kept from her and almost ignored by the members of the family who gather in his home. His heart is full of pain, of terrible unanswered questions about life and God and death. When his Uncle Andrew tells him about the funeral--"A cloud came over the sun and a butterfly was resting on the coffin as it was lowered. When it touched bottom, the sun came out and the butterfly flew up and out and straight into the sky. Don't you think that's wonderful, Rufus?"--he strikes his uncle and runs off to the place he had shared with his father.

His mother goes to him there. She realizes his need of her and responds with the perception of life that was the father's gift to Rufus as well as to herself. She speaks to him of his father, of himself, of the baby to be born, and of the force of love, not death.

As Rufus, Michael Kearney has considerable small-boy charm. He is believable when he discusses the death of his rabbits, God's way, or when he flattens pennies on the railway tracks and enjoys the cap his Aunt Hannah buys for him. During the long funeral sequence, he glares from his seat on the stairs at the minister seated in his father's chair, and when his mother cries, "Why?" he shouts, "Stop hurting my mother!" Among adults weeping, praying, and talking about "orphans" and "that wonderful man," the boy is bewildered and lost.

Like Tad Mosel's play All the Way Home, the film is less effective in portraying Rufus than was the original novel by James

Agee, A Death in the Family. Alex Segal's direction, Robert Preston's acting of the father, and Jean Simmons' of the mother lack distinction. But enough remains of Agee's theme to make All the Way Home an interesting picture of a child's reaction to death and to the tribal ceremonials which accompany it. The photography by Boris Kaufman is superb.

Also: From Literature
Religion

BIRCH INTERVAL, see p. 37

CHILDREN ADRIFT (LES ENFANTS DES COURANTS D'AIR)

France, 1958. 26 mins. b/w. (d/sp) Edouard Luntz. (CON, MMM)

With a minimum of dialog--"Attendez-moi!" ("Wait for me!") the boy cries out at the very end--with nothing more than a subtle camera, the play of light and shade, and editing, Children Adrift succeeds as well as many more ambitious, feature-length films in communicating to us the vitality of a child in the midst of deprivation and death. This documentary suggests one's experience of Forbidden Games, one's recognition of Anne Frank in the secret annexe.

A very charming small boy lives with his grandfather in a wretched foreign-refugee camp in the suburbs of Paris. They earn a bare livelihood with a pushcart. In the morning, after the child rises at dawn to fill his grandfather's water bottles, he breaks out into utterly joyous play; he and his gang delight in turning a junkyard into a source of high excitement. Their fun is photographed in brilliant sunshine.

Then the grandfather dies. There is no more sunshine. In the wet, dark streets, the other boys help him haul the body of his beloved companion to the hospital. When they leave him, completely alone, he cries out to the world, "Attendez-moi!"

A beautiful cinema statement about a child's reactions to life and death. The life is constricted and difficult, yet the child can play; when death brings loneliness, he still reaches out toward life.

THE CHRISTMAS TREE

France, Italy, 1969. 110 mins. col. (d/sp) Terence Young, from the novel L'Arbre de Noel by Michel Bataille (ph) Henri Alekan (m) Georges Auric (c) William Holden, Virna Lisi, André Bourvil, Brook Fuller. (BUD, WRS)

How does a ten-year-old with leukemia take the knowledge that he has six months to live? How does his father share the last days with his son? Watching The Christmas Tree, one wants to cry, "Oh no!" again and again, at an absurdity of plot or bizarre twist of meaning, but one stays with the movie out of interest in the child's approach to his own death.

Pascal (Brook Fuller) is exposed to radiation poisoning on a fishing trip in Corsica with his father, Laurent (William Holden), when a plane carrying an atomic weapon explodes overhead. Laurent, a middle-aged, widowed millionaire industrialist, takes the boy to his chateau in the country, and with his wartime friend Verdun (André Bourvil) and his mistress, Catherine (Virna Lisi), tries to indulge Pascal's every whim for the few months that remain. Because Pascal takes an interest in wolves, Laurent and Verdun steal two from a Paris zoo so that Pascal may train them. On Christmas Eve, with the adults away temporarily, the child begins to weaken. He dies at the foot of the Christmas tree, surrounded by unopened presents and guarded by his two howling pet wolves. His last gift to his father is a plaque wishing him and his friends good luck.

There are a lot of things you wish weren't in this picture--the Ford tractor Pascal is given to drive around in, the wolves, the unrealized theme about the dangers of nuclear accidents. But when it's on center--the boy's awareness that his illness is fatal--The Christmas Tree is revealing. Apparently, he is drawn to the animals because they symbolize primal life forces. In his conversations with Verdun, he learns all he can about the habits of wolves and the legends about them. And he gets as close as he can to nature during the last days in the country. His only explicit reference to his coming end is calm and elliptical; he seems to accept it and he wonders who and what will be around when he is gone.

The prizewinning French novel on which director-scriptwriter Terence Young based *The Christmas Tree* must have had clarity and sensitivity which eluded him in his adaptation. Involved with the production is the talent of photographer Henri Alekan, composer Georges Auric, and actor André Bourvil.

Also: Family Relationships

CRIA!, see p. 15

DEATH BE NOT PROUD

Westfall Productions, ABC-TV, 1975. 81 mins. col. (d) (sp) Donald Wrye, from the memoir by John Gunther (ph) Michael Chapman (m) Fred Karlin (c) Arthur Hill, Jane Alexander, Robby Benson, Linden Chiles, Ralph Clanton. (LCA)

In *Death Be Not Proud*, John Gunther's true story of his son's death, on which this film is based, there is an entry from the boy's diary: "*L' chaim.*" It is the Hebrew toast, "To life."

Johnny loved life and made the most of it. As Judith Crist said of *Death Be Not Proud*, it is a movie not to miss, because it is "a glowing affirmation of the nobility of even the shortest lives."

When he is sixteen, a junior at prep school, Johnny Gunther learns that he is dying of a malignant brain tumor. He celebrates his seventeenth birthday in a nursing home. Yet he says to his mother, "I have so much to do! And there's so little time!" He is determined to graduate with his class. And he does. Fourteen months after his death sentence, he walks up the aisle at Deerfield Academy, without staggering, partly blind and paralyzed, with his head in a turban of bandages, and receives his diploma, to thunderous applause.

"What did I think of him?" asks Johnny's father in the film. "I loved him the way fathers love their sons. But I'd never taken the time to know him...."

It is only when the boy is dying that both his parents become aware of what might have been, of the time none of them can have again. As writers often separated from their son, and now divorced, John and Frances Gunther have a deep sense of guilt.

This beautiful, moving film eschews heroics. It makes very real the boy's sensitivity and courage, the parents' emotional problems. The questions raised by the situation--whether to tell Johnny he is dying, whether to use passive euthanasia, whether to encourage the boy's drive to get into Harvard in the midst of imminent death--are treated intelligently.

Arthur Hill (The Andromeda Strain) and Robby Benson (Jeremy) are excellent as the father and son.

"One short sleep past, we wake eternally," from John Donne's sonnet "Death Be Not Proud," is true of Johnny Gunther. He has been alive for more than thirty years, in his father's book, and now he lives in a fine movie.

Also: Family Relationships
From Literature

ECHOES OF A SUMMER

Bryanston, 1975. 98 mins. col. (d) Don Taylor (sp) Robert W. Joseph (ph) John Coquillon (m) Richard Harris, Terry James (c) Richard Harris, Lois Nettleton, Geraldine Fitzgerald, William Windom, Brad Savage, Jodie Foster. (SWA)

"If I could be old. Old for one day ... twenty-five years old. Even a day of problems, a trip to the obstetrician or marriage counselor, a secret day with a married man, just to be twenty-five for a flash--that'd hold me forever."

That's twelve-year-old Deirdre speaking. She's a bright girl, she knows that her heart condition is incurable, that she must face up to death and dying. In her last summer, she does such a valiant and even fanciful job of it that she can teach acceptance of death to her parents and to the little boy next door who is her friend.

Deirdre celebrates life, understanding her own mortality as part of the pattern. That we are moved and charmed by this dying girl sustains the film. As Richard Eder of The New York Times put it, "Her composure, her toughness, her bleak eye that dissolves into a rare but total glee ... turn the good lines into arrows."

The good lines don't come often enough, for the script is weak and the direction uninspired, but Echoes of a Summer attempts to deal with an important subject and Jodie Foster plays it to the hilt.

The film was selected for the 1976 Cork Festival.

FORBIDDEN GAMES, see p. 211

LIES MY FATHER TOLD ME, see p. 91

MY UNCLE ANTOINE, see p. 25

THE SPIRIT OF THE BEEHIVE, see p. 275

WARRENDALE, see p. 266

WAR AND ITS AFTERMATH

ALL QUIET ON THE WESTERN FRONT, see p. 288

BALLAD OF A SOLDIER

USSR, 1959. 89 mins. b/w. (d) Grigori Chukhrai (sp) Chukhrai and Valentin Yoshov (ph) Vladimir Nikolayev, Era Saveleva (m) Mikhail Siv (c) Vladimir Ivashov, Shanna Prokhorenko, Antonina Maximova, Nikolai Kruchkov, Evgeni Urbanski. Russian dialog with English subtitles. (MAC)

Ballad of a Soldier is a simple, tender and tragic ballad about Alyosha, a soldier of nineteen. Before it is over, you know again that war murders our best. There are few boys you'd rather watch growing up than Alyosha, and it hurts to know that he will never grow any more than he does during his last leave from the front in World War II.

Not that Alyosha doesn't go a long way from innocent boyhood in those few days. Being a hero hasn't been hard; Alyosha doesn't want the medal the General offers him. What he'd prefer is a pass to go home to visit his mother on the farm and fix the roof. It is the journey back to the civilian front that is full of new experience.

He has much to learn. The wife of one comrade turns out to be unfaithful. The wife of a crippled veteran he has befriended is still happy her husband is alive. And Alyosha falls in love for the first time. He and seventeen-year-old Shura, drawn to each other in a few hours, know they never want to be apart again. But Alyosha and Shura are separated forever in a railway switching yard, casualties of the war.

Beautiful performances of the unsophisticated boy and girl are given by Vladimir Ivashov and Shanna Prokhorenko. When they meet in a box car on a troop train, the frightened girl cries, "Mama!" and the nice boy introduces himself with polite correctness. Their brief love is rich in humor as well as poignancy. This is the Soviet Union, and the movie was made in 1959; Alyosha and Shura do not sleep together.

Well directed and photographed, *Ballad of a Soldier* brings a young man to life before our eyes, telling us that no one will ever see him again after he goes back to the front. Among many other international honors, Chukhrai's film won a Cannes Festival award as the best film for human qualities.

Also: Finding Oneself
Love and Sex

THE BRIDGE

West Germany, 1959. 102 mins. b/w. (d) Bernhard Wicki (sp) Michael Mansfield and Karl-Wilhelm Vivier, from the novel Die Bruecke by Manfred Gregor (ph) Gerd von Bonin (c) Volker Bohnet, Fritz Wepper, Michael Hinz, Frank Glaubrecht, Karl Michael Balzer, Volker Lechtenbrink, Guenther Hoffmann, Cordula Trantow. Available in two versions: German with English subtitles or dubbed; specify when ordering. (CIN)

An exceptionally convincing picture about adolescents, Bernhard Wicki's The Bridge has few rivals among films which indict the shattering absurdity of war. Its schoolboy protagonists are the victims of a sniper's bullet, of falling debris, of shrapnel, of enemy fire, of open fire from their own side--but most of all they are victims of the assumptions which led to their senseless call-up. No less a victim is the American soldier, the "enemy," who is aghast at the need to kill one of them and cries out, "Kid, what are you doing in this war?"

In the last scene of The Bridge, a sixteen-year-old German soldier, drafted into the crumbling Nazi army in April, 1945, is staggering away from battle. His six comrades, all the same age, are dead. They have been defending a bridge that nobody told them was going to be destroyed by one of their own demolition squads. Two days later (as the sound track comments), the war in Europe is over. We remember the final moment of All Quiet on the Western Front, also just before the end of a war: the hand of nineteen-year-old Paul Baumer (Lew Ayres) is reaching out of the trenches toward a butterfly. There is a shot, and the hand falls.

The Bridge begins in the homes and school of the seven teenage friends from the same small German village. Every schoolboy is presented as an individual; we meet him with his parents and friends. Before they go into battle, the boys are vividly, economically introduced to us. We know the boy who despises his cowardly Nazi father, the boy who loves his father's mistress, the boy who becomes involved with Franziska, the boy who carries his father's pistol into battle, the boy who is the complete idealist. There are no stereotypes in the excellent screenplay by Michael Mansfield and Karl-Wilhelm Vivier based on Manfred Gregor's novel, and in Wicki's superb direction of the fine young actors. These teenagers are not actors who are ideological symbols in a slaughter of the innocents; they are people we have lived with. In battle, crowing over a direct hit against enemy tanks or weeping in terror, they are wholly believable.

Junker's son to washerwoman's son, they are eager to be called up to service for the fatherland; they have been well taught.

After only one day's training, they are ordered into combat. One of their teachers, who has been in charge of their military training, tries to keep them from being sent to the front. A friendly captain puts them in the command of a sympathetic corporal, with instructions to see that they are unharmed, and they are assigned to guard duty on a small bridge at the edge of the village. Before the corporal can tell them that they will soon be relieved and the bridge (of no strategic importance) will be razed by a German demolition squad, he is killed in the night by two SS men. Now on their own, the boys dig in to defend the bridge with bazookas and machine guns against approaching American tanks. They make a heroic stand but soon four of them are killed. After the Americans withdraw temporarily and the German demolition squad arrives to blow up the bridge, one of the boys, unwilling to admit that his comrades have given their lives in vain, kills the demolition sergeant. The squad returns the fire and kills one more boy. Only one of the seven survives.

Widely recognized at European festivals, The Bridge won an Academy Award nomination and an assignment for Wicki to direct the German episodes for The Longest Day. In The Bridge, Wicki's control of his craft is shown in the editing and in the use of direct cuts in the early domestic scenes and of special effects and sound in the final battle sequences. But he has turned his camera on more than shells bursting in air; his close-ups of each boy's face are saying more than "War is hell." Like the close-up of Paul Baumer's hand, they are saying, "I am me, and I must not be wasted."

CLOSELY WATCHED TRAINS, see p. 38

THE DIARY OF ANNE FRANK, see p. 297

FATHER, see p. 44

FORBIDDEN GAMES

France, 1952. 90 mins. b/w. (d) Rene Clement (sp) Jean Aurenche, Pierre Bost, René Clément, from the novel Les jeux inconnus, by François Boyer (ph) Robert Juillard (m) Narcisco Yepes (c) Brigitte Fossey, Georges Poujouly, Lucien Hubert, Suzanne Courtal. French dialog with English subtitles. (JAN)

A classic of children in war and of the gap between children and adults, René Clément's Forbidden Games (Jeux interdits) is from that great line of French films about children which includes Poil de Carotte, La Maternelle, The 400 Blows, and The Wild Child. Though it does not show a battlefield, it is also one of the great anti-war films; through the eyes of the children it mirrors man in war.

The forbidden games are played by a girl of five and a boy of eleven, spectators of the adult games of death, who see the world of their parents as grotesque and meaningless, without truth or safety. From the madness that adults have made for them, the children escape into the fantasy world they make for themselves.

The film begins with a strikingly edited sequence of a Stuka raid in June, 1940, on a road crowded with civilian refugees fleeing south from Paris. The column of men and women is being machine-gunned from the air. One of the refugees is a fragile, exquisite five-year-old, Paulette (Brigitte Fossey). She sees her parents killed instantaneously by shell fragments. Her dog is also killed. Bullets still spitting in the dust around her, Paulette wanders away from the bodies of her parents to recover the body of her dog from the stream into which an adult has thrown it. With the dead dog in her arms, Paulette is taken in and given shelter by a peasant family, the Dolles. Their eleven-year-old son, Michel (Georges Paujouly), becomes fiercely attached to her.

Michel speaks Paulette's language rather than his parents' and the two children create their own world. Affected by the carnage of the war and the burial of one of the Dolles sons, they build a secret graveyard to shelter small creatures from the night and the rain; they bury first her dog and then a dead mole, chick, stote, lizard, and beetle. The games are tender and innocent, but when the children steal crosses from Michel's brother's coffin and from the church altar to make their cemetery beautiful, the adults are shocked. The police come for the crosses. Michel agrees to tell where they are if Paulette is allowed to remain with the family. When he is betrayed by his father, who tells him she is to be taken away to the Red Cross refugee center, Michel destroys the crosses in his rage. At the refugee station, Paulette first cries, "Michel!" and then, "Maman!"

The artistry of Forbidden Games lies in its intellectual irony (the ignorant peasant family outraged by the children's game but not by the game of war) and in the extraordinary playing of the two children. Clément's achievement can be compared to that of Vittorio De Sica, who had also drawn remarkable characterizations from the unprofessional children in his three postwar films, Shoeshine, The Bicycle Thief, and Miracle in Milan.

Clément suggests but does not underline the contrasting attitudes toward death of the children and the adults. Contributing to his style is the understated music of Narciso Yepes, sixteenth century melodies for the mandolin. Robert Juillard's camera lingers on the animal cemetery in the deserted mill and on the despair in Michel's face when he has lost his little five-year-old love.

Because of the violence of the experiences which Brigitte Fossey was required to enact for Forbidden Games, a controversy arose in France about whether children should be allowed to appear in films of this type. The summer after the film was released, Monica

Stirling wrote in Films in Review: "A more pertinent question is whether small children should be allowed to live through events of this type. This, presumably, was the consideration that drove Clément to make this moving, exciting, and adult film."

One of the great performances by a child in world cinema, Brigitte Fossey's Paulette has heartbreaking impact. No one who sees it can ever think about children and war in quite the same way as before.

Also: Death
Family Relationships

THE HOUSE ON CHELOUCHE STREET

Israel, 1973. 88 mins. col. (d) Moshe Mizrahi (sp) Moshe Mizrahi and Rachel Fabien (ph) Gila Almagor, Shai Ophir, Yosseph Shiloah, Michal Bat-Adam, Avner Hizkiahou, Ofer Shalhin. Hebrew and Spanish dialog with English subtitles. (FNC)

Uprooted by death and war from their comfortable home in Alexandria, a family of Sephardic Jews emigrates to Palestine in the turbulent last days of the British Mandate, before the War of Independence in 1948. The beautiful widow Clara (Gila Almagor) tries to make a life for her four children in a one-room house. The head of the family, Clara's emotional as well as financial support, is her oldest son Sami (Ofer Shalhin). In the summer of 1946, when their story begins, Sami is fourteen and a half.

Sami knows many pressures. Chelouche Street echoes with the reverberations of the repressive British occupation, of poverty and strikes, of Arab violence, and of Irgun and Hagana underground terrorism. His uncle wants him to join the Irgun movement. Their neighbor Nissam courts the unwilling widow, who favors (to Sami's bewilderment) an Ashkenazic suitor who is stable, if unromantic.

The boy is initiated into work and sex experiences beyond his years. Resentful at having to leave school for a poorly paid job as an apprentice in a machine shop, Sami loses the job anyway when the older workers go out on strike. Meanwhile, he is humiliated to see his struggling mother scrub other women's floors. When he is not yet sixteen, Sami has a brief sexual relationship with an earthy, lovely librarian of twenty-five, Sonia (Michal Bat-Adam), who is separated from her husband. He is fortunate, for Sonia is able to make him understand why their relationship cannot be a lasting one.

Before the movie ends, Sami's younger brother is killed in an air raid, and Sami himself must go off to war. In a time of turmoil, he has been stretched in many ways; he has not really been able to face with his mother's dignity and grace the family's difficult new life in Chelouche Street. But he has not broken, and he is on the way to understanding some of the things a man is called on to accept.

Writer-director Moshe Mizrahi's semiautobiographical film has much to recommend it: warmth and delicacy in delineating the family relationships, excellent acting, and a good picture of the people in one courtyard in an explosive period and place. As Sami, Ofer Shalhin is completely credible, an adolescent forced to change with extraordinary circumstance.

The film was a 1973 Oscar nominee for best foreign film and an international festival selection.

Also: Family Relationships
Love and Sex

IF I HAD A GUN

Czechoslovakia, 1971. 90 mins. b/w. (d) Stefan Heher (sp) Milan Ferko, from his novel (ph) Stanislav Szomolanyi (m) Ilja Zelenka (c) Marian Bernat, Jozef Graf, Ludovit Kroner, Ludovit Reiter. Slovakian dialog with English subtitles. (MAC)

You're thirteen, a boy living safely enough with your family in a Slovakian village during the Nazi occupation. The local commandant has turned the place into a small fascist state. The things that go on--hauling away a Jewish woman, anti-Semitic games, petty cruelties, your uncle stashing away his black-market loot--you accept as the usual grown-up craziness, and as results of the war. You have your own affairs, war or no war; peeking at the girls bathing, playing tricks when you're serving as altar boy.

But the main thing right now is what you fantasize. If you had a gun, you would kill the Nazi commandant, take revenge on the Nazi neighbors, be the village hero.

Then your uncle hides a gun with you and you practice with it. What happens, after all your bravado? You wake up. The events of history and your dream life do not march in step, somehow.

More than one critic has called director Stefan Heher's boy's-eye view of war a minor classic. Though it closely resembles the earlier Czech film Long Live the Republic (Karel Kachyna, 1965), with the same kind of protagonist looking at the occupation and the same implied social criticism, Heher's personal style is unique.

If I Had a Gun is both broadly funny and tragic; its peasant characters are strongly defined; it artfully blends the boy's everyday experience and daydreaming with the realities of the time and place.

When the fall of Dubcek saw the collapse of the so-called New Wave of Czech filmmaking, Stefan Heher, in Slovakia, continued to experiment and to create individualized work. In If I Had a Gun, he has given us an original and assured drama with many memorable scenes and people, showing us how war changes a boy's dreams and turns a game into reality.

Also: Finding Oneself

LACOMBE, LUCIEN

Twentieth-Century-Fox, 1974. 141 mins. col. (d) Louis Malle (sp) Louis Malle and Patrick Modiano (ph) Tonino Delli Colli (m) Django Reinhardt and the Hot-Club of France (c) Pierre Blaise, Aurore Clément, Holger Lowenadler, Thérèse Giehse, Jean Bousquet, Gilberte Rivet, Pierre Decazes, Stéphane Bouy, Loumi Jacobesco, René Bouloc. French dialog with English subtitles. (FNC)

Director Louis Malle (A Man Escaped, The Lovers, Zazie in the Metro, Murmur of the Heart) has said of his 1974 film, "I decided to tell the story of a seventeen-year-old peasant who, as a result of a series of circumstances, joins the Gestapo and who, for three months, has a whale of a time with a police card, a machine gun, and money."

It is Malle's belief that Lucien could be any of us, given the same set of circumstances. He does monstrous things, but the old Jewish tailor, Albert Horn (Holger Lowenadler), looking at the adolescent who is destroying him and his family as he might pull the wings off flies, says, "I can't seem to entirely dislike you." And Horn's young daughter, France (Aurore Clément), has a brief love affair with him.

Is Lucien emotionally underendowed, a sadist, an opportunist? An example of the banality of evil? Proof that "It's like a disease," as his countrywoman, also working for the Gestapo, puts it?

"I am interested in ordinary people being mentally prepared to be monsters in time of crisis," is Malle's response. Lucien to him is "mediocre," without ideology, an adolescent who is playing with real guns, who loves as an act of animal pleasure, who feels his new power and shows no pity.

Malle confesses that he is fascinated by what he does not understand. Lacombe, Lucien gives us more questions than answers. Lucien (who presents his name in the bureaucratic way, surname first) provides us with the excitement of speculation. What is the psychological and social truth of the character?

Lucien (Pierre Blaise), in June 1944, is a bored and disgusted hospital orderly in the small town of Figeac in Occupied France. Swabbing the floor, a portrait of Pétain behind him, he turns to the window for escape, and with his slingshot pointlessly kills a bird singing in the sunlight.

His father is a prisoner of war and his mother sleeps with the landlord; Lucien knows the farm is no longer home. On an impulse one day, he shoots some rabbits and takes one as a gift to his former schoolteacher, Peyssac (Jean Bousquet), and asks to be accepted in the local maquis group. He is rejected; Peyssac thinks him stupid and irresponsible. Returning in discouragement to Figeac, Lucien is out after curfew because of a flat bicycle tire, and chances by the local headquarters of a French contingent of German police. They get Lucien tipsy and have no trouble extracting from him the name of the maquis leader. As Lucien is recovering from a hangover the next morning, Peyssac is brought in and tortured.

Far from feeling remorse, Lucien is delighted to be treated as an equal, as he thinks, by the swaggering group of social misfits in the French Gestapo group. He is impressed by Aubert (Pierre Decazes), a former cycling champion; by Jean-Bernard (Stéphane Bouy), an aristocratic type; by Jean-Bernard's mistress, Betty (Loumi Jacobesco), a prewar film starlet. He revels in his first taste of power and its rewards: a black beret, a pistol, and a tweed suit tailored by the famous Jewish Parisian, Horn, who is in hiding with his daughter and his mother.

Twenty-year-old France Horn at first sees the seventeen-year-old Gestapo recruit, who has accepted hunting human beings as casually as he does animals, as a means of getting her family to Spain. They become lovers and Lucien moves into the Horn apartment, where an ambivalent relationship between the Jewish family and Lucien develops.

Horn allows himself to be picked up by a zealous Gestapo man, Faure (René Bouloc), and is transported to a camp. His daughter France flees with Lucien and they hide in an abandoned farmhouse, where Lucien is in his natural element and they have a romantic interlude. (Before this, Lucien and a German officer were rounding up France and her grandmother. Why did Lucien kill the officer and drive the women to safety? Because the officer was trying to chisel him out of his gold watch, part of his spoils of war!)

Later, inevitably, Lucien is shot as a traitor. Malle finds his story no more incredible than any other story of the times, or of the majority of collaborationists, who had no opinions either way but were in it for the money.

The nonprofessional farm boy (Pierre Blaise) whom Malle cast as Lucien is, in a word, perfect. He *is* the sullen, swaggering, brutish, stupid, and yet somehow innocent seventeen-year-old Gestapo tool. Equally true is Aurore Clément as young France Horn, vulnerable emotionally as well as politically.

Lacombe, Lucien is a remarkable and controversial portrait of an adolescent who is far too troubling to be called ordinary. And while one is discussing Lucien, another character should not be forgotten: his mother. She was "shocked" by his Gestapo employment, but she took the money he earned.

LITTLE BOY LOST

Paramount, 1953. 95 mins. b/w. (d) (sp) George Seaton, from a story by Margharita Laski (ph) George Barnes (c) Bing Crosby, Claude Dauphin, Christian Fourcade, Gabrielle Dorziat, Nicole Maurey. (FNC)

Forget the title and Der Bingle's two or three bursts into song; this is no Hollywood formula molasses about a war waif. An extraordinary performance by eight-year-old Christian Fourcade sets it apart; once you've seen it (TV shows it occasionally) you'll class it with the most interesting screen images of childhood.

Crosby's an American reporter who returns to France after World War II to hunt for the child of his brief marriage to a French girl (Nicole Maurey) killed by the Nazis. The boy Jean (Christian Fourcade) may or may not be his son.

From the moment we meet him in the orphanage, and from all his tentative overtures to the man (equally cautious in reaching out to him) until their final understanding, the boy is complex and very moving. As the Mother Superior (Gabrielle Dorziat) says, he is a marked child. In his face and undersized body, he carries the signs of hunger, strain, loneliness--the signs of the war orphan. But he also has the mark of a child, and a very intelligent child at that.

When Christian Fourcade reacts to his first (borrowed) birthday, or a gift of gloves (which do not fit but which he doesn't want to exchange), or a man's humorous camaraderie, it is hard to believe he is acting. The delicate, unerring expressiveness of his characterization is a tribute not only to the boy but to director George Seaton's handling. (In later films, a comedy directed by Henri Decoin and a melodrama directed by Ralph Habbib, the child was less effective. Perhaps, like Jackie Coogan, he was better suited to portraying a "little boy lost.")

LONG LIVE THE REPUBLIC

Czechoslovakia, 1965. 133 mins. b/w. (d) Karel Kachyna (sp) Jan Prochazka and Karel Kachyna (ph) Jaromir Sofr (m) Jan Novak (c) Zdenek Lstiburek, Nadezda Gajerova, Iva Janzurova. Czech and Russian dialog with English subtitles. (MAC)

Director Karel Kachyna has captured the highly impressionable, uninhibited reactions of a twelve-year-old boy in a small Moravian village during the final days of World War II, with the camera moving back and forth from the real world around the child to the memories each event recalls to him. In something of the same way that _Zero for Conduct_ lets us into the secret imagination of its children, _Long Live the Republic_ penetrates into the magical elements of Olda's dreamy longings. All the time he sees how his elders behave--with a cruelty and selfishness which shock him--in the wartime village, he holds on to his own symbols of tenderness and compassion: his mother's love, his light-colored horse, some puppies.

Olda (brilliantly played by Zdenek Lstiburek) has many problems. He's short and has trouble with the other kids about that. His father cares more about his only horse than his only son and beats Olda. His only friend, a man who also likes animals, is ruined by the villagers. Olda loses his father's horse to a German fugitive in the woods and has to steal another from the Russian camp. And there are always so many conflicts to resolve--between his hunger for affection and his need to survive, for instance.

A multiple prizewinner abroad, Long Live the Republic is a most rewarding film for anyone interested in a child's understanding of his world and his need to rebel against its death and destruction in time of war.

MY FATHER'S HOUSE

Israel, 1946. 56 mins. b/w. (d) Herbert Kline (sp) Meyer Levin (ph) Floyd Crosby (c) Ronnie Cohen, Irene Broza, Isaac Danziger. English dialog. (MAC)

David, an eleven-year-old Polish Jewish survivor of the Holocaust (Ronnie Cohen), is obsessed with the idea that he will find his family alive in Palestine. Hadn't his father promised to meet him there?

But his father is long dead in Oswiecim. There is a new, extended family for David among the others in the newly settled land--including Miriam, a young woman brutalized by the Nazis who finds her own salvation through the boy and Avram, a young Jewish kibbutznik with a warm heart.

This is the first feature produced by the Israeli community. It has many rough spots, but it is a warm film and has the virtues of Floyd Crosby's photography, the Kline-Levin production, which knows where it's going, and performances by leading players of the Habima theatre company.

Dated (or historic, if you will) as it is, My Father's House is a small, touching tribute to the postwar travail of too many children.

MY NAME IS IVAN

USSR, 1962. 84 mins. b/w. (d) Andrei Tarkovsky (sp) Vladimir Bogomolov and Mikhail Papava, from Bogomolov's novel Ivan's Childhood (ph) Vadim Yusov (c) Kolya Burlaiev, Valentin Zubkov. Russian dialog with English subtitle. (MAC)

An intelligence scout for the Soviet army in World War II, he slips in and out of the enemy lines at the front, gathering information. On his last mission, he is captured and executed.

He is Ivan, twelve at the beginning of the war, fourteen at his death in service. But long before he was killed by the Nazis, Ivan was a casualty of the war. He could not even remember the only joyous days he had ever known, on the farm with his mother and sister. When they die early in the war, Ivan seeks revenge by joining the young people's intelligence unit. And when, after two years, his captain sends him back to school, Ivan is unable to remain. His childhood is over, destroyed by bloodshed and hatred.

Frail in structure and sometimes artificial in its straining for impressionistic effects, Andrei Tarkovsky's first film is interesting for its focal portrait of the boy, well played by Kolya Burlaiev. He is a valid symbol. Originally called Ivan's Childhood, after Bogomolov's novel, My Name Is Ivan is about the childhood of far too many children in our time.

NAKED AMONG THE WOLVES

East Germany, 1963. 100 mins. b/w. (d) Frank Beyer (sp) Bruno Apitz, from his own novel (c) Erwin Geschonneck, Fred Delmare, Armin Mueller-Stahl. German and Polish dialog with English subtitles. (UAS)

In Buchenwald in 1945, while the American army is advancing toward the camp, and the prisoners' underground (led by Communist stalwarts) waits for the moment to revolt, a Polish prisoner from Auschwitz smuggles in a three-year-old boy secreted in a suitcase. The prisoners are determined to keep the child alive and scrounge food for him. When they are alerted to his presence, the Nazi commanders torture several prisoners but nobody betrays the boy's hiding place. During a battle between prisoners and guards--the American planes and tanks are nearby--the prisoners are freed, and so is the child.

The child is not identified in the credits; he is The Child, as the protagonist of The Red Badge of Courage is The Youth. A symbol of life for the prisoners, the focal point of their struggle against their captors, he almost literally lights up the concentration camp. It's tough being hidden in one place after another in the men's barracks (once even in a pigsty) but this youngster is completely sunny and uncomplaining.

We never really believed that Shirley Temple won the Civil War, even though she was the only Confederate to climb into Lincoln's lap (see The Littlest Rebel, 1935), but we're ready to believe that this three-year-old could make even an SS guard turn a blind eye.

THE PIGEON THAT TOOK ROME

Paramount, 1962. 101 mins. col. (d) Melville Shavelson (sp) Melville Shavelson, from "The Easter Dinner" by Donald Downes (c) Charlton Heston, Elsa Martinelli, Harry Guardino, Baccaloni, Gabriella Pallotta, Brian Donlevy, Marietto. (FNC)

Last named in the cast, Marietto is the one good reason to catch The Pigeon That Took Rome next time around on television. In the midst of a synthetic comedy of American intelligence agents in occupied Rome--gag after gag in the Shavelson manner--this Italian kid of eleven is something else. He knows the score. To be half-starved, to beat the Nazis at their own game--and to scrounge for his Papa (Baccaloni), his beautiful, dumb sister (Elsa Martinelli), and the naive Americanos (Heston and Guardino)--that's Marietto's forte.

In It Started in Naples (q. v.), in 1960, Marietto's playing of the gamin inspired Variety's prediction, "He should go far in filmdom." He went only as far as The Pigeon, but in it not even the Paramount stereotypers could dim his characterization. He's still there, bursting out of the TV box with his precocious, bitter tirade against the war which has emptied all their bellies.

REACH FOR GLORY

Great Britain, 1962. 89 mins. b/w. (d) Philip Leacock (sp) John Kuhn, Jud Kinberg, John Rae, from the novel The Custard Boys by John Rae (ph) Bob Huke (m) Bob Russell (c) Harry Andrews, Kay Walsh, Oliver Grimm, Michael Anderson Jr., Martin Tomlinson. (GEN)

Like another film about British schoolboys, Lord of the Flies, Philip Leacock's Reach for Glory suggests that the evil of war comes from the evil in man. The boys here have learned to hate; they want the war to last until they get into it, though they have no idea why it's being fought and share some of the bigotry of the enemy; they can be led by any bully who knows the right slogans.

On the English coast during World War II, these adolescent evacuees from London, too young for the army, play at soldier by forming gangs to organize raids against stray animals. John Curlew, whose older brother--to the shame of his parents--is a conscientious objector, is a sensitive schoolboy, the only one in his gang to befriend Mark Stein, ostracized because he is a Jew and an Austrian refugee. During a gang foray, Mark panics and betrays the gang's position. The gang leader orders a "court martial" and an "execution," all part of a war game, but the game turns to tragedy: there is live ammunition, not blank cartridges, in one of the rifles. Mark is lying dead when the others join the townspeople to watch a parade for a returning war hero.

Obvious melodrama and symbolism? Much of Reach for Glory is like that, and all the adult characterizations are oversimplified. But director Philip Leacock, always good with young actors, gives us excellent insights into the friendship between two schoolboys and the sadism in some youngsters which can be triggered in time of war.

THE RED BADGE OF COURAGE

M-G-M, 1951. 69 mins. b/w. (d) John Huston (sp) John Huston, adapted by Albert Band (ph) Harold Rosson (e) Ben Lewis (m) Bronislau Kaper (a) Cedric Gibbons, Hans Peter, (c) Audie Murphy, Bill Mauldin, Douglas Dick, Royal Dano, John Dierkes, Arthur Hunnicutt, Tim Durant. (FNC)

This film was not released as director-scenarist John Huston originally conceived it; it was taken out of his hands, recut and reshaped, and some of the human elements are not clear, despite a prose commentary taken from the novel, which has been added at intervals. Nevertheless, in its present form--a vignette--it has impact; it is a classic portrait of The Youth, as Crane called his raw young recruit, discovering himself in the crucible of battle. When Crane wrote The Red Badge of Courage in 1892, when he was only twenty-one and knew war only at secondhand, he produced a masterpiece of sensibility. The film is far from a masterpiece, but the sensibility is here.

Henry Fleming, The Youth (Audie Murphy), is a Union volunteer in his teens. He is full of illusion about the glory of war. During the engagement of his regiment, part of Fighting Joe Hooker's Army of the Rappahannock, at Chancellorsville, he begins, Crane tells us, as "an unknown quantity." The day before his initiation into combat, dazed by drilling and endless waiting, confused by the veteran soldiers (who conceal their own fear under cocky boasts), he feels panic mount. How will he acquit himself in battle?

During a Confederate attack, The Youth turns and runs in terror, deserting his company. In the nightmare that follows, he tries to overcome his humiliation. (In the novel, at this point, he meets The Tall Soldier, from whose death he learns much, and The Tattered Man, a wounded soldier whose concern for him increases his guilt. In the film, these meetings have been so truncated that we miss the motivation for his inner development and discovery of the meaning of courage.)

On the next day, led back to his company with a wound received from a hysterical Union soldier also in flight, The Youth is accepted as an honorably wounded veteran. In the final battle, he fights like a wildcat, full of fury against the men trying to kill him, even retrieving a battle flag in the face of enemy fire. He has discovered that the true meaning of the "red badge" has nothing to do with courage; it is an acceptance of the facts. "He had been to touch the great death, and found that, after all, it was but the great death. He was a man."

Among the many excellences of the film are Harold Rosson's shots of haversacks and bayonets on grassy meadows, Huston's chaos of war with its yelling men and plunging horses--reminiscent of the Mathew Brady Civil War pictures--and good playing by most of the young actors. The viewer does not lose sight, underdeveloped as he may be in this version, of The Youth, green and growing, as he achieves the badge of his manhood.

Also: Finding Oneself
From Literature

RED SKY AT MORNING, see p. 57

THE ROAD TO LIFE, see p. 190

THE SEARCH

Switzerland, 1947. 103 mins. b/w. (d) Fred Zinnemann (sp) Richard Schweizer, David Wechsler, Paul Jarrico (ph) Emil Berna (m) Robert Blum (ed) Hermann Haller (c) Montgomery Clift, Aline MacMahon, Ivan Jandl, Jarmila Novotna, Wendell Corey. (FNC)

Produced in Switzerland and in the rubble of the postwar American Zone of Germany, The Search compassionately records the plight of Europe's refugee children, whose homes and lives were shattered in World War II.

In particular, it shows us nine-year-old Karel Malik (Ivan Jandl) and his mother (Jarmila Novotna), who has been desperately looking for him in the ruins of Germany. When we first see him, the Czech youngster is with a group of refugee children on their way to a home run by UNRRA, the organization formed to rehabilitate displaced children. Becoming panic-stricken because they think that the ambulance is a gas chamber, the children break out. Karel is found by an American soldier (Montgomery Clift), who "adopts" him and looks after him, with the help of a tireless UNRRA official (Aline MacMahon). Karel and his mother are reunited eventually--after he has been taught by his soldier friend to speak and to trust.

The scenes between Montgomery Clift and the unsmiling, traumatized boy are deeply affecting. Directed in semidocumentary style by Fred Zinnemann, The Search won an Academy Award for its story and a special award for Ivan Jandl.

SHOESHINE (SCIUSCIA)

Italy, 1946. 93 mins. b/w. (d) Vittorio De Sica (sp) Cesare Zavattini, Sergio Amidei, Adolfo Franci, C. G. Viola (ph) Archise Brizzi (m) Alessandro Cicognini (c) Rinaldo Smordoni, Franco Interlenghi. Italian dialog with English subtitles. (JAN)

Shoeshine is one of the great, enduring ones.

In his 1947 review, James Agee called it "one of the few fully alive, fully rational films ever made," and in the seventies, Orson Welles said he ran Vittorio De Sica's Shoeshine "and the camera disappeared, it was just life." In I Lost It at the Movies, Pauline Kael wrote that instead of "that feeling we get of human emotions that have been worked-over and worked into something ... we receive something more naked, something that pours out of the screen."

What pours out of the screen is the tragedy of two young boys in Rome in the first days of the American occupation after World War II. They are victims of the demoralization in the wake of the Fascist regime, of the war, of the Nazi occupation, and of the American liberation. They are destroyed--they destroy each other--because their innocence is no match for adult indifference, selfishness, and cruelty.

Giuseppe (Rinaldo Smordoni) and Pasquale (Franco Interlenghi) are close friends, earning their meagre living by shouting, "Sciuscia!" ("Shoe-sha!") to G. I. Joes in the streets. They are postwar gamins, but they have a romantic dream, to own a horse, a special white horse. Trying to earn enough money to buy it, they become involved in the black market. The two boys ride the white horse proudly down the street, but their black-market dealings are discovered by the police, and they are sent to a prison-like reform school for youth. Here the friends are purposely separated. Pasquale, the older boy, is tricked by the authorities into informing against their adult confederates, including Giuseppe's brother. The friends become bitter enemies, and Pasquale, as a police informer, sinks even deeper into the corruption of the prison. Giuseppe and the prison bully make their escape in the confusion of a fire that interrupts a film showing. They head straight for the stable where the horse is hidden. Pasquale leads the police there. The stable is empty, but Pasquale sees Giuseppe and the other boy riding off on the white horse. Pasquale kills Giuseppe.

"Then comes a cry of appalling anguish--a cry echoing the anguish of all children who have been neglected, hurt, or murdered--and this cry mingles with the sound of the hoofs of the horse they both loved as it canters into the night. It is one of the most unforgettable moments in all cinema." (Basil Wright, The Long View)

Vittorio De Sica's second postwar film, Shoeshine heralded the neo-realist movement. Its success enabled him to make his other great films. Shoeshine does not have the perfection of The Bicycle Thief--its melodrama and lack of clarity at the close are sometimes mentioned--but it is dateless, unique, and immensely moving. The physical and emotional injuries inflicted on children in a dislocated society have never been filmed with more depth and honesty.

De Sica has always been magnificent in showing us children. Watching Shoeshine today, we take for granted the reality of the Roman streets, the prison, the police interrogation of Pasquale. But we are surprised all over again by an example of something only he has given us: the small boy in the prison, who has tuberculosis, and who has always wanted to see the ocean. He is about to see it in a movie--and then the projector catches fire.

Also: Delinquency and Crime

THE SPIRIT OF THE BEEHIVE, see p. 275

THE TWO OF US

France, 1967. 86 mins. b/w. (d) Claude Berri (sp) Claude Berri, adapted by Gerard Brach (ph) Jean Penzer (m) Georges DeLerue (c) Michel Simon, Alain Cohen, Luce Fabiole, Roger Carel, Paul Preboist, Charles Denner, Jacqueline Rouillard. French dialog with English subtitles by Noelle Gillmor. (SWA CTH)

The Two of Us was called "a lovely, sentimental reminiscence of childhood in wartime.... The story impinges on peacetime childhood as well" by Renata Adler in The New York Times.

Beginning with a narrator recalling the way he was as a child in 1943, director-writer Claude Berri's film, originally called Le Vieil Homme et L'enfant (The Old Man and the Child) tells with warmth and delicacy the story of a friendship that arose far from the battlefield, and became one of the victories of the war.

The parents of eight-year-old Claude (Alain Cohen), a Jewish child in Paris in 1943, have represented themselves as Alsatians to avoid deportation to a concentration camp. They send Claude to a remote farm in the south of France, to be sheltered from the Nazis by an old couple, parents of one of their Catholic friends. The seventy-three-year-old peasant farmer, Gramps (Michel Simon), follows the Vichy line--particularly its antiSemitism--so they do not tell him that the boy is Jewish. They have given him a Christian surname, taught him the Lord's prayer, and warned him he must "always bathe in private."

An ignorant, gruff, contradictory old man who can't kill a rabbit, Gramps is savage about the Jews ("You can tell them by their smell"), he has a closed view of the world, and Claude doesn't understand it. But they roam the countryside together, go fishing with Gramps' dog, and are soon very close. They share experiences: Claude has his head shaved as a punishment in school, and Gramps comforts him with a hat and a release from school until everything has blown over; Petain's portrait is moved to the attic; Gramps' dog is buried in the garden. Each discovers something about himself. When France is liberated, they are "the two of us," full of love and sad they have to part.

The chief actors are superb. Alain Cohen, large eyed, grave, has dignity and mischievous charm. The great Michel Simon is greater than ever in a role cut to his enormous size. When The Two of Us was shown at film festivals in Panama, Cannes, and Berlin, Simon won acting awards at all three.

A former actor, Claude Berri won an Academy Award for his short about a boy and his pet, The Chicken. His first feature, The Two of Us has a feeling for all its people which some critics have found suggestive of the humanism in Jean Renoir's films.

Also: Cultural Conflicts

TWO WOMEN

Italy, France, 1960. 105 mins. b/w. (d) Vittorio De Sica (sp) Cesare Zavattini and Vittorio De Sica, from Alberto Moravia's novel La Ciociaria (ph) Gabor Pogany (m) Armando Trovaioli (c) Sophia Loren, Jean-Paul Belmondo, Eleanora Brown, Raf Vallone, Renato Salvatori. Italian dialog with English subtitles. (MAC)

Originally called La Ciociaria (Woman of Ciociaria) after Alberto Moravia's novel, and noted for Sophia Loren's prizewinning performance in the main role, the film is aptly titled Two Women, for it is the drama of mother and daughter, alienated and then united by the shocks of war.

During the bombings of Rome in 1943, Cesira (Sophia Loren), a young widow, and her thirteen-year-old daughter, Rosetta (Eleanora Brown), go back to Cesira's mountain village, tiny Sant' Eufemia in Ciociaria. Here the handsome, fiery widow becomes involved with a shy intellectual, the teacher Michel (Jean-Paul Belmondo), who has been trying to avoid involvement in the war. The romance is complicated by the fact that Rosetta has also fallen in love with him. When the teacher is forced to leave the village to guide enemy soldiers across the mountains, Cesira and Rosetta decide to return to Rome. On the way, in the ruins of a bombed-out church, they are raped by Moroccan soldiers. The horror of the experience numbs Rosetta. In Rome, consumed by a sense of disgrace, she sells herself to the first young man she meets, for a pair of stockings. In despair over her daughter's bitterness, Cesira is unable to crack her defenses, and they are far apart until news comes that the teacher whom they both loved has been killed by the Germans. Rosetta is dissolved in grief and comes to life again through the recollection of her love. She clings to Cesira and the bond of sorrow unites them.

No images of youth torn apart by war are stronger than the close-up of Rosetta's face that De Sica holds in the rape scene, or the picture of the mother's anguish as she tries in vain to penetrate to the shock in the young girl's mind.

Director Vittorio De Sica has drawn excellent performances from all his actors, but none is more moving than that of Eleanora Brown as Rosetta.

Also: Family Relationships
From Literature
Love and Sex

LES VIOLONS DU BAL

France, 1974. 110 mins. b/w and col. (d) (sp) Michel Drach (ph) Yann Le Masson and William Lubtchansky (m) Jean Manuel De Scarano and Jacques Monty (c) Marie-Josée Nat, Jean-Louis Trintignant, Gabrielle Doulcet, Michel Drach, David Drach, Nathalie Roussel, Christian Rist, Paul Le Person. French dialog with English subtitles. (FNC)

Director-writer Michel Drach's Les Violons du Bal is often linked with Louis Malle's Lacombe, Lucien, because they are both about young people in Vichy-held France, but they could not be less similar in intention, style, and emphasis. Perhaps their only similarity lies in the fact that they have both been enormous box-office hits in France, where their critical reception has been interesting. Malle's film is considered his chef-d'oeuvre and also his most controversial. (In one issue Le Monde called it a masterpiece and in another not long afterward took it severely to task for dealing only with the collaborationists and not with the Resistance.) Drach's film, also considered his best to date, was the official French entry in the 1974 Cannes festival, where Marie-Josée Nat won the Best Actress award; yet here and abroad it has been called by some critics too charming or too sweetly nostalgic about a terrible time.

Although Les Violons du Bal is about a terrible time in the lives of a family of French Jews fleeing from occupied France, the child who remembers the time is remembering not the political terror, which he was almost too young to grasp fully, but his family --a warm, loving, wonderful family. They were handsome and charming people, and despite the desperate situation in which they were caught, they did escape, they did survive. Is this a fairytale, as some have called it? Or is Les Violons du Bal a valid picture, made with grace and tenderness, of the boy's experiences? Is it too much to believe, for instance, in the totally lovable, almost magical mother he conjures up from childhood?

Michel Drach's feature is a film-within-a-film. First we see, in the present, Michel Drach, playing himself, as a filmmaker who cannot get financial backing for a film about a Jewish family in Nazi-occupied France "in which no one dies"--the story of his own childhood. When he agrees not to play himself and substitutes the star Jean-Louis Trintignant, a backer is found. As the adult Michel, Trintignant will wander around France, revisiting the places where Drach had been during his family's flight. Drach's son, David, will play Michel as a child; his wife, Marie-Josée Nat, will play both herself and the child Michel's mother.

When we are in the past, experiencing it on the child's level, we see it in romantic color (photography by William Lubtchansky); when we are in the present, we see it in cinéma-vérité black and white (photography by Yann Le Masson). The device is not intrusive; we are caught up in a compelling narrative about a beguiling and credible child.

Michel (played by the delightful David) is a very happy child of nine, whose Paris home is a warm, secure, joyous shelter. His mother (Marie-Josée Nat) is beautiful; his grandmother (Gabrielle Doulcet), loving. He has a sister (Nathalie Roussel) and older brother (Christian Rist). But very soon the war becomes more than a game and his home changes. His absent father (in the Resistance) is urging the family to leave Paris for Vichy. Their familiar, lovely things are packed and stored; they are refugees on the road. They try to establish a new home but nothing is the same now. Michel's older brother slips away to England to join their father; his sister, pregnant by a young man whose mother will not sanction his marriage to an "Israelite," returns to Paris. Michel finds out that he is Jewish and that that is not a particularly happy thing to be.

Briefly, the family follows his sister to Paris, but it's too dangerous, and Michel is sent off alone--with a new name--to be cared for in the country. He has plenty of food again, a motherly woman looking after him, and even a "cousin" his own age to play with. (The interlude is reminiscent of the experience of the child in Claude Berri's The Two of Us, also sheltered by a family in the country.) But soon another and much more hazardous adventure begins for Michel. With his mother and grandmother and a small party of men, he is to make an attempt, on foot, to cross the border into Switzerland. Before they reach the frontier they are robbed and abandoned by the men. Ahead of them, Grandmother, hidden in a hearse, is safe on the Swiss side. Behind them is a Nazi patrol. They are among the lucky ones; they make it through the barbed wire and are welcomed by a Swiss guard.

Some have seen in Les Violons no more than its charm, its color, its director's possible romanticizing of himself as a child. (If we grant that Drach is seeing his mother and his boyhood through a mist of love, is there nothing to learn from a man's vision of his best time as his time in his family, even in a time of war?)

Other films have dealt with the suffering of Jewish families, less fortunate than Drach's cultivated and elegant people, also evacuated from their homes and strafed with other refugees on the roads leading south from Paris. Les Violons du Bal gives us insight into a child's efforts to understand events beyond the charmed circle of his home.

Two scenes of special sensitivity are characteristic of the film's quality: his mother explaining to the nine-year-old Michel the difference between a Jew and a Christian; and his grandmother going into a church to pray for Michel's safety and being overcome with joy to find him hiding there.

Also: Family Relationships
Religion

WAR HUNT

United Artists, 1962. 81 mins. b/w. (d) Denis Sanders (sp) Stanford Whitmore (ph) Ted McCord (c) John Saxon, Robert Redford, Charles Aidman, Tommy Matsuda. (UAS)

In many films we have met children who turn against the soldiers invading their land. In War Hunt, the child is marred for life when he makes a hero of one of the soldiers in his country.

Tommy Matsuda plays Charlie, an eight-year-old Korean war orphan. He becomes the mascot of an American unit. His closest friend is Private Endore (John Saxon). At first Endore's captain calls him a "valuable man." But Endore soon develops into a psychopathic killer who goes on voluntary intelligence missions to satisfy his blood lust. After knifing enemy guards, he performs a dance over the corpses.

Another American soldier, Private Loomis (Robert Redford), who is appalled by Endore's influence over Charlie, struggles with Endore to gain the boy's favor. When the cease-fire comes, Endore refuses to obey it and attacks his own side. The captain (Charles Aidman) shoots him. The Korean child looks at his hero's dead body, and runs away.

Understated and excellently acted, War Hunt leaves one with a vivid understanding of one of the civilian casualties of war, the small boy who becomes attached to the psychotic soldier.

An ironic comment on the film's theme is made at the very beginning, in the title design. Close-ups of quivering reeds are accompanied by the sweet voices of a children's choir singing a pastoral Korean chant.

THE WAR OF THE BUTTONS (LA GUERRE DES BOUTONS)

France, 1962. 92 mins. b/w. (d) Yves Robert (sp) François Boyer, from the novel by Louis Pergaud (ph) André Bac (m) José Bergmans (c) Martin Lartigue, Jacques Dufilho, Jean Richard, André Treton, Michel Isella. French dialog with English subtitles by Noelle Gillmor. (MAC)

Based on Generals Without Buttons (1938), this is one of the rare remakes to achieve distinction (Le Prix Jean Vigo) and great popularity.

The story of a feud between the boys of two neighboring villages in the French countryside, it is fun for its own sake, with satirical meaning, for those who choose, about the start and finish of adult wars.

The war of the buttons starts with a shouted insult, escalates to pitched battles (buttons are the spoils that go to the victor, and each prisoner is stripped of his clothing), and ends with no true victory for either side, since the rival leaders are sent to the same reform school. (The feud really is ended when the parents of both towns, disgusted by all the trouble the kids are making, call a halt.)

One of the most amusing scenes in the movie occurs when one side launches a surprise attack in which they wear no clothes at all--and the surprise crumbles the enemy.

Whatever moral about warfare is to be gleaned from The War of the Buttons, it is undeniably an amusing and accurate picture about a hundred boys raising hell across the farmlands. If you understand French, you'll catch some words, in the heat of battle, which schoolboys chalk up on fences.

DELINQUENCY AND CRIME

BAD BOYS (FURYO SHONEN)

Japan, 1960. 90 mins. b/w. (d) (sp) Susumu Hani (ph) Mitsuji Kanau (m) Toru Takemitsu (c) Yukio Amada, Hirokazu Yoshitake, Koichiro Yamazaki, Masayuki Ito. Japanese dialog with English subtitles. (MAC)

Susumu Hani (Children Who Draw, She and He) was inspired to make Bad Boys by the book Pinioned Wings, a graphic confessional by some of the inmates of a reform school in Kurihama, near Tokyo Bay, which reflected the restlessness of city boys who stumble into crime.

The film is semidocumentary. Shooting in such actual haunts of juvenile delinquents as Asakusa and the Ginza in downtown Tokyo, with no formal script, Hani presented the basic dramatic situations to his cast, all non-professionals, former reform school pupils. He encouraged them to give free expression to their feelings. The improvisation works; we get true and often unexpected glimpses of street and reformatory life.

We follow Asai (Yukio Amada), seventeen and homeless, in the year he spends in reform school. He has been picked up on suspicion of robbery. Learning that the reformatory society is run on the gangster system, he rebels, but is punished by the inmate gang. Transferred to a woodworking course, he does very well and makes friends. Released on probation with 320 yen, Asai shouts farewell to the deserted porch of the reformatory. He is clearly ready for a different life; he has left his childhood behind.

The grandson of Motoko Hani, the famous woman educator of Japan, Susumu Hani has given us a film with many insights about bad boys. Whether the pupils of the Akehama Reformatory are down at the shore yelling at the ships passing their prison, or exchanging confidences in the workshop, they are real young people on whom we seem to be eavesdropping.

BAD COMPANY

Paramount, 1972. 94 mins. col. (d) Robert Benton (sp) David Newman, Robert Benton (ph) Gordon Willis (m) Harvey Schnidt (c) Jeff Bridges, Barry Brown, Jerry Houser, Joshua Hill Lewis, Damon Cofer, David Huddleston, Jim Davis, John Savage. (FNC)

Teenage Drew Dixon's journal, used as a commentary for Bad Company, has this early entry: "I had fallen in with some rough types, but I will always keep to the straight and narrow, so help me God. It is still a sunny day."

But Drew (Barry Brown) cons, steals, and finally kills. The movie--written by Robert Benton and David Newman, authors of Bonnie and Clyde--tells us how his virtue is gradually eroded.

In 1863, Drew is one of the young draft dodgers hunted by the Union Army for refusing to fight in the Civil War. He has been hidden by his strict Methodist parents, who give him $100 and their consent to flee from conscription. With his dead older brother's watch, Drew makes his way to Missouri en route to Virginia City. On the Missouri frontier, he is mugged by Jake Rumsey (Jeff Bridges), a petty thief of his own age, and is persuaded by him to join a gang of scruffy adolescent runaways, ranging in age from eleven-year-old Boog (Joshua Hill Lewis) to eighteen-year-old Jake. They set out to make their fortunes in the golden West.

But it's harder than they thought. Not all of them make it. Those who do manage to last go along with the rugged amorality of Jake, who has learned survival tactics in a tougher school than any of these basically naive kids have known.

A friendship grows between Jake and Drew, based partly on liking and partly on curiosity about their different backgrounds and values. Jake tells Drew, "I'm the crook and you're the liar."

Drew's pious maxims do not go very deep. The farther West they travel, hounded by a band of renegades under Big Joe (David Huddleston), sold a farmer's wife by the farmer himself for an introduction to sex, double-crossed by one another and by various frontier types, the easier it becomes for the good young man to adopt the lawless ways of the country and the times.

By the film's end, Drew is robbing banks and shooting hombres as efficiently as Jake. They are the only ones left of the original group of boys.

Very well directed by Robert Benton, the movie has considerable humor as well as its violent action photographed on the Kansas plains. It makes no moral comment; its characters are free from self-scrutiny; Jake is incorrigible and Drew is corruptible--a kind of myth of the West again, except that the heroes are kids in their teens.

Is it real, is it true? "It doesn't matter how it really was; nobody knows anyway," Benton said to an interviewer.

Bad Company can best be taken as British critic Tom Milne took it: "Horatio Alger mocked by Mark Twain."

Also: Finding Oneself

BADLANDS

Warners, 1974. 95 mins. col. (prod) (d) (sp) Terrence Malick (ph) Brian Probyn, Tak Fujimoto, Stevan Larner (m) George Tipton (c) Martin Sheen, Sissy Spacek, Warren Oates, Ramon Bieri, John Carter. (SWA)

In 1958 a real mass killer, Charles Starkweather, nineteen, and his girl, Carol Ann Fugate, fourteen, left a trail of murders across the Dakota Badlands. Starkweather was executed and the girl got life. (She is now out of prison.)

The very gifted filmmaker Terrence Malick has written and directed a version of their story, changing the boy's age to twenty-five and the girl's to fifteen. The killer is executed; his girl (an innocent victim, Malick implies) gets off free. The badlands through which we follow this fascinating, terrifying, and essentially enigmatic pair are their personal badlands of existential alienation. They move into violence, in and out of love, like affectless figures in a modern drama of amorality. We feel that everything they do takes place in an airless space--the vacuum of our times, perhaps Malick is saying. (The story presumably is set in 1960 in a South Dakota town, but it could be today, anywhere. And, as other commentators have noted, Badlands, unlike the movies it somewhat resembles--Bonnie and Clyde, Breathless, Thieves Like Us--does not comfort us with its glamor or nostalgia of the past; it is really now.)

The film is narrated by Holly (Sissy Spacek) in her empty little voice. Holly's weltanschauung is derived from Teen Romance and the fan magazines. Holly is a very bored motherless high school kid who has a strict father (Warren Oates). She's a sitting duck for the jobless, shiftless Kit (Martin Sheen), who falls for her. (He's a former garbage collector.) When Holly's father tries to prevent her from running off with Kit, Kit kills him and burns down the house.

Seemingly unmoved by her lover's slaying of her father, as she was unmoved by her father's slaying of her dog, Holly escapes with Kit to the forest and for a while acts out an idyll with him. He seems to be James Dean for her; she seems to be an audience and prop for him. It doesn't last more than a couple of weeks.

And while the "love" relationship lasts, it is frightening in its lack of sensibility. After Holly's sex initiation in the bushes, this bobby-soxer asks the man, "Did it go the way it's supposed to?" and when he answers, "Yeah," she asks, "Is that all there is to it?" "Yeah." "Gosh, what was everybody talking about?" "Don't ask me!"

Because he feels so little, Kit thinks of crunching their hands with a rock to make their experience memorable, but this idea falls of its own weight. (Holly objects that it would hurt.)

So much for romance. The rest of their adventure is just about as meaningless and easily dismissed by Holly. "I sat in the car and read my maps and spelled out entire sentences with my tongue on the roof of my mouth, where nobody could read them." (They have escaped from the forest, where they were discovered, and Kit had to kill a number of the posse. In their travels, they leave a trail of more murders.) Eventually, after they have driven across the Badlands in a stolen Cadillac, Kit lets himself be captured. (Holly has become completely estranged from him by this time; she's tired of playing the game.)

At no point does this fifteen-year-old show emotion for one of Kit's victims. This child, who says at one point that she would "never again hang out with a hell-bent type, no matter how much I was in love with him," is unexplained by writer-director Malick. There is no blame placed on her parents or society. What has made Holly is anyone's guess--and the psyche of this adolescent is worth guessing about, because for one reason or another, in one way or another, it keeps cropping up in our contemporary films.

But *this* alienated nonheroine is fifteen!

Badlands is a disturbing movie, as well as a movie so interestingly photographed and conceived that it promises well for Malick's future.

Also: Love and Sex

THE BAD SEED, see p. 290

THE BLACKBOARD JUNGLE, see p. 170

BORN INNOCENT

Tomorrow Entertainment (CBS-TV), 1974. 92 mins. col. (d) Donald Wrye (sp) Gerald DiPego, suggested by the book by Creighton Brown Burnham (c) Linda Blair, Joanna Miles, Kim Hunter, Richard Jaeckel. (LCA)

If Linda Blair is as hair-raising in Born Innocent as she was in The Exorcist, it is because she is the victim of a system of juvenile justice indicted in harrowing detail. As originally presented on NBC-TV, Born Innocent is the ordeal of a girl of fourteen who is placed by uncaring parents in a very tough detention home.

She has an alcoholic mother (Kim Hunter) who doesn't want her, and a father (Richard Jaeckel), a mechanic, who can make nothing of her. Chris (Linda Blair) runs away six times in two years. When her parents decide to make her a ward of the state, she is thrust through the courts and jail and placed in a juvenile detention home where the authorities don't seem to know what's going on.

After being made to submit to an intimate physical examination, the little girl, who is relatively innocent and a virgin, is put into a dormitory with a range of offenders including girls who were on drugs at nine and prostitutes at ten or eleven. The transformation of Chris's personality, her suffering, and the disintegration of her innocence, are brutally spelled out.

Joanna Miles plays a sensitive teacher, and Linda Blair is hard to fault as Chris. Born Innocent could lead to a closer and less melodramatic look, by students of our juvenile delinquency laws, at an important subject.

Also: Family Relationships
Special Children

BOY

Japan, 1969. 97 mins. col. (d) Nagisa Oshima (sp) Tsutomu Tamura (ph) Yasuhiro Yoshioka, Seizo Sengen (m) Hikaru Hayashi (c) Fumio Watanabe, Tetsuo Abe, Akiko Koyama, Tsuyoshi Kinoshita. Japanese dialog with English subtitles. (GRO)

Based on an incident which took place in Japan in 1966, the story of Boy is simple; a ten-year-old is taught by his parents to run into moving cars so that they can extort money for damages from the drivers. After pulling the trick all over the country, they are arrested.

But Oshima's superb film is not simple; it is deeply penetrating. Director and critics agree that it has social emphasis and symbolism.

"Besides saying something about a specific environment," wrote Harold Clurman in The Nation, "it leads us to know something about family feeling even in the absence of family, and about the tenderness even in degraded folk."

The boy is isolated from school, other children, and grandparents, in his own outlaw family: his father, wounded in war (Fumio Watanabe); his passive and unthinking stepmother, orphaned and raised by foster families (Akiko Koyama); his little brother (Tsuyoshi Kinoshita).

The ten-year-old's character is drawn beautifully, without any of the bid for sympathy for the mistreated child. The picture begins with the boy (Tetsuo Abe) playing hide and seek by himself, unaffectedly. With seeming matter-of-factness, he accepts his parents' instructions and is soon throwing himself in front of car after car. ("Work is work," says his father, who doesn't work.) We recognize a child's adaptation to the outrages perpetrated by his elders or by society. But the boy is not really stoical. He runs away to another town. (It only reinforces his loneliness.) He'd like to visit the country village where his grandmother lives, but who has the fare? He gets as far as a seaside resort and cries himself to sleep on the beach.

Later on, in the far North, during a family quarrel, the boy witnesses a real accident in the snow, a car wreck in which a girl is killed. The parents run away, but he stays. He is afraid that somehow he is responsible.

In the climax of the film, the boy sees a snow figure and tells his little brother he'd like to be a snowman from outer space, "invulnerable and fearless," with no mother or father, but he can't because he's just an ordinary boy. He attacks the figure and destroys it. Then, in an immensely moving sequence, he sits remembering the face of the dead child in the snow.

"Though I have taken an objective view," director Oshima has said, "I have also made the film as a prayer, as is the boy's tear in the final scene, for all human beings who find it necessary to live in a like manner."

Oshima has also explained his use of symbols in Boy: the Japanese flag with a black sun as a mark of the need for revolt against the state of things in his country; the boy's mother as an archetype of too-passive Japanese womanhood; the boy's silence during the police questioning as a statement that his society has not permitted him any alternative. The boy's feeling of guilt comes from inner direction, his memory of the child's death in the snow.

Exceptionally interesting for its child psychology, Boy also has a distinctive film style. Its complete convincingness, the air of reality it never loses, comes from Oshima's lifelike lapses in continuity, his open-ended sequences, and the brilliant color shots of modern Japan by cinematographers Yasuhiro Yoshioka and Seizo Sengen.

Also: Family Relationships

A CLOCKWORK ORANGE, see p. 271

THE COOL WORLD, see p. 293

DEAD END

United Artists, 1937. 92 mins. b/w. (d) William Wyler (sp) Lillian Hellman, based on the play by Sidney Kingsley (ph) Gregg Toland (art) Richard Day (m) Alfred Newman (c) Sylvia Sidney, Joel McCrea, Humphrey Bogart, Wendy Barrie, Claire Trevor, Allen Jenkins, Marjorie Main, Ward Bond, Gabriel Dell, Billy Halop, Leo Gorcey, Huntz Hall, Bobby Jordan, Richard Punsley, Minor Watson, Elizabeth Risdon. (AIM, BUD, MAC, TWY, WCF)

Because the critical and popular success of Dead End brought so many imitators, some serious and many more exploitative, it suffers a great deal on re-viewing. But it was a seminal film; it spawned the archetypal image of slum kids who graduate to the list of Ten Most Wanted Men. In the first screen appearance of The Dead End Kids--Gabriel Dell, Billy Halop, Leo Gorcey, Huntz Hall, Bobby Jordan, Richard Punsley--we see the inspiration for innumerable screen dramas about youngsters walking the avenue of good and evil and being pulled over to one side or the other by adult role models. The Dead End Kids followed the 1937 hit with Angels with Dirty Faces (1938), Crime School (1938), Angels Wash Their Faces (1939), and Hell's Kitchen (1939). Later on, the ensemble went on to star in countless comedy films of their own, as The Eastside Kids and The Bowery Boys.

The 1937 Goldwyn/United Artists publicity claimed that the six boys had all been found in the streets before being cast in the stage play which preceded the movie. Actually, they were all professional child actors. They were able to persuade audiences, however, that they bore the true marks of the gutter--in Dead End, if not in the comedy-series concoctions.

The theme of Sidney Kingsley's play, that crime-breeding slums recycle succeeding generations into vicious gangs, is well served by Lillian Hellman's screenplay and William Wyler's direction. Extremely effective is the multiple set designed by Richard Day, who had worked with Stroheim. Wyler had planned to shoot the film on location in a New York slum, but Goldwyn insisted on the use of studio sets. Day's set, photographed by Gregg Toland--the teeming slum at the edge of the East River, backdoor to a luxury apartment house--underscores the drama of social contrasts.

Kingsley's message is emphasized by the fact that the two men who represent the forces of good and evil battling for the kids--the aspiring architect (Joel McCrea) and the notorious gangster, "Baby Face" Martin (Humphrey Bogart)--are boyhood friends, both born in the slum. "Baby Face" has returned after ten years, unrepentant and unreformed; he represents the future of the Dead End kids, the story tells us, unless some social changes can be made in their environment.

Dead End has excellent performances; the six boys are as tough as the thirties had seen on celluloid, and "Baby Face" Martin is vintage Bogart. There is a remarkable scene in which Marjorie Main, as the gangster's bitter mother, excoriates her son. (The scene between Bonnie and her mother in Penn's Bonnie and Clyde is somewhat reminiscent of it.)

So many contemporary portraits of slum kids owe so much to Dead End that the original is worth taking a look at.

Also: From Literature

THE 400 BLOWS (LES QUATRE CENTS COUPS)

France, 1959. 98 mins b/w. (d) François Truffaut (sp) François Truffaut, helped with dialog by Marcel Moussy (ph) Henri Decae (m) Jean Constantin (c) Jean-Pierre Léaud, Patrick Auffay, Claire Maurier, Albert Rémy, Guy Decomble, Georges Flamant. Guest appearances: Jeanne Moreau, Jean-Claude Brialy. French dialog with English subtitles. (MAC)

Since his first feature won the director's prize at Cannes in 1959, François Truffaut has grown into one of the treasures of world cinema, and Jean-Pierre Léaud, who played his twelve-year-old Antoine Doinel, has grown up in Truffaut's films. A fascinating work, The 400 Blows improves with re-viewing; Truffaut's and Léaud's portrait of a living, breathing adolescent is undimmed.

Antoine Doinel is really Truffaut; the scenario is based on Truffaut's own childhood and experience in reform school. The title of the film can be translated, roughly, as "the school of hard knocks." Young Antoine has no snap course.

What propels Antoine from a Paris tenement into delinquency and reform school? The artist Truffaut offers no pat answer, only human beings going from day to day. The boy is no angel, the adults no monsters; like most of us, they are crawling between heaven and earth.

"I despair of teaching the ordinary parent how to handle his child," said B. F. Skinner--and Antoine's parents, who care for him less than most, handle him with little understanding. He is illegitimate and his mother (Claire Maurier) finds him a nuisance in her marriage to Doinel (Albert Rémy). Although he is a good-natured man, Doinel isn't happy with the way things are in his home. Antoine, whom he'd like to treat as his son, gives him cause for anxiety; he's doing badly at school. The teacher (Guy Decomble) is as insensitive as Doinel.

The boy catches his mother cheating on Doinel with her lover and knows she is indifferent to everything but her own pleasure. He plays hookey with his pal, René (Patrick Auffay). His excuse, that his mother has died, blows up in his face when both parents storm into the classroom. Afraid to go home, he hides out at René's and begins a life of petty thievery, roaming around Paris. Finally, he is caught trying to return a typewriter that he has stolen from Doinel's office and is jailed with adult criminals and prostitutes. Because his parents say they cannot cope with him, he is sent to reform school. His mother visits him and assails him for causing Doinel to lose his job. Desperate in the highly regimented institution, he seizes a chance to escape and runs away. He gets as far as the edge of the sea, the guards pursuing him; he pauses, feet in the water, and turns to face us. There is nowhere to go.

This final, famous "freeze shot" of Antoine is a coarsened still photograph, like the image on a Wanted poster or in a newspaper case history. It is directed at the viewer; it is the viewer who is haunted by the boy, responsible for him.

This twelve-year-old is remarkable, yet very true to adolescence. Treated like a child when he is no longer a child and like an adult (in jail, for instance) when he is not yet an adult, he takes off on his own. He lives a cool, independent existence. He suffers, but does not trust adults enough to explain or to plead. He alternately breaks our heart and stirs us to laughter. For The 400 Blows has its lighter scenes. When he goes to the movies and sits between his parents, for a moment he is a loved and smiling child and not the little troubled "old child" he is throughout most of the film. And there are also some very funny scenes; the gym class trailing behind the teacher on an outing and dropping away one by one; the pupil in class blotting his notebook pages and having to tear them all out.

The tragedy begins with the boy's arrest. Antoine's face, as he peers from behind the bars of the police wagon, the tears shining in his eyes, is one of the great speechless outcries of cinema. After his arrival at the police station, there is another famous Truffaut sequence, the interview with the psychiatrist. Facing the camera in a close shot, "telling all" (yes, even about sex) in man-to-man fashion, the boy is self-revealing within the frame. Later, in the mobile camera work of his run to the sea, we sense his flight to free himself from his whole life.

Despite the fact that the preoccupations of Antoine are no purer than those of other adolescent boys--for Truffaut does not sentimentalize his memory of himself--he is more honest than the adults who betray him as well as each other. For whose good do his parents take him to the police, for what reason does his mother reject him in reform school? When he lies in bed listening to his parents quarrel, or sees through his mother's self-serving attempt to be nice to him, he has the look of every sharp youngster who has learned about "Them": unsurprised. "This is the way 'They' are."

Every detail in The 400 Blows helps us to feel affinity with Antoine Doinel, at twelve years a complete individual. This superb film is rich in insight, young Jean-Pierre Léaud's as well as Truffaut's.

Also: Family Relationships
Generation Conflicts

GO ASK ALICE

Metromedia (ABC-TV), 1973. 74 mins. col. (d) John Korty (sp) Ellen Violett (ph) Earl Rath (c) William Shatner, Jamie Smith-Jackson, Jennifer Edwards, Mimi Saffian, Ann Ryman, Ruth Roman, Andy Griffith. (SWA, TWY, WCF, WHO)

Well directed by John Korty for television, this is a strong picture of the youthful drug culture. It is based on the real diary of a fifteen-year-old drug pusher which was published by permission of the girl's parents after she was found dead of an overdose. The title is taken from Grace Slick's song "White Rabbit," from "Surrealistic Pillow" (recorded by the Jefferson Airplane), in which Alice in Drugland pops pills and sees rabbits ten feet tall.

Alice (Jamie Smith-Jackson) moves with her family to a suburban town where her father will be dean of political science at the university. Mousey and shy, she makes only one friend, Beth, also a wallflower but, unlike Alice, "super cool about not being popular." When Beth is away, Alice goes to a party where her soft drink is spiked with LSD. For the first time in her life, she feels beautiful, free, and uninhibited.

When Beth returns, Alice is hooked and is one of the "heads" in her high school, with an addict lover who makes her push speed to grade-school kids. As a result, her younger brother learns more about Alice than her nice, blind parents do.

The film shows her rapid deterioration--running away, sleeping in parks from Texas to California, taking to prostitution with even younger girls, searching for the "perfect drug." Ill and despairing, she is told by a priest (Andy Griffith) in a church center for battered youth that her diary is what makes her different from others. He convinces her to go home.

Back at school, she is considered a "fink" by the speed freaks because she has gone over to the straight kids. The "heads" harass her and dose her again with LSD when she is baby-sitting; she winds up in a hospital with severe mental and physical injuries. An understanding doctor (Ruth Roman), private counseling, and group therapy seem to be hastening her rehabilitation. She returns to school and a potential boyfriend; her parents are supportive. And then, says an off-screen voice, Alice is dead of a drug overdose several weeks later.

The Alice of the real diary is more disturbed, more contradictory, more deeply given to street language and sexual degradation in the period away from home than the Alice of the film. The television script is considerably more structured. While this has reduced some of the characters, like the parents, to stereotypes, it has not weakened the underlying force of the material. John Korty leaves one with disturbing images of the progress of a nice girl to degeneracy and death. A typically effective scene is the one in which Alice and her friends are getting zonked at her birthday party while her folks are fussing with the birthday cake.

Also: From Literature
Generation Conflicts

HENRY, BOY OF THE BARRIO

U. S., 1970. 30 mins. b/w. (d) Bernard S. Selling. (ATL)

"Henry is too old to shine shoes and too young to get a job," says the narrator of this documentary. At fourteen Henry is not too young to be arrested for stealing a car; he has already been picked up for shoplifting.

Filmed over a period of two years, Henry's twelfth to fourteenth years, this cinéma-vérité short (musical score added) is neither novel nor remarkably well done, but its force comes from the boy's own words. He tells it the way it's been for him in his wretched ghetto home near the railroad yards, how he feels about losing his father, about having a mother who drinks and has a lot of men, about having a brother home from prison; about the law, and the Welfare, and school. Even about one good time "on the outside," when he went sailing.

Henry is Mexican-American, his mother is Indian, his environment Anglo urban slum. When he looks for his father's grave in the cemetery, he is looking for his own life. He started to drop out when he was twelve. Listen to Henry; his other name is legion. His speech is sometimes indistinct, but he gets through.

Also: Cultural Conflicts
Family Relationships

THE JUNGLE

U. S., 1967. 22 mins. b/w. (CHA)

Described as a sociological experiment, this documentary film was conceived and photographed by the 12th and Oxford Street Gang of Philadelphia. According to the distributor, its production initiated a major change in the life style of the members of the gang.

The teenage actor-gang members tell us how they feel about their lives and their environment--the loyalties, the violence, the gang wars, the drinking, and sense of aimlessness.

The Jungle is a contribution to our understanding of black ghetto youth. They give us their own point of view. The scenes of gang violence are harsh and effectively photographed; the "actors' " comments are revealing.

JUVENILE COURT

U. S., 1973. 144 mins. b/w. (prod) (ed) Frederick Wiseman (ph) William Brayne (asst. ph) Oliver Kool. (ZPH)

The seventh film of documentary filmmaker Frederick Wiseman (High School, Hospital, Basic Training, Law and Order, Essene, The Cool World) is again what he calls a "voyage of discovery" into a contemporary institution and, by indirection, into American society.

With his cameraman, William Brayne, Wiseman spent more than a month in Juvenile Court 616, Police City of Memphis, Tennessee, shooting more than sixty hours (about 125, 000 feet) of day-to-day episodes in the treatment of juvenile offenders, from their arrests and initial processing to the final disposition of their cases.

He later edited this footage to the final 144 minutes of Juvenile Court. This four percent, of course, is not objective but selective.

"Even though the audience is aware of my own point of view," Wiseman has said, "I try to present the material so that viewers can develop their own. It's pompous to suggest that film can provide solutions or will contribute to social change, but a film can provide information which might, in an undefined way, help in the development of new approaches to the issues the film presents. I try to make the final film reflect the complexity of the subject."

In Juvenile Court, he has tried to use a variety of situations and people to show us the problems of the court system from the vantage point of the judge, the social workers, and the lawyers, as well as the under-eighteen offenders who are the accused.

The film has no narration, no explanation, no identification of individuals by function or name. But the central figure in Juvenile Court is Kenneth A. Turner, a compassionate man; he is seen in the courtroom (where he judges 17, 000 complaints a year) and in his chambers, with the parents, parole officers, psychiatrists, et al, and with the young people whom he is counseling.

What comes through, in all this, is that a humane effort is being made to serve the interests of children who are delinquent or who have been victimized, although the juvenile court is operating in a maze of uncertainty. Decisions are made on the thinnest evidence. Though a young person's life hinges on their determinations, the well-meaning judge, social workers, and psychiatrists seem as far from certainty as the kids or their often uncomprehending parents.

Who are the children? A bespectacled fifteen-year-old white boy accused of sexually molesting a girl for whom he had been baby-sitting; a pimply young junkie; a pretty, blonde would-be suicide who had once charged her stepfather with making indecent advances but now cries to go home; a tiny black boy whose uncle poured hot grease on him; children accused of shoplifting, vagrancy, prostitution, possession of firearms, drug stealing. One case only is followed to its climax; a white, middle-class boy just short of eighteen, involved with an older boy in an armed robbery.

There are scenes of searing insight. The mother of the child whom the fifteen-year-old is accused of molesting is revealed in Judge Turner's chambers as sexually obsessed. The boy is given a lie-detector test. We do not learn the outcome of the case. Wiseman seems to say: you have heard these people speak for themselves; you judge.

Viewers of Juvenile Court are asked to be more than passive spectators. Swift camera movements--from a counselor's diatribe against prostitution to an intense close-up of the defendant; from the lawyers' plea bargaining to the children's reactions--underline the point that lives are being judged and being shaped. What is the viewer's reaction, according to his own values and prejudices?

Juvenile Court can awaken anyone to a vital aspect of the life of many of our children. A boy is seen telephoning: "If you love me, you want to come up here and get me out 'cause I ain't done nothing." What has he done, what are these people trying to do for him? Looking at him, in this documentary, you too must care.

THE LONELINESS OF THE LONG DISTANCE RUNNER

Great Britain, 1962. 103 mins. b/w. (d) Tony Richardson (sp)

Alan Sillitoe, adapted from his short story (ph) Walter Lassally (m) John Addison (c) Tom Courtenay, Michael Redgrave, Avis Bunnage, James Bolam. (GEN)

Eighteen-year-old Colin Smith (Tom Courtenay) is a Borstal Boy, who is in a reform school for robbing a bakery. He is a hardened, working-class adolescent from a Midlands slum. For most of Alan Sillitoe's story, he ticks away, and then he goes off like a time bomb. That final explosion of contempt for society, for the adult who represents its standards, is evidently echoed in the resentful breasts of a great many angry youngsters, for The Loneliness of the Long Distance Runner is one of their favorite films.

If there is a hero in the story, it is the eighteen-year-old. The adults are all sick, adulterous, sadistic, ignorant, superstitious, incompetent, or hypocritical. Nothing is the young man's fault. The world he never made is deemed responsible for his condition. His definitive act, most sympathetically presented, is his independent, symbolic thumbing of his nose at (choose one) the Establishment, the Bosses, the Governor.

The metaphor of the film is the running of a race. In the reformatory where Colin is sent, the pompous Governor (Michael Redgrave) believes in the rehabilitative power of physical activities. He decides to train Colin--a rebellious inmate with some distinction as a long-distance runner--to win a forthcoming match with a prominent public school. On the day of the race, Colin easily outdistances his rivals, but in sight of victory, he stops dead at the grandstand, and with a mocking bow, allows the others to pass him over the finish line. He smiles at the Governor; he has refused to yield to the authority he despises.

This is a rigged story, but it is most effectively filmed. Director Tony Richardson gives us a forceful drama on two levels simultaneously: Colin's career in the reform school and flashbacks of his family life before his crime. The climax brings both to a head. Tom Courtenay, a superb young actor, makes the film.

Specious as the character is (he refuses a job because he doesn't want Them to profit from his labor, steals so he can have money for fun, and of course blames Them for punishing him), Colin's hard-bitten delinquent boy is convincing enough, as are the smug Governor and the Borstal teachers and guards.

Avis Bunnage is excellent as his mother, whose extravagance, bad temper, and illicit sex have contributed to Colin's family experience.

The importance of The Loneliness of the Long Distance Runner is not so much in what it tells us of Colin, perhaps, as in what it tells us of other boys and girls, not from the slums and not in reform schools, who have made him a hero in the war of the generations.

Also: From Literature
Generation Conflicts
Teachers and Schools

LORDS OF FLATBUSH, see p. 21

ME (NAKED CHILDHOOD), see p. 119

MILES TO GO BEFORE I SLEEP, see p. 120

NOBODY WAVED GOODBYE, see p. 122

111TH STREET

U. S., 1962. 32 mins. b/w. (prod) (d) (sp) (ph) Arnold Federbush (m) Frank Cohen (c) Bob Rothenberg, Vic Purcell, Ellie Bovelle, The Angels. (MAC)

If the parents aren't around, says the social worker in this semi-documentary film about a teenage gang in the high-delinquency area on New York's upper East Side, the kids have to create a civilization all their own.

The Angels (played by themselves) want to look big, be big, take part in the jungle life of a big gang. The only source of identity any of them know is bigness, achieved by violent or criminal means, in the destructive environment of the inner city.

Other goals, education, middle-class values, are meaningless to them. They do not believe the youth worker who tells them he wants to help them; they kid him and try to fight or are simply indifferent. After repeated failures to make contact with The Angels, the social worker (Bob Rothenberg) achieves only a minor breakthrough.

Filmed in cooperation with the New York City Youth Board, 111th Street throws light on the very complex problem of juvenile delinquency and suggests one approach to its solution. It is not strong in dialog or production values, but its basic honesty and the uncolored reactions of The Angels make it a contribution to understanding and a jumping-off point for discussion.

THE QUIET ONE

Mayer-Burstyn, 1948. 67 mins. b/w. (d) Sidney Meyers (sp) Helen Levitt, Janice Loeb, Sidney Meyers (ph) Richard Bagley (c) Donald

Thompson, Clarence Cooper, Sadie Stockton, Estelle Evans, Paul Baucum, Sidney Meyers, the staff and boys of the Wiltwyck School. Commentary written by James Agee, spoken by Gary Merrill (m) Ulysses Kay. (GEN)

The Quiet One is a milestone documentary, still one of the most perceptive and eloquent studies of a boy's delinquency.

Donald Peters (Donald Thompson) is the quiet one. He is ten years old and black, has never known a father, has a mother who rejects him, and a grandmother (with whom he lives) who is disgusted with him. Like the young Jude in Thomas Hardy's Jude the Obscure, Donald feels his existence to be an undemanded one. Like that other unloved boy, Donald would have said, if he had any words,

> As you got older and felt yourself to be at the center of your time, and not at a point in its circumference, as you felt when you were little, you were seized with a sort of shuddering.... All around you there seemed to be something garish, glaring, rattling, and the noises and glares hit upon the small cell called your life, and shook it, and scorched it.

Donald wanders alone through the streets of Harlem, spending the long days in the alleys and tenements, skipping school, sleeping out--giving us an unforgettable image of that small cell seized with a sort of shuddering.

In its power to make us see the boy's private world and to evoke compassion for his misery, The Quiet One is reminiscent of those very great films about children, Poil de Carotte or La Maternelle. There are the same symbols of the feeling of rejection. The boy in Poil de Carotte, driving along a road and passing a happy family, whips his horse in a frenzy of loneliness and pain. The boy in The Quiet One, walking through a tunnel in the park and passing a solicitous mother and her little girl, bitterly mimics the girl's "Ma-ma, ma-ma" until his voice taunts him with its own reverberations.

Moments in the film sear us as they sear him. At home with Grandma--a home he hates so much he seldom returns to it even to sleep; a grandma who wishes she need never claim him again in Children's Court or look on his "mean, mopey, sassy little face" any more--he gets a beating and then swallows his breakfast, all in silence. "And that's how a day begins," says James Agee's commentary, which is everything a commentary should be. "The same old helpless fury, and rage and fear and hatred.... And the sick quiet that follows violence and duty without love."

When Donald returns briefly to school, he is so far behind that he fails. When he tries to buy his friends, he also fails. He turns wildly into and against himself, ashamed and self-hating; he strikes himself, smears cold cream across his face in the mirror, tears up beds, destroys property, steals.

The first half of the film explains the experiences which bring him, another delinquent child, to Wiltwyck School; the second half (which involves his Wiltwyck counselor, Clarence, and the school psychiatrist who narrates it) explains the painful first steps by which he is helped to heal himself. The problem is never oversimplified. He retreats completely into his shell at first. He has severe learning problems. He is jealous of any sign that his counselor is not utterly interested in him alone. Before he makes his final decision to remain at Wiltwyck, he runs away.

Everything in The Quiet One is significant; every visual detail takes us into Donald's heart and mind. "Circumstances have deformed them," says Agee's commentary about boys like Donald. The unrelenting camera eye shows us these circumstances--the ghetto streets, the bitter home, the weary people--and the other circumstances, Wiltwyck School or its like, which nurture rehabilitation.

Made on a shoestring by its highly gifted creators (Sidney Meyers, Richard Bagley, Helen Levitt, and Janice Loeb); with a sensitive score by Ulysses Kay; with Agee's superb commentary; and with good playing by some members of the American Negro Theatre and some nonprofessionals (including Donald Thompson and the boys and staff of the Wiltwyck School), The Quiet One is a rare film. Compared with the Hollywood clichés of the Dead End Kids, Donald is the prototype par excellence of the child of the slum, starved for understanding and love.

Also: Family Relationships
Finding Oneself
Teachers and Schools

REBEL WITHOUT A CAUSE, see p. 125

THE ROAD TO LIFE, see p. 190

SHOESHINE, see p. 223

SHOTGUN JOE

U.S., 1969. 25 mins. col. (d) Eric Camiel. (JAS)

Joe Scanlon, sixteen, is serving a nine-month term in Cheshire Reformatory, Connecticut. The camera follows him around, as he works in the kitchen, disrupts a class, raps with the filmmaker in his cell. He has a chip on his shoulder; his bravado seems forced.

"He's intelligent," say some reformatory caseworkers, "but his brashness is aimed in the wrong direction.... He has an image he has to defend."

What's inside Joe, who has broken the law, brawled, gotten drunk, is boastful about his shotgun exploits? He tells the interviewer about the sister he loves so fiercely, who loves him; about his pathetic mother. But he ends the interview sharply: "I don't want to talk about this any more."

Joe Scanlon raises more questions than he answers--like any other interesting, complex, deeply troubled adolescent. When he leaves reform school, where will he be headed? Where is he now? Still, this documentary is one of the best of many short films probing into the character and background of teenage rebels against the law. The film was a Golden Eagle prizewinner.

THIEVES LIKE US, see p. 161

THIS CHILD IS RATED X

NBC News, 1971. 53 mins. col. (TWY)

Winner of an Emmy Award for an outstanding news documentary program, this 1971 NBC News White Paper still has much to tell us about the inequities of the children's courts, training schools, and detention facilities in the United States today.

Two types of youngsters are the focus of the documentary: the child who is a truant from a brutal home or from school and the child who is guilty not of such juvenile delinquency but of very serious crime. Because both often are assigned to the same kind of indiscriminate facility, many emerge well schooled in major crime.

This well-substantiated factual presentation of the justice meted out to real children might be an interesting follow-up to a program featuring a classic fiction film like The 400 Blows (q. v.). It is also worth comparing with Frederick Wiseman's documentary about the same system, Juvenile Court (q. v.).

UNMAN, WITTERING, AND ZIGO, see p. 192

WEST SIDE STORY, see p. 139

WILD BOYS OF THE ROAD

Warners, 1933. 68 mins. b/w. (d) William Wellman (sp) Earl Baldwin from a story by Daniel Ahearn (ph) Arthur L. Todd (c) Frankie Darrow, Dorothy Coonan, Edwin Phillips, Rochelle Hudson, Sterling Holloway, Arthur Hohl, Minna Gombell. (UAS)

Although not on a par with Nikolai Ekk's earlier The Road to Life (q. v.), which had much the same theme, this hard-hitting film of Warners' "exposé cycle" in the thirties shows with considerable sympathy how young people during the Depression were forced out into the edge of society to live by their wits.

In Juvenile Court at the end of the film, the judge (sitting under the Blue Eagle of the NRA) wants to send the youthful defendants home. Eddie (Frankie Darrow) explains the plight of two or three hundred thousand like himself, loose on the nation's highways:

> I'll tell you why we can't go home. Because our folks are poor. They can't get jobs, and there isn't enough to eat. What good will it do to send us home to starve? You say you got to send us to jail to send us off the streets. Well, that's a lie! You're sending us to jail 'cause you don't want to see us. You want to forget us. Well, you can't do it. 'Cause I'm not the only one. There's thousands just like me and more hitting the road each day.

We first meet Eddie at Hilldale High's Sophomore Frolic with his pal Tommy (Edwin Phillips). They can't find a job to raise 75¢ for the tickets, and their folks are getting food from the Community Chest. They hit the road for the big city, riding the rods in the search for something better. With Sally (Dorothy Coonan) and other adolescents in the boxcar, they are herded off the train in Chicago ("we haven't got enough jobs for men, let alone kids"). The hope of a home with Sally's Aunt Carrie is shattered when the cops raid her "house."

Rolled off the boxcar again, the kids take advice from a bum: their "army" pelts the detectives with eggs and fruit and reclaims the train. They are now outlaws--even more definitely after they kill a brakeman who has assaulted and raped one of their number. In a Boys Republic outside Columbus, they build their own society, a "city" built with sewer pipes and egalitarian ideals, an adolescent radical alternative. When the city's merchants complain about their organized panhandling, the police and fire departments wash the kids from their city.

Next, in New York, Eddie, Tommy, and Sally have hopes of work but become involved in a delivery and pick up which is a holdup. They're carted off to jail.

Back to the kindly judge in Juvenile Court: he descends from the bench, assures the kids that things are going to be better and that Eddie's father will find work. He dismisses the charges against them and there is assurance (under that Blue Eagle and the NRA, by implication) that Eddie and Sally and Tommy will soon be back with their parents in their homes.

Wild Boys of the Road, for some, missed its chance to be a real social challenge by confusing drama with melodrama and by ending on a note of sentimental happiness, with FDR's "prosperity just around the corner." It impressed others, like William Troy of The Nation, as a more powerful criticism of the effects of the Depression than one might have expected from Hollywood. This sentence in his October 18, 1933, review sums up the historical importance of this film about adolescents:

"Never before does one remember having witnessed an American picture whose climax is made to consist in a pitched battle between a band of outlaws and the police, in which sympathy is manifestly with the former."

Also: Cultural Conflicts

THE YOUNG AND THE DAMNED (LOS OLVIDADOS)

Mexico, 1950. 88 mins., b/w. (d) Luis Buñuel (sp) Luis Buñuel and Luis Alcoriza (ph) Gabriel Figueroa (m) Rodolfo Halffter, from themes by Gustavo Pittaluga (c) Alfonso Mejia, Estela Inda, Robert Cobo, Miguel Inclan, Salvador Quiros. Spanish dialog with English subtitles. (MAC)

As it is difficult to categorize the great director Luis Buñuel except to place him in a class by himself, so it is impossible to find an equal for Los Olvidados ("The Forgotten Ones")--released here under the title The Young and the Damned--in the category of social films which express anger and concern over what poverty can do to devastate youth. It is, simply, one of the two or three most remarkable films inspired by childhood. One can never forget its adolescents spawned by the slum; they are destroyers as well as the destroyed.

The Young and the Damned is set in the outskirts of Mexico City. Among the savage, the depraved, and the victimized (the drunkards and the beggars, the pederasts, the thieves and killers, the starved and the hunted) in the world from which the only escape seems to be death, are the adolescent gangs fighting each other out of fear and hunger. Two boys are the center of the drama. The younger, Pedro (Alfonso Mejia), has a mother who has no use for him. The older, Jaibo (Robert Cobo), a vicious sadist, leader of a gang of small boys, pursues Pedro, taking him deep into violence and crime. At the end, Jaibo kills Pedro, whose body ends on a rubbish heap. When Jaibo himself is killed by someone whom he has terrorized, the dog that symbolizes his soul runs off into darkness.

There are sequences of shocking power in the film. Jaibo's gang tips a legless beggar out of his cart and torments a blind man, who lashes out at them with a stick tipped with a rusty nail. In the famous dream sequence, when Pedro is hungry, his mother offers him a disgusting piece of raw meat.

Brilliant and disturbing in its realism, The Young and the Damned also is fascinating in its surrealism. A web of symbols, of poetic images, overlays the real. A sick woman's back is caressed by a dove; into several brutal scenes, a rooster steps suddenly.

Buñuel once said to an interviewer in Mexico, "I am against conventional morality, traditional sacred cows, sentimentality and all that moral filth of society which comes into it."

The French title for this film is Pitié Pour Eux, but Buñuel shows that pity is ineffective because it bears no relationship to the problem. At one point, Pedro (for whom there is hope?) is sent to a reformatory. The director, a kindly man who trusts the boy--and Pedro is trustworthy--gives him fifty pesetas and sends him back into the city on an errand. But it doesn't matter that the director is a good man or that Pedro is a "juvenile delinquent" instead of an old hand at crime; Jaibo ambushes Pedro and steals the money. Back to the starting point. Buñuel believes that the only real reform in this jungle which is society is revolution, the complete obliteration of the status quo. He shows us that these children and adolescents are twisted at the roots and find expression only in perversion and crime; their one way out under the existing system is death.

Buñuel's film is not a conventionally humane social appeal. It is a work of art by a man who holds strong views about what makes the Pedros and the Jaibos. Through his vision, and the superb photography of Gabriel Figueroa, The Young and the Damned becomes a searing document on one level, a troubling poem-of-the-damned on another.

THE YOUNG RUNAWAYS, see p. 128

THE YOUNG STRANGER, see p. 128

SPECIAL CHILDREN

ADOLESCENCE

France, 1966. 22 mins. b/w. (d) Vladimir Forgency (sp) Agnes Van Parys (ph) Roger Bimpage (m) Chopin, Schubert, Paganini (c) Sonia Petrovna, Madame Egorova (Princess Troubetzkoy). Technical advisor: Jacques Rozier. French dialog with English subtitles. (MAC)

Sonia Petrovna, the French schoolgirl of fourteen, inhabits a world of special trials and special joys, the world of the budding artist. Ballet is her passion. At home and in school she is a lovely adolescent girl, responding like other girls her age. But once she enters the rehearsal hall, she belongs to the tradition of an art. She accepts its discipline. Taking ballet lessons in Paris from the great Madame Egorova (Princess Troubetzkoy), teacher of Massine and Maria Tallchief, Sonia learns absolute devotion.

When Sonia goes for an audition and is turned down for the place that she has worked for in a ballet company, she is as bitterly disappointed as any other adolescent whose first hope has failed. But she is no ordinary girl; she is a dedicated artist. She returns to the drafty rehearsal hall, ready to continue her lessons with the eighty-four-year-old Madame Egorova.

In this short documentary director Vladimir Forgency and his technical adviser, director Jacques Rozier, have given us insight into the bond between the generations. Seventy years may separate the two women, but they are one in their selfless absorption in their art.

Also: Teachers and Schools

AS WE ARE

U. S., 1973. 29 mins. col. (prod) Marty Gross. (PNX)

The excitement felt by retarded children when they first see new possibilities for themselves is matched by the excitement of adults who are working with them.

In the Tempus Art Center, an art program is being offered for such youngsters. The range of creative expression which opens for them, and to which they respond eagerly, leads to their self-knowledge.

An international prizewinner, As We Are is a most revealing documentary about the learning process.

Also: Finding Oneself
Teachers and Schools

THE BAD SEED, see p. 290

BALLET GIRL

Denmark, 1954. 23 mins. b/w. (d) Astrid Henning-Jensen (sp) (prod) Bjarne Henning-Jensen (ph) Gunnar Fischer (c) Kirsten Arnvig; Hans Brenaa, Inge Sand, Viveka Segerskog, and other leading members of the Royal Danish Ballet. Narrated in English by Claire Bloom. (MAC)

Through the eyes of ten-year-old Kirsten Arnvig, a student at the Ballet School of the Royal Danish Ballet, this documentary introduces us to the backstage life of the ballet. We see her hard work, her discouragement when she has difficulty with the intricate routines, her disciplined home life, and her final triumph when she appears before the footlights for the first time, one of the children being trained, in a centuries-old tradition, to take their place in the great ballet company.

The little girl and her classmates are convincingly drawn by Astrid and Bjarne Henning-Jensen, creators of those classic films about children Palle Alone in the World and Ditte, Child of Man (q. v.). The English narration, spoken by Claire Bloom, is informative about the children's schooling in the dance, and the young dancers' expression of their day-to-day hopes and anxieties is often charming. The plot is as unnecessary and obtrusive as it is in feature-length backstage movies.

Also: Teachers and Schools

BALLET SHOES, see p. 291

BAXTER, see p. 71

BENJY

U. S., 1951. 30 mins. b/w. (d) Fred Zinnemann (sp) Stewart Stern (ph) J. Peverell Marley. Narrated by Henry Fonda. (MMA)

Made possible by a grant from the League for Crippled Children, Benjy was a contribution to the work of the league made by director Fred Zinnemann and his staff of volunteer Hollywood professionals, which included narrator Henry Fonda, cameraman J. Peverell Marley, A. S. C., and scriptwriter Stewart Stern (author of Zinnemann's Teresa).

The story of a crippled child and his physical and mental readjustment; of his parents, who cannot understand his condition; and of the successful efforts of the Los Angeles Orthopedic Hospital in correcting the boy's condition and his parents' attitude toward it, Benjy is of interest to anyone concerned with handicapped children.

As is true of all Hollywood productions in which some professionals are involved, the element of staging interferes with the documentary approach to a subject like this, and the best moments, the most genuine emotions, remain those in which the children themselves convey an immediate sense of their problems.

BORN INNOCENT, see p. 235

BOYS IN CONFLICT

U. S., 1969. 72 mins. b/w. (d) (prod) Edward A. Mason, M. D., for Guidance Camps, Inc. (ph) D'Arcy Marsh (ed) Ben Achtenberg. Film Program, Harvard Medical School, 33 Fenwood Road, Boston, Mass. 02115.

Steve is a college junior, not only a dedicated human being but a charming one able to smile at himself. He is in his second year as a counselor in Camp Wediko, established by Dr. Robert Young of the Judge Baker Guidance Center to provide assistance in the treatment of emotionally disturbed boys and incidentally to provide their counselors with an experience for growth.

In this excellent documentary made by Dr. Edward A. Mason, child psychiatrist and mental health film director, we follow Steve through seven weeks of one summer as he lives and copes with a group of nine preadolescent boys with behavioral problems.

These youngsters have been referred to Camp Wediko by psychiatrists and agencies. The boys in Cabin 2, under Steve's care, are about ten years old. John has tantrums and fear of failure; Ronnie has disguised hostility; Dannie is withdrawn and uninterested in other children; David D., who has a hare lip, is academically retarded; Al, who is overweight, thinks of himself as a buffoon; David S. is awkward in social relationships; Steven, who has an unfortunate family background, has a basic chronic anxiety; Artie is something of a bully; Mark, the cabin leader, expresses frustration by running.

From the arrival at camp until the bus takes them home, the boys and their counselor are spied on by the cinéma-vérité camera. Though we see them at archery practice, swimming, camping out overnight, and preparing for a birthday party, it is the moments between camp activities that carry the impact of the film and give us compassion for these emotionally ill children. Their hysteria, suffering, yelling and swearing, fighting, withdrawals--as well as their moments of humorous or tender reaction--are shocking in their closeness to us. And we go along with Steve, hour by hour, as he attempts to grapple with the children's conflicts and estimate what is happening. Though it is overlong, the film records many revealing small events.

Intended to be shown to medical and psychiatric professionals, Boys in Conflict can be shown to parents by special arrangements. Useful as the documentary undoubtedly is to trained or in-training therapists who work with disturbed children or to teachers and parents who have similar responsibilities, it can be helpful as well to adults without special psychological background who deal not with emotionally ill children but with normal children who also, on occasion, have disturbed moments. Fighting, swearing, and tantrums occur in classrooms and in homes; we might all benefit from watching such counselors as Steve or Dorothy in Boys in Conflict.

Also: Teachers and Schools

A CHILD IS WAITING

United Artists, 1963. 102 mins. b/w. (d) John Cassavetes (sp) Abby Mann, based on his television play (ph) Joseph La Shelle (m) Ernest Gold (c) Burt Lancaster, Judy Garland, Gena Rowlands, Steven Hill, Bruce Ritchey. (UAS, BUD, MAC, WCF)

The people who made A Child Is Waiting could not have been more sincerely concerned with its subject or better intentioned--Stanley Kramer, producer; Phillip Langner, his associate; John Cassavetes, director; Abby Mann, scriptwriter. They obviously envisioned an honest dramatization of what can be done for the mentally defective child and what is being done. If their film often falls short of one's expectations, lay it to the fact that A Child Is Waiting also tries to be entertainment of a sort and utilizes far too many movie clichés.

Originally performed (in 1957) on CBS' "Studio One," the film still smells of the studio, although most of it was shot in the Pacific State Hospital in Pomona, California. Gena Rowlands and Steven Hill, as the divorced parents of one of the inmates, are stilted and reminiscent of too many hospital and soap-opera situations; Judy Garland and Burt Lancaster, as staff members of the institution, do their best but remain Garland and Lancaster.

Except for Bruce Ritchey, as a twelve-year-old borderline case, the children in the film are not actors, but actual patients at Pacific State. These forty real retardates, damaged children clinically classified as imbeciles and morons, are the finest thing in

A Child Is Waiting. For them, it is well worth tuning it in on television.

"These people have a right to life," the film is saying. Beyond their defects, one sees children much like other children. They desperately need to achieve something for themselves. ("No one ever needed to succeed in any little way so much as these children do," Dr. Clark says.) And the Thanksgiving show in which all the children participate, and Reuben's father hears Reuben (Bruce Ritchey) haltingly recite a poem and respond to the audience's applause, is a deeply moving sequence.

The spontaneous material, in which the retarded youngsters are seen at work in the school and emerge as individuals who are stunted but very responsive to affection, is always interesting; the rehearsed sequences, seldom convincing.

Far less valid and important than more recent documentaries about special children, A Child Is Waiting is more moving than the run-of-the-mill television doctor show. It's not Warrendale (q. v.), but its children are real and heartbreaking, and still capable of inspiring hope.

CRASH OF SILENCE (a. k. a. MANDY)

Great Britain, 1953. 93 mins. b/w. (d) Alexander Mackendrick (sp) Nigel Balchin, Jack Whittingham, from the novel by Hilda Lewis (ph) Douglas Slocombe (m) William Alwyn (c) Phyllis Calvert, Jack Hawkins, Terence Morgan, Godfrey Tearle, Marjorie Fielding, Dorothy Alison, Mandy Miller. (JAN)

Do you remember the appealing little girl in The Man in the White Suit who became Alec Guinness's accomplice when he was being pursued and who pointed the wrong way to his pursuers? She was Mandy Miller, a seven-year-old who has only to look into the lens to be eloquent. In this film, originally released under the title The Story of Mandy and directed by Alexander Mackendrick, Mandy is very moving as a deaf child who is taught to speak.

Shot in Manchester's Royal Residential Schools for the Deaf, Mandy is most interesting when it is showing us, in documentary style, the long and difficult process by which children are taught to lip-read and to formulate sound. Jack Hawkins gives a sympathetic performance as the kind of gruff, loving teacher who has a green thumb for youngsters in special need of understanding.

Fascinating as are all the scenes with Mandy and the other children, the film has a tedious, BBC soap-opera plot about her parents' misunderstandings, their disagreements about her education, a threatened divorce, etc.

It is worth your time, however, to watch what Mackendrick has done with close-ups of the children, the sound track, and Mandy's performance. Like little Helen Keller's mastery of her first word, Mandy's final ability to enunciate her name, when some strange children ask her, is one of the high spots in dramas about handicapped children.

Also: Teachers and Schools

DAVID AND LISA

Walter Reade, 1962. 94 mins. b/w. (d) Frank Perry (sp) Eleanor Perry, from the book by Theodore Issac Rubin (ph) Leonard Hirschfield (c) Keir Dullea, Janet Margolin, Howard Da Silva, Neva Patterson, Clifton James. (GEN)

Twice removed from scientific statement--Dr. Rubin's book was a fictionalized case history, Eleanor Perry's screenplay is deliberately free from technicalities--this story of two adolescents in a school for disturbed children is not a study in depth. Its psychiatric definitions are not its strong point; the psychiatric sessions are not illuminating. (Not that the plot eschews pseudo-scientific clichés about weak fathers, domineering mothers, and sexual deviates in the making.) Still, David and Lisa is a well-acted picture of two young people who reach out to each other by sharing their afflictions. We can accept the boy and girl, the parents, and the psychiatrist in human terms and go on to other sources for clarification of psychoneurosis and schizophrenia.

Seventeen-year-old David Clemens (Keir Dullea) is obsessed with the need for complete isolation. "A touch can kill," he believes. In the private boarding home for emotionally disturbed children in which his mother (Neva Patterson) places him, he rejects the other children and his psychiatrist, Dr. Swinford (Howard Da Silva).

Lisa (Janet Margolin) is a fifteen-year-old schizophrenic with two distinct personalities: as Muriel, she is mute; as Lisa, she talks only in rhymes.

As David becomes interested in Lisa, he enters her world and speaks to her in rhymes; he begins also to relax and to respond to Dr. Swinford. Because he seems improved, his mother removes him from the home, but he is unable to live under her domination and runs back to the clinic. Lisa is so delighted that she permits David to speak to her without rhyming and makes a drawing of her two personalities, connecting them with Me. Later, they quarrel and she runs away. After an all-night search, David finds her hiding in a museum. He persuades her to return to Dr. Swinford, showing her his love and trust by reaching out to her: "Take my hand."

Speaking not clinically but cinematically, this low-budget independent production, Frank and Eleanor Perry's first effort as a director-scriptwriter team, is often sensitive and convincing. Keir Dullea and Janet Margolin are appealing actors, able to communicate warmth even in trite moments (Lisa's flight, the museum scene).

Greatly overpraised in 1962 (Time went so far as to call it "a minor masterpiece"), David and Lisa won a Venice Film Festival Best Picture by a New Director award; in the context of more recent screen treatments of emotionally disturbed children (like the documentary Warrendale (q. v.) to name one), it may not seem to be as incisive as it did then. However, it stands up as a director's success in obtaining good performances in adolescent roles.

Also: From Literature

DITTE, CHILD OF MAN see p. 298

FLAVIO

U. S., 1962. 12 mins. b/w. (d) (sp) (ph) Gordon Parks. (CON, MMM)

Born black and poor, filmmaker Gordon Parks has wasted no time in self-pity; he has enriched us with his gifts and his compassion. He was the ideal man to make a documentary movie about a boy like Flavio.

Twelve-year-old Flavio lives with his family of eleven in one of the worst sections of Rio de Janeiro, where the rain soaks down on their decaying flavella, and with hard work adults can manage to feed the children one meal a day. He is seriously ill, but he cooks and cleans the house while his bitter mother is working and his father (resigned to his fate) is out with her. He keeps the home together with more than chores; he is capable of humor and hope.

At twelve, Flavio is brave, generous, and mature. "I look young," he says, "but I work like a man."

Combining stills and live action effectively, with its excellent musical score, Flavio is witness not only to Gordon Parks's skill as a photographer but to his understanding of people. Flavio is not a symbol of poverty's victims; he is a remarkable young human being with a sense of life's values. Watching him enjoying the evening meal with his family, following him through a typical day in the flavella, we learn much about the endurance of a boy's spirit.

Also: Family Relationships

I NEVER PROMISED YOU A ROSE GARDEN

Roger Corman/Edgar J. Sherick/New World Pictures, 1977. 94 mins. col. (d) Anthony Page (sp) Gavin Lambert and Lewis John Carlino, from the novel by Joanne Greenberg (ph) Bruce Logan (m) Paul Chihara (c) Bibi Andersson, Kathleen Quinlan, Sylvia Sidney, Signe Hasso, Diane Varsi, Susan Tyrrell, Darlene Craviotto, Ben Piazza, Lorraine Gary, Reni Santoni, Martine Bartlett, Norman Alden. (FNC)

That we share the torment of the schizophrenic girl of sixteen, in the film adapted from the 1964 autobiographical novel by Joanne Greenberg ("Hannah Green"), is due to the remarkable performance of Kathleen Quinlan as Deborah Blake. By the time she has made the trip back from suicidal schizophrenia, with the help of her calm, loving, woman psychiatrist Dr. Fried (Bibi Andersson), we have been prepared to accept the truth that life has not indeed promised us a rose garden.

Deborah is in a mental hospital because she cannot cope with bridging her inner reality--the hellish fantasy world of "Yr," her desert retreat peopled by demons and tyrants--and the reality of every day. The other patients and even some of the staff in the hospital are as lost as she. (The supporting cast offers portraits of varying degrees of sensitivity.) She clings to Dr. Fried with painful need, though she is sometimes flippant. Eventually, she is persuaded by Dr. Fried to relinquish the "Old Gods" who have been giving her such a hard time.

Those who have read the book will miss in the film the explanation of the causes of Deborah's conflicts--a complex of social and historical as well as family factors. Much is oversimplified in the screenplay.

However, on its own terms, _I Never Promised You a Rose Garden_ is a rewarding experience. The intelligence and courage with which this adolescent recognizes her pain and meets the compassionate woman doctor's challenge to come to terms with it are very moving. Cinematically, the visions of "Yr" are extraordinary.

Also: From Literature

THE MIRACLE WORKER, see p. 183

MOUCHETTE

France, 1966. 90 mins. b/w. (d) (sp) Robert Bresson, from the novel _La Nouvelle Histoire de Mouchette_ by Georges Bernanos (ph) Ghislain Cloquet (m) from the _Magnificat_ of Monteverdi (c) Nadine Nortier, Marie Cardinal, Paul Herbert, Jean-Claude Guilbert, Jean Vimenet. French dialog with English subtitles. (NLC)

"Mouchette is one of the most believable human beings on the screen and one of the few real children ever conceived in cinematic terms" (Chin, Museum of Modern Art, 1970).

When Sight and Sound compiled a list of the fifty greatest films ever made, Robert Bresson's Mouchette was among them. Certainly the moment of Mouchette's suicide--strangely joyful, seemingly predestined--is one of the most remarkable in modern cinema.

This peasant schoolgirl is fourteen when she kills herself. Bresson did not think her misery was unique. "She is found everywhere," he said, "[in] wars, concentration camps, tortures, assassinations."

Mouchette has lived a life of successive humiliations. Her drunken bootlegger father beats her because she has snatched some pleasure at the fairground. Her teacher mocks her first for not singing and then for singing out of tune. She has no friends; her bedridden mother is dying. Caught in a storm as she comes home from school through the woods, she is given shelter by a poacher. He responds to her compassion when she listens to his troubles, by raping her. Soon after she is orphaned, and the village women abuse her because she has been sexually assaulted. To free herself from the filth of her existence, Mouchette rolls herself down a hill into the pond below.

Bresson makes us see the world through Mouchette's eyes, which are not the eyes of a saint. (She is violent, flings mud, swears.) We never lose sympathy with her, and when she turns from malice and revolt and despair to free herself in death, with the sound of Monteverdi's Magnificat on the sound track like a paean, we accept it as release from suffering, not as destruction.

In the nonprofessional cast, Nadine Nortier is excellent as Mouchette. Her brief joys and profound terrors are made real not so much in dialog or music as in images and natural sounds. Bresson's artistry enlarges every part of her hostile universe. Though his film has no sentimentality, its emotion is intense. We feel that we cannot bear what is being done to Mouchette, but we never doubt that it is happening.

100 MEN AND A GIRL

Universal, 1937. 84 mins. b/w. (d) Henry Koster (sp) Bruce Manning, Charles Kenyon, Hans Kraly (ph) Joseph Valentine (m) Liszt, Tschaikovsky, Wagner, Mozart, Verdi; "It's Raining Sunbeams," Frederick Hollander and Sam Coslow; "A Heart That's Free," Alfred G. Robyn and Thomas T. Railey (c) Deanna Durbin, Leopold Stokowski, Adolphe Menjou, Alice Brady, Eugene Pallette, Mischa Auer, Billy Gilbert. (UNI)

Deanna Durbin, the Canadian girl singer who won worldwide success after her first film, Three Smart Girls (1936), was given a Special Academy Award in 1938 "for bringing to the screen the spirit and personification of youth."

And if youth is a sweet freshness of voice and manner, that she certainly did. When she was sixteen, her grateful studio, Universal, whose leading musical comedy star she had become, presented her in the lavish 100 Men and a Girl. It was her most popular movie. The Soviet Union called her the people's favorite American actress, and Americans got together with Leopold Stokowski after a little girl had led them.

In the story, Deanna is the daughter of a poor and unemployed violinist (Adolphe Menjou), whose friends, like Mischa Auer, are also out of work. With exuberant effectiveness matched only by the younger Shirley Temple, Deanna solves everything. She maneuvers 100 unemployed musicians, led by herself, into an encounter with Leopold Stokowski (himself) on his own stairway, where their performance of Liszt's Second Hungarian Rhapsody wins him over. He becomes their conductor, and there is a great deal of symphony, comedy, and happiness to follow.

Deanna weaves her way through all this with great simplicity and wholesomeness. In addition to the classical music, there are some songs written especially for her.

The teenage appeal of this very nice girl is at its peak in 100 Men and a Girl. Her career flourished through That Certain Age (1938) and Mad About Music (1938) but came to an end with her teens. Her last film was made in 1948.

THE OTHER

20th Century-Fox, 1972. 100 mins. color. (d) Robert Mulligan (sp) Thomas Tryon, from his novel (ph) Robert L. Surtees (m) Jerry Goldsmith (c) Uta Hagen, Diana Muldaur, Chris Udvarnoky, Martin Udvarnoky, Norma Connolly. (FNC)

Adapted for the screen from a novel by Tom Tryon, by the author himself, this occult shocker is a case study of a schizoid boy of eleven. So highly developed is his power of projection that he can conjure up his dead identical twin. Under the inspiration of "the other," Niles Perry (Chris Udvarnoky) systematically decimates members of his circle. Hardly anyone suspects that anything extraordinary is taking place, as Niles, in the name of his other incarnation, Holland Perry (Martin Udvarnoky), murders a hated playmate, a neighbor, and a child who threatens to displace him as the center of his family's love.

Niles, who has a calm exterior that barely hides the tensions of his other self, is a likeable child. He lives on a Connecticut farm (the time is 1935) with his mother (Diana Muldaur), crippled as a result of a fall caused by Niles himself when she began to guess the dreadful truth about him; and his Russian-born grandmother (Uta Hagen), who first taught him to imagine his dead twin's presence as a defense against loneliness. This "great game" enables Niles to experience sensations through others, while retaining his sense of self.

Indecisive in its picture of Niles, the film fails to explore the nature of his schizophrenia or of his motivations. It builds chiefly on the elements of horror--family madness, an ancestral curse, imaginary or ambiguous landscapes, blind alleys of symbol.

Robert Mulligan, the director, has won excellent performances from Chris and Martin Udvarnoky as Niles and his twin brother and from Diana Muldaur and Uta Hagen as the helpless adults. He and photographer Robert L. Surtees sometimes use camera angles from the child's perspective to make their point about relationships. The mood is always strong--indeed, to many the film style is pretentious and cluttered.

(In shooting the sideshow freaks, Mulligan is using his characteristic trick of symbolism; he underlines the contrast between the obvious grotesques and the handsome but psychologically warped Niles.)

Interesting as a horror tale using a child, *The Other*, like many horror tales, carries a whisper of truth. Niles is not every child, not even a child one sees clearly enough, but he suggests other children, particularly the youngest children in a large family, who wield power over their own lives through their extraordinary imaginations.

Also: From Literature

THE ROCKING HORSE WINNER, see p. 321

RUN WILD, RUN FREE

Great Britain, 1969. 100 mins. col. (d) Richard Sarafian (sp) David Rook, from his novel *The White Colt* (ph) Wilkie Cooper (c) Mark Lester, John Mills, Sylvia Syms, Gordon Jackson, Bernard Miles, Fiona Fullerton. (GEN)

Though the child's love for the white colt is reminiscent of *National Velvet* and the story's resolution is in the tradition of *My Friend Flicka*, the difference here is that ten-year-old Philip (Mark Lester) is a deeply disturbed boy when we meet him. Because of an early, unexplained trauma, he does not speak; he has retreated into psychosomatic muteness.

The only child of well-meaning parents who cannot reach him, he lives in Devonshire on the edge of Dartmoor. After a futile experience in a local clinic, Philip's mother (Sylvia Syms), nervous and self-blaming, and his puzzled father (Gordon Jackson) leave him free to roam on the moors he loves so much. They wisely do not interfere with the only human relationship he has--with the Moorman, a retired Army colonel who shares his affinity for animals and wild-life and who persuades a neighbor child, Diana (Fiona Fullerton), to let Philip share in training her kestrel (baby falcon). The Moor-man (John Mills) also helps Philip tame the beautiful, wild white colt whom Philip has named after himself, and to whom he devotes all his time, until the pony suddenly disappears. When Philip catches a glimpse of the runaway, he unwittingly injures the kestrel on his arm, in his pursuit; later, Diana's pet is accidentally killed, the colt is still missing, and Philip lapses into his former listless-ness.

But after the Moorman recaptures the colt and teaches Philip to ride, Philip speaks to him. At the end of the film, when the colt is struggling in a quagmire, and Philip's parents try to help him to rescue the animal, the boy recovers his voice completely; he is able not only to encourage the pony to get to his feet and free himself from the bog, but to speak to his father and mother.

Quite apart from one's acceptance of the means of Philip's recovery, Run Wild, Run Free is a sensitive and intelligent movie about a troubled child. Mark Lester (of Oliver!) is emotionally convincing. If the film ending pulls out all the stops, there are so many earlier scenes of simplicity and beauty that we remember best the Devonshire moors and the children and animals who inhabit them. Credit goes to Wilkie Cooper's brilliant color photography and Geoffrey Foot's editing.

Also: Animals and Nature

SARAH

Yorkshire TV, Great Britain, 1973. 60 mins. b/w. (d) John Frankau (sp) Buy Cullingford (c) Pheona McLellan, Richard Vernon, Ursula Howells, Kathleen Michael. (PBS-TV)

Sarah, seven and a half, is played by an extraordinary young actress called Pheona McLellan. You will not forget her; behind those owlish glasses, there is a fascinating person.

She is an adopted child, plain and unprepossessing, who lives in a small seaside town. To her pleasant parents and puzzled head-headmistress, she is a loner, a difficult child, possibly backward. She won't join in games and likes her lessons so little that she won't even try.

Having been chosen herself, Sarah decides to choose an adopted father for her own. On the sea front, she slips her hand into that of Mr. Clissold, a retired civil servant (Richard Vernon), and somewhat to his consternation, informs him that she has chosen him.

The story, in a nutshell, is Clissold's discovery that Sarah is an exceptionally gifted child. (It starts when she learns to play chess; when she says "Checkmate," Clissold is fascinated and shaken by the mind behind the child's facade.) He persuades others to recognize her potential and guides her education.

The relationship between the child and the man avoids the obvious. It is moving and provocative. What we take away from *Sarah* is wonder--at a child's character, at our own blindness to it, at the marvel that can be created when we at last see what has been there all the time.

Also: Teachers and Schools

A THOUSAND CLOWNS

United Artists, 1965. 118 mins. b/w. (d) Fred Coe (sp) Herb Gardner, from his own play (ph) Arthur J. Ornitz (m) Don Walker (c) Jason Robards, Barbara Harris, Barry Gordon, William Daniels, Gene Saks, Martin Balsam. (UAS)

It is a scriptwriter's axiom that out of the mouths of babes.... The precocious teenager, part monster, part mentor to his elders, is well represented in *A Thousand Clowns* in the character of Nick (Barry Gordon). This twelve-year-old "hip juve" (*Variety*), whose wisecracks appeared first in Herb Gardner's Broadway play and seem right at home on the screen, tries to monitor the eccentricities of his uncle, Murray Burns (Jason Robards).

Murray is a writer who has resigned from the rat race. He cares for his nephew, Nick, in a one-room apartment where they have lived in complete love and understanding since Nick was parked there by his mother seven years before. Unemployed and unmarried, Murray is frowned on not only by the neighbors, to whom he shouts out-of-window paeans of freedom at odd hours, but by the Child Welfare Board. Its representatives would like to take the boy out of his custody. Murray's brother (Martin Balsam), his girl (Barbara Harris), and his nephew himself would like Murray to get a job so he can keep Nick. But Murray finds it almost impossible to conform. When we are introduced to television's "Chuckles the Chipmunk"--a grotesque portrait superbly drawn by Herb Gardner and superbly played by Gene Saks--we don't wonder why Murray doesn't want to write for his show. (The cards are stacked against TV, advertising, and other media for which Murray might work; Chuckles is the only symbol of conformity that Mr. Gardner offers us.)

Nick delights in his uncle's hatred for the "dead people," as Murray calls the conformists. What teenager wouldn't enjoy going along with Murray's ideas? He favors playing the guitar or playing hooky, visiting the Empire State Building as a copout from problems, and scorning the Establishment. Their incredibly cluttered apartment nurtures twin souls. The special life that Nick shares with Murray is fun. After all, Nick is something of a nonconformist himself; the Child Welfare Board visitors are taken aback not only by his conversation but by his favorite plaything, a nude female figure with light-up breasts.

Underneath the gags, both verbal and visual, is a believable adolescent and a convincing man-boy relationship. Nick is a child in many ways, and so is Murray; yet Nick in essence is more mature and realistic than his uncle. He knows that pressure will drive Murray back to a job and to respectability (even if it means writing for "Chuckles the Chipmunk"), the pressure of his love for Nick, which demands sacrifice. Earlier than anyone else, the boy knows not only that Chuckles will get Murray, as the Child Welfare Board threatens to get him if he doesn't fit into the pattern, but that the girl will get him. If there is an escape for men like Murray, it must come from means other than those described by author Herb Gardner. It's not always clear what makes Murray Burns either as free or as charming as we're asked to believe, but it is always easy to see in Nick the "hip juve" of many a seventies family situation.

<u>Also</u>: Family Relationships

WARRENDALE

Canada, 1966. 105 mins. b/w. (d) Allan King (ph) William Brayne (ed) Peter Moseley (c) children and staff of Warrendale, House Two. (GRO)

"A great artist," was Jean Renoir's tribute to Allan King, who produced and directed this superb documentary; and Renoir wondered how the "animated professional actors" of fiction films could ever be as moving as the real children of <u>Warrendale</u>. Though there have been other films about emotionally disturbed children, this is the great film. It is totally involving and is a profound experience.

When it was shown at the Cannes Festival in 1967, where it won the International Film Critics' Prize, King said, "This film is not really about disturbed children. It's about anger, rage, and grief in everybody, particularly focused around the experience of loss and death. For some people the film threatens their emotional security, or at any rate challenges their view of themselves, their experience of childhood and their experiences of other people emotionally. We've found that the reaction to the film often reflects the personality problems of the viewer."

King's purpose, which was not to demonstrate treatment but to give the audience the intense experience of the lives of these children through the events he chose to represent, is in line with his favorite definition of art, John Dewey's "Art is a formed expression of emotion." Warrendale, a Canadian residential treatment center for emotionally disturbed children--an environment placing a high premium on direct and free emotional expression--was an ideal place to do this.

The children in Warrendale are not brain damaged or mentally defective; they cannot control their behavior, which is so disturbed that they are unable to live at home. Before becoming part of the "experiment and the frontier" of Warrendale, some of them have been in juvenile detention or psychiatric wards.

King spent a month getting to know Warrendale, then with his photographer, William Brayne, and sound man, Russel Heise, began shooting. After five more weeks, he had forty hours of film, edited by Peter Moseley to 105 minutes of extraordinary cinéma vérité.

We are in House Two, where twelve children live together as a family, with eight full-time staff people to care for them. Subject to fear and rage and guilt, these youngsters bite, kick, howl, weep, thrash about, suck baby bottles, curse and swear, withdraw. They are not stupid--many are remarkable as people. They have tempests inside them which they cannot calm.

When a child is shaken by one of these tempests, the Warrendale response is not repression or drugs, but "holding"--one or more adults will hold the child firmly and warmly in his arms, keeping him from harming others or himself, but allowing him free rein for the expression of the inner feelings that terrify him. The child is held in protective love.

(Is this the best treatment? We do not know. Warrendale itself became a controversy for Warrendale, which changed hands and techniques some time after the documentary was made.)

The most powerful experience in a film of many intense experiences is the children's confrontation with death. The young black cook, Dorothy, who is a beloved friend, dies suddenly. The news shatters the children--they are filled with guilt as well as fear. Their reactions range from hysteria to pretended unconcern and complete withdrawal. Later, when they attend the funeral with the staff, their faces are unforgettable.

Each of the youngsters in House Two is, literally, alive and kicking, six or seven feet from the camera. King, when asked if the children forgot the camera was there, said no, not at all.

"But the thing a person being filmed has to feel is that you are not judging him, you don't think him peculiar, you accept him as a valid person in his own right."

If, looking at the children in Warrendale, we do not judge them, don't think them peculiar, accept them as valid persons in their own right, we shall discover more than the experience of the children. What moves these children is not alien to any of us; we are one with them.

Allan King has not taken advantage of these children. He obtained their full consent to make the film.

"I told them that I thought our society was emotionally cold and ungiving.... People were seldom honest with each other, seldom able to express their feelings directly or meaningfully.... It seemed to me that the children had gained a great deal from the freedom of expression towards which they were working and that they lived with a feeling, a warmth, and a genuine humanity which was rare in our world; that this was something people should know about and feel for themselves."

And so they agreed to the film. And we can know about Irene, Tony, Carol; about Robert, Lori, Patrick, Pegi, Davey, Debbie, Freddie, Susan, and Bob, who are not unlike other children, not unlike ourselves.

Also: Death

WHO ARE THE DEBOLTS, AND WHERE DID THEY GET 19 KIDS?

Korty Films and Charles Schulz Creative Associates, 1978. 72 mins. documentary, col. (prod) (d) John Korty (c) Robert and Dorothy DeBolt and family. (PYR)

Adopted children with special handicaps, the youngsters in the DeBolt family are a moving and exuberantly inspiring group. The filmmakers spent nearly two years recording their day-to-day living together, and in the process the children lost their camera shyness. Here they are to the life--coping with very real problems, but growing in confidence and strength and becoming not "handicappers" but contributors.

The children derive their ability to swim in the mainstream from their adoptive parents' unfailing love, support, and patience. Robert and Dorothy DeBolt, who are founders of A. A. S. K., Aid to the Adoption of Special Kids, are remarkable people, and this is a remarkable film about them. Director John Korty's 1978 Academy Award-winning documentary is a beautiful job, and no one who sees Who Are the Debolts is likely to forget these parents and their 19 kids, or the lesson they have for us--that handicaps (in kids or in ourselves) are what we start with, not what we end with.

Also: Family Relationships

THE WILD CHILD (L'ENFANT SAUVAGE)

France, 1970. 85 mins. b/w. (d) François Truffaut (sp) François Truffaut and Jean Gruault, from the book Mémoire et Rapport sur Victor de l'Aveyron by Jean Itard (ph) Nestor Almendros (m) excerpts from Vivaldi (c) Jean-Pierre Cargol, François Truffaut, Jean Daste, Françoise Seigner, Paul Ville, Claude Miler, Annie Miler. French dialog with English subtitles. (UAS)

It is unlikely that many adults will be called on to effect the transformation of a wild child, one almost wholly alien to civilization. Yet no one should miss this beautiful, unsentimental film by the great François Truffaut, in which a "beast boy" incapable of communication is brought closer to human childhood. It is an account of development on the part of the educator as well as his pupil, and it is full of marvels about the spirit of the boy and of those who worked with him.

The film is based on the 1806 memoirs of the French physician Jean Itard, of the Paris Institute for the Deaf and Dumb, who had heard of Victor of l'Aveyron, a boy of about twelve who had managed to survive in the forest after having been left there to die at the age of three or four. The wild boy (Jean-Pierre Cargol) has been imprisoned by the peasant villagers and is tormented when he tries to escape. At the Institute, to which he is brought by Itard (François Truffaut) for examination and testing, he is exhibited as a curiosity to visitors by the orderlies and mocked by the other children.

Itard's colleague, Professor Pinel (Jean Daste), believes the boy is "an inferior being ... an idiot," but Itard believes his deaf and dumbness is the result of isolation; he turns around when he hears a nut cracked.

Eager to educate him, Itard takes the boy into his bachelor home; his housekeeper, Madame Guerin (Françoise Seigner), cares for him.

Itard notes in his diary, "All he does he is doing for the first time"--bathing, walking erect, eating with utensils, wearing clothes--and, another time, "Each day gives me fresh proof of his intelligence."

When the doctor, striving for objectivity, works the boy like a machine, the child rebels with a tantrum--and Itard is pleased not only to see that human sign but also to be reminded that he, too, must be human. Again, when he punishes the boy without reason "to see if his reaction is rebellion" and Victor reacts bitterly, Itard notes, "The very pain of his hate filled me with delight--savage man elevated to the full stature of a moral being."

Victor learns to say "lait" (milk), can associate some words with objects, and shows signs of affection. There are many moments of failure and discouragement. ("I wish I had never seen you!" the doctor cries, and the boy weeps.) But Victor invents a chalk holder and his teacher exults to see this spark of imagination.

One day, feeling rejected because the man has gone out without taking him along, the boy runs away. But he has lost the ability to exist on his own. In his social adaptation, he has lost the freedom of the wild child. Cold, half-starved, terrified, he returns to the doctor, who welcomes him joyfully: "You're no longer a wild boy.... You're an extraordinary boy with great expectations, and this is your home."

It is an open-ended film; the "great expectations" are questionable, the child's loss of his self-sufficiency clear. But he knows love and security.

Truffaut has maintained a meticulous and unemotional style both in the role of the teacher and in the direction of the film. With the recitations from the loving doctor's journal, however, and his genius for bringing people to life, he achieves a moving drama, not a cold case history. As the wild child, a dark-eyed gypsy boy, Jean-Pierre Cargol, is very effective.

Dr. Itard never, in fact, succeeded in transforming Victor into a completely normal, rational child. He established teaching methods and procedures, however, that are still used today by followers of the Montessori School.

This Truffaut film is both "rigorous and tender" (Godard's description of Truffaut's quality as a director) and there is fascination in it for all who work with children of any sort.

Also: Teachers and Schools

FANTASY

A CLOCKWORK ORANGE

Great Britain, 1971. 137 mins. col. (d) (sp) Stanley Kubrick, based on Anthony Burgess's novel (ph) John Alcott (m) Walter Carlos (c) Malcolm McDowell, Patrick Magee, Michael Tarn, Warren Clarke, Adrienne Corri, Miriam Karlin, James Marcus, Aubrey Morris, Godfrey Quigley, Sheila Raynor, Philip Stone. (SWA)

Fifteen-year-old Alex, the violence freak, is presented as the child of a nightmare world of the near future. Is he a prefiguration of the adolescent of our times? Is A Clockwork Orange a cautionary fable about our youth?

Alex (Malcolm McDowell) roams the London streets in a mad period that may be the end of the seventies. There are influences from Russia. After milk-plus at the Korova bar, Alex and his "droogs" (teenage hoods) are sharpened up for a bit of "the old ultra-violence." They're good at bashing senior citizens in the eyes with bicycle chains. They beat up an ancient drunk in a tunnel, steal a car, and roar out into the country, running everyone else off the road. In between, they've bloodied Billy-boy and his gang, and tied up and gagged a man in a private home while they raped his wife. They're a bit "shagged and fagged and fashed" by their fun.

The characters speak in "nadsat," the language of Anthony Burgess's 1963 novel on which the film is based: a mixture of current slang, archaic English, and anglicized Russian. It is more effective, and clearer, on the page than on the sound track, where it has no time to reverberate in the imagination.

Imprisoned for a random murder of a woman, Alex is chosen as a guinea pig for a rehabilitative technique: a behavioristic barrage of electronic impulses, film, and music (particularly his favorite, Beethoven's Ninth). He is "cured" of sex or violence urges; he is an automaton, with no free will of his own. But he is soon threatened on all sides by "an almost magical coincidence of retribution" (Kubrick)--menaced by the old drunk, by his former droogs (now policemen), and by the husband of the woman he raped. Eventually, Alex recovers from the scientific cure and is ready to embark on a life of ultra-violence with the blessing of the Minister of the Interior (a fascist type).

The message (according to the novel as well as the film) is that any attempt to make man into a mechanical creation is to be deplored more than his freedom to choose his own sinful acts, ultra-violence not excepted.

The chief departure in Kubrick's film from Burgess's novel has been summed up by Stanley Kauffmann (The New Republic): "The modest moral resonance of the book is reduced: partly because of certain small changes, like converting a murder victim from an old woman to a sexy broad and killing her with a giant ceramic phallus (thus changing sheer heartlessness into sex sensation); mostly because Kubrick has to replace Burgess's linguistic ingenuity with cinematic ingenuity, and he doesn't."

Winner of the New York Film Critics Awards for Best Picture and Best Director and nominated for Academy Awards in both categories, A Clockwork Orange was nevertheless greeted by a mixed press, unlike Kubrick's earlier Dr. Strangelove and 2001: A Space Odyssey. At first, terms like "dazzling to the senses and the mind" and "Kubrick's true genius of cinema" were used. Then some cooler voices objected. Stanley Kauffmann found the Kubrick film invention weak and repetitive, his musical tricks less appropriate than in his earlier works, and Alex's fantasies not so much witty as "mostly hand-me-down silent-film dreams with fewer clothes and more violence." He thought it all boring. Clayton Riley said in The New York Times of the film's style that it was gimmicky, mindless symbolism. In the same paper, Fred Hechinger deplored Kubrick's message that man isn't a noble savage but an ignoble one, irrational, brutal, weak; and that any attempt to create social institutions on a false view of his nature is doomed. This, said Hechinger, is the voice of fascism. Pauline Kael (The New Yorker) was most vehement in her dislike of the film. While Burgess is a humanist horrified by a society in which men lose their capacity for moral choice--a dehumanized society in which adolescents have no way to release their energies except in crime and vandalism--Kubrick (says Kael) "has learned to love the punk sadist ... Alex is the only likable person we see ... and the movie puts us on his side. Alex, who gets kicks out of violence, is more alive than anybody else in the movie, and younger and more attractive, and McDowell plays him exuberantly.... The look in Alex's eyes at the end tells us that he isn't just a mechanized, choiceless sadist but prefers sadism and knows he can get by with it."

Obviously, A Clockwork Orange is a film to see and to respond to on a very personal level. How much does it tell us about the adolescent Alex (played by McDowell, incidentally, when he was twenty-seven) that is illuminating about boys in our culture?

A friend has told us that when he and another teacher saw the film in a Staten Island, New York, neighborhood theater, the approval of Alex expressed by the young people in the audience reached such raucous levels that it had to be controlled by the management. Many people who are not admirers of Kubrick's "bloody boring" approach think that A Clockwork Orange, far from being a social satire or responsible comment, is a self-indulgent director's experiment with film dynamite.

Also: Delinquency and Crime
From Literature
Generation Conflicts

A KID FOR TWO FARTHINGS

Great Britain, 1955. 91 mins. col. (d) Carol Reed (sp) Wolf Mankowitz, from his own book (ph) Edward Scaife (m) Benjamin Frankel (c) Celia Johnson, Diana Dors, David Kossoff, Brenda de Banzie, Joe Robinson, Jonathan Ashmore, Primo Carnera, Lou Jacobi, Vera Day. (JAN)

There are two worlds in A Kid for Two Farthings. One is the slum world of Petticoat Lane, in London's East End. In and around the tailoring shop of Kandinsky (David Kossoff), an old Jewish philosopher with a vivid fancy, swarm an assortment of colorful characters. Sam the muscle man (Joe Robinson) while he assists in the shop dreams of becoming Mr. World. Sonia (Diana Dors) dreams of becoming Mrs. Sam. Python Macklin, a fearfully ugly wrestler (Primo Carnera), eggs Sam into a fight. And there are many more --Madam Rita, who is a man, and Lady Ruby, who is no lady, and Blackie Isaacs (Lou Jacobi). Fascinated by all of them and by the stories that Kandinsky tells, is a six-year-old, Joe (Jonathan Ashmore), who has recently come to live in Petticoat Lane with his mother, Joanna (Celia Johnson), who boards and works with the tailor.

The other world is the six-year-old's imaginary life. Joe is a collector of pets. One day he buys a young kid from a vagrant. Because of its single horn, Joe is certain that it is a unicorn; Kandinsky has told him all about the magical powers of unicorns. The child is conned by the gentle old tailor into believing that he can fulfil all the wishes of his neighbors and friends in Petticoat Lane through the magic of this unicorn. Soon things begin to happen, Sam beats the Python and is able to buy Sonia a ring; Kandinsky gets a steam presser; there is a hint that Joe's father, who has been abroad, may return.

Who is to say that the unicorn was not a unicorn, that it did not work all this magic? Surely not six-year-old Joe.

OUR MOTHER'S HOUSE

Great Britain, 1967. 105 mins. col. (d) Jack Clayton (sp) Jeremy Brooks and Haya Harareet, from the novel by Julian Gloag (ph) Larry Pizer (m) Georges Delerue (c) Dirk Bogarde, Margaret Brooks, Pamela Franklin, Louis Sheldon Williams, Mark Lester, Sarah Nicholls, Parnham Wallace, John Gugolka, Gustav Henry. (FNC)

Our Mother's House is a superbly directed and acted Gothic tale of seven extraordinary children who build a world of their own, making fantasy real until an adult appears and demolishes it with an ugly truth.

In the old Victorian house in which they live with their bedridden mother, the seven Hook children, never having known a father, center their existence on "Mothertime" each night in her room. They learn to take care of themselves. When their mother dies, they are fearful of the outside world. Burying her in the garden and building a shrine in a shed in the backyard, they keep her death a secret from everyone--the maid, their teachers, the neighbors. They forge their mother's signature on her annuity checks and run the household by themselves. Every night they celebrate "Mothertime" with supernatural meaning, for the oldest girl, Diana (Pamela Franklin), communes with the dead woman's spirit.

All this fantasy of adoration is destroyed when Charlie Hook, their father (Dirk Bogarde), arrives. A dissolute, lecherous charmer who captivates the children at first, he finally becomes their enemy. Not only does he attempt to overthrow their mother's shrine but he confronts them with knowledge they cannot bear: their mother was a shameless slut and they are all illegitimate. Diana kills him with a poker, and the children leave their fantasy home to tell the secret they have guarded up to now.

Yes, this adaptation from Julian Gloag's novel is weird; but director Jack Clayton (The Innocents) is brilliant with his child players. Attractive, credible, and touching, they are a beautiful lot, from the adolescent Diana (Pamela Franklin) stirred by mysticism and sex, to Gerty, who rides a motorcycle (Sarah Nicholls), and stuttering Jiminee (Mark Lester). Each is an individual. Together they persuade one that it might have happened, that anything is possible for children who will have it so.

As for Diana's beaning Charlie with the poker--well, remember Lord of the Flies and A High Wind in Jamaica. These are, after all, literary British children, and everyone knows what they're like.

Also: From Literature

THE RED BALLOON

France, 1956. 34 mins. col. (d) (sp) Albert Lamorisse (ph) Edmond Séchan (m) Maurice Le Roux (ed) Pierre Gillette (c) Pascal Lamorisse. No dialog. (MAC)

This marvelous film is a poetic fantasy, a lovely miniature, about a small boy and a bright red balloon in the gray streets of Paris. The Red Balloon is a revelation of a child's imagination and sense of wonder and has been considered a classic since it won the Grand Prix at Cannes in 1956.

There is no dialog, only music. The boy (Pascal, Lamorisse's son) discovers the balloon and tames it for his own. They play together, and go together to church and school, where the adults do not feel about the balloon the way Pascal does. Neither do some street urchins, who try to snatch it away. There is a struggle and Pascal wins for a little while, but in the end the balloon is destroyed; it dies, a limp, red rag in his hand. But suddenly all the balloons in Paris leave their owners' hands and come to Pascal. Joyously, they lift him into the sky.

Edmond Séchan's photography, Albert Lamorisse's direction and writing, and the child's playing are all beautiful. The balloon, its destruction, the ending, can mean anything you want them to mean.

THE SPIRIT OF THE BEEHIVE (EL ESPIRITU DE LA COLMENA)

Spain, 1973. 98 mins. col. (d) Victor Erice (sp) Francisco J. Querejeta from an idea by Victor Erice and Angel Fernandos Santos (ph) Luis Cuadrado (m) Luis de Pablo (c) Ana Torrent, Isabel Telleria, Fernando Fernan Gomez, Teresa Gimpera, Juan Margallo. Spanish dialog with English subtitles. (JAN)

"Not since René Clément's Forbidden Games has any movie entered so deeply into the perilous country of children's nightmares and fantasies." Vincent Canby's judgment has been echoed by critics here and abroad, who have found this subtle, complex Spanish film one of the most haunting ever made about children.

In the aftermath of war, the children in Clément's and Erice's films survive by creating their own world, in a distorted mirror of the terrible world of adults.

The Spirit of the Beehive is set in 1940, in a remote, bleak village in Castile to which an upper middle class family has fled from the civil war. Its devastation is still with them: their big house is almost bare of possessions, a daily troop train passes, a movie audience is made up of old women and children. The father (Fernando Fernan Gomez) is an intellectual in retreat from reality; he keeps bees by day and writes metaphysical comments about them in his journal at night. The mother (Teresa Gimpera) sends a letter off on the troop train every day to a long-lost lover, probably dead. Left to their own devices are the two children: Ana, eight (Ana Torrent); and Isabel, ten (Isabel Telleria), who amuses herself in her boredom by tricking her sensitive, credulous little sister.

After seeing James Whale's movie Frankenstein, the children talk about it in bed. Ana asks why the little girl and the monster were killed; Isabel tells her they're not really dead, the monster is a living spirit. You only have to announce yourself, and he will come.

Because Isabel tells her the monster lives in an old barn,

Ana measures a mysterious footprint there. But Isabel has fooled her before, playing dead and frightening her. Ana continues the search alone. Finally, the monster materializes--a wounded fugitive soldier (Juan Margallo). Ana gives him food and her father's coat with his chiming watch in it. After Ana's "spirit" is shot by the Guardia Civil and his corpse is laid out in the village hall, Ana's father recovers his property from the soldier's body. Seeing him with the watch again, Ana goes to the barn, which is bloodstained. She runs away. Search parties go out, as in Frankenstein, with dogs and torches. Near a stream, Ana sees the true monster, but loses consciousness when he embraces her. She is found at the foot of a ruin and brought home in shock, refusing to eat or speak. As the moon rises, she comes out of her coma, gets a drink of water, and calls softly through the open windows, "It is Ana. It is Ana."

The film is fascinating on many levels. Is it an indictment of the war's devastation of families like Ana's? Is the isolation of her home and village a metaphor for Spain's isolation under Franco? Is the "beehive" (a reference to Maeterlinck's comparison of life to a beehive) a metaphor for her family's introverted existence, her parents' senseless busywork? The little girls stand between innocence and evil, on the brink of destruction (jumping over bonfires, defying oncoming trains). Is this suggestive of the political situation of Spain? Since the film is lyrical, the viewer is free to think what he will.

Artistically, there are no questions. The Spanish mood of repression is recreated in stunning visuals. There are probably no more than fifty lines spoken in the entire film. Few are needed, for the children are eloquent and beautifully drawn. As Forbidden Games gave us the haunting little Brigitte Fossey, The Spirit of the Beehive gives us a performance by Ana Torrent which belongs with the greatest ever seen in a film about children.

Also: Death
Family Relationships

VALERIE AND HER WEEK OF WONDERS (VALERIE A TYDEN DIVU)

Czechoslovakia, 1970. 75 mins. col. (d) Jaromil Jires (sp) Jaromil Jires, Ester Kumbachova, from Vitezslav Nezval's novel (ph) Jan Curik (m) Jan Klusak (c) Jaroslava Schallerova, Helena Anyzkova, Petr Prymek. Czech dialog with English subtitles. (JAN)

"It is a week in the life of a child in which she becomes a girl, when something she did not know till then is born in her and something of a child remains," says director Jaromil Jires. "It is not, however, a realistic psychological drama with the real torments of adolescence ... rather about the things an adolescent girl longs for."

A poetic tour de force, in which fantasy blends with reality, and folklore, myth, and cinematic invention symbolize the inner life of the characters, it is based on a black novel by the Czech poet and surrealist Vitezslav Nezval, which Jires says he transposed to a more humorous plane in the film, so that horror is unreal.

Thirteen-year-old Valerie (Jaroslava Schallerova) sublimates her real life in bizarre gothic dreams. Her innocence and awakening sexuality merge lyric tenderness and disturbing eroticism. Her mysterious grandmother is vampire, mother, cousin; there are flagellants, lustful priests, masked magicians.

Jan Curik won an award at the Chicago Film Festival for his color cinematography (the film also won the top prize at Bergamo). The images are often lovely--Valerie floating among flowers in a running stream, followed by a close-up of daisy petals blooming drops of blood; Valerie resting in a wood and reentering her dream: the lovers disappear from the countryside and her bed stands alone on the leafy ground, dissolving into whiteness.

Also: Love and Sex

WHITE MANE, see p. 284

WILD IN THE STREETS

American International, 1968. 96 mins. col. (d) Barry Shear (sp) Robert Thom (ph) Richard Moore (m) Les Baxter, Barry Mann, Cynthia Weil (c) Christopher Jones, Shelley Winters, Ed Begley, Diane Varsi, Hal Holbrook, Millie Perkins, Richard Pryor. (GEN)

Preposterous and raucous though it is, Wild in the Streets makes its points about the freaked-out youth of the sixties and is often very funny.

Max Flatow (Christopher Jones) is a fifteen-year-old so completely alienated from his mother that he poisons the dog, blows up her car, and leaves home. Seven years later, he is Max Frost, millionaire rock-and-roll star, whose mansion is filled with hippies. Hal Holbrook, Congressman from California (where else?), wants support for his campaign. He promises if elected to lower the voting age to fifteen. But the kids run their own candidate for Congress, former child star and present LSD convert Diane Varsi. Then they pour LSD into Washington's water supply.

This is the beginning of a reign of terror. (Pauline Kael thought it quasi-Fascist.) Turned-on congressmen lower the eligibility age for President to fourteen. Max, more than seasoned at twenty-two, becomes President, and youth sweeps into power. Max proclaims mandatory retirement at thirty. All citizens over thirty-five are condemned to serve life sentences in concentration camps, compelled to take LSD.

At the end of Wild in the Streets, Max feels that the future is threatened. He has just run into a pair of activist seven-year-olds.

Under this satirical fantasy, who shall say what message is being flashed to those of us over thirty-five? Anyway, Renata Adler of The Times is only one of many who have found the movie entertaining.

Also: Generation Conflicts

THE WIZARD OF OZ

M-G-M, 1939. 101 mins. col. (d) Victor Fleming (sp) Noel Langley, Florence Ryerson, and Edgar Allan Woolf from the book by L. Frank Baum (m) Herbert Stothart, Harold Arlen (lyr) E. P. Harburg (sp. eff) Arnold Gillespie (c) Judy Garland, Frank Morgan, Ray Bolger, Bert Lahr, Jack Haley, Billie Burke, Margaret Hamilton, Charles Grapewin. (FNC)

After making Thoroughbreds Don't Cry and Love Finds Andy Hardy (1938) and Babes in Arms and The Wizard of Oz (1939), Judy Garland received a special Academy Award "for her outstanding performance as a juvenile."

Judy was over age for Dorothy in The Wizard, being all of seventeen, but she is just about perfect as the child in Hollywood's most popular fantasy. "A pert and fresh-faced miss," said Frank Nugent in The New York Times, "with the wonder-lit eyes of a believer in fairy tales."

The wonder doesn't fade for a moment, as we watch the cyclone lift Dorothy and her little dog Toto out of Kansas, far away from Aunt Em, and into the magical company of Professor Marvel (The Wizard), The Scarecrow, The Cowardly Lion, The Tin Woodman, The Good Witch, and the Wicked Witch.

After thirty-eight years, adult eyes see through the special effects: the Munchkins are only the Singer Midgets, and The Good Witch's skyborne chariot is a bumpy bubble. But age has not withered nor custom staled the infinite charm of Judy as the little girl "Over the Rainbow."

ZERO FOR CONDUCT, see p. 195

ANIMALS AND NATURE

BLESS THE BEASTS AND CHILDREN, see p. 114

A DOG OF FLANDERS, see p. 299

THE GREAT ADVENTURE

Sweden, 1953-1954. 78 mins. b/w. Doc. (d) (sp) (ph) Arne Sucksdorff (m) Lars Erik Larsson. English narration written by J. MacLaren-Rose, spoken by Norman Shelley. (c) Arne Sucksdorff, Anders Norborg, Kjell Sucksdorff, Sigvard Kihlgren. (MMA, WRS)

Arne Sucksdorff thought _The Great Adventure_ might be compared in some ways to _Forbidden Games_:

> "[In both] there are children turning life into a fairytale which they take in earnest.... In my film they live on a farm, surrounded by a forest, which is a world without compassion, and their secret is a small otter cub whom they try to save from danger. I have tried to show nature as a whole, as a world of good and evil in which human beings eventually have to make a choice. My film, therefore, is probably more primitive, more sensual [than _Forbidden Games_]."

The _Great Adventure_ is an incomparable poetic documentary, made by a great film artist, of the life during the four seasons of the farm year of the animals in the woods and the lake and of the children nearby.

We watch Anders, who is ten, buying herrings to feed the greedy otter the boys have trapped and tamed; and Kjell, who is six, and Sucksdorff's own child, fishing in a hole in the ice with the magnificent dark woods behind him. Fox cubs, great black grouse, a vixen racing in a cornfield, baby owls, the boys coming on a dead roebuck in the snow--all are actors in the "great adventure" of the seasons. The film is very slow, very serene and unhurried in its observation, yet you may agree with British documentary filmmaker Grierson that the stories of daily living are "more dramatic and more vital than all the false excitements you can muster."

In the spring, Kjell leaves his family to live in the woods with his pet, but the otter slips away from him. The boy learns that "no one can cage a dream for long, no matter how kind the keeper." This is Sucksdorff's allegory, man's relation to his lost paradise.

The photography (Sucksdorff) and music (Lars Erik Larsson) are beautiful. It might all be a fairy tale, but it is no less real than the adult world we return to when the film is over. Though it was not on this farm in central Sweden that we were ten and six years old, we recognize Anders and Kjell, we know the calls of the summer woods: "This was what it was like ... a summer morning, when we first woke up."

The Great Adventure is a rediscovery of the wonder of the moods of childhood and the cycles of nature.

"J. T.", see p. 20

KES

Great Britain, 1969. 109 mins. col. (d) Kenneth Loach (sp) Barry Hines, Kenneth Loach, Tony Garnett, from the novel _A Kestrel for a Knave_ by Barry Hines (ph) Chris Menges (m) John Cameron, (c) David Bradley, Colin Welland, Lynne Petrie, Freddie Fletcher, Brian Glover, Bob Bowes. (UAS)

Kes is a child-and-animal movie with a difference. The original British title, _A Kestrel for a Knave_, from the novel on which it is based, suggests the reason. Billy isn't the usual youngster who turns to a pet for consolation when he is unhappy at home and at school; he is a fifteen-year-old Yorkshire kid trying to rebel against the grimness of life in the northern British mining town of Barnsley.

Billy starts out with a problem or two: he's short for his age, clumsy, bad at soccer; he lives (more or less abandoned) with a flighty working mother and an older brother who bullies him. He's not attentive in school. The only good thing that ever happens to Billy--and it doesn't transform his life for the conventional happy ending of other child-and-animal stories--is that he finds a kestrel (baby hawk), as wild and fierce and free as he would like to be himself. With the encouragement of the only one of his teachers who's ever taken an interest in him, Billy trains the hawk and is caught up in the fascination of the ancient sport of falconry. But nobody will let them be. When his brother viciously kills the kestrel, Billy's grief is reminiscent of the boy's in _The Yearling_.

Kes has good unstressed comedy, like a chaotic soccer game with unenthusiastic boys, and lovely scenes showing Billy's training of the kestrel; but it is largely a reminder of how hard and unfair life can be for a boy of Billy's age--a not particularly endearing boy, but one who knows he wants more out of life than going down the mine.

Shot entirely on location in Barnsley, mostly with nonprofessional locals or semiprofessional actors, Kes has some remarkable performances by adolescents who look and sound right (sometimes so Yorkshire sounding that they're hard to understand). An international festival selection, it is the work of former British-TV director Kenneth Loach (Poor Cow, 1967; Wednesday's Child, 1972).

For its lack of sentimentality and its rare realism in the children-and-animals genre, this film of a neglected child is worth seeing. David Bradley is excellent as Billy.

Also: Growing Pains

THE LITTLEST HORSE THIEVES

Disney, 1976. 104 mins. col. (d) Charles Jarrott (sp) Rosemary Anne Sisson (ph) Paul Beeson (m) Ron Goodwin (c) Alastair Sim, Peter Barkworth, Maurice Colbourne, Susan Tebbs, Andrew Harrison, Chloe Franks, Benjie Bolgar, Prunella Scales, Geraldine McEwan. (DIS)

It's hard not to let one's Anglophile prejudice show in talking about The Littlest Horse Thieves. British made and British played, it's topnotch Disney--many cuts above the domestic productions. Its three child "thieves" are natural, earnest, charming; its script (by Rosemary Anne Sisson, who's written TV's Elizabeth R and Upstairs, Downstairs) and direction (by Charles Jarrott, who's done Anne of the Thousand Days, among other good movies) are first-rate. The late Alastair Sim heads an admirable cast.

In a coal mining town in Yorkshire in 1909, a new manager decides to make a profit by replacing with machinery the pit ponies that haul coal to the surface and live underground. A miner's two young stepsons and the manager's eleven-year-old daughter, to save the beloved ponies from the slaughterhouse, match adult intransigence with daring, youthful ingenuity.

Andrew Harrison, Benjie Bolgar, and Chloe Franks are appealing children. Their characterizations--and those of the aristocratic mine owner blinded by class differences, the boys' stepfather, and the ice-cold manager who is a loving father--lift the film above others of its type.

THE LITTLEST OUTLAW

Disney, 1955. 75 mins. col. (d) Roberto Gavaldon (sp) Bill Walsh, from a story by Larry Lansburgh (ph) Alex Phillips (m) William Lava (c) Pedro Armendariz, Joseph Calleia, Rodolfo Acosta, Andres Velásquez, Pepe Ortiz. (GEN)

The engaging Andres Velásquez as ten-year-old Pablito and the location photography near San Miguel Allende in Mexico that gives him a frame make this a little more than the routine boy-horse adventure.

Filmed by the Disney company with the facilities of the Churubusco Studios, the story tells of a youngster whose stepfather is the brutal horse trainer of a Mexican general. When the general's prize jumper, Conquistador, fails in a test and is threatened by the general with destruction, Pablito runs away, taking the horse with him.

With the police on his trail, Pablito finds refuge in a small city cathedral, where the padre (Joseph Calleia), accepts the horse as one of his parishioners. There are adventures with gypsies and outlaws, a fight in the bull ring (featuring Pepe Ortiz), a horse show in Mexico City, and the blessing of the animals by the priest on the Feast of St. Anthony.

Pablito is brave and kind, and (as _Variety_ said) the portrait of the little outlaw never descends to maudlin sentimentality.

LOUISIANA STORY, see p. 54

MY FRIEND FLICKA

Twentieth Century-Fox, 1943. 90 mins. col. (d) Harold Schuster (sp) Lillie Hayward, Francis Edwards Faragoh, from the novel by Mary O'Hara (c) Roddy McDowall, Preston Foster, Rita Johnson, Jeff Corey. (FNC)

Your name is Ken McLaughlin, you're ten years old, and you tame an outcast colt on your father's Wyoming ranch. What happens after that? You turn into the prototype of all the Hollywood movie children who reclaim (and are reclaimed by) animals.

As Ken, Roddy McDowall does well enough. He daydreams, gets poor grades in school, and puzzles his father, a strict West Point man. When he is offered a colt of his own to train, he disturbs his father by selecting a filly bred of a loco mare. But he is full of faith in his friend Flicka, and after weeks of training her with loving gentleness, he is proved right. Father, of course, has new faith in son Ken.

Rather simply done, with a minimum of sentimentality except at the end, _My Friend Flicka_ follows Mary O'Hara's story with fidelity, though it tones down some of its force. It has interest chiefly as the first of many movies about children who relate more to their animal friends than to their families.

Also: From Literature
Growing Pains

MY SIDE OF THE MOUNTAIN, see p. 56

NATIONAL VELVET

M-G-M, 1944, 123 mins. col. (d) Clarence Brown (sp) Theodore Reeves and Helen Deutsch, from the novel by Enid Bagnold (m) Herbert Stothart (ph) Leonard Smith (c) Elizabeth Taylor, Mickey Rooney, Jackie ("Butch") Jenkins, Donald Crisp, Anne Revere, Reginald Owen, Arthur Treacher. (FNC)

Once upon a time, there was a butcher's little girl and a vagabond boy who believed they could turn an unknown jumper, a beautiful sorrel gelding, into a champion. And so they trained the horse themselves, and she rode it in the Grand National Steeplechase at Aintree, and it won.

Enid Bagnold's story of Velvet Brown and her love for her horse is a classic of the genre and has been made into a film of taste and charm. Velvet Brown is not just any twelve-year-old, she is Elizabeth Taylor, fresh and completely enchanting. Mickey Rooney, as her rascally friend Mi Taylor, and Jackie ("Butch") Jenkins, as the youngest of the family, are fine, too.

Clarence Brown has given us some lovely views of the children and the hunter on the English downs near the sea. Their absorption and belief in the horse they love, common to many children in life as well as fairy tales, make Velvet Brown and Mi Taylor memorable prototypes.

Also: From Literature

OLD YELLER

Disney, 1957. 83 mins., col. (d) Robert Stevenson (sp) Fred Gipson and William Tunberg, from Gipson's novel (ph) Charles P. Boyle (m) Oliver Wallace (c) Dorothy McGuire, Fess Parker, Tommy Kirk, Kevin Corcoran. (DIS)

The first of many Disneys about a boy and his dog, Old Yeller is still one of the best of the breed, well received by the critics, and phenomenally popular. It gave young Tommy Kirk his only good role, before he was cast in a string of formula comedies.

The pioneer Coates family in Texas in 1869 temporarily loses father Jim (Fess Parker) when he goes on a cattle drive, and fifteen-year-old Travis (Tommy Kirk) becomes the head of the house. His lonely little brother, Arliss (Kevin Corcoran), adopts a big stray dog, Old Yeller, who wanders onto the farm and becomes a part of their lives. When this faithful protector and friend catches rabies from some wild pigs on a trapping expedition, he must be shot. Travis does it and is devastated. But he makes friends finally with one of Old Yeller's pups.

It might have been caramel custard, but Fred Gipson's script from his novel retains the pleasant frontier flavor of the boy and his family.

THE RED PONY, see p. 319

RUN WILD, RUN FREE, see p. 263

WHITE MANE (CRIN BLANC)

France, 1953. 40 mins., b/w. (d) Albert Lamorisse (sp) Albert Lamorisse, adapted by Denys Colomb de Daunant (ph) Edmond Séchan (m) Maurice Le Roux (c) Alain Emery, Crin Blanc. Commentary by Albert Lamorisse and James Agee, spoken by Frank Silvera. (MMA)

This documentary was photographed in the Camargue, in the south of France, with the local ranchers, a beautiful, wild white stallion named Crin Blanc ("White Mane"), and a small boy who knows that the horse can be captured only by gentleness. This beautifully photographed and poetically conceived adventure was made by Albert Lamorisse, Edmond Séchan (The Red Balloon), and Denys Colomb de Daunant (Dream of Wild Horses, also about the Camargue).

"We enter and experience the child's domain," wrote Pauline Kael. We share his joy in discovery of the animal, and when a choice must be made, we understand why the two free and proud creatures choose their own world, far from the world of men.

The boy (Alain Emery) loses Crin Blanc when he runs out of the makeshift corral to rejoin his herd. The lesson for the child is the same as the one young Kjell learns in The Great Adventure (q. v.), when his tamed otter slips back into the forest. After a terrific battle with the leader of the herd, White Mane returns to the Camargue marshes. The ranchers try to trap him with fire. The boy rescues him, and they gallop to the river, which sweeps them both out to sea.

James Agee collaborated with Lamorisse on the commentary, which does not get in the way of the images.

THE YEARLING, see p. 62

FROM LITERATURE

ABIDE WITH ME, see p. 109

THE ADVENTURES OF HUCKLEBERRY FINN

M-G-M, 1960. 107 mins. col. (d) Michael Curtiz (sp) James Lee, from the novel by Mark Twain (c) Tony Randall, Eddie Hodges, Archie Moore, Josephine Hutchinson. (FNC)

There has never been a good movie about the most famous boy in American literature. We've had Mickey Rooney (1939) and in this adaptation we have Eddie Hodges, but we've never had Huck Finn. The thirteen-year-old who hated all the restraints of civilization, who understood what his creator called "the damned human race," and who observed it in all its pious humbug during his river odyssey with Jim has escaped screening.

There has been nobody to capture him as David Lean captured Pip and David Copperfield. The wise Hollywood money wanted a vehicle for Mickey when he was a hot child star; their version of Huck included Abolitionist speeches that would have turned the original Huck green. Now, the box-office watchers have turned out a vehicle for Eddie Hodges, full of too-bright color and some music and a lot of sentimental hokum. Eddie is a cute little boy who was considerably better in Frank Capra's _A Hole in the Head_ (1959), but he's not Huck Finn. He's nowhere near the "great-spirited boy among mean-spirited men" that one critic called Huck.

Some day, a filmmaker will look at the boy in the book, not at stereotypes of entertaining characters in the public domain, and will discover a masterpiece of insight. Until then, you might look at this as an example of everything they did _not_ understand about Mark Twain's boy.

THE ADVENTURES OF TOM SAWYER

United Artists, 1938. 91 mins. col. (d) Norman Taurog (sp) John Weaver, from the novel by Mark Twain (ph) James Wong Howe (c) Tommy Kelly, Jackie Moran, May Robson, Walter Brennan, Ann Gillis, Victor Jory. Spring Byington, Donald Meek, Margaret Hamilton, Nana Bryant. (GEN)

Most of the movies made from Mark Twain's Tom Sawyer look too much like the illustrated classics editions, or second-rate Norman Rockwell. Which one of the five different screen Toms you prefer will depend on your age and nostalgia quotient.

Eliminating on grounds of taste, the recent musical adaptation sponsored by The Reader's Digest, which is more saccharine and less tart than we like our Twain, we could go all the way back to 1917, when Jack Pickford was Tom. In 1920, Jackie Coogan played the role. Often seen on television, the Coogan film, though dated, is set in a Missouri village that the author would have the least trouble in recognizing. In 1938, Billy Cook was not bad in Tom Sawyer, Detective. But, all things considered, the most satisfactory available film to date is Selznick's film starring Tommy Kelly (also 1938). He is convincing in all the classic scenes of boyhood and so is the Becky Thatcher (Ann Gillis). Working well with the famous children are a good Aunt Polly (May Robson) and Injun Joe (Victor Jory).

The best books, of course, seldom make the best movies, and one of the effects of even this Technicolor try is to send one back to the children of the printed page, as alive as dialog and our imaginations can make them.

AH, WILDERNESS!

M-G-M, 1935. 101 mins. b/w. (d) Clarence Brown (sp) Albert Hackett, Frances Goodrich, from the play by Eugene O'Neill (c) Wallace Beery, Lionel Barrymore, Aline MacMahon, Eric Linden, Cecilia Parker, Mickey Rooney, Spring Byington, Charles Grapewin, Frank Albertson, Bonita Granville, Helen Flint. (FNC)

Eugene O'Neill's "comedy of recollection"--still widely read and performed by little theater groups--is a dated movie with some incidental glimpses of adolescence as it possibly was on July 4, 1906, in a town very much like New London, Connecticut. It takes some suspension of disbelief.

Mrs. Miller (Spring Byington) urges father Nat Miller (Lionel Barrymore) to discipline their seventeen-year-old son Richard (Eric Linden), who is in the grip of the life force and burning to overthrow the shackles of his family--shackles that have been defined for him by Swinburne, Omar Khayyam, Oscar Wilde, and Bernard Shaw. Valedictorian of his high school class, he plans a speech that will revolutionize man's thinking. To his sweetheart, Muriel (Cecilia Parker), Richard confides that he has been born a century ahead of his time. She is a little frightened by the news.

Meanwhile, Muriel's father (Charles Grapewin) has got hold of a love letter from Richard to the girl; bits of poetry with sexual overtones copied from Swinburne convince him that his daughter's friendship with this flaming rebel must end. Richard, in a mood of

tragic cynicism about his own and Muriel's family, goes to the Pleasant Beach House and tries to embark on the road to ruin. A few gin fizzes later, he finds he cannot accept the invitation of the coarse and worldly Belle (Helen Flint) to go up to her room. He is thrown out by the bartender because he is underage. At home, things do not turn out as badly as Richard fears; after his father's fumbling attempt to find out whether the boy has had relations with the prostitute, and his man-to-man warning about the "whited sepulchres" of loose women, the crisis passes.

Played for comedy and sentiment, with an M-G-M cast of familiar faces, Ah, Wilderness! is so faithful to the original that the camera underscores its weaknesses. It becomes a comedy of nostalgia for a simpler time rather than a comedy of true recollection--for the young Eugene O'Neill was not like Richard; he was more like the Edmund of Long Day's Journey into Night--and is an entertaining fairy tale of adolescence. Richard, we feel, is a young man made in fancy; O'Neill said the idea for Ah, Wilderness! came to him in a dream.

Also: Finding Oneself
Love and Sex

ALL QUIET ON THE WESTERN FRONT

Universal, 1930. 103 mins. b/w. (d) Lewis Milestone (sp) Del Andrews, Maxwell Anderson, George Abbott, from the novel by Erich Maria Remarque (ph) Arthur Edeson (m) David Broekman (c) Lew Ayres, Louis Wolheim, John Wray, Raymond Griffith, Slim Summerville, Russell Gleason, William Bakewell. (CWF, SWA, TWY, UNI)

Drafted into the Kaiser's army at eighteen, Erich Maria Remarque wrote the classic war novel of our time, about four boys who go straight from the schoolroom into the trenches as eager volunteers and are brutalized and destroyed by the reality of battle. Lewis Milestone's 1930 movie, in great sympathy with the novel, is still one of the most powerful antiwar films.

Two of its scenes, at least, scar the memory. (It is no wonder that Lew Ayres, who played Paul Baumer, the nineteen-year-old protagonist, became a lifelong pacifist.) A boy is dying in hospital after a leg amputation; his friends wait beside his bed to take the boots he won't need any more. Paul is trapped in a foxhole with the Frenchman he has just killed, and in the soldier's wallet sees pictures of his enemy's wife and children.

Baumer, Kropp, Muller, Leer--how idealistically they responded to their teacher's urging to enlist, in 1914! Four years later, back home on leave, Paul Baumer cannot face other boys in that schoolroom. How can he tell anyone about the war? Only comrades who have shared filth, fear, and death can understand. One of his comrades is shot in the lungs, another in the stomach, a third goes insane. In October, 1918, on a day when the front has been so inactive that the communiqué has reported "all quiet," Paul reaches a hand out of the trenches to catch a butterfly and is killed.

The novel says that on Paul's face is "an expression of calm, as though glad the end had come." An end had come to him and his friends long before their deaths--an end to illusion, faith, youth, ties with family and home. On leave, they found nothing in common with the adults who had made the war that they were fighting.

(In training, griping about a sadistic corporal, dunking him in a dirty pool; stealing food as an older soldier, Kat, teaches them; sneering at even younger recruits; hunting girls--that is the only life they have known, outside of the terror of the guns. No longer youths, never fully men, they have been shut off forever from the world of the others.)

Director Lewis Milestone began to shoot All Quiet as a silent film; continuing it after the advent of sound, he still concentrated on the visuals, retaining many of the rhythms and values of the best work of an earlier period. Though the horrors of screaming shells are present in this "audible picture," as a reviewer of 1930 called it, there is no straining after the new effects at the expense of the interior drama. Here is the war, through the eyes and in the eyes of its young soldiers and their older comrades.

Also: War and Its Aftermath

ALL THE WAY HOME, see p. 203

ALMOS' A MAN

PBS/TV, 1976. 39 mins. col. (d) Stan Lathan (sp) Leslie Lee, from the short story by Richard Wright (ph) Tak Fujimoto (m) Taj Mahal (c) LeVar Burton, Madge Sinclair, Robert Doqui, Garry Goodrow. (PER)

Teenage David Glover, the protagonist of Almos' a Man, is played by LeVar Burton, who was the young Kunta Kinte in the television series based on Alex Haley's Roots. Robert Geller, executive producer of The American Short Story: A Film Series, a project of the National Endowment for the Humanities, of which Almos' a Man is a part, says,

> In Roots he portrayed a young man filled with hope--destined, he is sure, to be a warrior and a leader. That hope was torn from him. In Almos' a Man, he plays another young man nearing adulthood--but without hope, expecting to continue his present life behind the plow. In the Richard Wright story, he only fantasizes a future.

The original title of Wright's story was The Man Who Was Almost a Man. David Glover, a Black farm worker in the Deep South in the 1930s, is seventeen. Like other adolescents, he is searching for his identity, pitting his inner desires against the indifference or the prohibitions of his elders. His parents are overprotective and deny him his independence.

One day, pushing a plow, David hears gunshots while his white employer is hunting. David dreams of owning his own gun--now, that would be something like a man--but is ridiculed by the other farmhands. However, the boy is able to coax his mother into letting him use two dollars of his earnings to buy a used handgun from a mail-order catalog. While timidly practicing with the gun, David accidentally kills a mule. He confesses, is publicly humiliated by his father, and is bondaged by the landowner to work twenty-five months to pay for the mule.

But David will not be bondaged. Retrieving his gun, he hops aboard a passing train, filled with notions of a very different future for himself. In the box car where we last see him, with no money, and the unloaded gun in his pocket, fantasy enwraps him; he is going "somewhere, somewhere he could be a man."

"All kids go through the same trips," says LeVar Burton, "the same changes, growing pains, anxieties. Everybody can relate to the occasional humiliations, the care of parents, the closeness to mother. It's natural and universal."

Opening up the world of Richard Wright's fiction, Almos' a Man is sensitive and cinematically interesting. It owes much to a good script by Leslie Lee (winner of an Obie for the play "The First Breeze of Summer") and to good direction and a good cast. Taj Mahal's music and Tak Fujimoto's photography are effective.

Also: Finding Oneself

AND NOW MIGUEL, see p. 8

THE APU TRILOGY, see p. 69

THE BAD SEED

Warners, 1956. 129 mins. b/w. (d) Mervyn LeRoy (sp) John Lee Mahin, from the play by Maxwell Anderson and the novel by William March (m) Alex North (c) Nancy Kelly, Patty McCormack, Henry Jones, Eileen Heckart, Evelyn Varden, William Hopper, Paul Fix, Jesse White, Gage Clarke, Joan Croydon, Frank Cady. (MOG, SWA)

Adapted from the play by Maxwell Anderson and the novel by William March, with the story unchanged except for the very end, The Bad Seed emerges as little more than a shocker. Its major premise is that some children are born all bad, and that the apparently sweet little eight-year-old Rhoda (Patty McCormack) is a psychopathic child who has murdered an old woman before the start of the film and who kills two more victims during the course of the story. Slowly, we learn that she has caused the drowning of a little classmate.

Whether the premise would be easier to swallow if the production had been better remains debatable. Neither the girl's mother, played by Nancy Kelly, nor the drowned boy's mother, Eileen Heckart, is persuasive in her mounting frenzy. The school principal (Joan Croydon) is little more than a caricature. Patty McCormack, as the bad seed, is a somewhat overgrown specimen and, again, not particularly convincing.

As if to assure us that none of this grotesquerie is meant seriously, the film's producers and scriptwriter have substituted an epilogue for the play's original ending: the cast is called out for bows, and Miss Kelly playfully spanks Patty. Just in case you believed that anyone with pigtails could be so horrid.

<u>Also</u>: Delinquency and Crime
Special Children

BALLET SHOES

BBC, 1975. 180 mins. b/w. (d) Tim Combe (sp) John Wiles, adapted from Noel Streatfeild's novel (c) Angela Thorne, Mary Morris, Terence Skelton, Elizabeth Morgan, Jane Slaughter, Sarah Prince. (TIM)

Since its publication in 1936, Noel Streatfeild's <u>Ballet Shoes</u> has charmed children and adults all over the world. Now the novel has achieved one of those smooth-as-silk BBC dramatizations and was brought to American television audiences by PBS as a Christmas 1976 treat.

The three little Fossils, orphan girls adopted as infants by an absentminded explorer (fond of collecting fossils) and left with his niece in London before he disappeared on an expedition, are enchanting children. Real, natural, highly individual, they make a secret vow "to become famous and put our names in the history books." Each in her own way struggles to fulfil her goal. Posey, ten (Sarah Prince), is a ballerina; Pauline, twelve (Elizabeth Morgan), is an actress; Petrova, eleven (Jane Slaughter), is a born mechanic, fascinated by cars and planes. Money is scarce in the Depression, but their guardian's lodgers take a hand and help them prepare for their careers. There are adventures and discoveries at Madame Fidolia's dance school, self-doubts, dreams, awakening to adult reality.

What makes the filmed <u>Ballet Shoes</u> so good is that each one of the British Little Women is played to perfection, and John Wiles's adaptation of the Noel Streatfeild characters is refreshing. The children are as much fun to watch--and as understandable--as a trio of one's friends' offspring. Provided, that is, that one's friends are fortunate enough to have three very talented little girls. These are not stage children, but youngsters stepping on to the stages of special vocations.

<u>Also</u>: Special Children

THE BATTLE OF THE VILLA FIORITA, see p. 112

BAXTER, see p. 71

THE BLACKBOARD JUNGLE, see p. 170

THE BROWNING VERSION, see p. 171

CAPTAINS COURAGEOUS

M-G-M, 1937. 116 mins. b/w. (d) Victor Fleming (sp) John Lee Mahin, Marc Connelly, Dale Van Every, from the novel by Rudyard Kipling (ph) Harold Rosson (c) Freddie Bartholomew, Spencer Tracy, Lionel Barrymore, Melvyn Douglas, Mickey Rooney, John Carradine. (FNC)

The spoiled rich man's son in the original novel was nineteen; in this excellent film adaptation, he is twelve, and Freddie Bartholomew makes him surprisingly obnoxious in the early scenes when he is supposed to be obnoxious and unsurprisingly moving in the scenes after he has been turned into a very decent small boy. The metamorphosis occurs, as you may remember, in the course of Harvey Cheyne's schooling at the hands of the crew of the fishing schooner We're Here. Taken aboard off the Grand Banks, he is whipped into shape by Manuel (Spencer Tracy), the stern Portuguese fisherman, who learns to love his "little fish" as much as Harvey loves him. When Manuel dies, the boy is unreconciled to his loss, and it is hard for him to overcome the estrangement between himself and his father, who would help him if he were allowed.

The life of the boy in the old Gloucester fishing fleet is superbly photographed (by Hal Rosson, who shot The Red Badge of Courage)--rowing, trawling, fishing, steering, dressing down herring and cod, chopping bait.

Mickey Rooney is good, too, as the boy Dan. But it is young Harvey's "sea change" that registers. Kipling sails a smooth course.

Also: Family Relationships
Growing Pains

THE CHALK GARDEN, see p. 116

CHEAPER BY THE DOZEN

Twentieth Century-Fox, 1950. 85 mins. b/w. (d) Walter Lang (sp) Lamar Trotti, from the autobiography by Frank B. Gilbreth, Jr., and Ernestine Gilbreth Carey (ph) Leon Shamroy (c) Clifton Webb, Myrna Loy, Jeanne Crain, Mildred Natwick, Edgar Buchanan, Sara Allgood. (FNC)

The most improbable thing about the family of six sons and six daughters in Cheaper By the Dozen is that it was a real family that lived in Montclair, New Jersey, in the 1920s. Papa was a motion-study engineer, mama was bright as well as charming, and life was full of planned domestic efficiency that looked (and sounded) a lot more like farce.

The original book of family reminiscences, written by Frank B. Gilbreth, Jr., and Ernestine Gilbreth Carey, has always been extremely popular. Sometimes a pretty good book can make a much better movie. In this case, while the film is such broad and sentimental stuff that it's not always easy to swallow, it's all in fun. In the book the spirited children of Mr. and Mrs. Gilbreth were all individuals, defying any attempt at regimentation. In the movie, each is still himself, from the youngest to the adolescent miss (Jeanne Crain), but the mass effect is the one that counts. Nothing on the printed page was ever as hilarious as the movie's vision of a wholesale tonsillectomy or the twelve kids packing into the family car.

As for the original Mr. Gilbreth's metamorphosis into Clifton Webb--well, it's hard to believe that he had all those children, but having had them, he's a very firm head of the household, without being as cock-of-the-walk as his predecessor in best seller land, Father Day of Life with Father.

Also: Family Relationships

CHILD'S PLAY, see p. 173

A CLOCKWORK ORANGE, see p. 271

THE COOL WORLD

Fred Wiseman, 1963. 104 mins. b/w. (d) (ed) Shirley Clarke (sp) Shirley Clarke, Carl Lee, from the novel by Warren Miller (ph) Baird Bryant (m) by Mal Waldron with Dizzy Gillespie, Yusef Lateef, Arthur Taylor, Aaron Bell (c) Hampton Clanton, Yolanda Rodriguez, Bostic Felton, Gary Bolling, Carl Lee, Clarence Williams III, John Marriott, Gloria Foster, Georgia Burke. (ZPH)

The Cool World is the world of Harlem in 1963, the world as it is seen by a fourteen-year-old black boy, Duke Custis. The story is told in the first person, as in Warren Miller's brilliant novel, from which Shirley Clarke's unsparing and angry semidocumentary is taken.

We first meet Duke (Hampton Clanton) on a class trip to the Stock Exchange. He and his friends ignore the white teacher, who has handed them a pamphlet, "How to Own a Share of America." They are more interested in the difference between a Colt and a Luger. Duke's dream is to become somebody by getting hold of a gun and leading his gang, the Royal Pythons, in a rumble. As Duke Custis, "a cold killer," he will be as big a man as Priest (Carl Lee), the gangster who trades in guns and drugs.

When Blood (Clarence Williams III), leader of the gang, brings the boys a fifteen-year-old prostitute, LuAnne (Yolanda Rodriguez), Duke takes his turn with her. Later, after he has kicked out Blood and succeeded him as leader, Duke talks quietly and fondly with LuAnne and takes her to Coney Island to see the ocean.

But LuAnne vanishes. His friend Littleman is dead. Priest is on the run. Duke finally decides, reluctantly, to lead the Pythons in a rumble. A boy is killed; Duke is dragged off by the police and beaten. His voice comments on the new "cold killer" as he passes his mother and her new lover on the street, unnoticed by them. (Earlier, Duke hasn't been able to remember which of his mother's lovers cared enough about him to take him to the zoo.)

We have had revealing glimpses of Duke's family: his mother (Gloria Foster) talking about ghetto hardship; a brother illustrating the fact that he has educated himself out of the Harlem jungle; a grandma (Georgia Burke) crooning "Jesus was a black man."

Some of the shadings of Warren Miller's novel, such as the middle-class black home and Duke's feeling for his teacher, are missing in Shirley Clarke's film. But no aspect of misery, vice, or childhood "games" of sex and violence is ignored. Rather, The Cool World bears down unrelentingly on the social conditions of Duke's childhood.

The first feature film produced by Frederick Wiseman (High School, Juvenile Court) and a successor to Shirley Clarke's 1961

The Connection and many prizewinning shorts, The Cool World is marked by excellent camera work. The personal lives of many of the young nonprofessional actors parallel the story of the film. Most effective is the musical contribution to the Harlem scene. Written by Mal Waldron, it is played by Dizzy Gillespie and others of the Jazz Group.

Also: Delinquency and Crime

THE DARK AT THE TOP OF THE STAIRS

Warners, 1960. 123 mins. col. (d) Delbert Mann (sp) Harriet Frank, Jr., Irving Ravetch, from the play by William Inge (ph) Harry Stradling, Sr. (m) Max Steiner (c) Robert Preston, Dorothy McGuire, Eve Arden, Angela Lansbury, Shirley Knight, Frank Overton, Lee Kinsolving, Robert Eyer. (GEN)

Reenie Flood (Shirley Knight) is sixteen. She hasn't begun to put up her braids yet and wears a middy blouse over a dyed blue skirt or an old cardigan buttoned wrong. A thoroughly introverted, lonely girl, she is so sure that nobody can like her that she throws up in the bathroom at the prospect of going on a blind date.

Reenie's younger brother, Sonny (Robert Eyer), is also very lonely. A mama's boy who is the butt of the kids on the block, he collects fireflies and movie stars' pictures.

Reenie and Sonny are the children of Rubin Flood (Robert Preston), who's just lost his job as salesman for a saddlery firm in a small Oklahoma town in the 1920s; and his wife, Cora (Dorothy McGuire), who's grown tired of scrimping along on too little money and being alone while Rubin's on the road. Recently, Cora has been unwilling to make love with her husband; and, even more than ever, she has fiercely and possessively concentrated on her children.

The Floods, in William Inge's 1957 play, are a family in which each member has some fear about himself or the others, a fear not always clearer than the mysterious "dark at the top of the stairs." In the movie, which has been adapted and directed with heavy-handed overstatement, the theme gets lost in the welter of Freudian stereotypes and Hollywood formulas. In 1960, it seemed daring to show Rubin and Cora in bed together (Mr. Preston's bare chest was one of the earliest breakthroughs in screen realism) and liberal to suggest that a Jewish adolescent, a cadet in a military school who is the neglected son of a Hollywood actress, can be triggered emotionally to commit suicide when he is asked to leave a dance at a restricted country club. The film introduces a character not in the play, a warmhearted widow who runs a beauty shop, Mavis (Angela Lansbury), and who gives Cora advice on how to hold her husband.

The movie does not improve on the original; it blunts whatever delicacy Inge achieved in showing the relationship of his people to one another. It says everything literally and says it at least twice. In case you didn't get the point that Reenie is her mother's hope for hanging on to her youth and that Sonny is suffering from an Oedipus complex, director Delbert Mann nudges you with a sharp finger.

Shirley Knight is excellent, however, as Reenie, particularly in her meetings with the young cadet. They are convincing as two lonely and sensitive adolescents. "I know you're a nice girl," he says to her, "because there are tears in your eyes when somebody tells you something sad." She's a thoroughly nice girl, and what's a nice girl like Reenie doing in a movie like this?

(It is characteristic of the Hollywood formula that the Jewish cadet, Samuel David Golden, is played by Lee Kinsolving, who looks and acts exactly like Lee Kinsolving, not Samuel David Golden.)

Also: Family Relationships

DAVID AND LISA, see p. 258

DAVID COPPERFIELD

M-G-M, 1935. 133 mins. b/w. (d) George Cukor (sp) Howard Estabrook, from Hugh Walpole's adaptation of Charles Dickens's novel (c) Freddie Bartholomew, W. C. Fields, Lionel Barrymore, Maureen O'Sullivan, Edna May Oliver, Roland Young, Basil Rathbone, Elsa Lanchester, Lewis Stone, Madge Evans, Jessie Ralph, Hugh Williams. (FNC)

In his book about child performers of the screen, Those Endearing Young Charms, Marc Best tells how Freddie Bartholomew of London, when he was ten years old, came to the United States with his Aunt Millycent. Not many months afterward, he entered David Selznick's office dressed as David Copperfield. "Sir," he said, removing his beaver hat, "I am David Copperfield." Taking Freddie in his arms, Selznick replied, "Right you are. You are David Copperfield."

He always was. Though he was good in Captains Courageous and Little Lord Fauntleroy and Kidnapped and several other films, his most lasting screen image is that of the Victorian child, Dickens's self-pitying recollection of himself (written when he was old and rich and famous) as the sensitive, superior little gentleman who suffered so much from the injuries of crass adults. That child is meant to wring your heart, but thanks to Freddie's wistful delicacy and Mr. Cukor's taste, he is moving without descending to bathos. Almost adult as he converses with the Micawbers in London or Mr. Dick at his Aunt Betsey Trotwood's in Dover, he is very much the child in his home with Peggotty after his mother's death, or in school with his hero, Steerforth. And the frightened boy who forgets his lesson under the Murdstones' steely glares is not just Mrs. Copperfield's little boy; he might be yours.

DEAD END, see p. 237

DEATH BE NOT PROUD, see p. 206

THE DIARY OF ANNE FRANK

Twentieth Century-Fox, 1959. 170 mins. b/w. (d) George Stevens (sp) Frances Goodrich and Albert Hackett, from their play based on the book _Anne Frank: The Diary of a Young Girl_ (ph) William C. Mellor, Jack Cardiff (m) Alfred Newman (c) Millie Perkins, Joseph Schildkraut, Shelley Winters, Ed Wynn, Richard Beymer, Lou Jacobi, Diane Baker, Douglas Spencer. (FNC)

> It would be wrong to leave the impression that all in _Diary_ is grim, disheartening, or angering. On the contrary, most of it is devoted to close and superbly honest revelations of family life or the growing up of this charming girl. It would be hard to recall a more touching portrait in film of the pains and joys of adolescence, and the slowly developing first love between Anne and Peter is as delicate and penetrating as anything of the kind I can remember. Their first kiss is a classic in sensitive picture making. (Paul V. Beckley, _The New York Herald Tribune_)

As everyone knows who has read the original book, _Anne Frank: The Diary of a Young Girl_ (1952), from which Mr. and Mrs. Hackett derived their Pulitzer Prize play and this film, the scene is the "secret annexe," the small attic on the upper floors of Kraler's spice factory in which eight Jews of Amsterdam are being hidden from the Nazis. For two years, until the Green Police patrol comes for them, two families and Mr. Dussell the dentist remain there in cramped, terrified--yet somehow brave and dignified--living.

The father, Otto Frank (Joseph Schildkraut), and the thirteen-year-old daughter, Anne (Millie Perkins), are the most individualized of the refugees. He is the tower of maturity and wisdom and faith; she is youth, green and growing even there.

The pangs of thirteen to fifteen that Anne experiences are those of a sensitive, gifted girl feeling the emotional and instinctive drives of puberty. She is beginning to question, to rebel, to talk back. "Mother still doesn't understand me," Anne says, "but then I don't understand her." She is jealous of her older sister, Margot (Diane Baker), and rude and impatient as she sees the weaknesses of Mr. and Mrs. Van Daan (Lou Jacobi, Shelley Winters) and Mr. Dussell (Ed Wynn). What is taking place inside her, says Anne, is making her a different person. She has begun to accept her own uniqueness but has not yet learned to respect the uniqueness of adults; she is slowly but not always successfully developing tolerance.

With Peter Van Daan (Richard Beymer), a year or two older than herself, she is first the kid he knew at school, the girl everyone called "Quack Quack." Then, as they grow closer in a lyrical tenderness, they are united against the older generation. Not for them is the "Think of the misery outside"; even in the secret annexe, they show the affirmation of youth.

Anne, of course, is no ordinary girl; as the diary reveals, she is exceptional. Years after the war, her father returns and reads her famous words, "In spite of everything, I still believe that people are really good at heart." Weeping, he says, "She puts me to shame."

Millie Perkins, as Anne, never has the glow, the exquisite expressiveness, that Susan Strasberg had in the stage production. But George Stevens's direction is outstanding. The ensemble acting, the illusion of action and suspense despite the constriction of space, are remarkable.

Above all, the essential character of Anne Frank shines through. It does not need an actress to make us understand and feel the power of her truth.

<u>Also</u>: Family Relationships
Generation Conflicts
Growing Pains
War and Its Aftermath

DITTE, CHILD OF MAN

Denmark, 1946. 104 mins. b/w. (d) Bjarne Henning-Jensen, assisted by Astrid Henning-Jensen (sp) Bjarne Henning-Jensen, based on the novel by Martin Andersen Nexo (ph) Werner Jensen (m) Herman D. Koppel (c) Tove Maes, Karen Poulsen, Rasmus Ottesen, Karen Lykheus, Ebbe Rode, Preben Neergaard, Kai Holm, Lars Henning-Jensen. Danish dialog with English subtitles.

A beautiful novel, translated into most of the world's languages, Martin Andersen Nexo's <u>Ditte Menneskebarn</u> is also a classic of the screen, Bjarne and Astrid Henning-Jensen's <u>Ditte, Child of Man</u>. From the moment their film walked off with the grand prizes at half a dozen film festivals, the husband-and-wife team took a place in the first rank of international directors.

In <u>Ditte</u>, as in all their films which followed (the shorts <u>Ballet Girl</u> and <u>Palle Alone in the World</u>; the documentary feature <u>Where Mountains Float</u>; the feature <u>Boy of Two Worlds</u>, originally <u>Paw</u>), the Henning-Jensens have been concerned with the dramas in the lives of children.

And <u>Ditte</u> is a classic, for perception, for tenderness, for strong feeling without melodrama. The story might have lent itself to bathos in other hands: a baby girl, unloved and unwanted, is abandoned by her mother. She grows up in a country village, becomes a servant, and is seduced, like her mother, by a rich farmer's son. The Henning-Jensens are artists; Ditte's growing up and Ditte's character have simple beauty and inner passion.

All the children we see in the little North Sealand village are vital and true. The village itself is memorable; beginning their career as directors of documentaries, the Henning-Jensens utilized their experience in the making of their feature. These peasants, young and old, move in a setting we believe.

Not a little credit for the infinitely moving quality of Ditte herself, in her adolescence, is owing to the performance (her first on the screen) of Tove Maes. The other players, down to the bit parts, are members of Copenhagen's Royal Theatre.

<u>Also</u>: Love and Sex
Special Children

A DOG OF FLANDERS

Warners, 1959. 97 mins. col. (d) James B. Clark (sp) Ted Sherdeman, from the novel by Ouida (m) Paul Sawtell and Bert Shefter; St. Cecilia Academy of Rome Orchestra and Chorus (c) David Ladd, Donald Crisp, Theodore Bikel. (GEN)

When Ouida's cherished story was affectionately and tastefully produced by Robert B. Radnitz, it established the pattern of critical praise, international awards, and box-office success that all of Radnitz's subsequent films have followed. It won the Grand Prix (Golden Lion) at the Venice Festival, an award of merit from the Belgian Government, and a gold medal from Parents' Magazine.

The youngster in <u>A Dog of Flanders</u> (David Ladd) is enchanted by art. He dreams of becoming a great painter like his adored Rubens. When he and his grandfather (Donald Crisp), who sells milk to the townspeople, find a beaten mongrel in the road, the boy names him Patrasche, which was the name of Rubens's dog. After his grandfather's death, the boy devotes himself to Patrasche. In the end, he is adopted by a painter (Theodore Bikel), who makes him his apprentice.

David Ladd is unassuming but convincing as Nello Daas, the twelve-year-old. The producers "have drawn a genuinely loving portrait of childhood set against pastoral backgrounds that would entrance a Dutch or Flemish master." (A. H. Weiler, <u>The New York Times</u>) For those who care, it should be noted that Patrasche is played by the dog who was previously starred in Disney's <u>Old Yeller</u>.

The story was colorfully shot in authentic settings in the

Netherlands and Belgium, principally in the picturesque public squares and country meadows of Antwerp.

EAST OF EDEN, see p. 77

THE FALLEN IDOL

Great Britain, 1948. 92 mins. b/w. (d) Carol Reed (sp) Graham Greene, from his short story "The Basement Room" (ph) Georges Perinal (m) William Alwyn (c) Ralph Richardson, Sonia Dresdel, Michele Morgan, Bobby Henrey, Denis O'Dea, Dora Bryan, Walter Fitzgerald. (BUD, EMG, IMA, KPF, WHO, WRS)

One of the subtlest revelations of a child's behavior ever filmed, The Fallen Idol was adapted by Graham Greene from his short story "The Basement Room" and directed to perfection by Carol Reed. The performance obtained by the director from the child actor Bobby Henrey is one of the marvels of cinema, on a par with those that De Sica and very few others have achieved.

The boy, Felipe (Bobby Henrey), who is eight, is the lonely son of a diplomat living in a vast London embassy. Outside of a pet snake, MacGregor, the child has few interests. His close, understanding companion is the butler, Baines (Ralph Richardson), in whose basement room he listens to wonderful apocryphal stories of Baines's past adventures. Mrs. Baines (Sonia Dresdel) is a stern wife and an unsympathetic figure to the boy. As the housekeeper, she is designated to look after him in his parents' absence, but the child manages to slip away with Baines on a visit to the zoo. He becomes aware of a connection between his idol and the lovely Julie (Michele Morgan).

During an overnight absence of his wife, Baines and Julie make love. Mrs. Baines returns unexpectedly, and accidentally falls to her death on the huge staircase of the mansion. The boy, aware of hidden adult drama without understanding it, frightened by events and yet fascinated by them, runs out of the house. When he is found and brought back, his one desire is to protect Baines. Assuming that he has killed his wife, Felipe attempts to save him and thus throws suspicion on him.

Winner of the award for best direction given by the New York Film Critics, Carol Reed has brilliantly followed all the turns of the child's mind; The Fallen Idol is crystal clear in every inflection, every glance.

In the adult roles, Richardson and Miss Morgan are excellent. When the boy runs away, there are wonderfully true moments with a streetwalker (Dora Bryan) and some policemen.

The greatest tribute that one can pay to this film is that one often forgets that Bobby Henrey is acting a work of fiction.

FIRST LOVE, see p. 146

GIGI

M-G-M, 1958. 116 mins. col. (d) Vincente Minnelli (sp) Alan Jay Lerner, from the novel by Colette (ph) Joseph Ruttenberg (m) Frederick Loewe (lyr) Alan Jay Lerner (cos) Cecil Beaton (c) Leslie Caron, Maurice Chevalier, Louis Jourdan, Hermione Gingold, Eva Gabor, Jacques Bergerac, Isabel Jeans. (FNC)

There is a legend that Colette, seeing the young Audrey Hepburn for the first time, exclaimed, "That is my Gigi!" And truly, everyone who saw Miss Hepburn in the Broadway production of the play from Colette's novel forever after thought of the fifteen-year-old heroine in terms of that special coltish grace and delicate sexuality that are hers. But Leslie Caron is very believable in this lavish musical film. She is certainly a better Gigi than Daniele Delorme in the tame French film directed by Jacqueline Audry in 1949. She convinces with her artlessness and her wisdom.

Gigi, again according to legend, was a real girl, her story the same as the one Colette made so famous. Certainly, in Paris, at the turn of the century, she might have been just such a schoolgirl bred in a far from unworldly family. Trained by her grandmother (Hermione Gingold) and her aunt (Eva Gabor) for the role of *grande cocotte*, Gigi refuses to accept the convention of the women of her family ("We do not marry"). When she falls in love with the family friend, the roué Gaston (Louis Jourdan), and receives an offer from him to be his luxuriously coddled mistress, she refuses. It is to be wedlock or nothing--for romantic, not calculating, reasons. And Gaston, long since enchanted by Gigi's directness, zest, and individuality, asks for her hand in honorable matrimony.

The character of Gigi, even in the welter of color and song and special effects of a musical (one which won nine Academy Awards), is still one of the memorable portraits of a young girl tumbling out of childhood into womanhood; the Colette charmer, as portrayed by Leslie Caron, still appeals.

GO ASK ALICE, see p. 240

THE GO-BETWEEN, see p. 17

THE GORKY TRILOGY

U. S. S. R., 1938-1940. (d) Mark Donskoi (sp) Mark Donskoi, I. Gruzdev, based on Gorky's autobiographical works (ph) Pyotr Yermolov (m) Lev Schwartz (c) Alexei Lyarsky, Varvara Massalitinova, Nikolai Valbert, Mikhail Troyanovsky. Russian dialog with English subtitles. (MAC)

For its detailed, beautiful evocation of a man's growth from early childhood, this three-part biography of Maxim Gorky--extremely faithful to Gorky's memoirs--won international recognition for director Mark Donskoi. To film historian Roger Manvell,

> This group of films is still ... the outstanding example in the whole Soviet cinema of the expression of humane feelings and characterization. Social propaganda, though present, always takes second place to this most moving biography of a boy who gains his understanding of life through years of terrible poverty and suffering.

The three parts of the trilogy are *The Childhood of Maxim Gorky* (1938, 100 mins. b/w); *My Apprenticeship--Out in the World* (1939, 101 mins. b/w); and *My Universities*, a. k. a. *University of Life* (1940, 101 mins. b/w). The last film deals with the experiences of the grown man; so we shall limit ourselves to considering only the first two films here, but since themes and symbols recur throughout the trilogy, the viewer gains much from seeing all three parts.

The Childhood of Maxim Gorky (*Detsvo Gorkovo*), which is the most famous part of the trilogy, depicts Gorky's boyhood in Tsarist Russia in the 1870s. Gorky, whose real name was Alexei Pushkov, was raised from the age of four by his authoritarian, cruel grandfather; his life-loving, brave, and sympathetic grandmother; and two rival uncles. When his grandfather's dyer's business fails, Alexei must help the family by ragpicking. His home makes an indelible impression on him. He reacts against the poverty and searches for escape--a rescue through education. One day he leaves his grandparents to make his own way in the world.

My Apprenticeship--Out in the World (*V lyudlakh*) shows Alexei beginning to earn his living, at the age of eight. He works as a servant for a bourgeois family who promise him an education but make him a drudge. In secret, he reads books borrowed from the mother of a little girl who is his friend--Gogol, Dumas, Pushkin. For a time, he works as dishwasher on a Volga boat, where he is persecuted by the steward, but protected by the cook, to whom he reads *Taras Bulba* at night. Next he is an apprentice in a studio of icon painters. Returning home for a visit to his grandparents before setting off again on his travels, he is ignored by his petulant grandfather; but as the paddle steamer pulls away from the jetty, he sees his wise and loving grandmother wave. She says, "I shall never see you again."

Tsarist Russia, the young boy's shaping environment, is magnificently evoked in the ignorance and poverty, the filth of poorly lit streets, the brutalities of drunkards, the squalor one almost smells. Yet there is also the kindness of ordinary people and the lyricism of the Volga in what has come to be known as Gorky country, between the heights and the Tartar Steppes.

In his love for the boy Gorky and his power to film Gorky's surroundings, Donskoi is comparable to Satyajit Ray, whose Apu Trilogy (q. v.) creates the same sense in the viewer of closeness to a child in a particular culture.

GREAT EXPECTATIONS

Great Britain, 1946. 118 mins. b/w. (d) David Lean (sp) David Lean, Ronald Neame from the novel by Charles Dickens (ph) Guy Green (m) Walter Goehr (c) Anthony Wager, Jean Simmons, John Mills, Valerie Hobson, Francis L. Sullivan, Finlay Currie, Bernard Miles, Martita Hunt, Alec Guinness, Freda Jackson. (GEN)

A technical masterpiece--the opening sequence is required viewing in cinema courses for David Lean's editing and composition--this is also, in the first half at least, the best example of Dickens's characterization on the screen. Since the first half deals with Pip and Estella as children (Anthony Wager and Jean Simmons), Great Expectations might well be required viewing for those fascinated by Dickens's larger-than-life view of childhood.

Director Lean told Roger Manvell,

> The scene of the boy Pip lying terrified in his bedroom and then after a night of fear creeping downstairs at dawn and stealing food for the convict on the moors was something Dickens wrote as if he were right inside the boy himself. We tried in the film to make the audience share Pip's fear.

We also share, as in the boy's imagination, his first shock at meeting Magwitch on the marshes; and his early, loving closeness, when he is still uncorrupted, to the blacksmith, Joe Gargery. When he is summoned to play in Miss Havisham's great musty mansion with the already-corrupted child Estella, we share his infatuation for her, and his determination, despite her gibes, that he will become a gentleman.

The phantasmagoric world of childhood, its shuddering at the grotesque; its innocence and experience--they are all here, in an almost perfect film that captures the atmosphere and the essence of the novel, which remains one of the most memorable evocations of childhood in English literature.

THE HEART IS A LONELY HUNTER

Warners-7 Arts, 1968. 124 mins. col. (d) Robert Ellis Miller (sp) Thomas C. Ryan, from the novel by Carson McCullers (ph) James Wong Howe (m) David Grusin (c) Alan Arkin, Sondra Locke, Chuck McCann, Cicely Tyson, Stacy Keach, Laurinda Barrett, Biff McGuire, Percy Rodriguez, Wayne Smith. (GEN)

Carson McCullers' story, which centers on the influence of a deaf mute on a group of restless and unfulfilled people in a small Southern town, has a portrait of a young tomboy, Mick Kelly, which is another of her compassionate studies of youth. Like The Member of the Wedding (q. v.), this fine film from her novel speaks of the anguish of growing up.

In the original, Mick was fourteen. Here, played by newcomer Sondra Locke at twenty-one, she is seventeen. Since the locale is now Selma, Alabama, the story has been somewhat updated, as well as streamlined, to accommodate the changes of time. Portia, daughter of the black physician, Dr. Copeland, for example, is played by Cicely Tyson with a modern bite.

John Singer, the deaf mute (brilliantly drawn by Alan Arkin), is able to communicate with others, through touch and gesture, and to make them aware of their inner selves. One of the people for whom he unlocks the doors of loneliness and inarticulateness is Mick --rough, gangly, hungry for a response which she gets neither at home nor in her high-school crowd. Mick loves music and identifies it with sympathetic John Singer, whom she idolizes. She clings to him, and like the others, she clothes him with mythical, superhuman powers constructed in the image of her own needs.

Mick is fated for disillusionment here; and even in the one brief experience of love that she knows, she is disappointed. When she has a sexual encounter with a boy of her own age, Harry (Wayne Smith), it is no answer to her needs, and she is alone again.

Touching as she gropes for self-knowledge, Mick is a compelling screen image. Sondra Locke is excellent as the girl, as are Laurinda Barrett and Biff McGuire as her troubled parents.

Photographed interestingly by James Wong Howe and played by a very good cast, The Heart Is a Lonely Hunter is very satisfying as a film from a subtle novel. It won the Prix Femina of Belgium, and Alan Arkin was named best actor of the year by the New York Film Critics.

Also: Finding Oneself

HEIDI

NBC-TV, 1968. 120 mins. col. (d) Delbert Mann (sp) Earl Hamner, from the novel by Johanna Spyri (ph) Klaus Von Rautenfeld (m) Johnny Williams, performed by the Hamburg Symphony Orchestra (c) Maximilian Schell, Jean Simmons, Michael Redgrave, Walter Slezak, Peter Van Eyck, Jennifer Edwards, Zuleika Robson. (TV)

Made for television, this is the best film so far of the three or four adapted from Mrs. Spyri's book about the little orphan in the Alps whose heartaches and happiness have been classic since 1880. Shot on location in Switzerland and Germany, it is lovely to look at, and the cast would be hard to match. Michael Redgrave is Heidi's grandfather; Maximilian Schell, her uncle, Herr Sessemann; Jean Simmons, kind Fraulein Rottenmeir; Walter Slezak, Father Richter. Heidi herself is a spunky modern child of ten, Jennifer Edwards, who is not intimidated by period costume; her characterization is not lollipop, like Shirley Temple's in 1937, but very believable, especially in such scenes as her bedroom fight with cousin Klara (Zuleika Robson).

Warners-7 Arts, 1968. 95 mins. col. (d) Werner Jacobs (sp) Richard Schweizer, from the novel by Johanna Spyri (c) Eva Maria Sinhammer, Gustav Knuth, Ernst Schroder, Margaret Trooger, Gertraud Mittermayr. Dubbed version. (ROA, SWA)

Another recent adaptation, also filmed in the Swiss Alps, this is a German production available in a dubbed version. The photography is attractive, and the demure (if not pretty) little girl who plays Heidi, Eva Maria Sinhammer, is just as forlorn and homesick as ever when she is transported to Frankfort, although it has been updated to the city of today. This is the only streamlining; the story is still nineteenth-century.

A HERO AIN'T NOTHIN' BUT A SANDWICH, see p. 82

A HIGH WIND IN JAMAICA

20th Century-Fox, 1965. 104 mins. col. (d) Alexander Mackendrick (sp) Stanley Mann, Ronald Harwood, Denis Cannon, from the novel by Richard Hughes (c) Anthony Quinn, Lila Kedrova, James Coburn, Gert Frobe, Nigel Davenport, Isabel Dean, Dennis Price, Deborah Baxter. (FNC)

Richard Hughes's 1929 novel is a masterpiece, chilling in its mounting climaxes as the children's amorality is revealed. While director Alexander Mackendrick's 1965 film is not a masterpiece, it is a fine, restrained interpretation and chilling enough. It could not be closer to the original without straining credulity; the Thornton children, as Hughes described them, would be too much for the screen image.

"They are just not like English children!" their mother exclaims in dismay, when we first meet them in Jamaica, after the big blow of the title. The storm has killed Old Sam, a friend of theirs; they have just seen his body; yet they are singing and playing in the puddles the rain has left. It's not that death hasn't moved them. Ten-year-old Emily (Deborah Baxter) has lost her Tabby. She will remember the cat's death for a long time.

Perhaps Mrs. Thornton is right, that the island primitivism

and savagery have changed them. The littlest girl is fascinated by voodoo ghosts whose heads are on backwards. At any rate, the five children--with a Creole boy and his older sister--are soon packed off to England aboard the Clorinda. Attacked by pirates a few days out, the ship escapes, but the children are inadvertently left in the hold of the pirate vessel.

To pirate Captain Chavez (Anthony Quinn) and his raffish mate (James Coburn), the children are a nuisance. But they must be protected from the superstitious, dissolute crew, to whom the children are unlucky omens. Soon, with Emily as the most outspoken and fearless, the children have made a world of their own aboard the ship, adapting to the pirates' ways, no more incomprehensible than the ways of all adults. Absorbed in their own survival they watch lust, cruelty, and violence as if they were games. When one of the boys, John, is accidentally killed during a short stay ashore in Tampico, they do not question what has happened, but Emily asks, "If John's not coming back, can Edward have his blanket?"

In a fit of terror, Emily kills a Dutch captive taken by the pirates. After the children are safe again in England and the pirates are on trial, Emily says it was Captain Chavez who committed the crime. When their former captors are swinging on the gallows, the little Thorntons are watching toy sailboats on a pretty pond.

It was all believable on Richard Hughes' pages; it is believable in Alexander Mackendrick's direction--especially of child actress Deborah Baxter, as gifted a player as the young Hayley Mills. Her eyes are full of terror, of duplicity, and of innocence, and she is more than a match for Chavez the pirate (to whom she is a source of uneasy attraction) or for her father and mother. It is a stunning characterization of a famous novelist's creation: the heroine of The Innocent Voyage, as the 1943 Broadway play ironically called it.

HOW GREEN WAS MY VALLEY

20th Century-Fox, 1941. 112 mins. b/w. (d) John Ford (sp) Philip Dunne, from the novel by Richard Llewellyn (ph) Arthur Miller (m) Alfred Newman (art) Richard Day and Nathan Juran (c) Donald Crisp, Roddy McDowall, Sara Allgood, Walter Pidgeon, Maureen O'Hara, Barry Fitzgerald, John Loder, Patrick Knowles, Anna Lee, Rhys Williams, Arthur Shields, Ethel Griffies, The Welsh Singers. (FNC)

A Welsh mining family in the late nineteenth century is seen in this film through the eyes of the youngest, little Huw. The story is told as a recollection of the past by Huw Morgan in his old age. The film, very faithful to Richard Llewellyn's novel, is beautifully done, and its many awards are well merited.

Before their lives are disrupted by the changes which come to the coal mines, the Morgans are a close-knit family, headed by a Welsh father of another day (Donald Crisp, in a prizewinning performance) and a spirited mother (Sara Allgood) whose sons and daughters inherit her liveliness. The small boy of the family, Huw, sensitive and frail (a remarkable, tender characterization by Roddy McDowall, in his second screen role), is an observer of many dramas--unrequited love, social disruption, the conflict between generations.

Director John Ford won his fourth award from the New York Film Critics for How Green Was My Valley. Perfectly integrated in its style, it is especially moving in its picture of boyhood. Perhaps the portrait of young Huw is so moving not only because of Roddy McDowall's rare skill but because of Ford's close understanding of his position in the Morgan family. "I'm the youngest of thirteen," Ford said. "I was a fresh young kid at the table." Huw is not a fresh young kid, but he is one of the memorable sensitive children in films made from novels.

Also: Family Relationships
Growing Pains

HUGO AND JOSEFIN, see p. 19

THE HUMAN COMEDY

M-G-M, 1943. 120 mins. b/w. (d) Clarence Brown (sp) Howard Estabrook, from the novel by William Saroyan (m) Herbert Stothart (art) Cedric Gibbons (c) Mickey Rooney, Donna Reed, Van Johnson, Marsha Hunt, Robert Mitchum, Frank Morgan, Fay Bainter, Jackie ("Butch") Jenkins. (FNC)

Quite faithful in tone to the Saroyan novel about the simple Macauley family of Ithaca, California, during World War II--which means two hours of the Saroyan special mixture of goodness and goo.

There are two excellent characterizations. As Homer the high school boy and family breadwinner (father is in heaven and the older son is at war), Mickey Rooney is at his best, which can be very good indeed and not at all broad. His scenes with the drunken old telegrapher are as tender as his classroom "nose"-speech scene is hilarious. And five-year-old Jackie ("Butch") Jenkins, as Ulysses, the Macauleys' youngest, made child-actor history in this first starring role. Remember him waving to the trains, and pleading with Homer not to leave home? "Butch" went on to win the Critics Award for three later roles, in National Velvet, Our Vines Have Tender Grapes, and The Bride Goes Wild. When he retired from the screen in 1947, at the age of nine, he had created a very pleasant small-boy image, freckled and joyous, in the public mind.

Also: Family Relationships

I NEVER PROMISED YOU A ROSE GARDEN, see p. 260

I REMEMBER MAMA

RKO, 1948. 134 mins. b/w. (d) George Stevens (sp) DeWitt Bodeen, from the play by John Van Druten based on Kathryn Forbes' novel Mama's Bank Account (ph) Nicholas Musuraca (m) Roy Webb (c) Irene Dunne, Barbara Bel Geddes, Oscar Homolka, Philip Dorn, Cedric Hardwicke, Edgar Bergen, Florence Bates, Rudy Vallee, Ellen Corby, Barbara O'Neill. (FNC)

The Hansons, an immigrant Norwegian-American family of San Francisco at the turn of the century, appear first in Kathryn Forbes's autobiographical chronicle novel, Mama's Bank Account, then in John Van Druten's play and George Stevens's film, and finally in the television series of the fifties. The movie, like the play, concentrates on Katrin, "the dramatic one," who wants to be a writer.

Katrin does grow up to be a writer. She narrates and participates in her family drama, remembered in sentimental tranquility.

The flashbacks might well be called "I Remember Katrin," for they recreate a more trustworthy portrait of the adolescent girl than of her mother, whom she romanticizes in retrospect. Nobody, not even Irene Dunne, could be that self-sacrificing.

Katrin--in the glowing performance of Barbara Bel Geddes--is the observant, gifted child who never misses a detail of character, who is intensely empathetic in the joyous or sad events of family life, and who is finally ready to learn (from a famous authoress and from Mama) that she must write about what she knows.

Credit goes to director George Stevens for meticulous attention to every detail and shading. The many good character actors respond with obvious zest to the challenge of this popular saga.

Also: Family Relationships
Finding Oneself

I'M A FOOL

PBS/TV, 1975. 38 mins. col. (d) Noel Black (sp) Ron Cowen, from the short story by Sherwood Anderson (ph) Jonathan Else (m) Ed Bogas (c) Ron Howard, Amy Irving, Santiago Gonzales. (PER)

"I don't care nothing for working, and earning money, and saving it for no such boob as myself," says Andy at the end of Sherwood Anderson's 1922 story, in reluctant insight into the confusion he has made of an adult relationship for which he is not ready.

Andy is in his late teens. Like Anderson at his age, he has spent the 1900 summer wandering around the rural Ohio racetrack circuit as a "swipe." With Burt, who is older, he drives horses from track to track and tends them on the way. He has chosen this life in rebellion against his mother and sister, who have a more respectable job in mind for him.

One day, Andy sees a race from the grandstand. He's out of his depth; he's had a couple of drinks and bought fine cigars, after being taunted by a dude in a bar. He meets a lovely young girl, Lucy, and tries to impress her, boasting about his position in life, his wealth, and his experience. When Lucy later lets him know she's fond of him and would like to continue their relationship, Andy daren't tell her the truth. His lies lose him the hope of seeing her again. Ironically, the first time he's met a nice girl, he's posed as the respectable, successful man of his mother's values.

Andy's initiation into the complexities of class and sex is gently and understandingly filmed by director Noel Black (Pretty Poison, 1968; the prizewinning Reflections and Skater Dater of the sixties), an old hand at portraying adolescents in process of maturing. Ron Howard (Andy) is known to us, of course, as Fonzie's pal on television's "Happy Days," and as Steve in American Graffiti; he is ably supported by Amy Irving (Lucy) and Santiago Gonzales (Burt). Jonathan Else's photography and Ed Bogas's music recreate the period; the film was shot at the Sonoma and Santa Rosa tracks.

The original rambling monologue of Anderson's story becomes, in Ron Cowen's teleplay, good dialogue and a clear time sequence. The revelation of Andy's character through artless colloquial conversation is testimony to Anderson's debt to Mark Twain; Andy is a 1900 Huck Finn of the middle class.

I'm a Fool tells us again what we have all felt about our job, our family, and our co-workers, and reminds us what a terrible talent we used to have of tripping ourselves up by our youthful pretensions.

Also: Growing Pains

THE INNOCENTS

20th Century-Fox, 1961. 99 mins. b/w. (d) Jack Clayton (sp) William Archibald and Truman Capote, based on William James's novel The Turn of the Screw and William Archibald's play The Innocents (ph) Freddie Francis (m) Georges Auric (c) Deborah Kerr, Megs Jenkins, Martin Stephens, Pamela Franklin, Peter Wyngarde, Isla Cameron, Clytie Jessop, Michael Redgrave. (FNC)

Like Henry James's novel The Turn of the Screw, on which it is based (via William Archibald's 1950 Broadway play, The Innocents),

The Innocents has a mystery within its mystery. Were the ghosts of Peter Quint and Miss Jessel real ghosts or the products of governess Miss Giddens's sexually repressed psyche? Were the children of Bly House really bewitched by these spirits beyond the grave or driven to tragedy by Miss Giddens?

It is a compliment to the subtlety of director Jack Clayton and writers William Archibald and Truman Capote that, as James said, "We cannot possibly ever directly know." As The Turn of the Screw is read on many levels--as a tour de force of occult suspense, or a horror entertainment (without ever knowing what the horror is), or a Freudian analysis of the governess (or of Henry James)--so the film can be enjoyed as ghost story or as psychology.

The Innocents seems to lean to the Freudian interpretation, that the ghosts are figments of Miss Giddens's neuroticism; that only she sees them. And yet, and yet--how do you explain the tear, the visible tear, that the ghost of Miss Jessel drops?

(Henry James, about The Turn of the Screw: "[It was] ... a piece of ingenuity pure and simple, of cold, artistic calculation ... to catch those not easily caught.")

Whatever the nature of the forces that possess them, the children are possessed, their innocence corrupted. If they are not really perverted by the spirits of evil in the shape of Quint (Peter Wyngarde) and Miss Jessel (Clytie Jessop), in the way that their governess, Miss Giddens (Deborah Kerr), is convinced they are, then they are unwittingly destroyed by this disturbed woman herself. She uses shocks to make the children admit that they are being haunted and that their souls are being damned.

Martin Stephens, as Miles, the ten-year-old expelled from school for an unnamed wickedness, is an exquisite boy, moving through the decaying Edwardian mansion like a doomed angel. He is precocious, like eight-year-old Flora (Pamela Franklin), and is the most beautiful child Miss Giddens has ever seen. Whether we know the Jamesian plot or not, we know these strange young figures are moving to strange ends; we are not surprised that Miles, after Miss Giddens forces him to cry out the name of Quint, whom she is sure they both can see, should fall dead.

The Innocents is a beautiful film, beautifully handled in its translation from novel to screen. The photography by Freddie Francis, the music by Georges Auric, and Jack Clayton's direction all have the requisite style for such highbred horror. Conveying hysteria with quivering finesse, Deborah Kerr is utterly convincing as the spinster who destroys the children she loves by her demand that they save their little souls.

IN THIS HOUSE OF BREDE, see p. 199

INTRUDER IN THE DUST, see p. 49

ISLAND OF THE BLUE DOLPHINS, see p. 50

ISLANDS IN THE STREAM, see p. 88

KIM

M-G-M, 1950. 113 mins. col. (d) Victor Saville (sp) Leon Gordon, Helen Deutsch, Richard Schayer, from the novel by Rudyard Kipling (ph) William Skall (m) Andre Previn (c) Errol Flynn, Dean Stockwell, Paul Lukas, Cecil Kellaway. (FNC)

Though no comparisons are possible between the two novels in which they figure, comparisons have been made between the character of the boy Kim and that of Huckleberry Finn. Both are independent, resourceful thirteen-year-olds who hate the restrictions of civilization and find their own adventures in the adult world. They hate school and slip away to learn lessons to their own taste.

Huck belongs to Mark Twain's Mississippi, Kim to Kipling's India. We meet Kimball O'Hara, orphan son of a trooper of the Queen, in the colorful, teeming alleys of Lahore. He joins forces with a Tibetan lama, promising to take him to the holy city of Benares. Later, on the Grand Trunk Road stretching across India, the holy man and Kim, his _chela_ or servant boy, come across the Irish regiment of the boy's late father. Its chaplains almost trap Kim into going to school, but Kim, unhappy with military regimentation, at last escapes into more adventure. Told by Mookerjee, an Indian employed in the British secret service, that he, too, can become a secret agent if he resumes his education, Kim returns to school for a time. After resuming his Indian disguise, Kim plays the great game of spying on the frontier, working to forestall the Russian infiltration of the Khyber Pass.

Dean Stockwell is a warmhearted, self-sufficient Kim, much smarter than the grown-ups. His apprenticeship under Mahbub Ali, the crafty Indian horse trader spying for the British (Errol Flynn), is a famous tale of adolescent experience. The film is faithful to the original, perhaps too much so for its pace, and is rich in the atmosphere of Kipling's nineteenth-century bazaars and caravans.

LAST SUMMER, see p. 149

THE LITTLE ARK, see p. 53

LITTLE WOMEN

RKO, 1933. 107 mins. b/w. (d) George Cukor (sp) Sarah Y. Mason and Victor Heerman, from the novel by Louisa May Alcott (ph) Henry Gerrard (m) Max Steiner (c) Katharine Hepburn, Joan Bennett, Paul Lukas, Frances Dee, Jean Parker, Edna May Oliver, Douglass Montgomery, Henry Stephenson, Spring Byington, Samuel Hinds, John Davis Lodge, Nydia Westman. (FNC)

To a women's liberation collective working for the emancipation of young children from sex stereotypes and role models would this beautifully orchestrated film from Miss Alcott's classic be no more than a horror story from the Dark Ages?

Gentle Beth, tender Meg, dainty Amy, ardent Jo--that close-knit band of sisters growing into womanhood, with father away at war and Marmee holding the home together--are they only antique bisque dolls today?

If the answer is no, it is because Louisa May Alcott herself was one of the earliest women's libbers, in deed if not (shades of papa Bronson Alcott!) in word: a vigorous spinster who had always earned her own living and who managed to retain some humor, some degree of artistic independence, while achieving the success and conformity demanded by her times. In the character of Jo March, if in no other, Miss Alcott transcended her milieu. Jo's gloves, Jo's dress, Jo's hair, Jo's manners were unwomanly, but even in Miss Alcott's lifetime, Jo's mentality was acknowledged to be the most interesting in the novel. A hundred years after her creation, the girl who cried out, "Look at me, World, I'm Jo March, and I'm so happy!" is alive and well and living in the heart of most young readers and filmgoers.

In the New England of Civil War days, the New England of the genteel tradition, we see the joys and sorrows, loves and dreams, of four very proper young ladies. This is the society against which the careers of the suffragettes were a continuous protest. Yet in it Jo March flourished. For all its quaintness, Little Women lays less stress on being ladylike than on being human.

For their adaptation of a literary classic Sarah Y. Mason and Victor Heerman won an Academy Award. George Cukor's direction is in such good taste that this is the definitive version of the story. (The 1949 remake, directed by Mervyn LeRoy, which stars June Allyson, Peter Lawford, Margaret O'Brien, Elizabeth Taylor, Janet Leigh, Rossano Brazzi, and Mary Astor, is second-best. Cukor's film, "the Katharine Hepburn version," now most often available on television, is the odds-on favorite.)

The film is recommended as an evocation of girlhood in a bygone period, and as a faithful screening of a book that in one way or another affects every reader.

Also: Family Relationships

LOLITA

M-G-M, 1962. 152 mins. b/w. (d) Stanley Kubrick (sp) Vladimir Nabokov, based on his novel (ph) Oswald Morris (m) Nelson Riddle (c) James Mason, Sue Lyon, Shelley Winters, Peter Sellers. (FNC)

Black comedy, social satire, slapstick free-for-all--yes, Lolita is all of these. And yes, it has brilliant performances by Peter Sellers (as Clare Quilty), James Mason (Humbert Humbert), and Shelley Winters (Charlotte Haze). But is Vladimir Nabokov's nymphet character, Lolita, a byword for sexual precocity, not to say depravity? No, not really.

And that despite the fact that Nabokov wrote the screenplay from his novel. Whether the change in the main character was suggested by censorship/box-office expediency, or casting problems, or a feeling that the original might be a little gamey for American taste, the change was made. In the book Lolita was twelve years old. The point was that she was twelve. In the film, the part is played by Sue Lyon, a newcomer of fourteen who looks at least seventeen and is dressed and interpreted as if she were seventeen. That makes her no nymphet--but a starlet, heaven defend us. The thrust of the novel is lost. Instead of the fascinating picture of a mature man lusting after a more-than-nubile child who is apparently readier to seduce him than he is to seduce her, we have another story of sex between the older man and the younger woman. The movie Lolita hasn't been written well enough to suggest complexity; she's an ordinary-enough, sensual young woman. Maybe she's going to Camp Climax, like the original Lolita, but she seems much more suited for a junior counselor's position than for the nymphet role.

What remains of Nabokov's story is still vastly entertaining. It has a great deal of understanding of Humbert Humbert as a man and of his passion for the girl. Director Stanley Kubrick and Peter Sellers between them have created scenes of superb comic invention. To those who do not know or care about the novel's justly famous invention of the character of nymphet Lolita, the film, just possibly, may also provide insight into an older adolescent girl who is no more naive, no less aggressive and calculating, than her bikini.

In her scenes with her mother, the movie Lolita is especially knowing. This is a real seventeen-year-old woman watching an older woman making advances to a reluctant male. In her moments with the amorous Humbert Humbert, the girl is far less interesting than the man--testimony not only to James Mason's superior artistry but to the weakening of the Lolita character.

Also: Love and Sex

THE LONELINESS OF THE LONG DISTANCE RUNNER, see p. 243

LORD OF THE FLIES

Great Britain, 1963. 90 mins. b/w (d) Peter Brook (sp) Peter Brook, based on the novel by William Golding (ph) Tom Hollyman (m) Raymond Leppard (c) James Aubrey, Tom Chapin, Hugh Edwards, Tom Gaman. (GEN)

William Golding's parable of evil (1954), according to the novelist, "is an attempt to trace the defects of society back to the defects of human nature. The moral is that the shape of a society must depend on the ethical nature of the individual and not on any political system however apparently logical or respectable."

When they are free from adult restrictions and alone on their island, the boys in Golding's story, who begin with hopes of creating their own Utopia, end by reverting to primitive savagery. The seeds of evil are in the children, says Lord of the Flies.

The time is the outbreak of a future war. Thirty-five British schoolboys who are being evacuated to the South Pacific are stranded on an uninhabited island when their plane crashes on its shore and is washed out to sea. There are no adult survivors.

The boys try to set up a society which will survive. Chief among the group are the leader, Ralph (James Aubrey), who is the most sensible; asthmatic Piggy (Hugh Edwards), who is the most vulnerable; the bully, Jack (Tom Chapin); and the quiet, imaginative Simon (Tom Gaman).

By the time the boys are rescued, they have suffered, competed, surrendered reason to instinct, performed ritual orgies, and murdered both Simon and Piggy. The sailors on an English cruiser are appalled to find that English schoolboys are now savages. "In the middle of them, with filthy body, matted hair, and unwiped nose, Ralph wept for the end of innocence, the darkness of man's heart, and the fall through the air of the true, wise friend called Piggy."

Director Peter Brook had a difficult assignment, in translating this chilling fable into cinematic language. A great deal, unfortunately, has been lost in the translation, particularly the power, subtlety, and directness of the original. Taking his group of unprofessional youngsters to Puerto Rican jungles and beaches for the shooting, Brook had no screenplay but relied on improvisation based on the novel. The result doesn't work. The boys can't act, they seem to be aimless, the film's structure is fragmentary and sagging. (Lord of the Flies explodes the myth that children are natural actors; only superb directors of children can make them appear real.)

The title is a translation of the Hebrew Ba'alzevuv, a name for the devil (Beelzebub in Greek). The devil is implicit in the novel; in the key scene, the dead sow's head decaying on a stake in the hot sun seems to tell the imaginative Simon that "everything was a bad business." Brook gives us, instead, from the beginning, the literal buzzing on the sound track.

Despite its inadequacy as a film, Lord of the Flies has enough of the original in it--Piggy telling the true story of his home, the littl'uns' bad dreams at night, the terrible turning of the boys on their friends, the cruelty of children--to stir thought about Mr. Golding's vision of evil inherent in the human heart. What are little boys made of, indeed!

LOSS OF INNOCENCE, see p. 151

MEET ME IN ST. LOUIS

M-G-M, 1944. 113 mins. col. (d) Vincente Minnelli (sp) Irving Brecher, Fred J. Finkelhoffe, from the New Yorker stories and book by Sally Benson (ph) George Fosley (m) George Stoll (c) Judy Garland, Margaret O'Brien, Mary Astor, Lucille Bremer, June Lockhart, Tom Drake, Marjorie, Harry Davenport, Leon Ames. (FNC)

Margaret O'Brien, at seven, achieved some sort of first for a child actress; critic James Agee mentioned her in the same sentence as Garbo and said he couldn't wait until she was ready to play Hedwig in Ibsen's The Wild Duck. The public was right up there with the critics; when Margaret was eight, she was among the ten top-grossing stars in pictures.

As Tootie Smith, the youngest of the nice middle-class St. Louis family in this candy-box musical based on Sally Benson's New Yorker stories and book, little Miss O'Brien is simply terrific. With an intensity that reaches its climax in the famous Halloween scene, she runs the gamut of small-girl theatrics. Her 1944 Oscar (a special award) was a foregone conclusion.

The Smiths, in 1903, do not want to leave their beloved home and their way of life, just because papa has been called to a new position in New York. When sister Esther (Judy Garland) sings "Skip to My Lou" or "The Trolley Song" and when mama (Mary Astor) and the girls in their long white dresses are out on the lawn in spring, Meet Me in St. Louis is a romantic, nostalgic fairy tale. But when Margaret O'Brien--when Tootie--buries her dolls in the backyard, or destroys a snowman, or sings "Drunk Last Night" in her nightgown at a party, or sits up next to the driver of the carriage, or screams and screams after that walk on Halloween--reality bursts through.

Tootie is one of the most alive, imaginative, impish little girls in the movies. Nothing in Miss Benson's autobiographical sketches can match her.

THE MEMBER OF THE WEDDING

Columbia, 1952. 91 mins. b/w. (d) Fred Zinnemann (sp) Edna and Edward Anhalt, from the play by Carson McCullers (c) Julie Harris, Ethel Waters, Brandon de Wilde, Arthur Franz, James Edwards. (BUC, MAC, SWA)

"The funniness and the grief are often coexistent in a single line," said Carson McCullers about the tragicomedy of adolescent Frankie, the girl whom she first introduced in a novel. She was doubtful about the way it would go as a play. It went so well that it ran for sixty-two weeks on Broadway. The film version, directed by Fred Zinnemann, still works--because the character of Frankie transcends all problems of adaptation.

Frankie (for Frances) Addams (played in the theater and in the film by Julie Harris) lives in a small southern town, the daughter of a widower. His wife died when Frankie was born, and Mr. Addams has never had much time for the child. The summer of the play is an especially lonely time for Frankie; her best friend has moved away, and the neighborhood girls ignore her. A scrawny twelve-year-old, Frankie is as awkward as a boy; she's cut her hair so short she even looks like one.

Most of the time, Frankie sits around talking, eating, or playing cards in her father's kitchen with her two friends, Berenice Sadie Brown (Ethel Waters), the Addams' black cook, a deeply understanding and maternal woman; and John Henry (Brandon de Wilde), Frankie's odd little cousin and neighbor, who is seven. Very little happens during the play, except inside Frankie. Her moods are her drama. Time passes, Frankie speaks of her longings and fantasies, Berenice of her fears and memories.

Frankie, neither child nor woman, without strong family ties or friends, does not have a sense of identity. She cannot be clearly defined as a boy or a girl; she is neither Berenice's mistress nor her charge; neither John Henry's companion nor his merely tolerant babysitter.

Frankie feels that everyone except herself belongs to a group, and by belonging, knows who she is. "The we of me" is the theme of her heart; she's tired of having been "just an 'I' person" and now she is ready to belong to a "we."

The "we" is Jarvis, Frankie's older brother, a soldier of twenty-one, and Janice, his nineteen-year-old fiancée. Enraptured by the idea of their coming marriage, Frankie is determined to break out of her narrow life and leave with them after the wedding. Obsessed by her dream, she buys herself cheaply glamorous clothes for the ceremony, gives away her toys to John Henry, conjures up the coming excitements of her travels and experiences with Jarvis and Janice, and brushes off Berenice's attempts to dissuade her from her delusion.

In the end, of course, Frankie does not go with the couple. Exhausted and now aware of her folly, she changes her mind about suicide. Reality is crowding in--Berenice has grave troubles, John Henry dies, much happens to adults around her. When we last see Frankie, she has made a new friend. She will move away, she is growing up.

The novel published in 1946, the play produced in 1950, the film released in 1952--The Member of the Wedding is ageless, for it is one of the most beautifully realized works in contemporary American literature. Frankie is the prototype of isolated, awkward girlhood, and her need to identify with something is as lyrical and powerful today as it ever was.

Although the camera plays harshly with Julie Harris, who cannot be expected to look like twelve in close-ups, it hardly matters; the characterization is brilliantly clear, a classic of adolescence.

Also: Finding Oneself

MY FRIEND FLICKA, see p. 282

NATIONAL VELVET, see p. 283

OLIVER TWIST

Great Britain, 1947. 116 mins. b/w. (d) David Lean (sp) David Lean and Stanley Haynes, from the novel by Charles Dickens (ph) Guy Green (art) John Bryan (ed) Jack Harris (c) John Howard Davies, Robert Newton, Alec Guinness, Kay Walsh, Francis L. Sullivan, Henry Stephenson, Mary Clare, Kathleen Harrison, Anthony Newley. (JAN)

Following his splendid Great Expectations, David Lean made Oliver Twist, a film which ran into trouble in some quarters because of Alec Guinness's portrayal of Fagin but which has endured for its perfect young Oliver, the delicate-faced British child actor John Howard Davies. After playing Oliver, Davies was seen in The Rocking Horse Winner and Tom Brown's Schooldays, then left the industry to become a BBC television director. For everyone who sees Lean's film, he will forever be the image of Dickens's workhouse child.

"Oliver Twist's ninth birthday found him a pale, thin child, somewhat diminutive in stature, and decidely small in circumference" --that is the boy we first see, a parish orphan, a half-starved drudge in his Poor Law clothes of the 1830s. Farmed out to the coffin maker, he runs away, and the wide, harsh world of the city engulfs him. In his isolation he is the natural prey of The Artful Dodger (Anthony Newley) and Fagin (Guinness). As he had cried out to Mr.

Bumble (Francis L. Sullivan) on his way to the Sowerberry establishment, "I am a very little boy, sir; and it is so lonely, sir! So very lonely!"

From the evil company of Bill Sikes (Robert Newton) to the kind protection of Mr. Brownlow (Henry Stephenson), everything that happens to Oliver is seen acutely, with Dickens's heightened dimension of reality; we know the world of Oliver Twist, as we know the world of Pip in Great Expectations, through the eyes of the child. It is deeply felt, almost unrelenting drama, like the novel itself.

THE OTHER, see p. 262

OUR MOTHER'S HOUSE, see p. 273

POLLYANNA

Disney, 1960. 134 mins. col. (d) David Swift, from the novel by Eleanor H. Porter (c) Hayley Mills, Jane Wyman, Karl Malden, Agnes Moorehead, Donald Crisp, Richard Egan, Nancy Olson, Adolphe Menjou, Kevin Corcoran. (GEN)

Every popular book is rewritten each time a new movie version comes out. When Mary Pickford played the Glad Girl in this story of an incurably optimistic child bent on seeing the good in everyone, she was all coyness and curls. When Hayley Mills plays her she is a very different twelve-year-old.

Miss Mills had demonstrated, in 1958 in Tiger Bay, that she could act. Until she went on to adult roles, she charmed audiences with her teenage individuality and mother wit in such pictures as The Parent Trap, Whistle Down the Wind, and The Chalk Garden. In the setting of the little Napa Valley town near Santa Rosa where Pollyanna was filmed, she is refreshing. Though she does the conventional things little girls have been doing in the movies since the beginning--melting ogres, leading those who have gone astray, rekindling love in the stonyhearted--she is such a lively, unaffected youngster that you can take her. She butters and salts the Porter-Disney corn with seeming effortlessness. She's always been a pro.

In the role of Jimmy Bean, the orphan adopted by lonely recluse Adolphe Menjou, Kevin ("Moochie") Corcoran is as appealing as he was in Old Yeller and The Rabbit Trap.

THE RAILWAY CHILDREN

Great Britain, 1971. 106 mins. col. (d) (sp) Lionel Jeffries, from the novel by E. Nesbit (ph) Arthur Ibbetson (m) Johnny Douglas (c) Dinah Sheridan, Jenny Agutter, Bernard Cribbins, William Mervyn, Sally Thomsett, Gary Warren. (MOD, UNI)

British actor Lionel Jeffries has directed and scripted The Railway Children from E. Nesbit's classic children's novel of 1906, and the film has been recommended warmly as entertainment for youngsters. However, like a beautiful antique toy of a bygone era, it may be enjoyed with greater appreciation by adults. Gentle, slow, impeccably produced, it observes its Edwardian scene very closely. We are rewarded not only with pictures of old carriages, trains, and paper chases, but with glimpses of three very attractive Edwardian children.

Bobbie (Jenny Agutter) is fifteen, her sister and brother, twelve and ten. When their father is mysteriously taken away one day (later, they learn he has been falsely charged with treason, but it all comes right in the end), their mother (Dinah Sheridan) tells them they must all now "play at being poor." And so they go to live, happily, in a quaint cottage in a Yorkshire village. Despite hardship, illness, and longing for father, they are brave children, with time to make friends, to amuse themselves with a railway train game, and to express family affection. One day they even are heroes. They flag down a train and prevent a collision and receive awards from the Old Gentleman who has been their fairy godfather many times in the story. "Very beautiful and wonderful things do happen, and we live in the hope of them, don't we," the Old Gentleman says at one point. These children never do stop hoping, and loving, and they are finally rewarded.

The adolescent Bobbie, well played by Jennie Agutter of Walkabout, is interesting in her childish errors and her growing insights. Because she is moved by a surprise birthday party her friends and family give her, she busily organizes the same thing for Perks, the poor railway clerk with whom the children have a close understanding. She collects presents from the village people and is astonished when Perks' pride is wounded and he wants to refuse what he thinks is charity. At the end of the film, Bobbie shows the sensitivity of a woman. When her father comes back, she takes him to their cottage and remains outside while her parents are reunited. Then, to give them some time together, she rounds up the younger children and romps off through the fields with them to the railway station.

Also: Family Relationships
Growing Pains

THE PRIME OF MISS JEAN BRODIE, see p. 188

THE RED BADGE OF COURAGE, see p. 221

THE RED PONY

Republic, 1949. 89 mins. col. (d) Lewis Milestone (sp) John Steinbeck, from his novel (m) Aaron Copland (c) Robert Mitchum, Myrna Loy, Shepperd Strudwick, Peter Miles. (GEN)

Though Steinbeck wrote the screenplay, his story about a rancher's boy has been prettied up disappointingly.

The life and death of his new pony, which gave nine-year-old Jody a bitter taste of mortality, is still here. But where is Jody? Jody, who needed a haircut, who smashed a green melon and hid it in the dirt, who drank from a wooden tub in the cold spring? Jody (now called Tom) has been given a haircut; he is Peter Miles, a cute child actor like a dozen others. And Jody's friend, Billy Buck, the bandy-legged hired man with a walrus moustache? Billy Buck is Robert Mitchum. Grandfather ("the leader of the people") is intact, thanks to Louis Calhern, and so are the foothills of the Salinas Valley, but the movie is less Steinbeck than sagebrush. Nevertheless, it is closer to the original than the 1974 version, which first was shown on TV, that starred Henry Fonda and Maureen O'Hara; and it is a better film.

Also: Animals and Nature
Growing Pains

THE REIVERS

National General, 1969. 107 mins. col. (d) Mark Rydell (sp) Irving Ravetch and Harriet Frank, Jr., from the novel by William Faulkner (c) Steve McQueen, Mitch Vogel, Rupert Crosse, Will Geer, Ruth White, Sharon Farrell, Juano Hernandez, Lonny Chapman, Michael Constantine, Clifton James. Narrated by Burgess Meredith. (SWA)

William Faulkner's last novel, which won a posthumous Pulitzer Prize in 1963, is one of his pleasantest and most truly comic. The film adaptation by Ravetch and Frank is equally pleasant and funny, if somewhat simpler, and its blend of the innocence of youth and the experience of age is very true to Faulkner's intent. An adventure story, a farce, a magical dream anchored in reality, The Reivers is also about an eleven-year-old boy's coming to terms with values, responsibilities, consequences.

In the archaic dialect of Faulkner's Yoknapatawpha County, reivers are thieves. The three thieves here are Boon Hogganbeck, of whom Lucius's grandfather says, "He knows no obstacles, counts no costs, and has no fears" (Steve McQueen); Ned, a shrewd black servant (Rupert Crosse); and eleven-year-old Lucius (Mitch Vogel). The adventure is being narrated in retrospect. Lucius as an old man (Burgess Meredith) tells us about the wonderful journey in 1905, when he was a boy and stole his grandfather's Winton Flyer and drove from Jefferson, Mississippi, to Memphis, Tennessee, where he lived for a couple of days in Miss Reba's whorehouse. He lost the car, won it back in a horse race, and parted forever from his boyhood.

When Lucius is home again, "after all the lying and deceiving and disobeying and conniving" that have destroyed his innocence, he knows that a whipping from his father is not good enough to balance out his score. His grandfather (Will Geer) tells him that no experience can be forgotten. Nothing is ever lost. It's too valuable. "Live with it," grandfather says.

Lucius doesn't see how he possibly can.

"Yes you can," grandfather answers. "A gentleman accepts the responsibility of his actions and bears the burden of their consequences, even when he did not himself instigate them but only acquiesced to them, didn't say No though he knew he should."

The Reivers is sometimes a fairy tale, as when Boon Hogganbeck marries Everbe (Sharon Farrell), one of the girls from Miss Reba's house, and they name the first baby after Lucius. But in essence it is a true picture of the boy's learning about more than one code. (An interfaith citation awarded to the movie spoke of its affirmation of the values of acceptance, understanding and compassion.)

And Lucius's trip in the yellow Winton Flyer is one of the funniest rites of passage you could find.

Also: Growing Pains

THE RIVER, see p. 57

THE ROCKING HORSE WINNER

Great Britain, 1950. 91 mins., b/w. (d) Anthony Pelissier (sp) Anthony Pelissier, from the short story by D. H. Lawrence (ph) Desmond Dickinson (art) Carmen Dillon (c) Valerie Hobson, John Howard Davies, John Mills, Hugh Sinclair, Ronald Squire, Cyril Smith. (JAN)

D. H. Lawrence's superb, macabre story of a doomed child is a superb, macabre film; like The Fallen Idol, from Graham Greene's story, it is proof that superior cinema can be made from unusually sensitive writing.

John Howard Davies, who was a perfect Oliver Twist, plays the fragile ten-year-old of Lawrence's story with a brilliance worthy of an actor of much greater experience. Little Paul Grahame is the son of a couple (Valerie Hobson, Hugh Sinclair) always short of money; he imagines the very walls are shrill in their demands for it. He especially would like to satisfy his mother, a cold, beautiful, extravagant woman with little real feeling for her three children. And, in Lawrence's tale, a way opens for the child to rescue his parents, at the cost of his life.

Given a toy rocking horse for Christmas, the boy soon demonstrates that he is using it as a kind of devilish instrument; riding it hard, he is able to predict winners at the track. With the help of the handyman (John Mills) and his Uncle Oscar (Ronald Squire), he sets himself up in the handicapping business and arranges for his winnings to be given secretly to his mother. But still the walls cry, "We need more money," and the strain is too much for him. Whipping the rocking horse far beyond his strength in order to pick the Derby winner, he dies.

The portrait of an overwrought, highly imaginative child caught up in an obsession has never been better drawn than in this masterful film directed and scripted by Anthony Pelissier.

Also: Special Children

ROMEO AND JULIET

Great Britain, Italy, 1968. 138 mins. col. (d) Franco Zeffirelli (sp) Franco Brusati, Masolino D'Amico and Franco Zeffirelli, from the play by Shakespeare (ph) Pasquale De Santis (m) Nino Rota (c) Leonard Whiting, Olivia Hussey, Milo O'Shea, Michael York, John McEnery, Pat Heywood, Natasha Parry. (FNC)

Is there a better story of adolescent passion than Romeo and Juliet? Thirteen movies were made from the play between 1908 and 1968; among those still available, you have only to choose the one to your taste.

Traditionalists still have a good word to say for the 1936 M-G-M version, with Norma Shearer and Leslie Howard as a well-bred if overage pair, and John Barrymore as a fine Mercutio. Many relish the Renaissance settings and style of Renato Castellani's 1954 film, in beautiful color, with a very young Juliet, Susan Shentall; Laurence Harvey as her Romeo; and a mixed British-Italian cast. A British film (1965) creditably presents the Royal Shakespeare Academy Players, reading the verse with more understanding than any of the actors in more cinematic versions. And there are two excellent ballet films: the Bolshoi Ballet of Romeo and Juliet (1954), with Ulanova dancing an exquisitely moving Juliet; and the Paul Czinner ballet film (1966), a tribute to the 1965 London premiere presented by the Royal Ballet Company, which stars Rudolph Nureyev and Margot Fonteyn in magical performances.

But all young audiences, and many contemporary adults, prefer the film of Franco Zeffirelli. "I wanted to bring the story to the attention of young people," the director has said. "The story is of two urchins crushed by a stupid, banal quarrel with origins even the adults don't know. In love the young people found an ideal--one they could die for--and youth today is hungry for ideals."

Indisputably the urchins crushed by adults are the sixteen-year-old Juliet (Olivia Hussey) and the seventeen-year-old Romeo (Leonard Whiting). They are very beautiful youngsters, in or out of their clothes, and hot with love. They do not know how to act, they flatten all the best lines, and they cannot rise to any heights, but Zeffirelli's cinematic head of steam carries them along. If there is no shading in his film, there is plenty of color. His adaptation is a rich fifteenth-century tapestry, with brawling youth in the streets and passionate youth in the bedchamber.

Also: Love and Sex

A SEPARATE PEACE

U. S., 1972. 104 mins. col. (d) Larry Peerce (sp) Fred Segal, based on the novel by John Knowles (ph) Frank Stanley (m) Charles Fox (c) John Heyl, Parker Stevenson, Victor Bevine, Peter Brush, William Roerick, Scott Bradbury, Frank Wilich, Jr. (FNC)

The prep school boys at Devon Academy have volunteered to clear the snow from the railroad tracks so a troop train can pass. The GIs yell and laugh at the kids; then, leaving for the adult front--it is the start of World War II--they become grave.

The adolescent front at Devon is shadowed by this war and by the private wars of schoolboys. And for the separate war, there will be a separate peace.

Finny (John Heyl) is antiwar: "The fat old men have made it up." But when he wants to serve his country and can't, he's desolate. At sixteen, Finny is a born leader, the school's best athlete. His roommate Gene (Parker Stevenson), is his opposite, bookish and quiet. They are best friends. But as you know if you know John Knowles's novel--and it seems sometimes that almost everyone since 1960 has read it--their relationship is ambivalent, encompassing not only affection and hero-worship but jealousy and--is it really hatred? Does Gene want to kill Finny when he impulsively pushes him out of the tree, breaking his leg and ending all rivalry? The schoolboy kangaroo court dismisses the charge against Gene, but he feels his guilt and travels to Boston to admit to Finny that it was no accident.

Director Larry Peerce (Goodbye, Columbus) has done well by the popular book. Shooting at Phillips Exeter Academy in New Hampshire, which was John Knowles's school, and using nonprofessional schoolboys as his actors, Peerce has been successful in making large and small details ring true. His players, especially John Heyl as Finny, turn in excellent performances. These upper-class American preppies look and sound right for their times.

Occasionally they sound authentically childish. When Finney learns that Leper (Peter Brush), who has enlisted in the Army, has had a nervous breakdown, he says, "If war can drive somebody crazy, then it's real, all right." Quackenbush (Frank Wilich, Jr.) is left high and dry on the tide of school popularity; he's so unpopular he doesn't have a nickname, not even an unfriendly one. The War Game that Finny and Gene play, jumping from the top of the tree into the river, is part of their uneasy adolescence. Like Gene's combined loyalty to and resentment of his friend Finny, like all the boys' gropings for the meanings of things, it is testimony to Mr. Knowles's accurate recollection.

The novel told the story in the first person. The beginning of the movie gives us the adult Gene, fifteen years after the event, returning to the school and remembering the past. Gene has made his separate peace with himself and with the world.

For its insights into adolescent friendship and feelings of guilt, A Separate Peace is recommended. It can be given a gentleman's pass mark even by those who have made a cult of the book.

Also: Growing Pains
Teachers and Schools

SHANE, see p. 28

SOUNDER, see p. 100

THESE THREE

United Artists, 1936. 92 mins. b/w. (d) William Wyler (sp) Lillian Hellman, from her play The Children's Hour (ph) Gregg Toland (m) Alfred Newman (c) Miriam Hopkins, Merle Oberon, Joel McCrea, Bonita Granville, Marcia Mae Jones, Margaret Hamilton, Walter Brennan, Alma Kruger, Catherine Doucet. (MAC)

Because the Hays Office, in 1936, would not approve any film which mentioned lesbianism, Lillian Hellman's play The Children's Hour could not be screened without a change. But so good was Hellman's script from her original work that the core of the drama remained untouched. The liaison between the two women teachers that the child hinted at was changed to a liaison between one of the teachers and Joel McCrea, but These Three is still a well-acted, well-written story about two little girls who almost destroy adult lives by their lying. And it is a much better version of the Hellman play than The Children's Hour, 1962, also directed by William Wyler, with the original accusation plainly mentioned, but very few cinematic or literary values.

Little Mary Tilford (Bonita Granville), a venomous, spoiled child of twelve who is coddled by her grandmother, tells the lie about one of her teachers (Merle Oberon and Miriam Hopkins) in order to escape punishment at school. She is backed up by her vassal, another little girl, Rosalie (Marcia Mae Jones), whom she has reduced to absolute terror. Though one's credulity may be strained by the situation in the story--that a whole community will believe a child's charge--it is never strained by the character of the little girls. In the same year that Shirley Temple was dimpling her way into the hearts of America in The Poor Little Rich Girl, Bonita Granville and Marcia Mae Jones were creating superb characterizations of two other kinds of children entirely, a natural bully and her victim.

A TASTE OF HONEY, see p. 158

THIEVES LIKE US, see p. 161

TOBY TYLER

Disney, 1960. 96 mins. col. (d) Charles Barton (sp) Bill Walsh and Lillie Hayward, from the novel by James Otis Kaler (ph) William Snyder (m) Buddy Baker (c) Kevin ("Moochie") Corcoran, Richard Eastham, Henry Calvin, Tom Fadden, Barbara Beaird, Mr. Stubbs. (GEN)

"A minor classic among children's movies," Paul V. Beckley called this, in The New York Herald Tribune. Among adult movies about children, it holds a nostalgic place. On the biggest day of the year, when the big show comes to town, what youngster doesn't dream of running away to join the circus?

Kevin ("Moochie") Corcoran, who plays Toby, looks like a kid who'd run away to join the circus. But then he looked right in The Shaggy Dog and Pollyanna, too.

Entirely faithful to the book, Toby Tyler gives us the child's-eye view of Col. Castle's Great American Circus at the turn of the century. Not the greatest show on earth--but the one-ring travelling troupe has oily concessionaires and kindly clowns, bareback riders (Monsieur Ajax and his lovely partner Mademoiselle Jeanette), a gruff strong man with a warm heart, and a wildly mischievous monkey named Mr. Stubbs. When the young orphan runs away from his aunt and uncle on the farm to join them, he becomes Monsieur Toby, Equestrian Extraordinaire, for an interlude of adventure.

Kevin Corcoran won an award for top juvenile acting of the year for his performance as Toby.

TEA AND SYMPATHY

M-G-M, 1956. 122 mins. col. (d) Vincente Minnelli (sp) Robert Anderson, from his own play (ph) John Alton (c) Deborah Kerr, Leif Erickson, John Kerr, Darryl Hickman, Edward Andrews, Norma Crane. (FNC)

Robert Anderson, author of the original play, also wrote the screenplay for Tea and Sympathy. Made before the era of sexual permissiveness on the screen, the film lets no suspicion linger about the heterosexuality of Tom Lee (John Kerr). In a postlude, ten years after the story, he is married and the father of three.

The film is still an effective protest against insensitivity toward young people who are different and against the conformities demanded in adolescent male society. And those two noisy, insecure adults, Tom's father (Edward Andrews) and his housemaster, Mr. Reynolds (Leif Erickson), can still be found, insisting that a regular guy should meet their predetermined jock standards of masculinity and scorning everyone who doesn't. As Reynold's wife, Laura (Deborah Kerr), says to comfort Tom, "The tribe has to find a scapegoat to affirm their own shaky position."

In his New England prep school, Tom is an eighteen-year-old who doesn't mind being alone in his room. He reads poetry and has a great collection of folk songs. In '56, that was enough to get him branded Sister Boy. The tone of the student body is set in one of two new scenes Anderson added to the film, a grotesque torchlight ritual in which the upperclassmen attack the other students and tear off their pajamas. Tom is the butt of their cruelty, but even if he hadn't been, he would not have joined them. An exception to the others is his kinder roommate and friend, Al (Darryl Hickman), who is still not immune to group-think; he tries to teach Tom how to walk "right." It is a moving scene, despite Al's acceptance of Ivy League infantilism.

In an attempt to prove his masculinity, Tom visits the local floozie, Ellie (Norma Crane), but she has heard the rumors about him, too, and the episode (especially written for the screen by Anderson) is so agonizing that Tom tries to commit suicide. When Laura Reynolds finds him and learns that he has accepted the others' judgment of him and doesn't want to live, she gives herself to him to prove to him that he is able to love a woman. Laura says to the boy, "Years from now, when you talk about this--and you will--be kind."

Twenty years afterward, Tea and Sympathy is a little dated but one can be kind in talking about it. Vincente Minnelli's direction offers many insights into adult and adolescent character, and the film is still illuminating about sexual role playing and group pressures in family and school.

Also: Love and Sex

TO KILL A MOCKINGBIRD

Universal, 1962. 129 mins. b/w. (d) Robert Mulligan (sp) Horton Foote, from the novel by Harper Lee (ph) Russell Harlan (m) Elmer Bernstein (c) Gregory Peck, Mary Badham, Phillip Alford, John

Megna, Frank Overton, Rosemary Murphy, Brock Peters, Ruth White, Collin Wilcox, James Anderson, Alice Ghostley, Robert Duvall, William Windom, Richard Hale, Estelle Evans. (CWF, SWA, TWY, UNI)

Adapted from Harper Lee's semiautobiographical novel which won a Pulitzer Prize in 1960, To Kill a Mockingbird won a great many awards on its own in 1962-1963--Cannes, Brussels, Parents' Magazine, American Bar Association, Academy Awards to Gregory Peck and scriptwriter Horton Foote. Several citations mentioned its humane values and celebration of individual rights. Yet today, seen in the perspective of other films dealing with the issues of black and white in the South in the 1930s, the film seems to merit the description of Stanley Kauffmann, who found most of it pleasant but called it "a sort of soft-caramel Intruder in the Dust." We think its chief distinction is its picture of three delightful kids.

In the summer of 1932 in a small town in Maycomb County, Alabama, six-year-old Jean Louise (Scout) Finch (Mary Badham) is growing up with her ten-year-old brother, Jem (Phillip Alford), and their kooky seven-year-old visitor, Dill (John Megna).

Atticus Finch (Gregory Peck), the widowed father of Scout and Jem, is raising them as individuals, in the face of general disapproval of his permissiveness toward them. When Atticus, who is a not-very-prosperous lawyer, defends a black (Brock Peters) against a false charge of rape, and the case goes to trial in the overheated rural courtroom filled with prejudice, Scout and Jem stand by him with spunk and initiative. They find out that their father is not only the best shot in the county but a man of principle, who can understand his neighbors' beliefs while defending his own against them. They learn something about their own prejudices, too. They have been nursing a fear of old man Radley (Richard Hale), who lives in the "haunted" house next door with his retarded son, Boo (Robert Duvall) and making a great game of tracking him down with their friend Dill. But when Scout and Jem are attacked by Bob Ewell (James Anderson), their father's enemy, they are saved by the one person in the town they have dreaded most, Boo Radley.

The story is seen through the eyes of six-year-old Scout. Many of the warmest and most vivid scenes involve her initiation. From farmer Cunningham, who pays her father in hickory nuts quietly left at the back door, and his boy Walter, who spreads molasses all over his food, she discovers something about poverty. From Calpurnia (Estelle Evans), the black Finch housekeeper who tries to teach Scout a lady's manners, she unwillingly takes a lesson or two in the limits of adult patience with a tomboy. And from her father she learns how to be courteous to a Confederate grand dame and to look at other adults with compassion.

Scriptwriter Foote and director Robert Mulligan give us three children who are sharply drawn, often funny, and always believable, whether making up summer games or looking on at such adult rites as the courtroom scene where blacks rise in homage to their father because he is a white man who has defended a black in a bigoted town in which he must go on living.

John Megna, a Broadway child actor, is a remarkable Dill; Mary Badham and Phillip Alford are children always worth watching. Sometimes, as with kids, they mumble their words. But nobody will doubt what's going on.

Also: Family Relationships
Growing Pains

TREASURE ISLAND

Disney, 1950. 96 mins. col. (d) Byron Haskin (sp) Lawrence Edward Watkin, from the novel by Robert Louis Stevenson (c) Robert Newton, Bobby Driscoll, Basil Sydney, Finlay Currie, Geoffrey Wilkinson, John Gregson. (GEN)

In the days of silent movies, long before women's lib, the part of Jim Hawkins in Treasure Island was twice played by a girl. So let us just admit that the child in Stevenson's book is the prime example of the young hero-person in English literature. The sex, like the face, does not matter, as long as it is suffused with the life-glow of romance.

The first boy to play Jim, Jackie Cooper, was just about perfect in Victor Fleming's 1934 talkie for M-G-M, but unfortunately, the rest of the cast, overfamiliar M-G-M stars, were not. Far livelier is this 1950 Disney adaptation.

Made in England, it has an incomparable British cast, with Bobby Driscoll, the only American import, fitting right in as Jim. Robert Newton is a superb Long John Silver. It is a rousing saga in which a brave, clever boy takes his part in the adventures of men. From the first moments in the Admiral Benbow Inn, to the skullduggery aboard the beautiful square-rigger Hispaniola, plowing across the Atlantic from Bristol to the stockade on Skeleton Island, Jim is at the center of things. To Long John Silver, to the captain and the doctor, to the pirates and Ben Gunn, he is no mere child, not just a cabin boy to be condescended to. He is somebody to be reckoned with, a hero. Through Stevenson's genius, something is illuminated for us. This is the way a youngster sees himself: terrified, perhaps, but triumphant in the perilous situation.

A TREE GROWS IN BROOKLYN, see p. 103

TRUE GRIT

Paramount, 1969. 128 mins. col. (d) Henry Hathaway (sp) Marguerite

Roberts, from the novel by Charles Portis (ph) Lucien Ballard (m) Elmer Bernstein (c) John Wayne, Glen Campbell, Kim Darby, Robert Duvall, Jeremy Slate, Dennis Hopper, Jeff Corey. (FNC)

There is more to be learned about a fourteen-year-old pioneer girl in the 1880s in Charles Portis's popular novel True Grit than in the Henry Hathaway movie that writer Marguerite Roberts and an uneven cast made of it.

In the original, which is a stylized fairy tale Western adventure filtered through the child's eyes, Mattie Ross has style. She takes no guff from anyone, does Mattie; when this shrewd and unsentimental and spunky little girl hires Rooster Cogburn, a one-eyed whiskey guzzler of a U. S. marshal, to track down the hired hand who murdered her pa, she gets him for his "children's rate," $100, and insists on taking part in the hunt. Her conversation is quaintly formal, but it's straight out of the 1880s, and everything hangs together.

In Marguerite Roberts's screenplay, in Kim Darby's playing, and in Henry Hathaway's direction, there is no style in Mattie Ross. To start with, Kim Darby is a little too pretty and nubile and not wiry enough. Her lines are stilted, and they sound not like a girl of the 1880s but like a starlet in a period entertainment feature.

True Grit is entertaining, but not because it is Mattie's movie as Portis's novel was Mattie's. The movie is all John Wayne's. Rifle in one hand, six-gun in the other, reins between his teeth, spurring his horse to do sagebrush combat against half a dozen bad guys, Wayne is playing all the Western heroes of his career rolled into one, playing them with exuberant and self-conscious panache that won him an Oscar at last.

Hathaway (The Sons of Katie Elder, The Desert Fox) has handled the action better than the relationship between Mattie and Rooster Cogburn (Wayne), or between Mattie and the Texas Ranger, Le Boeuf (Glen Campbell), the other man pursuing the outlaw killer. Briefly, here and there, we see a growing closeness between the generations, and a suggestion (not in Portis) of tenderness in the girl--perhaps as a concession to movie audiences.

But True Grit is for Wayne watchers, not for girl watchers. "You're too old and too fat to be jumping horses over a four-post fence," says Mattie to Rooster. "Come and see a fat old man sometime!" calls back Wayne, clearing the four-post fence as he rides off.

If the film lacks the insight into child character of its source, it remains (for those who catch it on television) as part of the Western myth: the pubescent heroine who helps to manage pa's Arkansas ranch and who is capable not only of firing a couple of bullets from his gun into his killer's body but of surviving such a mishap as being knocked backwards by the gunfire blast into a rattlesnake pit. True grit.

TWO LOVES

M-G-M, 1961. 100 mins. col. (d) Charles Walters (sp) Ben Maddow, from the novel Spinster by Sylvia Ashton-Warner (ph) Joseph Ruttenberg (m) Bronislau Kaper (c) Shirely MacLaine, Laurence Harvey, Jack Hawkins, Nobu McCarthy, Juano Hernandez, Edmund Vargas, Neil Woodward, Alan Roberts. (FNC)

Very illuminating--in flashes--about children and adolescents, Two Loves is a murky mess in every other way. It is a quasi-Freudian drama, with an absurd character (Paul Lathrop, played by Laurence Harvey) and a very poorly acted major role (Anna Vorontosov, alias Shirley MacLaine). It does no credit whatsoever to the excellent novel Spinster by Sylvia Ashton-Warner on which it is based. But just as the original had a wonderful picture of a New Zealand infants' school (for small children), the film has glimpses worth catching. Next time Two Loves is on television, watch the first twenty minutes.

There are forty-six Maori and white children, "blooming and blossoming at the tops of their voices," in Miss Vorontosov's schoolroom. The child named Seven, rubbing sand in another child's eyes, says, "I want to kill her." He is sick of practicing writing. "Then practice writing 'I am sick of writing,' " orders Miss Vorontosov. The class is learning to read from the book it has written itself: "My father is in jail. When he comes out, he cuts my mother with a knife." Mark Cutter, who is white, has been instructed by his mother not to take off his shoes when the teacher asks him to; only Maori boys do that. Mark's closest friend is Matawhero, grandson of the Maori chief.

When W. W. J. Abercrombie, the new senior school inspector for the district (Jack Hawkins), comes to visit, Miss Vorontosov, on the defensive, tells him furiously that she has no rollbook, no plan book, she doesn't like anything that comes between her and the children, and she'd rather be fired than stifled. Very much aware of the joyousness of the children who are being warmed by Miss Vorontosov's fire, Mr. Abercrombie is more than sympathetic. He has a spark himself. Turning to leave the classroom, he surprises the children by suddenly sticking out his tongue, and they roar in delight.

Miss Vorontosov has a teacher's aide, the fifteen-year-old Maori girl Whareparita (Nobu McCarthy), who is more woman than adolescent, a lovely portrait. When the children are being deloused and one is terrified ("Don't burn me!"), Whareparita cradles her gently, singing and rocking her. Soon she will be pregnant herself. Since the Maori relatives are happy a new child is coming, nobody except Miss Vorontosov is distressed that the father is not known.

(The father is Mr. Lathrop, teacher in the upper school, a highly neurotic war veteran who is a nuisance in the plot until he kills himself. A very weak teacher, he attempts authority by pain, using a stick on the chief's grandson.)

The best performances in Two Loves, by Juano Hernandez as Chief Rauhula and all the children as themselves, put Miss MacLaine and Mr. Harvey to shame. Remember--the first twenty minutes.

Also: Cultural Conflicts
Teachers and Schools

TWO WOMEN, see p. 225

UP THE DOWN STAIRCASE, see p. 193

WEE WILLIE WINKIE

20th Century-Fox, 1937. 99 mins., b/w with tinted sequences (d) John Ford (sp) Ernest Pascal and Julian Josephson, from the story by Rudyard Kipling (ph) Arthur Miller (m) Louis Silvers (c) Shirley Temple, Victor McLaglen, C. Aubrey Smith, Cesar Romero, June Lang, Constance Collier. (FNC)

How to choose one early Shirley Temple from that incredible career (see Introduction)?

In her prime at nine, Shirley is still fun in Wee Willie Winkie, quintessential Ford and Kipling as well as Temple. It's nice to see her peel a banana in calm self-assurance as she goes off to persuade the villainous Hindu rebel (Cesar Romero) to sign a peace treaty.

It was her favorite movie, because she had a wooden gun and was allowed to march and drill with the big soldiers. If many of her fans admire it, too, it's probably because of the script and direction. As Jeanine Basinger points out (Shirley Temple, Pyramid, 1975), she is given moments in it of genuinely childlike innocence, as when she sings Victor McLaglen to "sleep" in the hospital, not knowing he has died.

But Wee Willie Winkie has its share of familiar Temple contrivances. Shirley's grandpa, C. Aubrey Smith, is Colonel at an 1890s British Army post in Raipore, India, and Shirley is kept busy thawing out his strict regime. She has to find a husband for her widowed mother, too. And there's the regiment to be saved and a war to be prevented. Mainly, she has to keep her great, gruff friend Sergeant Victor McLaglen in line.

The kilted little figure in the foreground of Ford's movie is appealing enough to tickle the shade of Rudyard himself, even though the original Private Winkie was a boy.

WHERE THE LILIES BLOOM, see p. 105

THE WILD DUCK (DIE WILDENTE)

West Germany/Austria, 1976. 105 mins. col. (d) Hans W. Geissendorfer (sp) Geissendorfer, from the play by Henrik Ibsen (ph) Robby Muller (c) Peter Kern, Jean Seberg, Anne Bennent, Bruno Ganz, Martin Floerchinger, Heinz Moog. German dialog with English subtitles. (NYF)

Hedwig, the grave little girl whose tragedy climaxes Ibsen's The Wild Duck, is beautifully played by Anne Bennent in this excellent film by the young German director Hans W. Geissendorfer. This Hedwig is a classic portrait completely understandable in modern terms: the adolescent who has few illusions about her father, who adores him, and who is shattered by his rejection of her.

Her mother, Gina (Jean Seberg), runs the Ekdals' photographic studio, and Hedwig, though she is going blind, helps her. Hjalmar Ekdal (Peter Kern) is a selfish, self-deluding man living in the fantasy of being an inventor. He has never invented a thing. His little daughter, coming on him sound asleep in his "workroom" (with its bare table), preserves the family fantasy. The depth of poignant, loving acceptance in her eyes is womanly beyond her years. Hedwig has a treasured possession, the wounded wild duck in their attic, where Old Ekdal (Martin Floerchinger) pretends to hunt wild game.

The placid contentment of the Ekdal home is destroyed when Hjalmar's school friend, Gregers Werle (Bruno Ganz), "suffering from an acute attack of integrity," tells Hjalmar that Gina was the mistress of Consul Werle (Heinz Moog), and Hedwig is not Hjalmar's child. Far from restoring the Ekdals to the bliss of noble truth, the disclosure is the death of the desolate, gentle Hedwig. Hjalmar brutally turns her away. When Gregers assures her that she will be accepted once more by Hjalmar if she will sacrifice her most cherished possession as a sign of her love, Hedwig shoots the wild duck, and then takes her own life, her "most cherished possession," of which the wounded bird is the symbol.

Geissendorfer's The Wild Duck is good cinema, good screen translation of an interesting play, and good psychology. The Hedwig of Anne Bennent remains the definitive portrayal of one of the most moving adolescents in literature.

Also: Family Relationships

THE YEARLING, see p. 62

DIRECTORY OF FILM COMPANIES AND DISTRIBUTORS

Distribution information is based on James L. Limbacher's _Feature Films on 8mm, 16mm, and Videotape_, 6th edition, 1979 New York, R. R. Bowker Company.

Since distribution rights change frequently, film users should check with the distributors' catalogs (usually free on request), as well as with the collections of local public libraries, university audiovisual centers, and foreign consulates.

ABC-TV	American Broadcasting Corp. 1330 Avenue of the Americas New York, NY 10019 (212) 581-7777
AIM	Association Instructional Materials 866 Third Avenue New York, NY 10022 (212) 935-4210
ATL	Atlantis Productions 1252 La Granada Dr. Thousand Oaks, CA 91360 (213) 495-2790
	Audio Brandon--see MAC (Macmillan Films)
AUS	Film Australia Australian Information Service 636 Fifth Ave. New York, NY 10020 (212) 245-4000
BAU	Bauer International 119 N. Bridge St. Somerville, NJ 08876 (201) 526-5656
BEN	Benchmark Films, Inc. 145 Scarborough Rd. Briarcliff Manor, NY 10510 (914) 762-3838

BFA	BFA Educational Media 2211 Michigan Ave. Santa Monica, CA 90404 (213) 829-2901
BIL	Billy Budd Films 235 E. 57th St. New York, NY 10022 (212) 755-3968
BUD	Budget Films 4590 Santa Monica Blvd. Los Angeles, CA 90029 (213) 680-0187
CAL	University of California Extension Media Center Berkeley, CA 94720 (415) 642-0460
CAR	Carousel Films 1501 Broadway New York, NY 10036 (212) 279-6734
CBS-TV	Columbia Broadcasting System 51 W. 52nd St. New York, NY 10019 (212) 975-4321
CCC	Cine-Craft Company 1720 W. Marshall Portland, OR 97209 (503) 228-7484
CFS	Creative Film Society 7237 Canby Ave. Reseda, CA 91335 (213) 881-3887
CHA	Charard Motion Pictures 2110 E. 24th St. Brooklyn, NY 11226 (212) 891-4339
CHU	Churchill Films 662 N. Robertson Los Angeles, CA 90069 (213) 657-5110
CIN	Hurlock-Cine World 13 Arcadia Rd.

	Old Greenwich, CT 06870 (203) 637-4319
CMC	Center for Mass Communications 562 W. 113th St. New York, NY 10025 (212) 865-2000
CON	Contemporary/McGraw Hill Films 1221 Avenue of the Americas New York, NY 10020 (212) 997-6831
	Princeton Rd. Hightstown, NJ 08520 (609) 448-1700
COR	Coronet Films 65 E. South Water St. Chicago, IL 60601 (312) 322-7676
CTH	Corinth Films 410 E. 62nd St. New York, NY 10021 (212) 421-4770
CWF	Clem Williams Films 2240 Noblestown Rd. Pittsburgh, PA 15205 (412) 921-5810
DIS	Walt Disney Productions 800 Sonora Ave. Glendale, CA 91201 (213) 845-3141
EMC	Extension Media Center--see CAL
FIM	Film Images/Radim Films 17 W. 60th St. New York, NY 10023 (212) 279-6653
	1034 Lake St. Oak Park, IL 60301 (312) 386-4826
	44530 18th St. San Francisco, CA 94114 (415) 431-0996

FFM	Films for the Humanities, Inc. Box 378 Princeton, NJ 08540
FNC	Films Incorporated 440 Park Ave. So. New York, NY 10016 (212) 889-7940 1144 Wilmette Ave. Wilmette, IL 60091 (312) 256-3200 476 Plasamour Dr. Atlanta, GA 30324 (404) 873-5101 5625 Hollywood Blvd. Hollywood, CA 90028 (213) 466-5481
GAM	Gamma III Distributing Corp. 711 Fifth Ave. New York, NY 10022 (212) 486-8888
GEN	General availability, on a non-exclusive basis, from many national rental sources. Also check library and university collections.
GRE	Joseph Green Pictures Co. 200 W. 58th St. New York, NY 10019 (212) 246-9343
GRO	Grove Press Film Division 196 W. Houston St. New York, NY 10014 (212) 242-4900
IMA	Images 2 Purdy Ave. Rye, NY 10580 (914) 967-1102
IMP	Impact Films 144 Bleecker St. New York, NY 10012 (212) 674-3375
IVY	Ivy Films/16 165 W. 46th St. New York, NY 10036 (212) 765-3940

JAN	Janus Films 745 Fifth Avenue New York, NY 10022 (212) 753-7100
JAS	Jason Films 2621 Palisades Ave. Riverdale, NY 10463 (914) 884-7648
KPF	Kit Parker Films Box 27 Carmel Valley, CA 93924 (408) 659-4131
LCA	Learning Corporation of America 1350 Avenue of the Americas New York, NY 10019 (212) 397-9330
LIB	Libra Films Corp. 150 E. 58th St. New York, NY 10022 (212) 838-7721
LUC	Lucerne Films 7 Bahama Rd. Morris Plains, NJ 07950 (201) 538-1401
MAC	Macmillan Films/Audio Brandon 34 MacQuesten Pkwy. So. Mount Vernon, NY 10550 (914) 664-5051
	1619 N. Cherokee Los Angeles, CA 90028 (213) 463-1131
	3868 Piedmont Ave. Oakland, CA 94611 (415) 658-9890
	8400 Brookfield Ave. Brookfield, IL 60513 (312) 485-3925
	2512 Program Dr. Dallas, TX 75220 (214) 357-6494
MCG	McGraw-Hill Films --see CON (Contemporary/McGraw-Hill)

MEG	The Media Guild Box 881 Solana Beach, CA 92076 (714) 755-9191
MMA	Museum of Modern Art Film Dept. 11 W. 53 St. New York, NY 10019 (212) 956-4209
MMM	Mass Media Ministries (a. k. a. Mass Media Associates, Inc.) 2116 N. Charles St. Baltimore, MD 21218 (301) 727-3270
MOD	Modern Sound Pictures 1402 Howard St. Omaha, NB 68102 (402) 341-8476
MOG	Mogull's 235 W. 46th St. New York, NY 10036 (212) 757-1411
MOT	Mottas Films 1318 Ohio Ave., N. E. Canton, OH 44705 (216) 494-6058
NBC-TV	NBC Educational Enterprises 30 Rockefeller Plaza New York, NY 10020 (212) 664-4444
NEA	National Education Association 1201 16th St., N. W. Washington, DC 20036 (202) 833-4000
NFB	National Film Board of Canada 1251 Avenue of the Americas New York, NY 10020 (212) 664-4444
NGA	National Gallery of Art Extension Services Washington, DC 20565 (202) 737-4215

NLF	New Line Cinema 121 University Pl. New York, NY 10003 (212) 674-7460
NYF	New Yorker Films 16 W. 61st St. New York, NY 10023 (212) 247-6110
NYU	New York University Film Library 26 Washington Place New York, NY 10003 (212) 598-2250
PAR	Paramount Pictures Corp. Non-Theatrical 5451 Marathon St. Hollywood, CA 90038 (213) 874-7330
PBS-TV	Public Broadcasting Service 15 W. 51st St. New York, NY 10019 (212) 489-0945
PER	Perspective Films 369 W. Erie St. Chicago, IL 60610 (312) 332-7676
PIC	Pictura Films 111 Eighth Ave. New York, NY 10011 (212) 691-1730
PNX	Phoenix Films 267 W. 25th St. New York, NY 10001 (212) 684-5910
PRU	Productions Unlimited 1301 Avenue of the Americas New York, NY 10020 (212) 541-6770
PYR	Pyramid Films Box 1048 Santa Monica, CA 90406 (213) 828-7577
RAD	Radim Films--see FIM/RAD (Film Images/ Radim Films)

REM	Rembrandt Films 267 W. 25th St. New York, NY 10001 (212) 675-5330
ROA	Roa's Films 1696 N. Astor St. Milwaukee, WI 53202 (414) 271-0861
SAL	Salzburg Enterprises 98 Cutter Hill Rd. Great Neck, NY 11021 (516) 487-4515
SAN	Sanrio Communications 1505 Vine Hollywood, CA 90028 (213) 462-7248
SCO	Scotia American 600 Madison Ave. New York, NY 10021 (212) 758-4775
STE	Sterling Educational Films (Division of Walter Reade) 241 E. 34th St. New York, NY 10016 (212) 683-6300
SWA	Swank Motion Pictures 60 Bethpage Rd. Hicksville, NY 11801 (516) 931-7500 220 Forbes Rd. Braintree, MA 02184 (617) 848-8300 7926 Jones Branch Dr. McLean, VA 22101 (703) 821-1040 1200 Roosevelt Rd. Glen Ellyn, IL 60137 (312) 629-9004 201 S. Jefferson Ave. Saint Louis, MO 63103 (314) 534-6300

	4111 Director's Row Houston, TX 77092 (713) 683-8222
	6767 Forest Lawn Dr. Hollywood, CA 90068 (213) 851-6300
TIM	Time/Life Multimedia 100 Eisenhower Dr. Paramus, NJ 07652 (201) 843-4545
TWF	Trans-World Films 332 S. Michigan Ave. Chicago, IL 60604 (312) 922-1530
TWY	Twyman Films 329 Salem Ave. Dayton, OH 45401 (513) 222-4014
UAS	United Artists/16 729 Seventh Ave. New York, NY 10019 (212) 575-4715
UNF	United Films 1425 S. Main Tulsa, OK 74119 (918) 584-6491
UNI	Universal 16 445 Park Ave. New York, NY 10022 (212) 759-7500
	425 N. Michigan Ave. Chicago, IL 60611 (312) 822-0513
	205 Walton St. Atlanta, GA 30303 (404) 523-5081
	810 S. St. Paul Dallas, TX 75201 (214) 741-3164
	2001 S. Vermont Ave. Los Angeles, CA 90007 (213) 731-2151

WCF	Westcoast Films 25 Lusk St. San Francisco, CA 94107 (415) 362-4700
WGBH-TV	WGBH Distribution 125 Western Ave. Boston, MA 02134 (617) 492-2777
WHO	Wholesome Film Center 20 Melrose St. Boston, MA 02116 (617) 426-0155
WIL	Willoughby-Peerless 110 W. 32nd St. New York, NY 10001 (212) 564-1600
WOR	World Northal 1 Dag Hammarskjold Plaza New York, NY 10017 (212) 223-8169
WRS	Walter Reade 16 241 E. 34th St. New York, NY 10016 (212) 683-6300
XER	Xerox Films 245 Long Hill Rd. Middletown, CT 06457 (203) 347-7251
ZPH	Zipporah Films 54 Lewis Wharf Boston, MA 02110 (617) 742-6680

SELECTED BIBLIOGRAPHY: GOOD READING ABOUT FILM

Agee, James. Agee on Film. 2 vols. Vol. 1. Reviews & Comments. Vol. II. Five Film Scripts. McDowell Obolensky, 1958/1960. Grosset & Dunlap reprint, 1969, pa.

Alpert, Hollis. The Dream and the Dreamers: Adventures of a Professional Movie Goer. Macmillan, 1962.

Artel, Linda and Susan Wengraf. Positive Images: A Guide to Non-sexist Films for Children. Booklegger Press, 1976.

Balázs, Béla. Theory of the Film. Roy, 1953. Dover reprint, 1970, pa.

Baldwin, James. The Devil Finds Work. Dial, 1976.

Barnouw, Erik. Documentary: A History of the Non-Fiction Film. Oxford University Press, 1974.

Basinger, Jeanine. Shirley Temple. Pyramid, 1975, pa.

Bazin, André. What Is Cinema? 2 vols. University of California Press, 1967/1971, cl. and pa.

Best, Marc. Those Endearing Young Charms: Child Performers of the Screen. A. S. Barnes, 1971.

Bogle, Donald. Toms, Coons, Mulattoes, Mammies and Bucks. Viking, 1974.

Braudy, Leo. World in a Frame: What We See in Films. Anchor, 1977, pa.

Capra, Frank. The Name Above the Title. Bantam, 1972, pa.

Corliss, Richard. Talking Pictures: Screenwriters in the American Cinema. Penguin, 1975, pa.

Cowie, Peter. A Concise History of the Cinema. 2 vols. A. S. Barnes, 1971, pa.

Chaplin, Charles. My Autobiography. Simon and Schuster, 1964.

Crist, Judith. The Private Eye, the Cowboy and the Very Naked Girl: Movies from Cleo to Clyde. Holt, Rinehart and Winston, 1968, pa.

Crowther, Bosley. Vintage Films. Putnam, 1976.

Denby, David, ed. Awake in the Dark: An Anthology of American Film Criticism, 1915 to the Present. Vintage, 1977, pa.

Edgar, Patricia. Children and Screen Violence. University of Queensland Press, 1977.

Eisenstein, Sergei M. Film Form. Harcourt Brace, 1949, pa.

________. The Film Sense. Harcourt Brace, 1942, pa.

Everson, William K. The Art of W. C. Fields. Bobbs, Merrill, 1967.

________. The Bad Guys: A Pictorial History of the Movie Villain. Citadel, 1964, cl. and pa.

________. The Films of Laurel and Hardy. Citadel, 1964, cl. and pa.

Fenin, George N. and William K. Everson. The Western: From Silents to the Seventies. Grossman, 1973. Penguin, pa.

Friedlander, Madeline S. Leading Film Discussions. The League of Women Voters, 1972, pa.

Gaffney, Maureen. More Films Kids Like: A Catalog of Short Films for Children. American Library Association, 1977.

Geduld, Harry M., ed. Film Makers on Film Making. Indiana University Press, 1967, cl. and pa.

Gelmis, Joseph. The Film Director as Superstar. Doubleday, 1970, cl. and pa.

Gessner, Robert. The Moving Image: A Guide to Cinematic Literacy. Dutton, 1970, cl. and pa.

Gilliatt, Penelope. Unholy Fools. Viking, 1973.

Goldstein, Ruth M. and Edith Zornow. Movies for Kids: A Guide for Parents and Teachers.... Rev., Frederick Ungar, 1980, cl. & pa.

Griffith, Richard and Arthur Mayer. The Movies. Rev. ed., Simon and Schuster, 1973, pa.

Hall, Stuart, et al., Film Teaching. The British Film Institute, 1968, pa.

Halliwell, Leslie. The Filmgoer's Companion. 6th ed., rev. Hill & Wang, 1977.

Haskell, Molly. *From Reverence to Rape: The Treatment of Women in the Movies.* Holt, Rinehart and Winston, 1974. Penguin, pa.

Higham, Charles and Joel Greenberg. *The Celluloid Muse: Hollywood Directors Speak.* Signet, 1972, pa.

Houston, Penelope. *The Contemporary Cinema.* Penguin, 1963, pa.

Huff, Theodore. *Charlie Chaplin.* Henry Schuman, 1951. Arno reprint.

Huss, Roy and Norman Silverstein. *The Film Experience: Elements of Motion Picture Art.* Harper & Row, 1968, pa.

Jacobs, Lewis, ed. *The Documentary Tradition: From Nanook to Woodstock.* Hopkinson and Blake, 1971, cl. and pa.

________. *The Emergence of Film Art.* Hopkinson and Blake, 1962.

________. *Film As Medium.* Farrar, Straus and Giroux, 1970. Octagon reprint, pa.

________. *The Rise of the American Film.* Harcourt, Brace, 1939, 1948. Teachers College reprint, 1968, pa.

Kael, Pauline. *Deeper into Movies.* Little, Brown, 1973.

________. *Going Steady.* Little, Brown, 1970.

________. *I Lost It at the Movies.* Little, Brown, 1965. Bantam, pa.

________. *Kiss Kiss Bang Bang.* Little, Brown, 1968. Bantam, pa.

________. *Reeling.* Little, Brown, 1976. Warner, pa.

Kauffmann, Stanley, ed. with Bruce Henstell. *American Film Criticism from the Beginnings to 'Citizen Kane.'* Liveright, 1972.

________. *Figures of Light: Film Criticism and Comment.* Harper & Row, 1971. Colophon, pa.

________. *Living Images: Film Comment and Criticism.* Harper & Row, 1975, cl. and pa.

________. *A World on Film.* Harper & Row, 1966. Delta, pa. Greenwood reprint, 1975, cloth.

Kay, Kathryn and Gerald Peary. *Women and the Cinema: A Critical Anthology.* Dutton, 1976, pa.

Kaye, Evelyn. The Family Guide to Children's Television. (Action for Children's Television) Pantheon, 1974.

Kerr, Walter. The Silent Clowns. Knopf, 1975.

Knight, Arthur. The Liveliest Art: A Panoramic History of the Movies. Rev. ed. Macmillan, 1977.

Leyda, Jay. Voices of Film Experience, 1894 to the Present. Macmillan, 1977.

Lindgren, Ernest. The Art of Film. 2nd ed., rev. Macmillan, 1963. Collier, pa.

MacCann, Richard Dyer, ed. Film and Society. Scribner, 1964, pa.

Madsen, Axel. The New Hollywood. Crowell, 1975.

Maland, Charles J. American Visions: The Films of Chaplin, Ford, Capra and Welles, 1936-1941. Arno Press, 1977.

Mallery, David. Film in the Life of the School. National Association of Independent Schools, 1968, pa.

Manvell, Roger and Lewis Jacobs, eds. The International Film Encyclopedia. Crown, 1972.

Manvell, Roger. Experiment in the Film. Grey Walls Press, 1949. Arno reprint.

Mayer, Arthur. Merely Colossal: The Story of the Movies from the Long Chase to the Chaise Longue. Simon and Schuster, 1953.

Maynard, Richard A. The Celluloid Curriculum: How to Use Movies in the Classroom. Hayden, 1971, cl. and pa.

Monaco, James. How to Read a Film: The Art, Technology, Language, History, and Theory of Film and Media. Oxford University Press, 1977.

Nichols, Bill, ed. Movies and Methods. University of California Press, 1977, cl. and pa.

Patterson, Lindsay, compiled by. Black Films and Film-Makers: A Comprehensive Anthology from Stereotype to Superhero. Dodd, 1975.

Ramsaye, Terry. A Million and One Nights: A History of the Motion Picture. 2 vols. Simon and Schuster, 1926; 1 vol. ed., 1964, cl. and pa.

Reilly, Adam. Harold Lloyd: The King of Daredevil Comedy. Macmillan, 1977.

Renoir, Jean. My Life and My Films. Atheneum, 1974, cl. and pa.

Rhode, Eric. Tower of Babel: Speculations on the Cinema. Chilton, 1967.

Rice, Susan. Films Kids Like; A Catalog of Short Films for Children. American Library Association, 1973.

Robinson, W. R., ed. Man and the Movies. Louisiana State University Press, 1967. Penguin, pa.

Ross, Lillian. Picture. Rinehart, 1952. Dolphin, Avon, pa.

Sarris, Andrew. The American Cinema: Directors and Directions, 1929-1968. Dutton, 1968, cl. and pa.

Schickel, Richard. The Disney Version: The Life, Times, Art and Commerce of Walt Disney. Simon and Schuster, 1968. Avon, pa.

________. Harold Lloyd: The Shape of Laughter. The New York Graphic Society, 1974.

Schillaci, Anthony and John M. Culkin, eds. Films Deliver. Citation Press, 1970, pa.

Sheridan, Marion C. with Harold H. Owen, Jr., Ken Macrorie and Fred Marcus. The Motion Picture and the Teaching of English. Appleton-Century-Crofts, 1965, pa.

Simon, John. Private Screenings. Macmillan, 1967; Berkeley, pa.

Sklar, Robert. Movie-Made America. Random House, 1975; Vintage, pa.

Stephenson, Ralph and J. R. Debrix. The Cinema As Art. Penguin, 1965, pa.

Talbot, Daniel, ed. Film: An Anthology. 2nd ed. University of California Press, 1966, pa.

Taylor, John Russell. Directors and Directions: Cinema for the Seventies. Hill & Wang, 1975, pa.

Thompson, Howard, ed. The New York Times Guide to Movies on TV. Quadrangle, 1971, pa.

Truffaut, François. The Films in My Life. Simon & Schuster, 1978.

Tyler, Parker. Classics of the Foreign Film. Citadel, 1962, cl. and pa.

________. The Hollywood Hallucination. Touchstone Books, 1970, pa.

Unesco, ed. The Influence of the Cinema on Children and Adolescents, 1961. Greenwood reprint.

Vogel, Amos. Film As a Subversive Art. Random House, 1976, pa.

Walker, Alexander. Sex in the Movies: The Celluloid Sacrifice. Penguin, 1970, pa.

Warshow, Robert. The Immediate Experience. Anchor, 1964, pa.

Weinberg, Herman G. Saint Cinema: Selected Writings 1929-1970, Drama Book Service, 1970; Dover reprint, 1973, pa.

Weiner, Janet. How to Organize and Run a Film Society. Macmillan, 1973, pa.

White, David Manning and Richard Averson. The Celluloid Weapon: Social Comment in the American Film. Beacon, 1972.

Wright, Basil. The Long View. Knopf, 1974.

CATEGORY INDEX

Documentaries

Family Relationships

Fantasy

Generation Conflicts

<u>Growing Pains</u>

Teachers and Schools

War and Its Aftermath

TITLE INDEX

ABOUT THE AUTHORS

RUTH M. GOLDSTEIN, a pioneer teacher of film in high schools, is the retired assistant chairman of English at Abraham Lincoln High School, Brooklyn, New York. For many years the film chairman of the New York City Association of Teachers of English and the film reviewer for the Board of Education magazine *High Points*, she directed the educational campaigns for major films. She writes discussion guides for teachers on films and plays, and reviews 16mm features for *Film News*. She now resides in New Smyrna Beach, Florida.

EDITH ZORNOW, film producer of *Sesame Street* for the Children's Television Workshop, New York, and artistic director of the very successful "Movies for Kids" series at Lincoln Center, has had a varied and distinguished career in film and television. She has been associated with the distribution of outstanding theatrical and non-theatrical films, and her television series, "The Art of Film" (National Educational Television), was awarded an "Emmy." A trustee of the Flaherty International Film Seminars and a member of the Board of Directors of the Media Center for Children, New York, she lives in New York City and Warren, Connecticut.

Ruth M. Goldstein and Edith Zornow are co-authors of *Movies for Kids: A Guide for Parents and Teachers on the Entertainment Film for Children*. (Revised ed.) Frederick Ungar Publishing Company, 1980.